# NEW YORK CITYSCAPES

***Seven Top Photographers Explore the Classic Landmarks & Hidden Spaces***

**Peter Alessandria** *with*
**Bill Bernal, Gina Brake, Viktor Buriak, Max Guliani, Jason Risorto & Karine Sayegh**

AMHERST MEDIA, INC. ■ BUFFALO, NY

Photographs by: Peter Alessandria (front and back covers, pages 1, 3, 4, 5–25, plus all contributor head shots); Bill Bernal (pages 26–41); Gina Brake (pages 42–57); Viktor Buriak (pages 58–77); Max Guliani (pages 78–93); Jason Risorto (pages 94–109); and Karine Sayegh (pages 110–126).

Published by:
Amherst Media, Inc., P.O. Box 538, Buffalo, N.Y. 14213
www.AmherstMedia.com

Publisher: Craig Alesse
Senior Editor/Production Manager: Michelle Perkins
Editors: Barbara A. Lynch-Johnt, Beth Alesse
Acquisitions Editor: Harvey Goldstein
Associate Publisher: Katie Kiss
Editorial Assistance from: Carey A. Miller, Rebecca Rudell, Jen Sexton-Riley
Business Manager: Sarah Loder
Marketing Associate: Tonya Flickinger

ISBN-13: 978-1-68203-380-7
Library of Congress Control Number: 2018953356
Printed in The United States of America.
10 9 8 7 6 5 4 3 2 1





www.facebook.com/AmherstMediaInc
www.youtube.com/AmherstMedia
www.twitter.com/AmherstMedia

# Contents



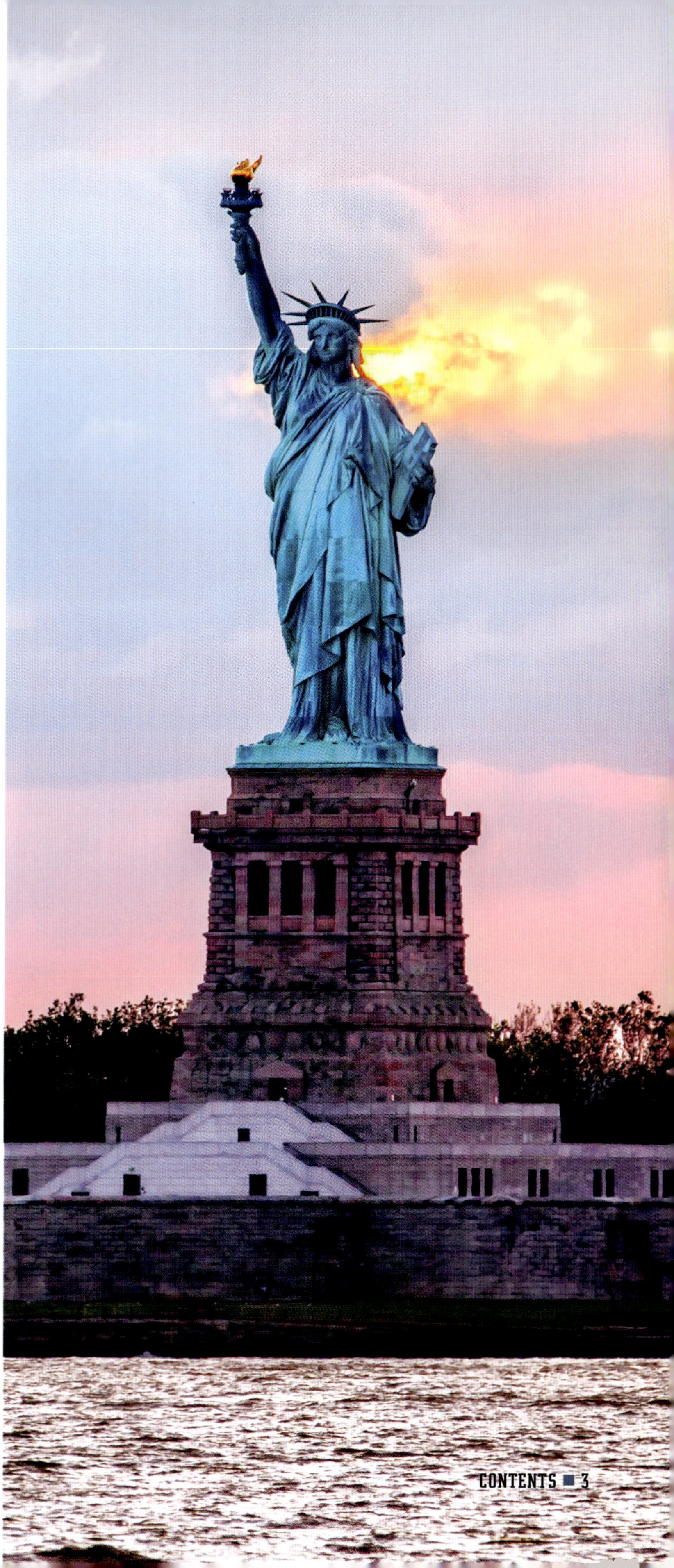

***Statue of Liberty.*** *(right)* The only way to get this view of the Statue of Liberty is to travel to Brooklyn. On a good day with no traffic it takes ninety minutes. On a bad day? Well as they say in Brooklyn, "Fhageddaboutit."

# Introduction

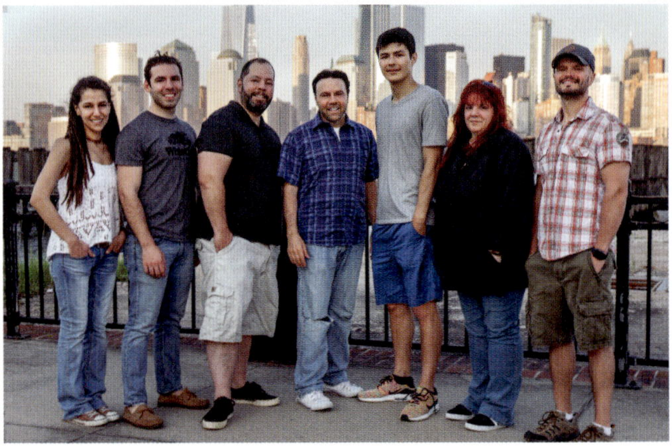

**Contributing Photographers.** *(left to right)* Karine Sayegh, Jason Risorto, Bill Bernal, Peter Alessandria, Max Guliani, Gina Brake, and Victor Buriak.

I never set out to be a photographer—I started out along a more conventional career path as an attorney. In fact, I didn't even pick up a still camera until I was in my late thirties. But when I did, it was love at first sight. I was instantly aware I had found my passion in life. When the Global Financial Crisis hit in 2008, I lost my law business and came to a crossroads: what I was going to do with the rest of my life? While the money was good, I had never loved being a lawyer. So I made the decision to pursue photography full-time. It hasn't been easy—in fact, it's been really hard at times. But I've never really looked back and am glad that I get to do what I love every day for a living.

This book is an expression of my love of photography. While I have been inspired by the work of many of the masters—people such as Ansel Adams, Henri Cartier-Bresson, and Alfred Stieglitz—it is my peers who influence me the most. The rise of social media has been a revelation for me. I am awed by the level of talent and creativity I see from my fellows photographers on Instagram and Facebook. Social media has also been a wonderful way for me to get to know other photographers personally. Through Instagram and Facebook, I've met dozens of wonderful and talented people—and, in fact, that's how I came to know each of the six other photographers featured in this book. Both their work and who they are as individuals has impacted me in powerful and positive ways. They are not only immensely talented, they are also wonderful people. I am honored that they all agreed to take this journey of doing a book with me.

As a reminder, we are all working artists. This means we sell prints of our work and license images for commercial or other uses. If you like a particular image or two—or twelve!—you can reach out to us directly (contact info is provided with each artist's biography). Also, please make sure to follow us on social media to stay abreast of our latest work.

I also want to give a shout-out to the wonder that is New York City. As with the six other photographers in this book, the Big Apple has been an ongoing source of inspiration for my art. The skyline of the World's Greatest City has been an unending canvas for our photographic expression. From any and every angle, New York City is quite simply awesome!

Finally, a special thanks to you, the reader, for taking the time to enjoy this book. I am always in awe when people say they like my work and I know my fellow photographers love it too. I hope each and every photo in this book speaks to you in profound and meaningful ways.

All the best!

*—Peter Alessandria*

# CHAPTER 1

# Peter Alessandria

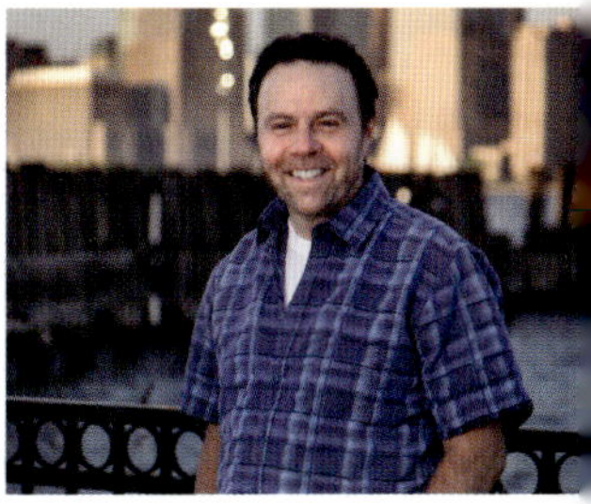

Instagram: @peteralessandria ■ www.peteralessandriaphotography.com ■ www.facebook.com/PeterAlessandriaPhotography

I grew up in the New York City area and was blessed with a good upbringing. My parents provided my siblings and I with everything we needed to succeed in life. I decided to become a lawyer. After law school, I moved to Los Angeles and worked in the entertainment business. At one point, I worked for a couple of film and television production companies. One of the perks of my job was that I got to visit the television and movie sets. I was fascinated with all the camera and lighting equipment, as well as with how movies and television shows were made. (I'll never forget—the first time I visited a movie set, they were filming the last scene of the movie on the first day of production. I had no idea they didn't make a film in the same order as you watched it!) Looking back, I can see it was these experiences that sparked my passion for the art of visual storytelling.

Eventually, I had my own law practice. I was doing mostly intellectual property law (trademarks and copyright), and since I was now my own boss, I was able to make time to explore my own creativity—first by becoming an independent filmmaker and eventually with photography. The filmmaking was a lot of fun; I wrote, produced, directed, and edited six short films in the span of five years. Then, near the end of 2004, I picked up a still camera for the first time and fell in love. It was a semiprofessional model, the kind with interchangeable lenses and a viewfinder you could see through. To this day, I still love the sound of a camera shutter opening and closing when you take a picture.

After getting that camera, suddenly all I wanted to do was take pictures. In the first couple of years, I took over 200,000 images. And when I wasn't taking pictures, I was on the Internet connecting with other people about taking pictures. I was in my late thirties and I had found my passion in life.

Then came the Global Financial Crisis of 2008. Remember that? ("How could I forget!" you might answer.) The Fed, the Treasury Department, and

**All Lined Up.** *(below)* This odd but photographically-fortuitous collection of pilings can be found on the Brooklyn side of the East River. A favorite spot for taking photos (among natives and tourists alike), the pilings create wonderful leading lines across the water to Lower Manhattan.

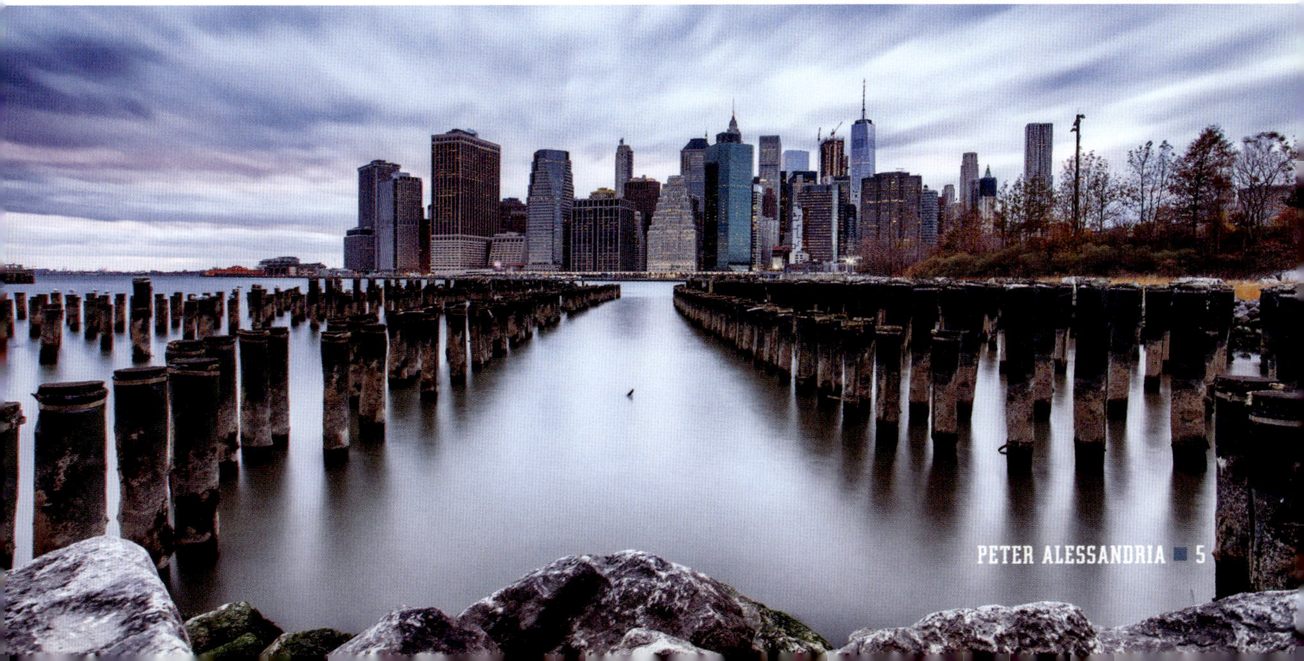

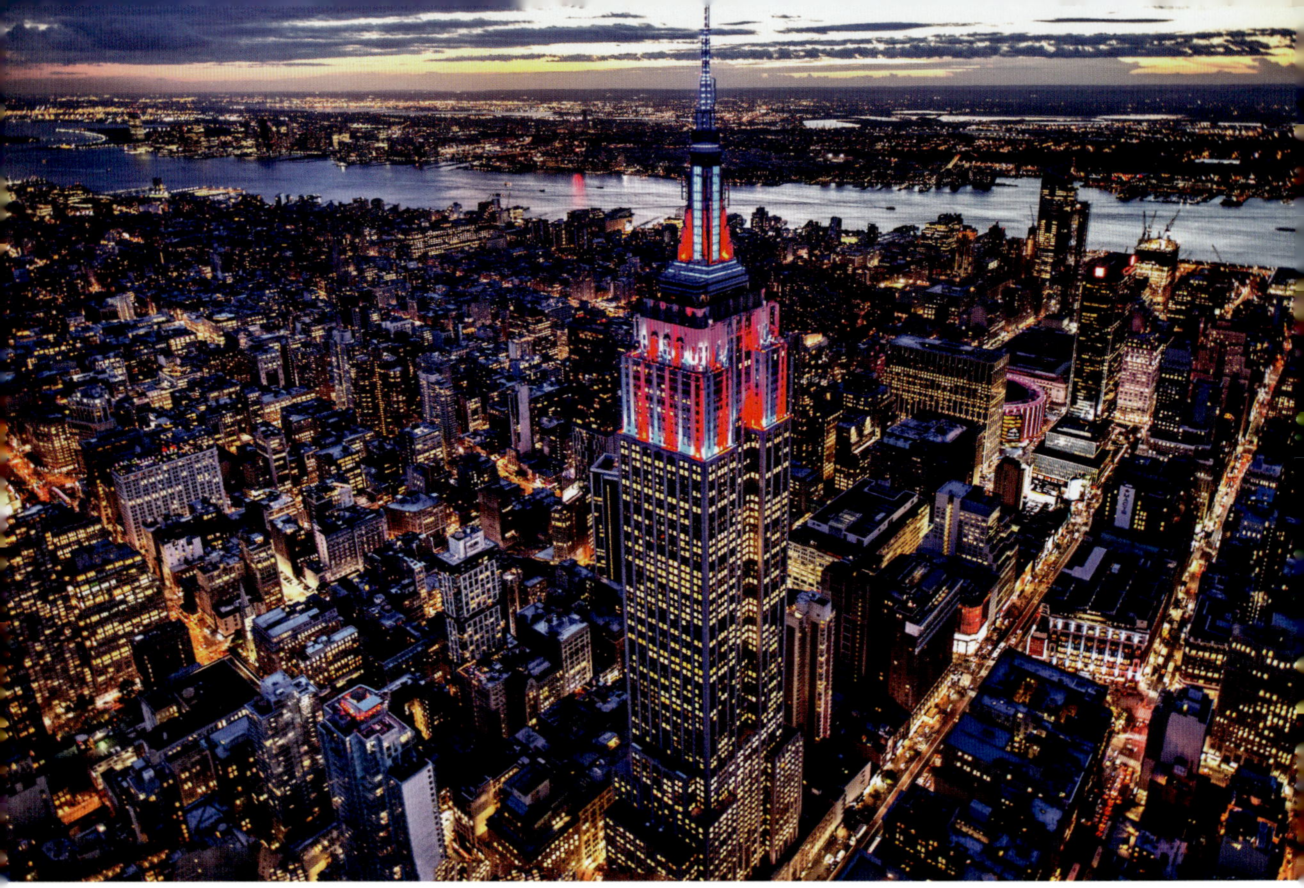

**_Magenta Empire_**. Magenta and blue dominate the tower lights of the Empire State Building in this aerial helicopter shot. When we fly over New York City, we have to take the doors off to avoid glare. There is no better feeling than flying around New York City at night, 1,500 feet up with no doors!

eventually the President told us the nation was on the edge of financial collapse. TARP and other corporate bailouts ensued.

Almost immediately, my law business was thrown into turmoil. My main client of nearly twelve years underwent an internal regime change and suddenly I was out of work. It was very shocking—and, honestly, I was scared.

After spending six months trying to find other clients, it became clear the law thing wasn't going to change anytime soon. I thought, "What am I going to do with the rest of my life?" I asked this question over and over. One day the answer came: *photography*. Wait. What? That made no sense. I had never even taken a photography class and knew nothing about the business of being a photographer. Could I really do this?

Maybe I had read too many books, like *Do What You Love and the Money Will Follow,* but after several weeks of agonizing, I decided I was going to leave the law behind. I had also been contemplating a move back to the East Coast. My sisters had all had kids (I have no kids of my own) and family was becoming more of a priority. So in the summer of 2009, I decided to start my photography career and move back East.

Truth is, there's a lot more to running a successful business than passion and creativity. It has been a lot harder than I anticipated to make a living as a photographer. But I can honestly say that most days I am the happiest I have ever been. I joke that my worst day as a photographer is still usually better than my best day as a lawyer. Every time I pick up a camera I know I made the right choice.

One of the most important things I've learned over the past few years is that having confidence and a belief in myself makes all the difference. I've found that it's not how I handle the successes that matters, but how I handle the failures, rejections, and disappointments. Those are what can derail any career, not just a photography one. I've had to learn—sometimes the hard way—how to pick myself up and dust myself off when things are tough.

That said, I have done pretty well so far. I've won many awards for my photography and had my work published in newspapers and magazines around the world. I've shown my photos in solo and group exhibitions and sold many fine art prints of my work. I've travelled as far as South America and the Middle East for my photography and am very active on social media, where all kinds of wonderful opportunities and people (including the six other photographers featured in this book) have come my way. I also teach one-on-one and lead photography workshops for professionals and beginners alike.

So while the road has been rocky at times, I am happy to be doing work that I love. Whether it took a Global Financial Crisis—or personal mid-life crisis—to get here, I'm all for it. And from where I sit today, the future looks quite bright indeed!

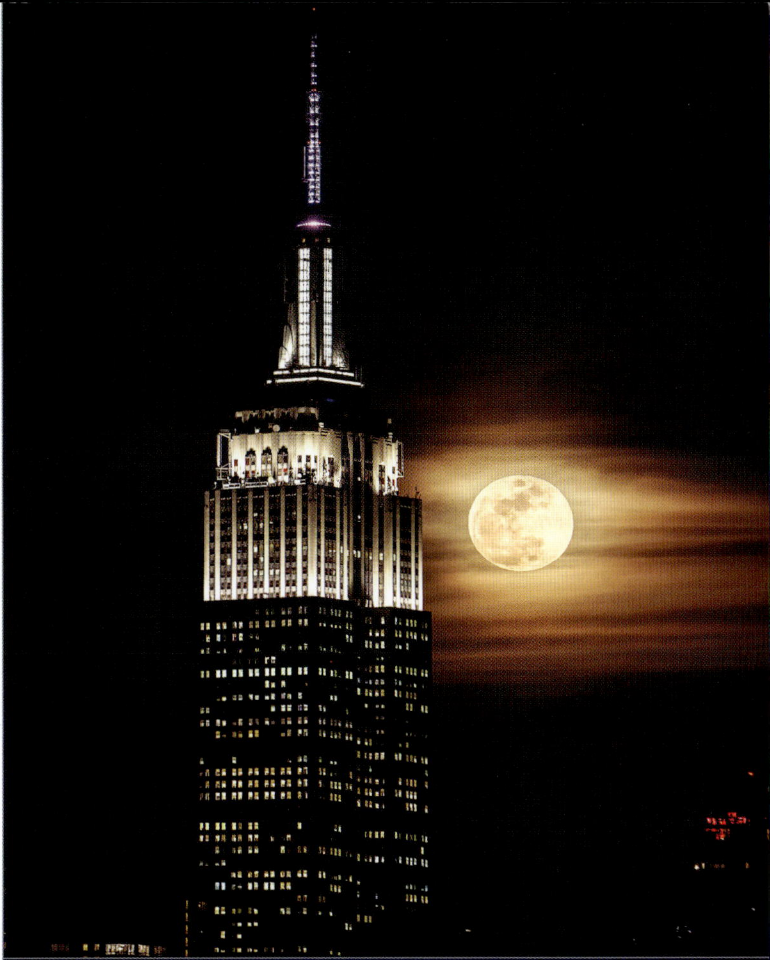

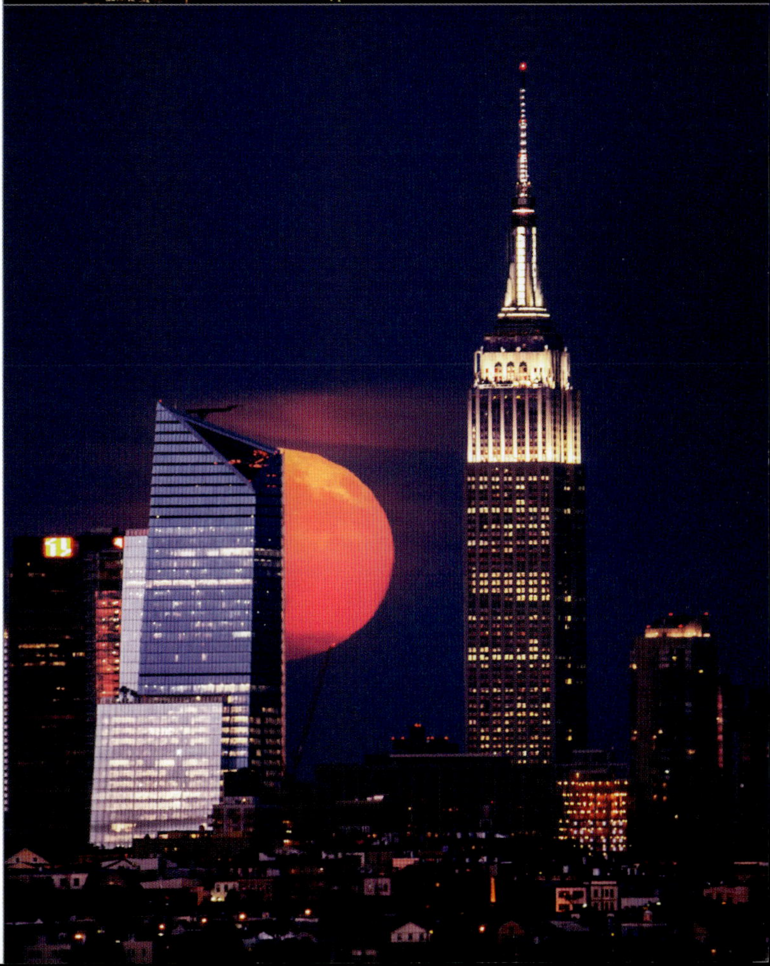

**Snow Moon.** *(top right)* The February "Snow Moon" rises behind the Empire State Building. Naming the full moons was one way the Native Americans kept track of the seasons.

**Sturgeon Moon.** *(bottom right)* August's full moon carries the same name as a fish popular with Native Americans living in the Northeast. This shot was taken from nearly seven miles away in a New Jersey landfill. Photographing the moon in relation to New York City's landmarks often requires travelling to exotic locations such as landfills, swamps, and the suburbs of Hoboken (just kidding!).

**Freedom Shines 9/11.** This is an aerial shot looking south from Midtown to Lower Manhattan. The Empire State Building is lit in red, white, and blue to commemorate the anniversary of 9/11. The two Tribute Lights grace Lower Manhattan where the Twin Towers used to be.

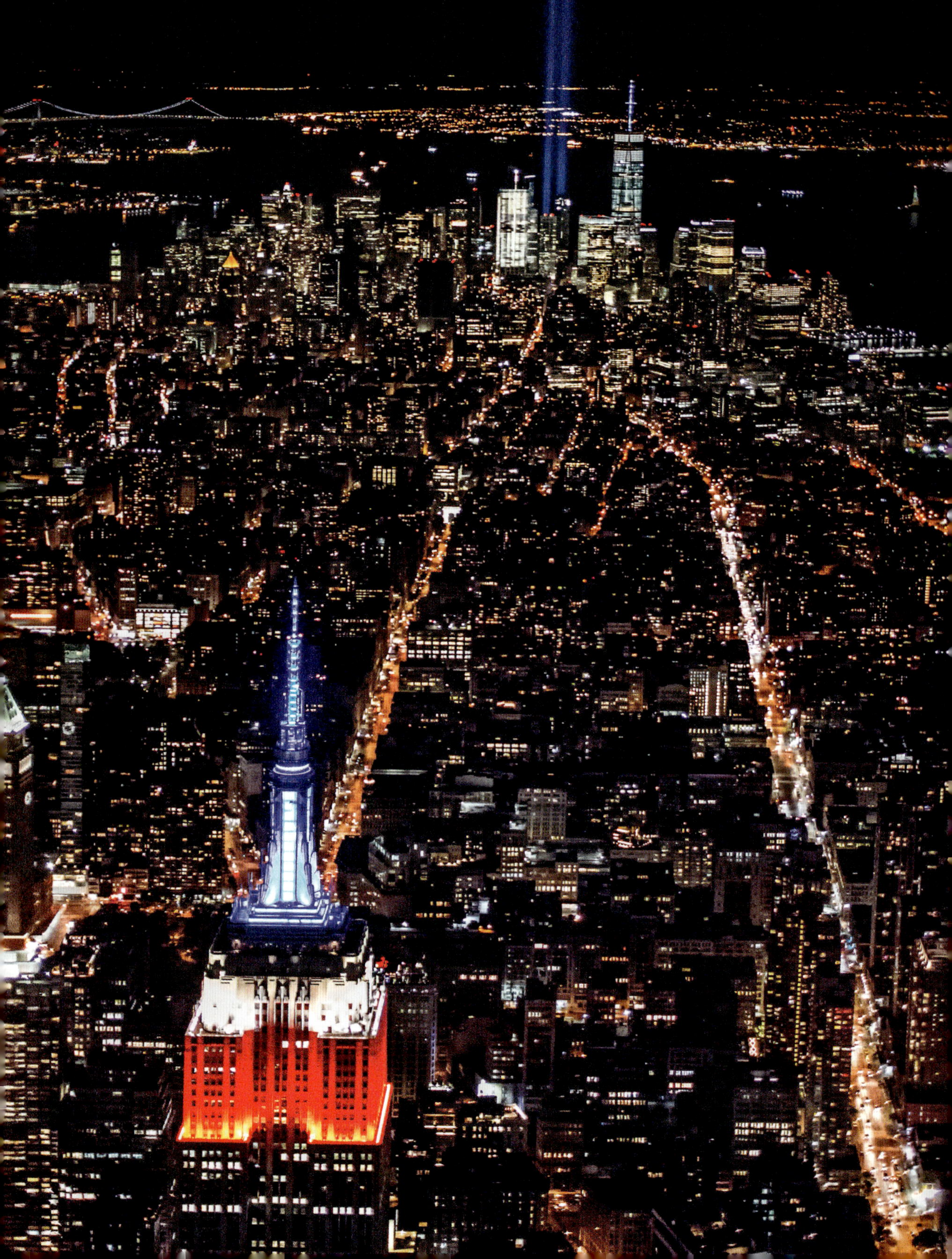

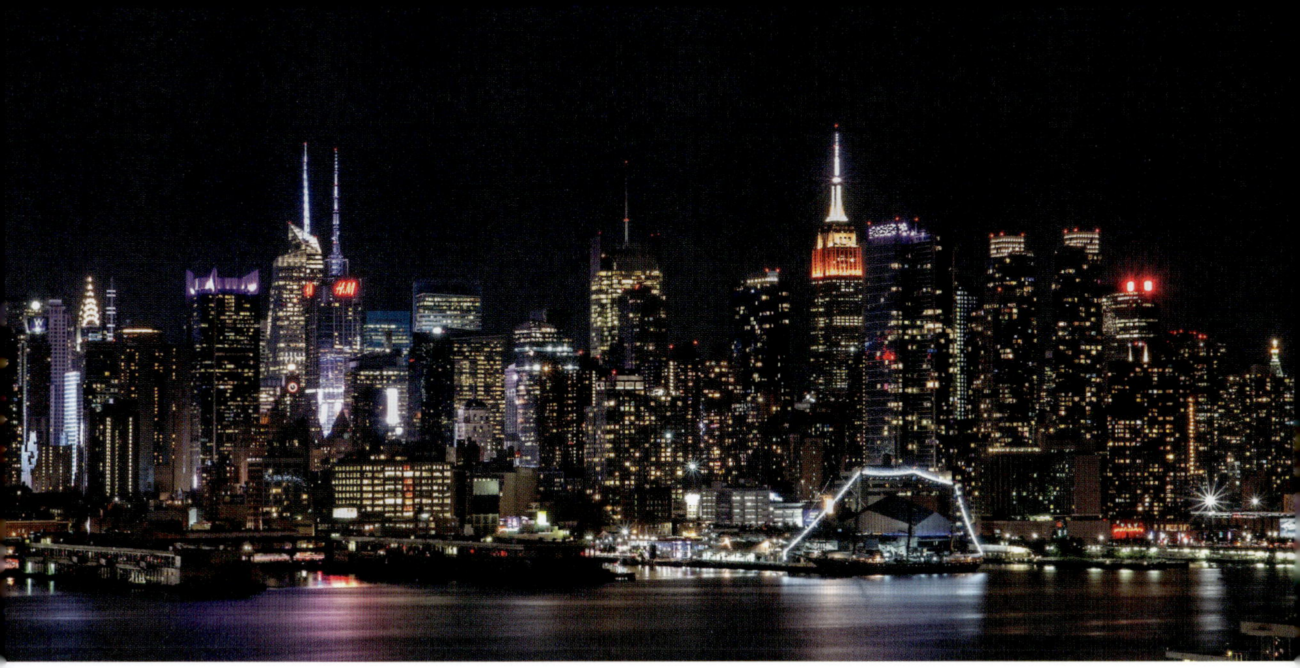


**Midtown West.** *(above)* From left: The Chrysler Building, Bank of America Tower, H&M Tower, New York Times Building, and Empire State Building define the view of Midtown Manhattan from Weekawken, New Jersey.

**Night Light.** *(bottom left)* Located across the Hudson River in Newport, New Jersey, the historic LeFrak Lighthouse once guided ships in and out of New York Harbor. While modern technologies make lighthouses unnecessary, here it makes a nice centerpiece to the Empire State Building on the left (simultaneously illuminated for Hanukkah and Christmas) and the Chrysler Building on the right.

**Statue of Liberty and Empire State Building.** *(bottom right)* Taken from Bayonne, New Jersey, this photo confuses a lot of people. Using a telephoto lens, I was able to compress the apparent distance between these two landmarks. The Statue of Liberty is actually two miles away from where I took this photo and the Empire State Building is another five miles beyond that. So we are seeing more than seven miles of compressed distance in this shot.

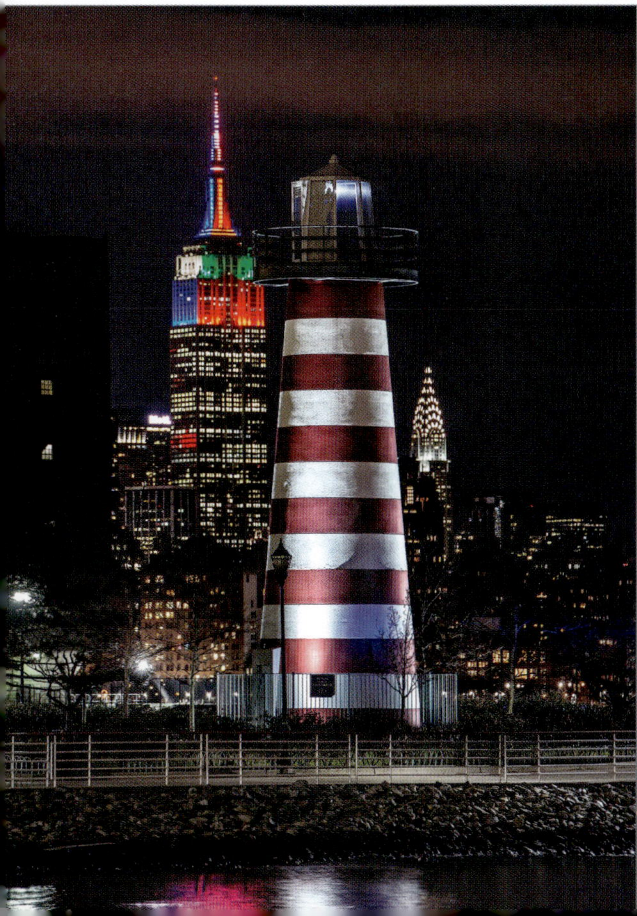

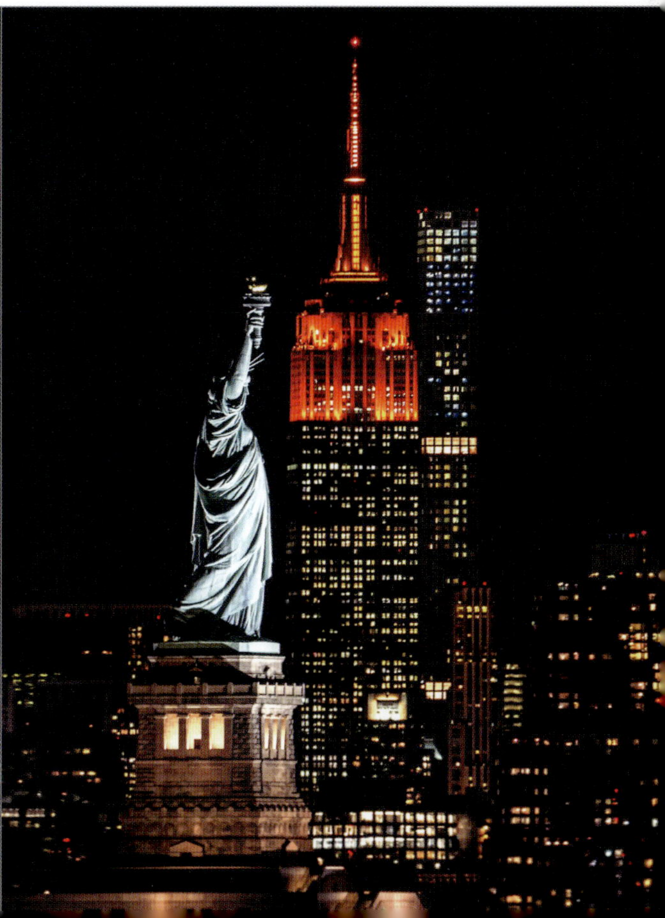

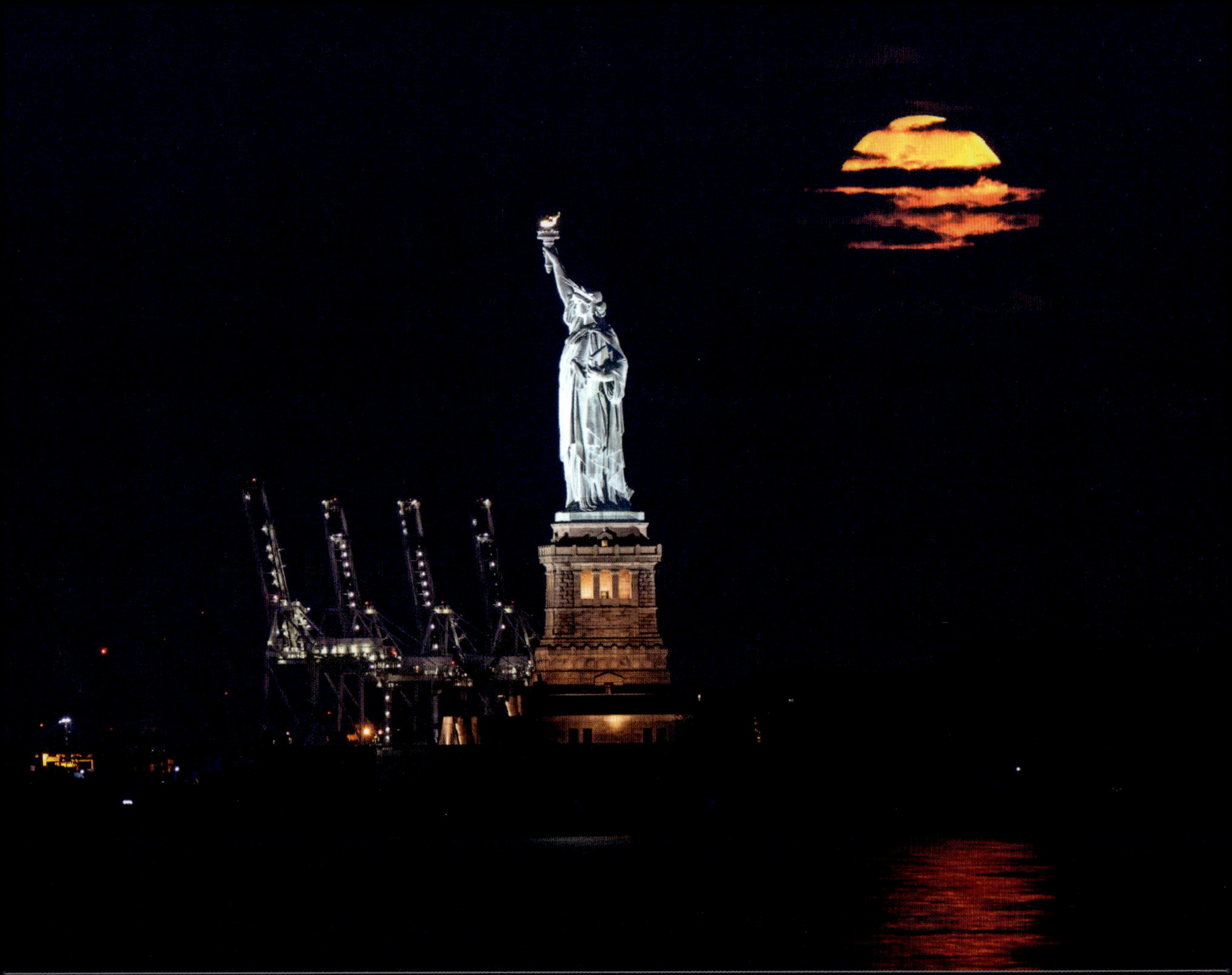

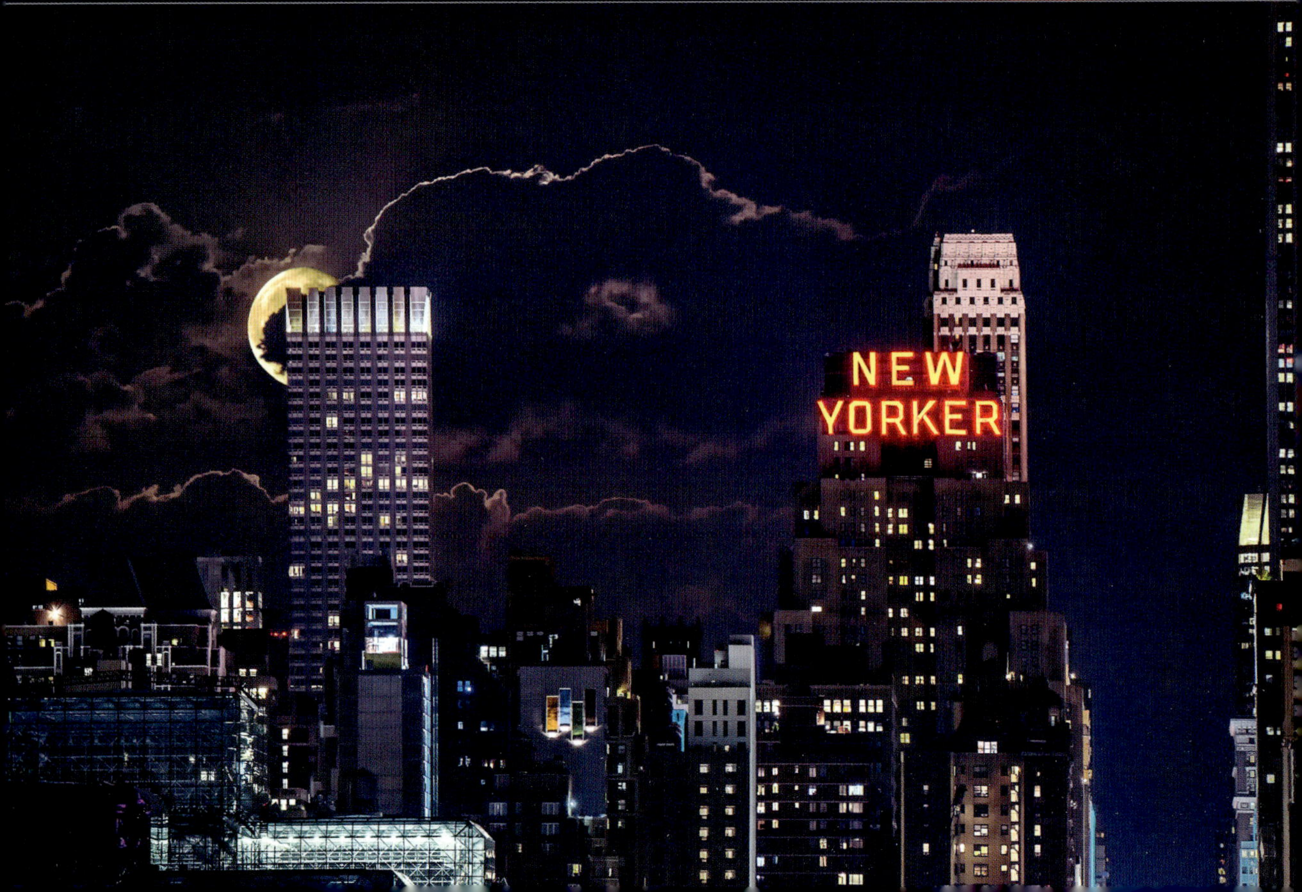
NEW
YORKER

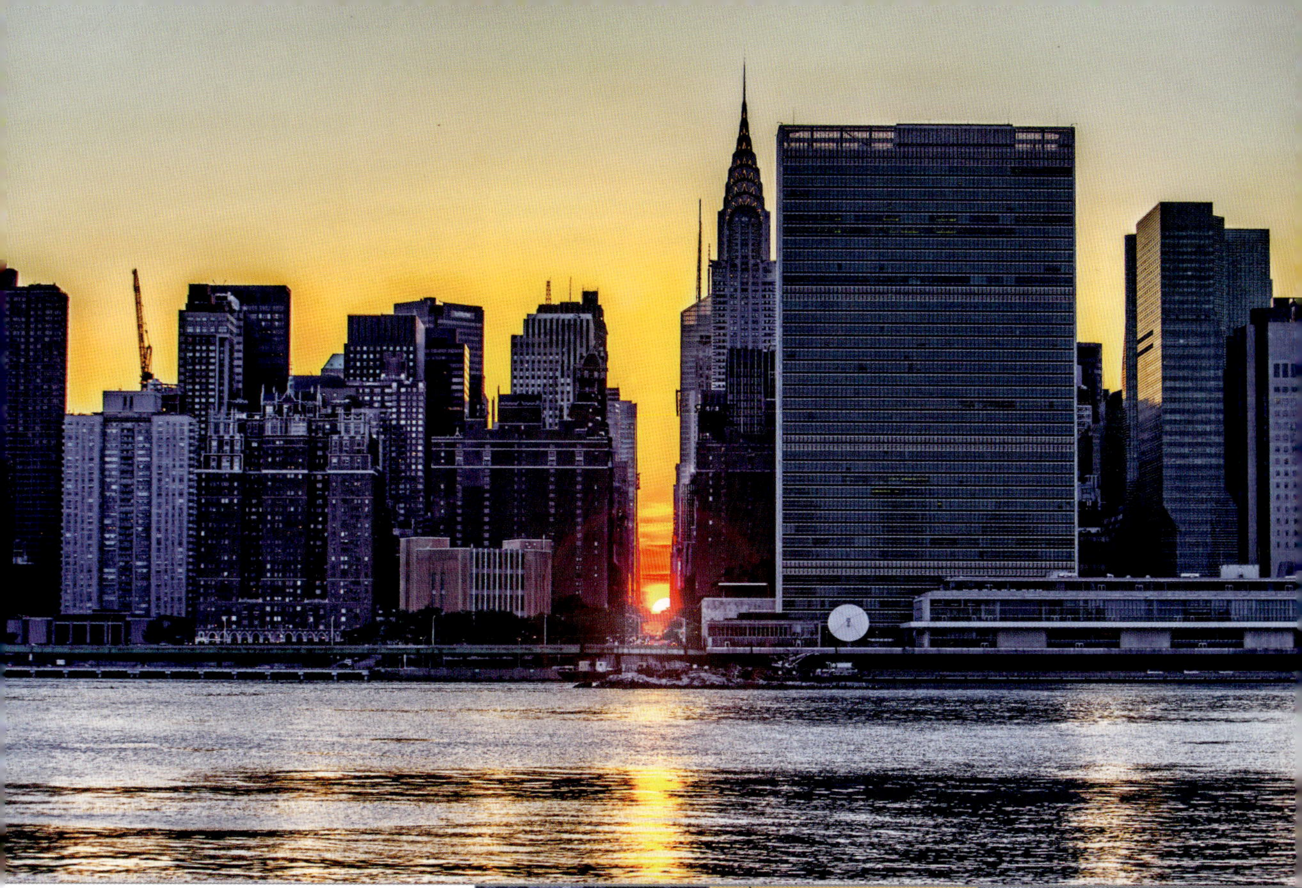

**Mr. Moonlight #1.** *(facing page, top)* A favorite pastime of mine is chasing the moon to line it up with some of New York City's better known landmarks. Here, it is setting behind the Statue of Liberty.

**Mr. Moonlight #2.** *(facing page, bottom)* From New Jersey looking east, the moon can be seen rising behind the historic New Yorker Hotel. Built in the art deco style of the 1930s, the New Yorker has played host to luminaries like Nikola Tesla, Queen Elizabeth, John F. Kennedy, and Muhammad Ali. I love the way the clouds partially obscure the moon in this photo. The New Yorker liked the photo so much they purchased a copy for their executive suite.

**Manhattanhenge #1 and #2.** *(above and right)* Stonehenge, England's prehistoric stone monument, has long been a center of conjecture. One theory is that ancient peoples marked the seasons by tracking the sun's alignment with its stone columns. A parody of its namesake, "Manhattanhenge" is celebrated by the New York City faithful when the setting sun aligns with the east/west street grid of Manhattan. The top photo shows the United Nations building, behind which is the top of the Chrysler Building. In the photo to the right, you see a pedestrian bridge that spans 42nd Street. Every "Manhattanhenge," that bridge is filled with (often) intoxicated, camera-phone-waving citizens. Any excuse to party in the Big Apple!

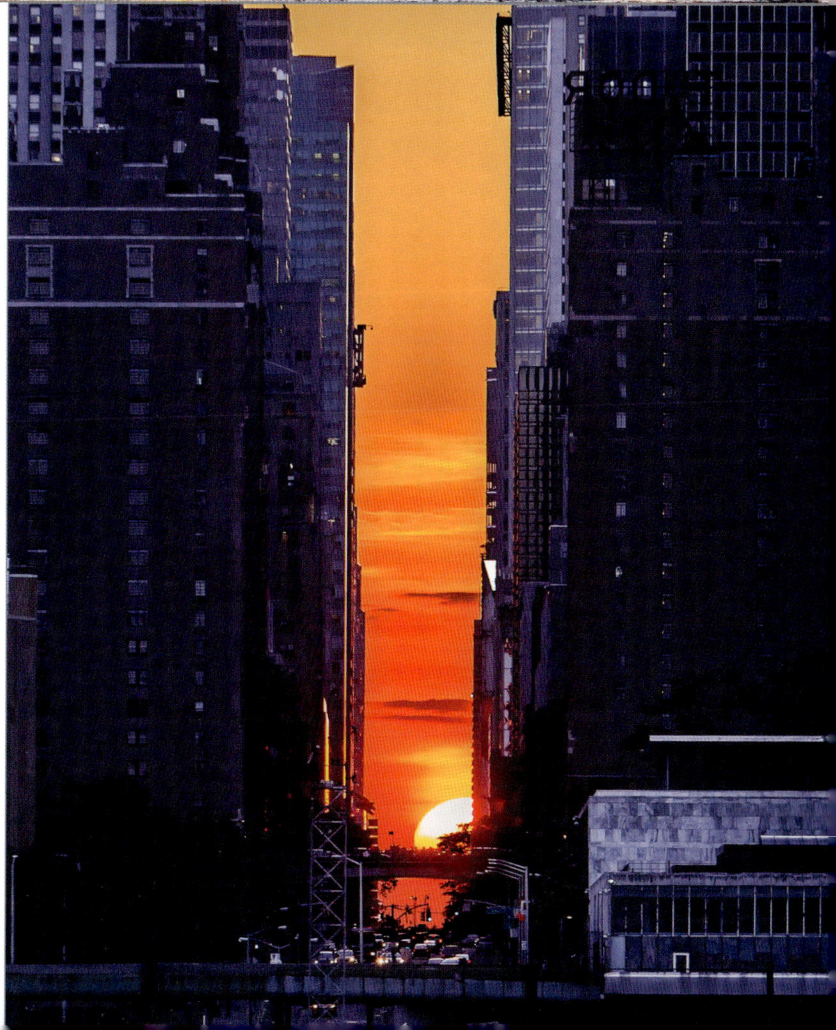

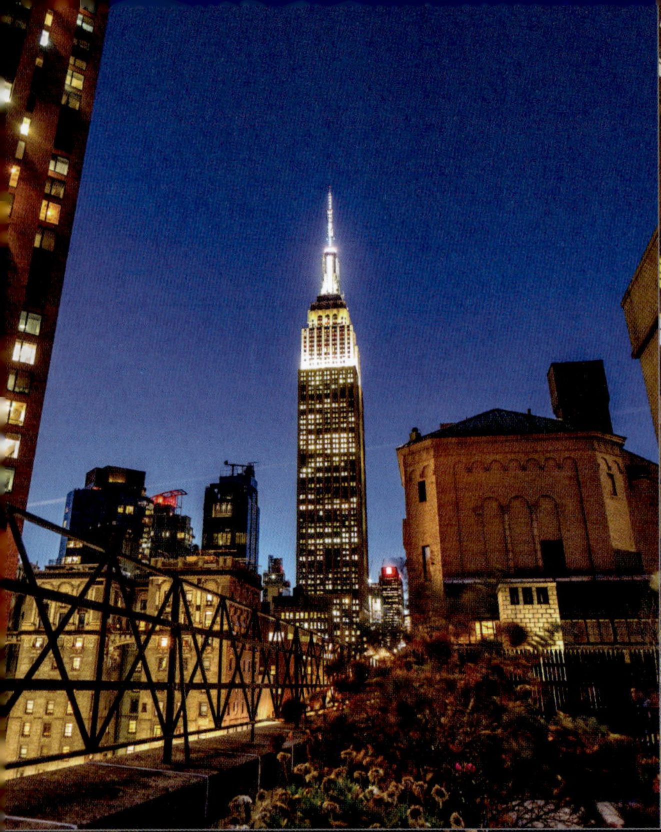

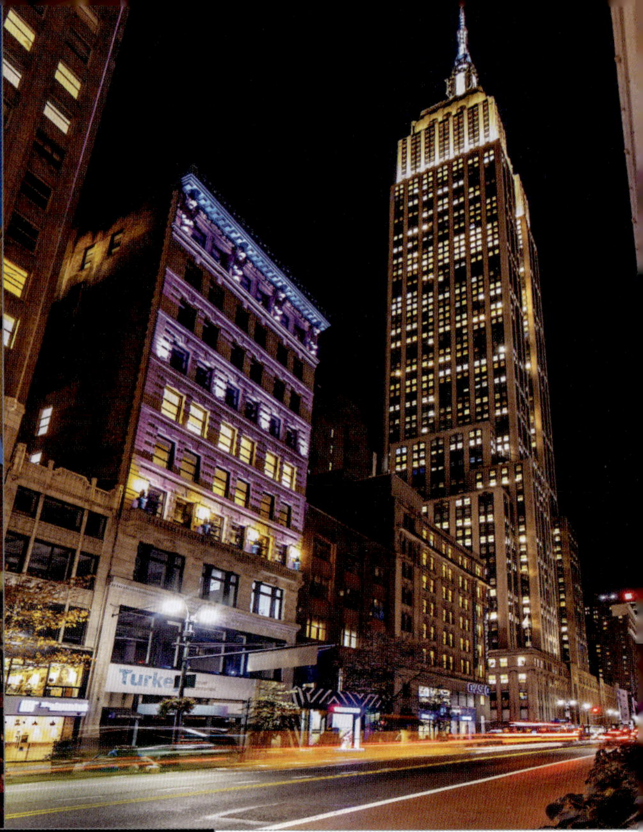

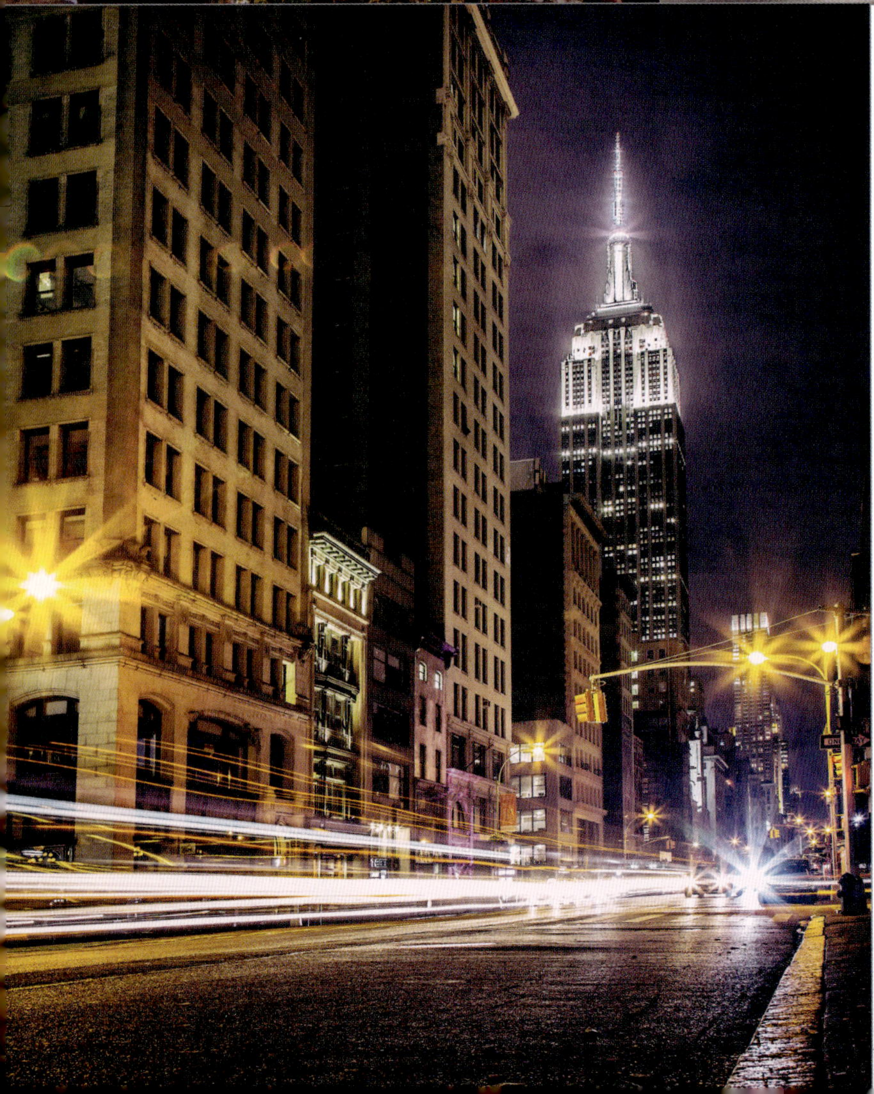

***Rooftop Oasis.*** *(top left)* With open space at a premium, New Yorkers often take advantage of their rooftops to create outdoor space. This particular rooftop garden offers a view of the Empire State Building.

***Empire State of Mind.*** *(top right)* Completed in 1931, the Empire State Building was the world's tallest building until 1970. At 1,454 feet, it captured the imagination of people all around the globe. Being climbed twice by King Kong in the movies only sealed the deal in terms of this building's iconic stature.

***Empire Statement.*** *(bottom left)* A long exposure captures the movement of traffic along Fifth Ave. The Empire State Building stands tall in the background.

***The World Is Flat.*** *(facing page)* A perennial favorite of locals and tourists alike, the Flatiron Building was constructed in 1921. This 22-story, wedge-shaped building resembles an old cast-iron clothes iron. Using a long exposure captured the movement of passing traffic as well as the full moon off to the left.

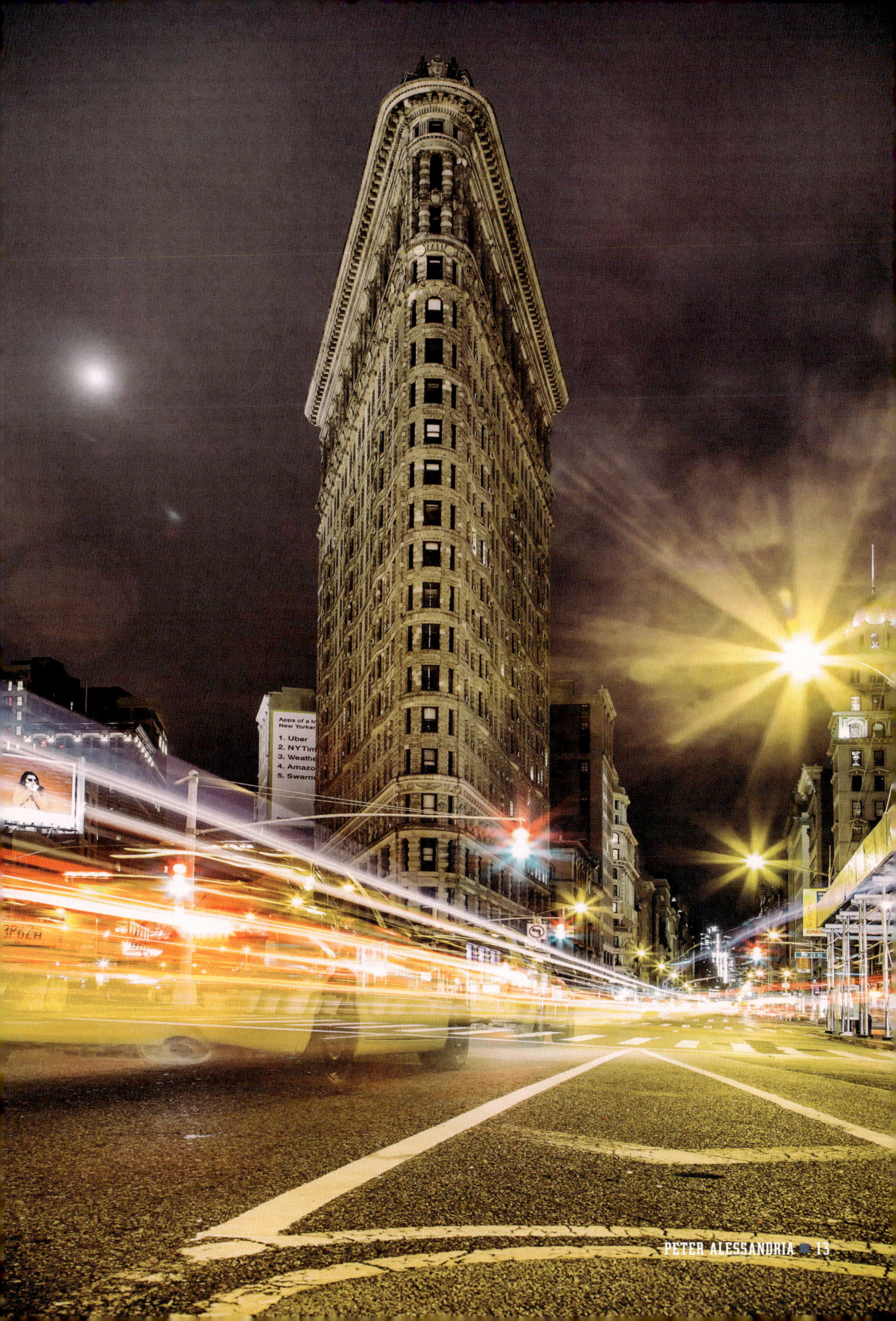
1. Uber

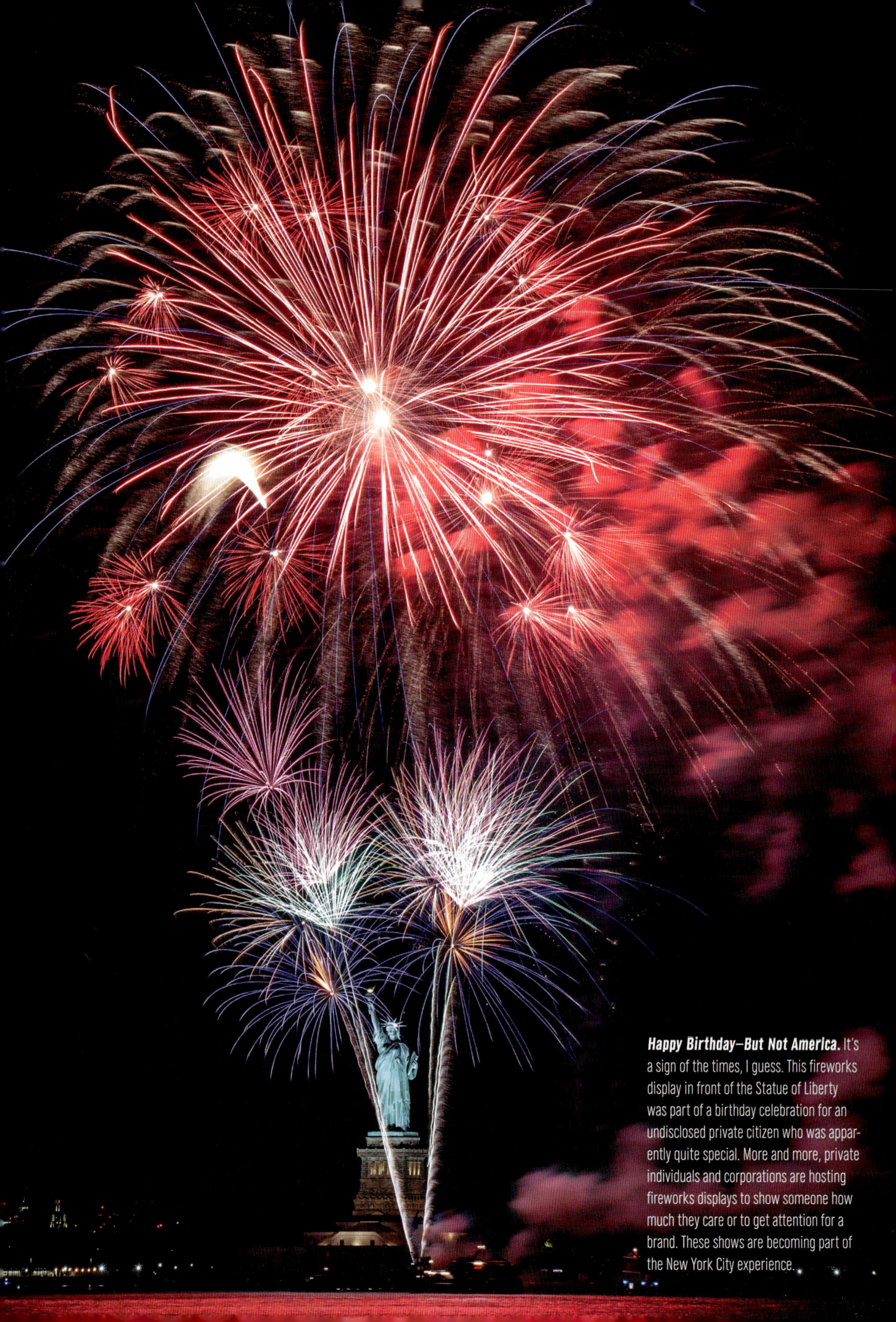

***Happy Birthday—But Not America.*** It's a sign of the times, I guess. This fireworks display in front of the Statue of Liberty was part of a birthday celebration for an undisclosed private citizen who was apparently quite special. More and more, private individuals and corporations are hosting fireworks displays to show someone how much they care or to get attention for a brand. These shows are becoming part of the New York City experience.

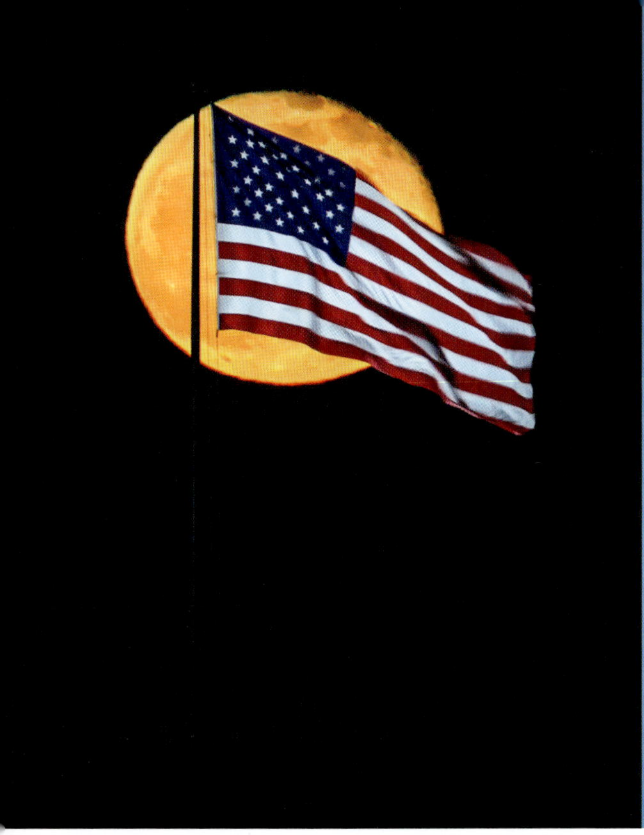

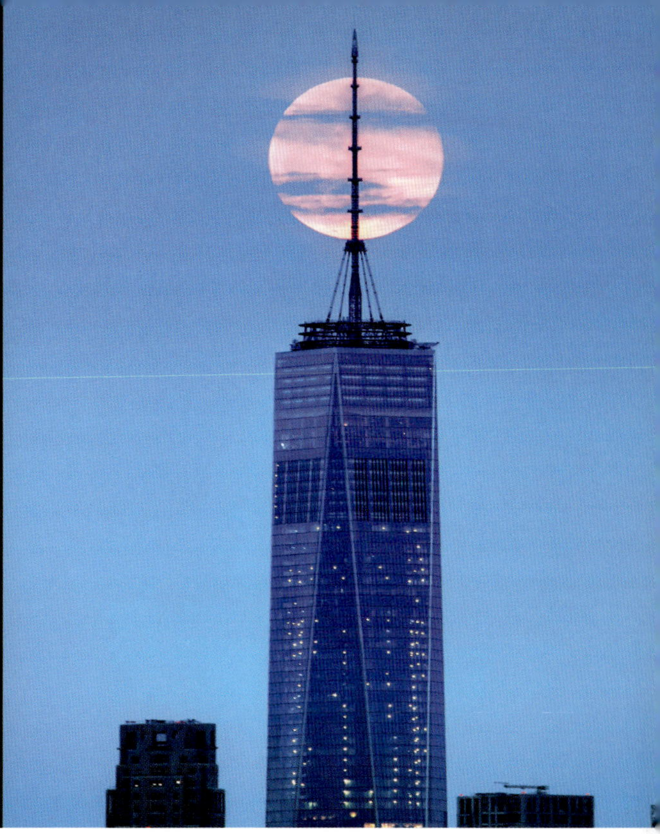

***Old Glory, Liberty Island.*** *(top left)* Just behind the Statue of Liberty on Liberty Island is a courtyard with a lone American flag. I took this photo one night while waiting for the moon to rise above the statue.

***Pink Moon.*** *(top right)* The April full moon creates a beautiful scene above One World Trade Center, near the site of the original Twin Towers. The Freedom Tower stands as a reminder of our strength and resilience as a nation.

***A Slow Night in Times Square.*** *(below)* New York City is what it is because people from all over the world come to live, work, and visit. This was the first night I had been in Times Square for many years. I was amazed by the size of the crowd and by the variety of accents and languages I heard. There were at least a dozen different languages being spoken!

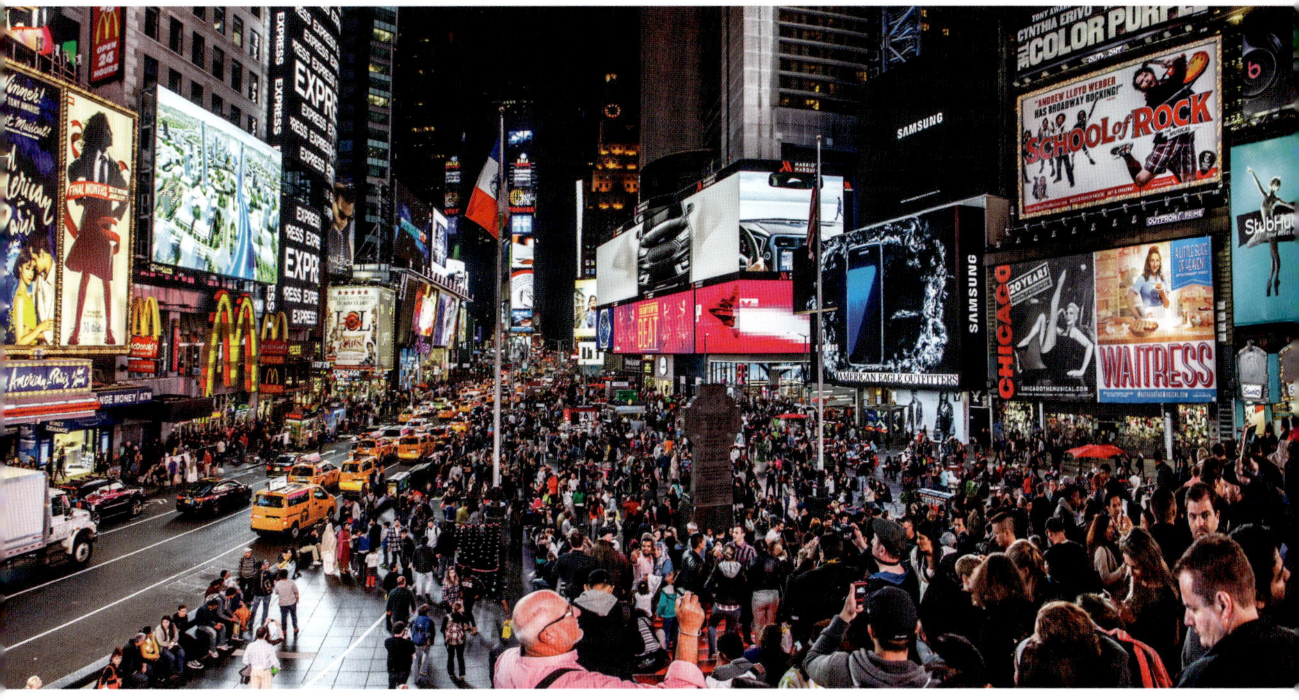

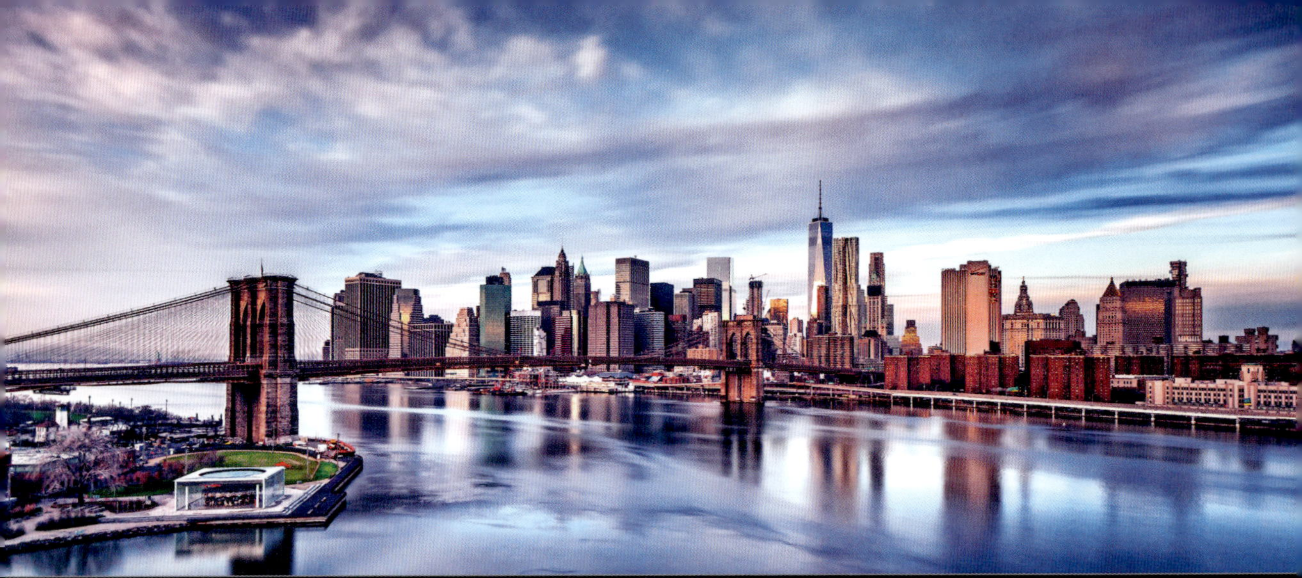
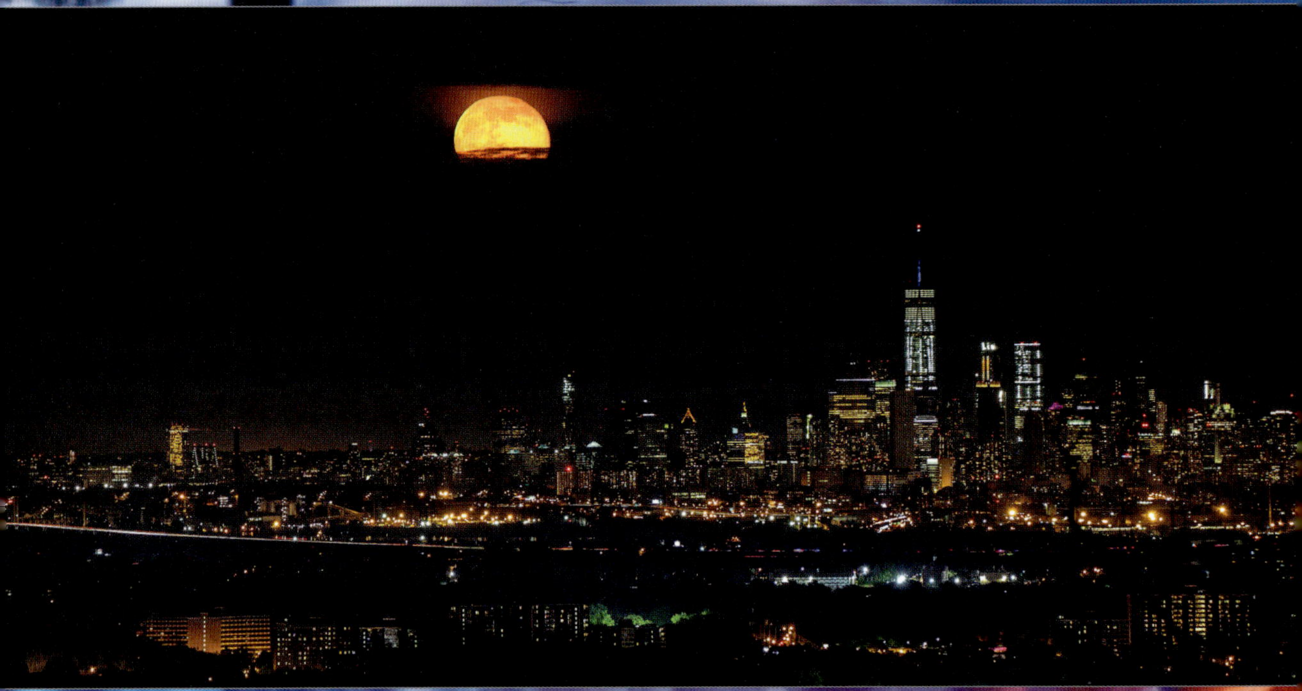
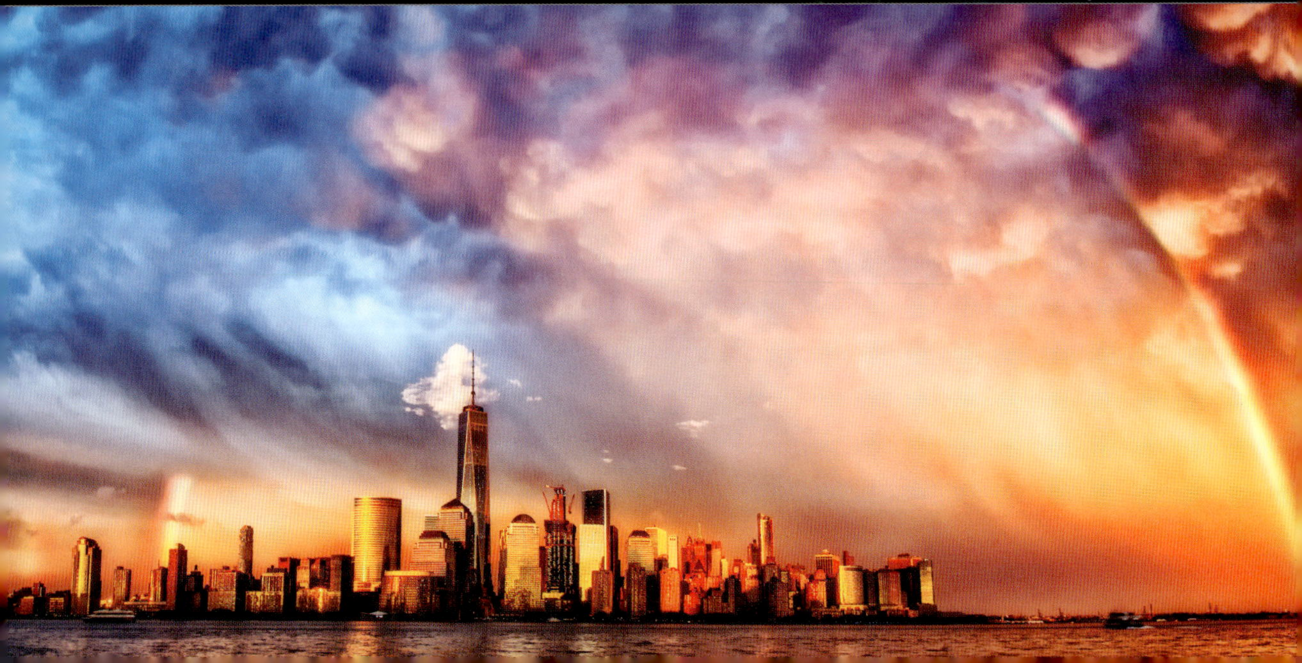

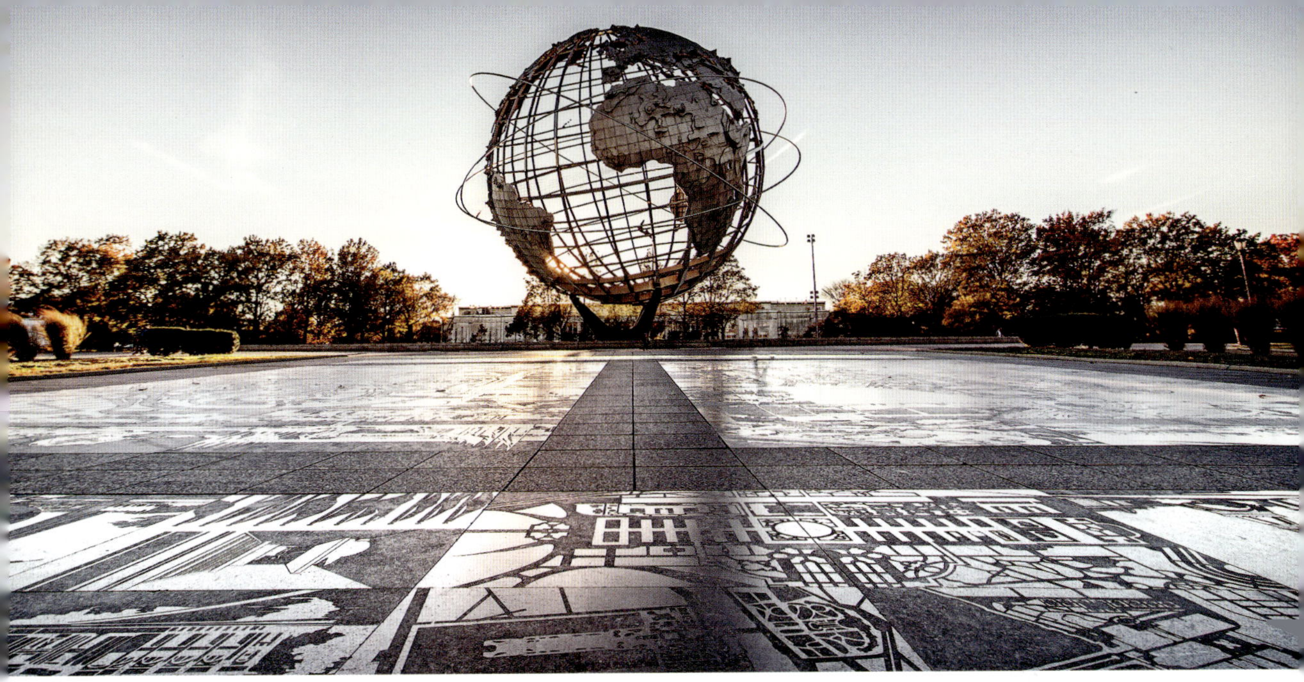

**Manhattan Blue.** *(facing page, top)* Lower Manhattan and the Brooklyn Bridge are seen from the walkway of the Manhattan Bridge on a tranquil Christmas morning, just after dawn.

**Under a Yellow Moon.** *(facing page, center) Lower Manhattan sits under a full moonrise as seen from nearly fourteen miles away in West Orange, New Jersey.*

**Rainbow City.** *(facing page, bottom)* In the aftermath of a huge thunderstorm, a massive rainbow, partially obscured by the clouds, enclosed the city.

**Unisphere.** *(above)* In 1964, the World's Fair came to New York. At its center was the Unisphere, a 12-story, stainless-steel model of the earth that still stands as a reminder of this coming-together of over eighty nations.

**Empty Sky Memorial.** *(below)* Opposite Ground Zero, across the Hudson River in New Jersey, the Empty Sky Memorial honors New Jersey residents lost on 9/11. The setting sun creates the illusion of a ring of fire and captures the ghosted figures of visitors taking in the etched names.

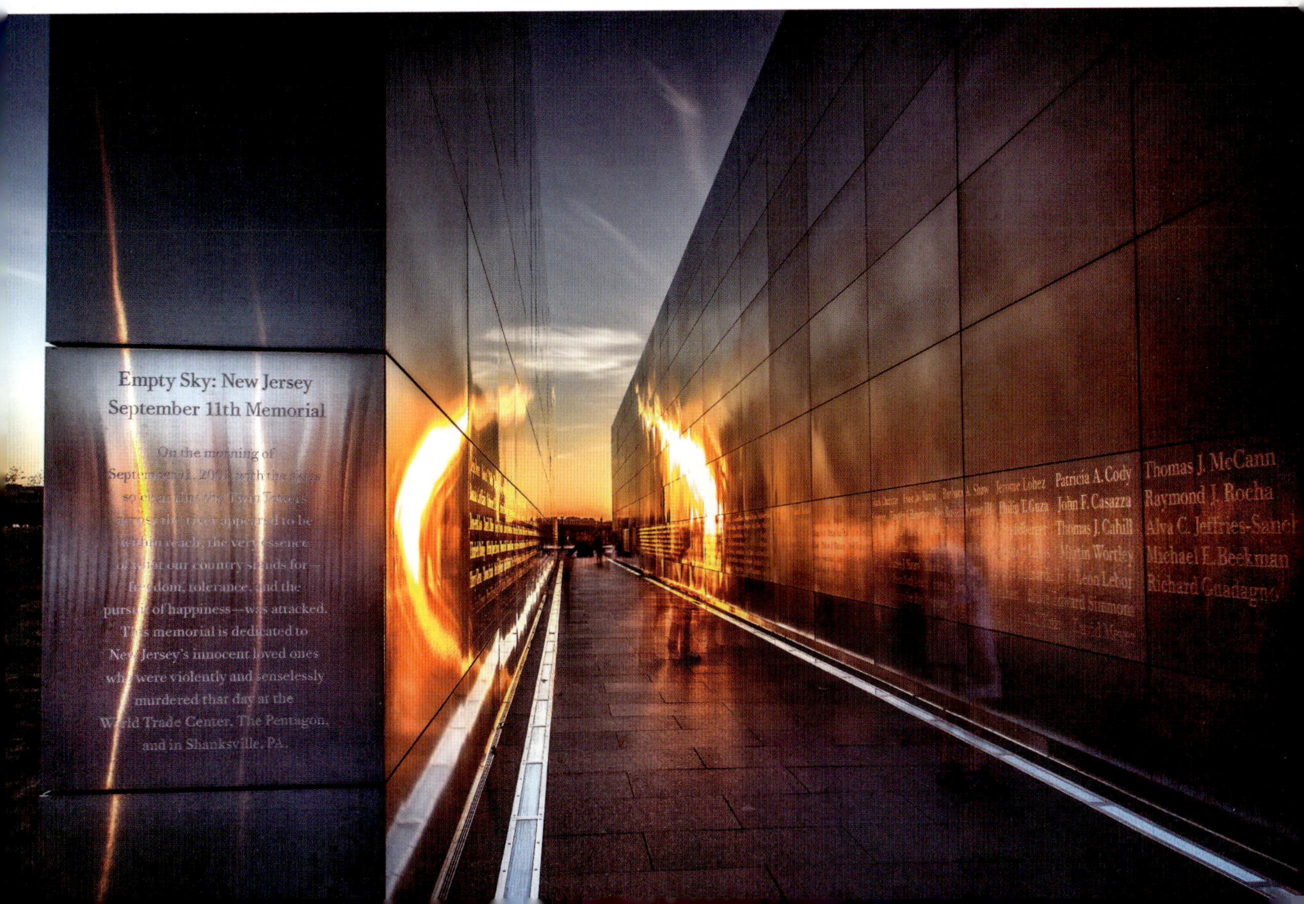

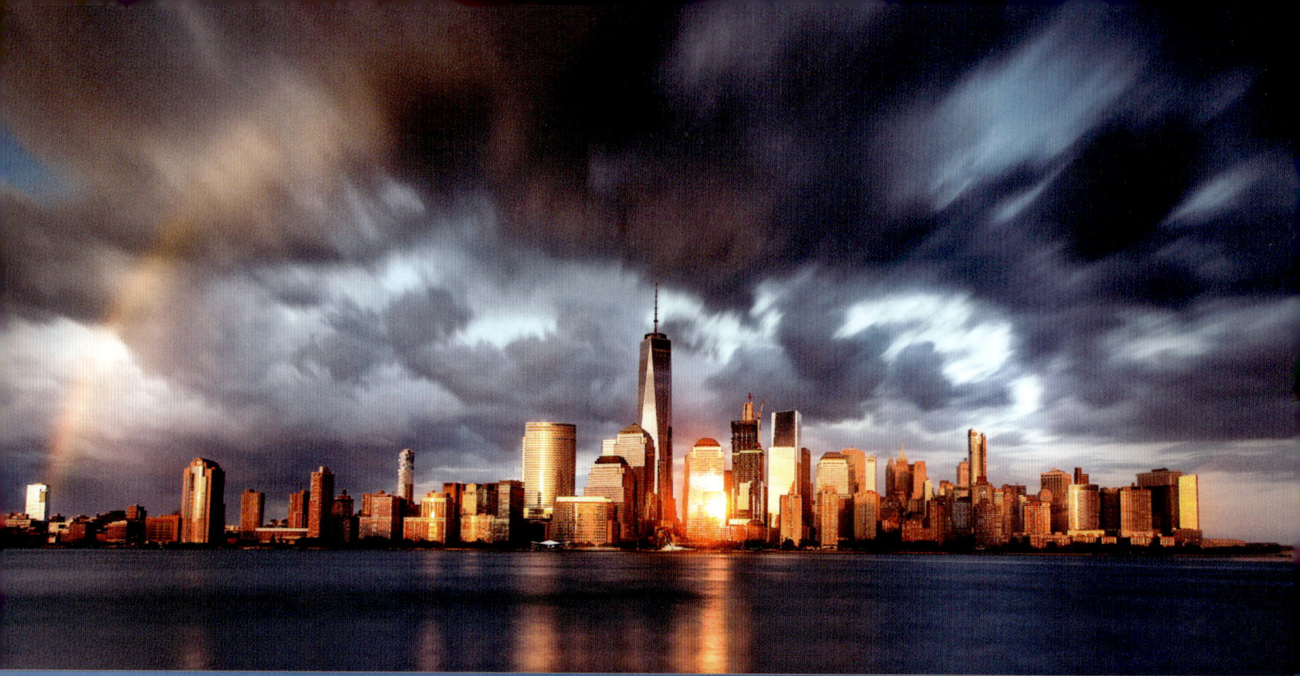

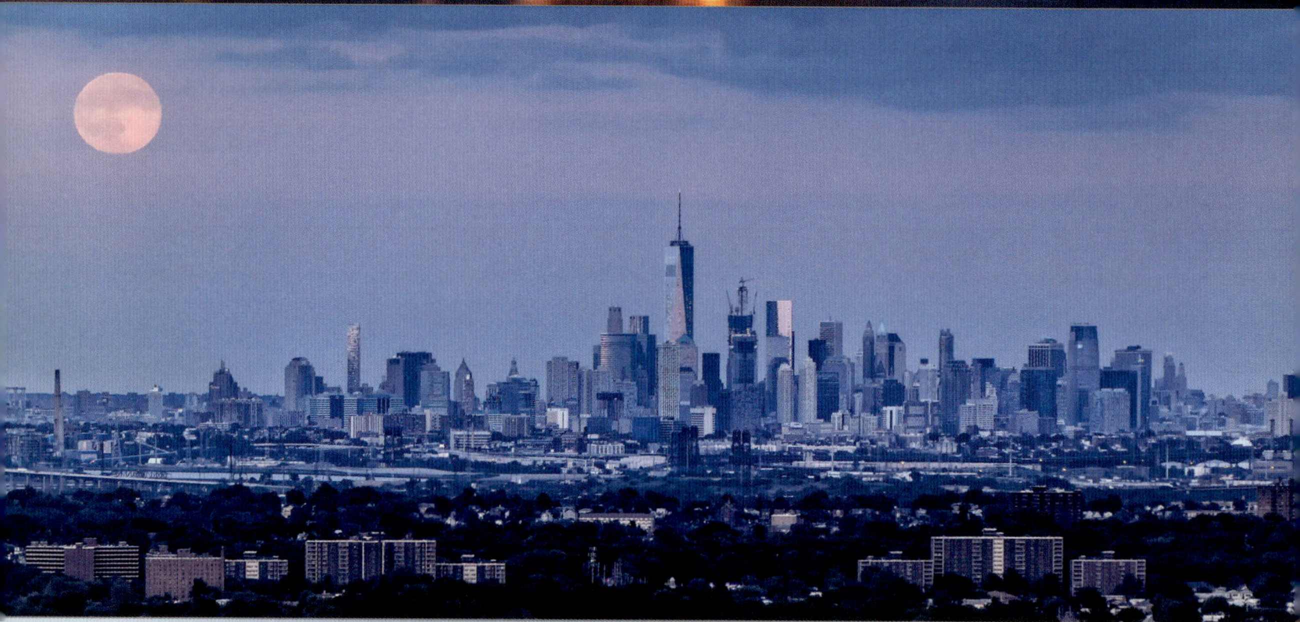

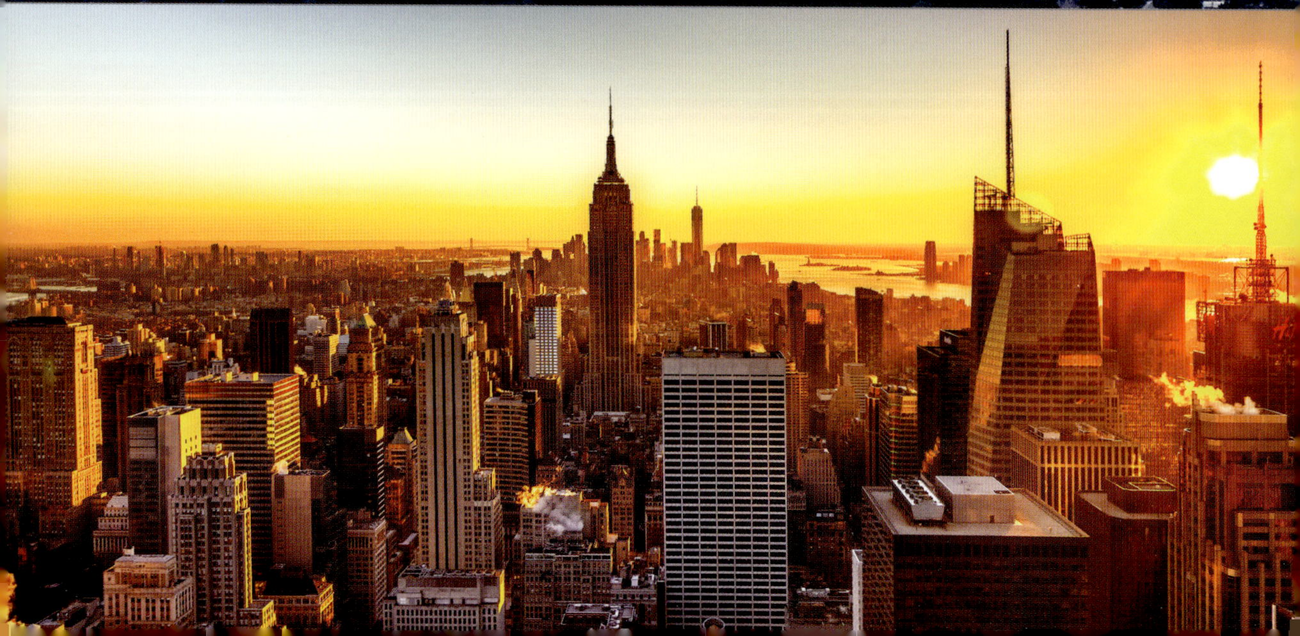

**Rainbow Gold.** *(facing page, top)* A rapidly moving summer storm leaves a golden rainbow over Lower Manhattan. Turns out New York City is a great place for photographers to storm chase.

**Blue Moonrise.** *(facing page, center)* This photo of the full moon rising over Manhattan was taken just after sunset, a time known in photographic circles as "blue hour." This photo was taken from nearly fourteen miles away in West Orange, New Jersey.

**The View From the Top.** *(facing page, bottom)* Rooftop shots like this give a true insider's perspective on the world's greatest city. Looking south, we see the Empire State Building, then Lower Manhattan and One World Trade Center. In the far distance, the Statue of Liberty stands in New York Harbor.

**Golden Hour.** *(right)* A setting sun meets the golden illumination of the Empire State Building's tower lights. I love how the pink sky compliments the yellow glow of the building's offices and crown.

**34th Street By the Dawn's Early Light.** *(below)* Photographing a New York City sunrise is always fun. This is the view looking east across the Hudson River from Hoboken, New Jersey. I was waiting for the sun to come up along 34th Street. The famed Wyndham New York Hotel is to the left and the Empire State Building is to the right.

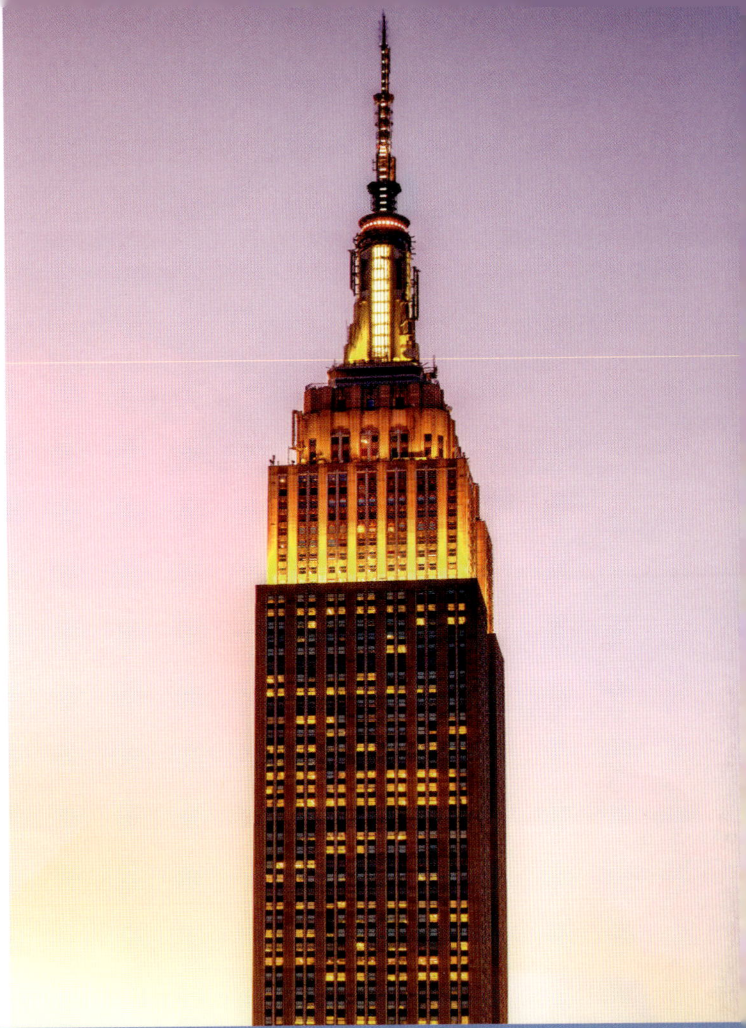

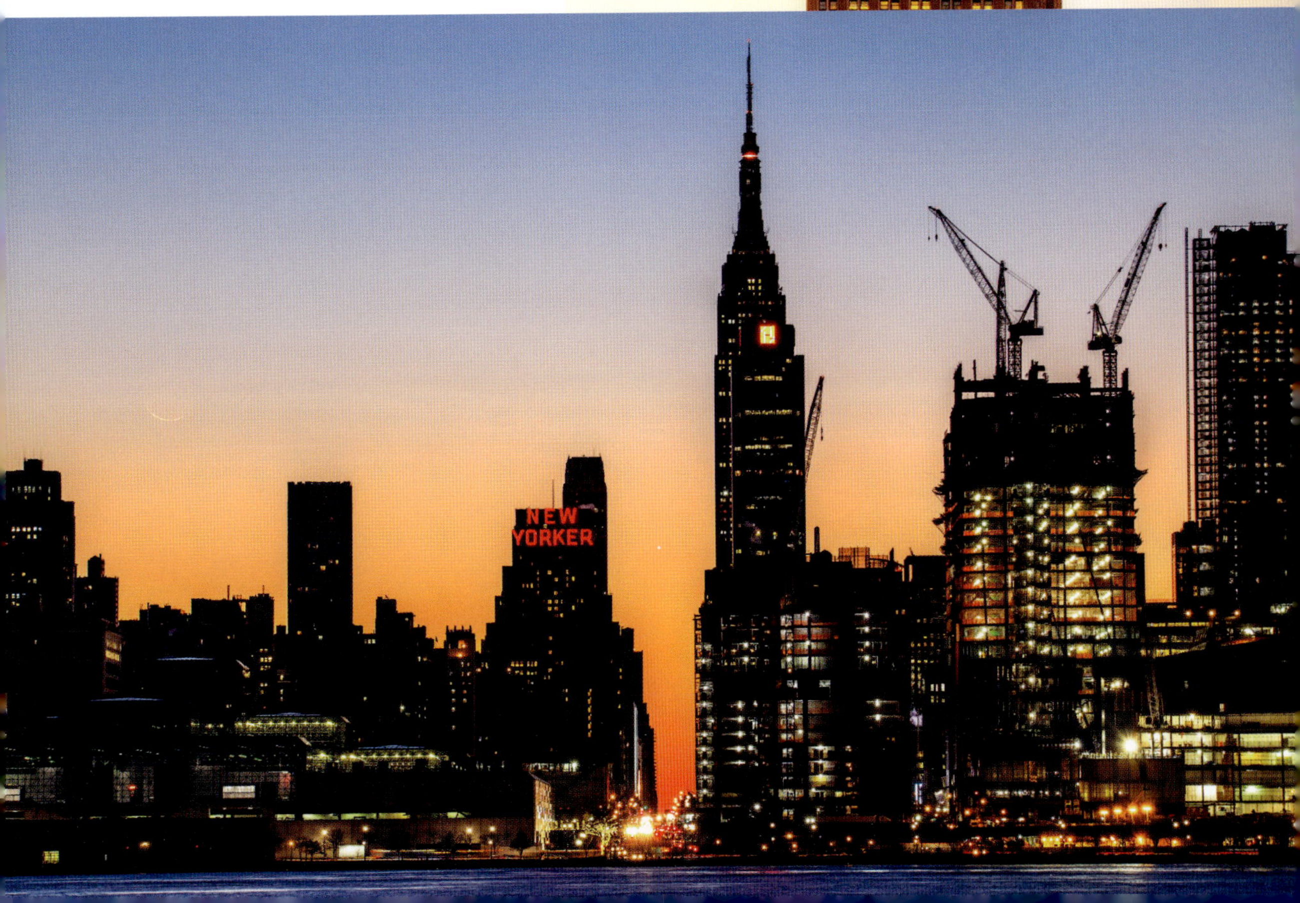

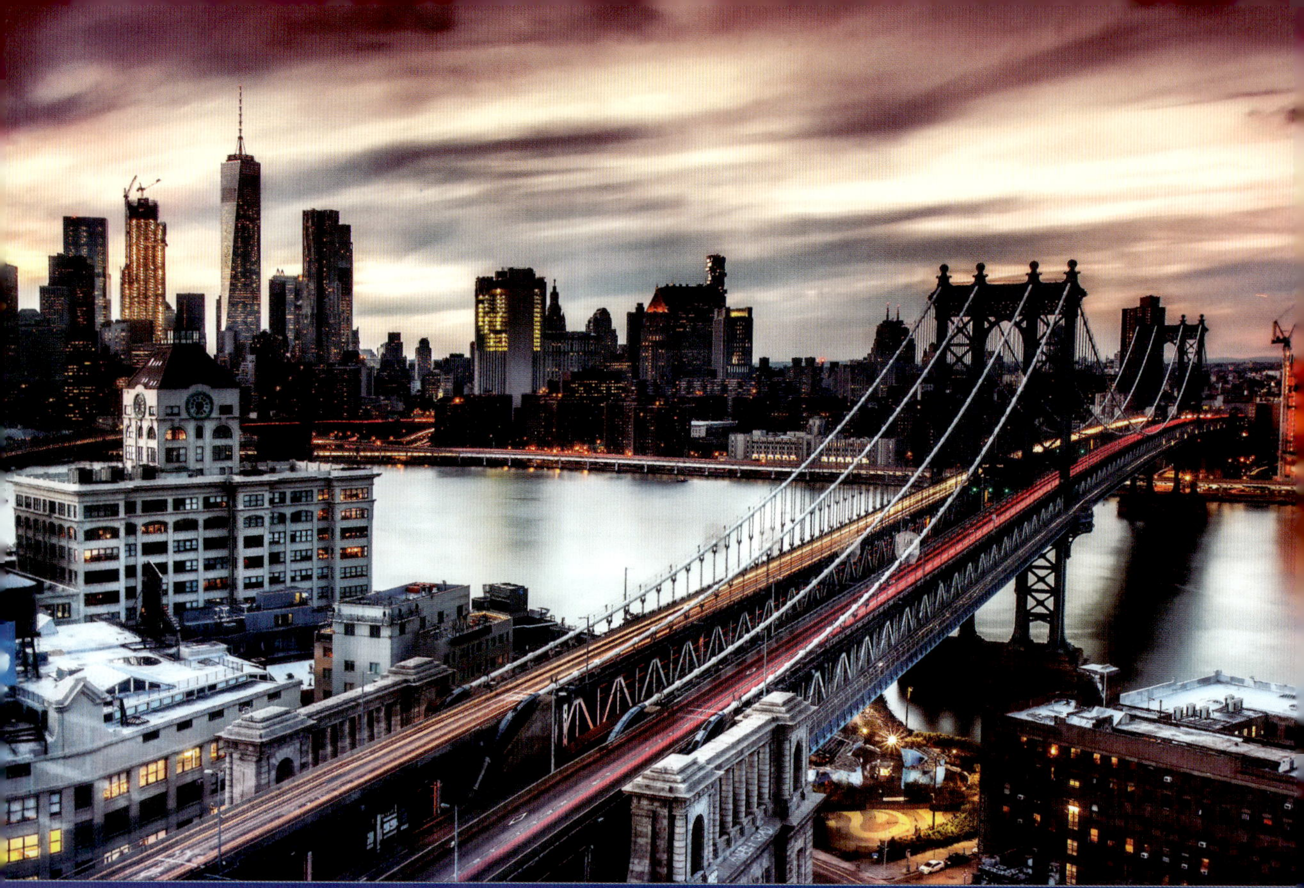

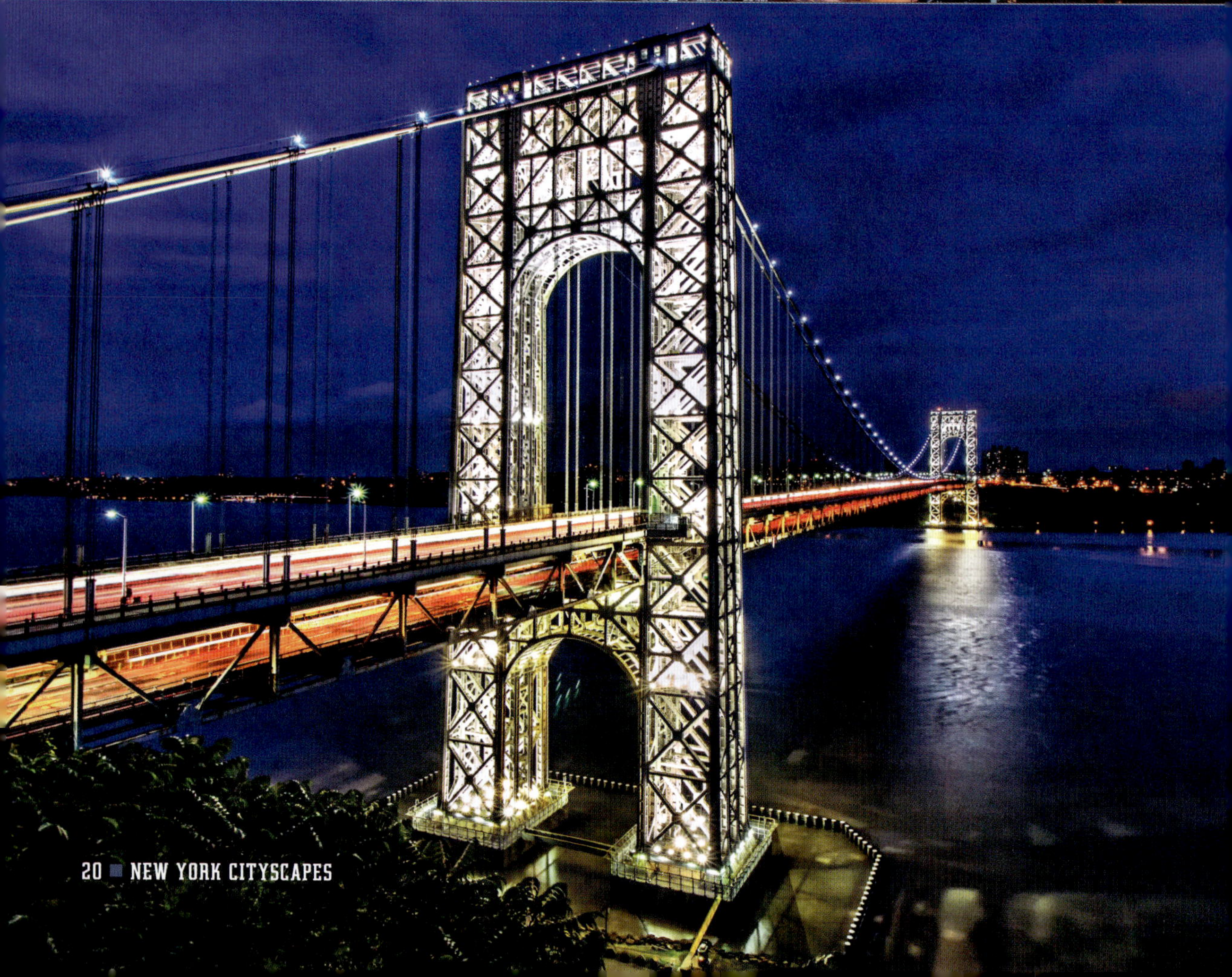

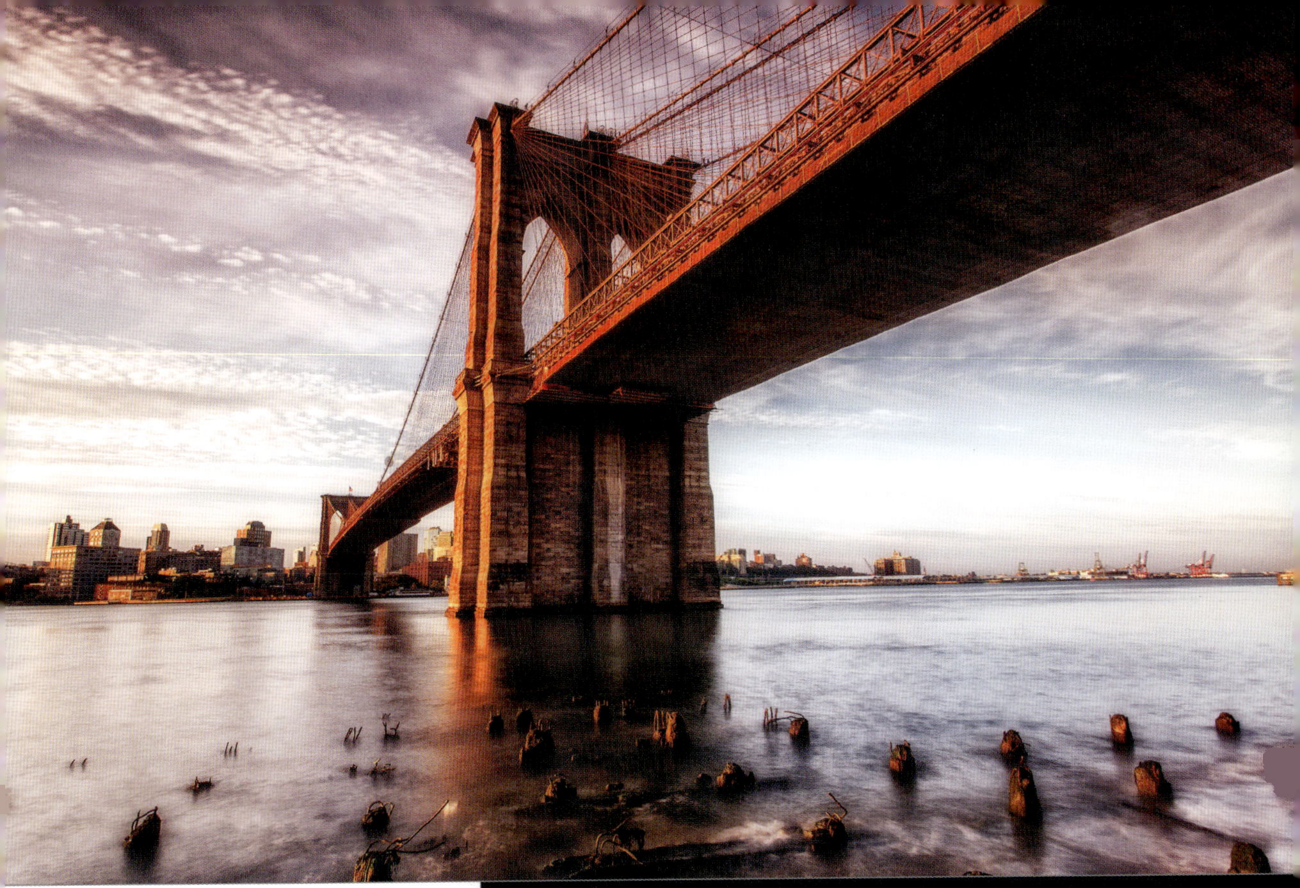

**Manhattan Bridge.** *(facing page, top)* This is a view of the Manhattan Bridge and Lower Manhattan from a rooftop in Brooklyn. The 1909 bridge was the first to employ an innovative truss design that was later used in many suspension bridges. I love the beautiful hues in the sky from the setting sun.

**Lit Up.** *(facing page, bottom)* When the George Washington Bridge was completed in 1933, the towers were supposed to be enclosed in sheet metal. However, at the last minute the decision was made to leave them uncovered. Lights were added to the internal structure and now, on national holidays, the towers are illuminated from within.

**"I Have a Bridge for Sale."** *(above)* The Brooklyn Bridge, opened in 1883, spans the East River between Brooklyn and Lower Manhattan. It carries more than 100,000 vehicles every day, but the bridge's center-span pedestrian walkway is so popular that it's often more congested than the roadway below!

**Verrazano Nights.** *(right)* The Verrazano-Narrows Bridge spans the entrance to the New York Harbor, connecting Staten Island and Brooklyn. To capture this photo, I waited for the moon to rise above the horizon and cross through the uprights of the bridge's tower.

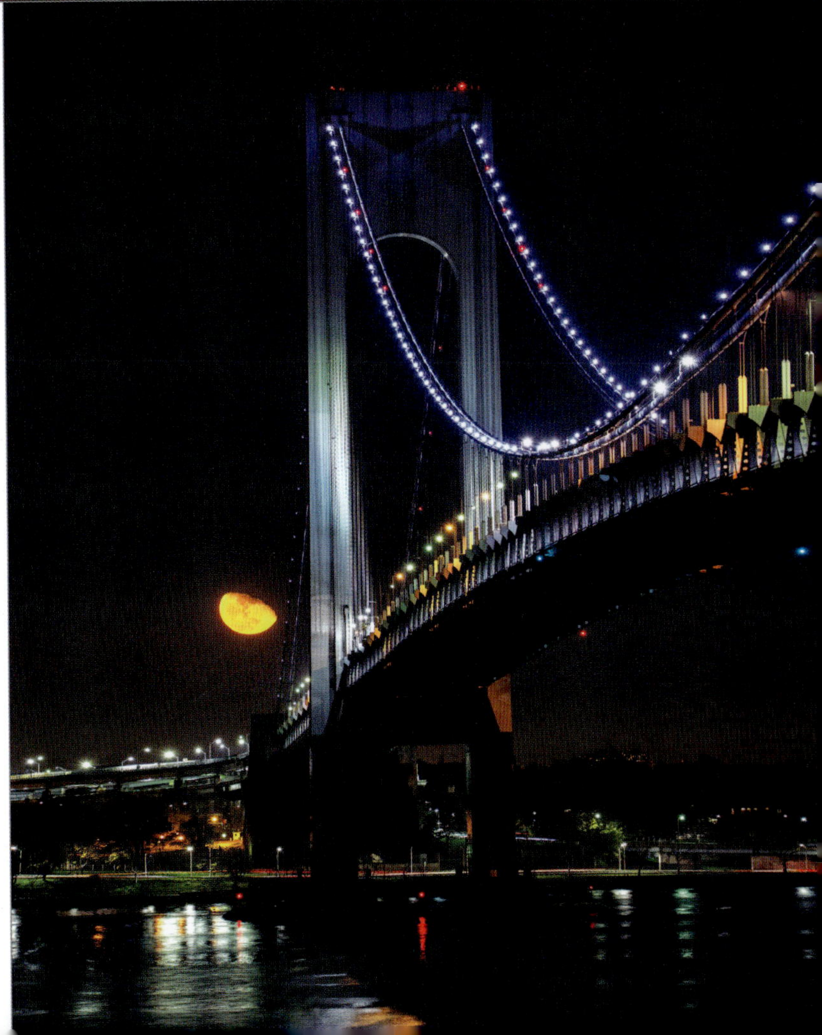

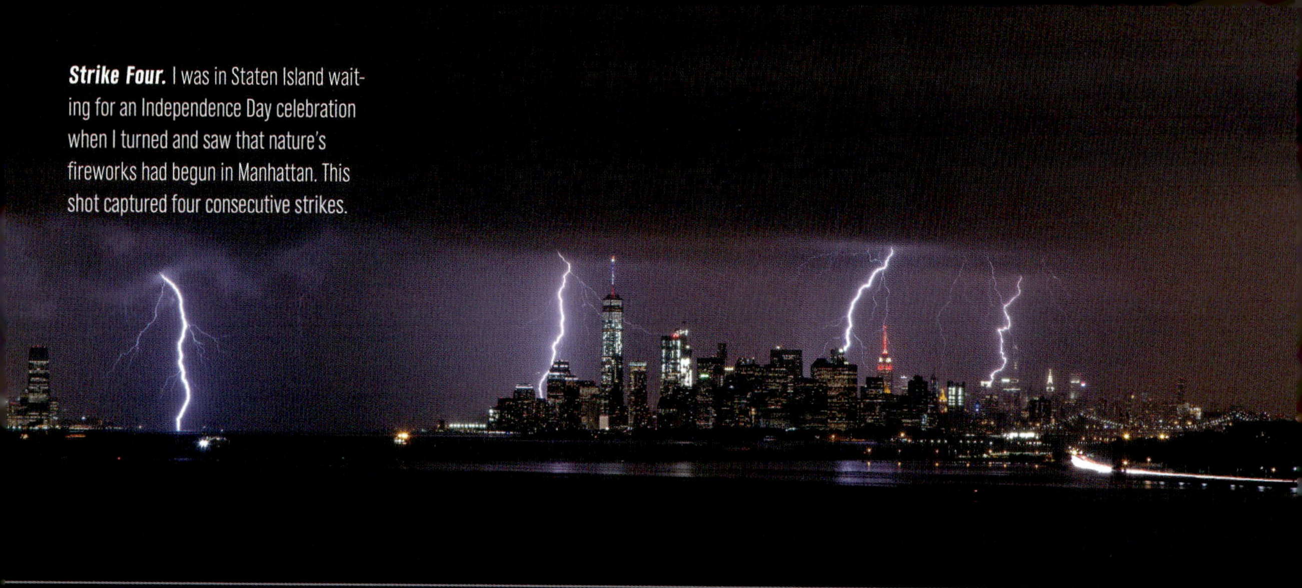

***Strike Four.*** I was in Staten Island waiting for an Independence Day celebration when I turned and saw that nature's fireworks had begun in Manhattan. This shot captured four consecutive strikes.

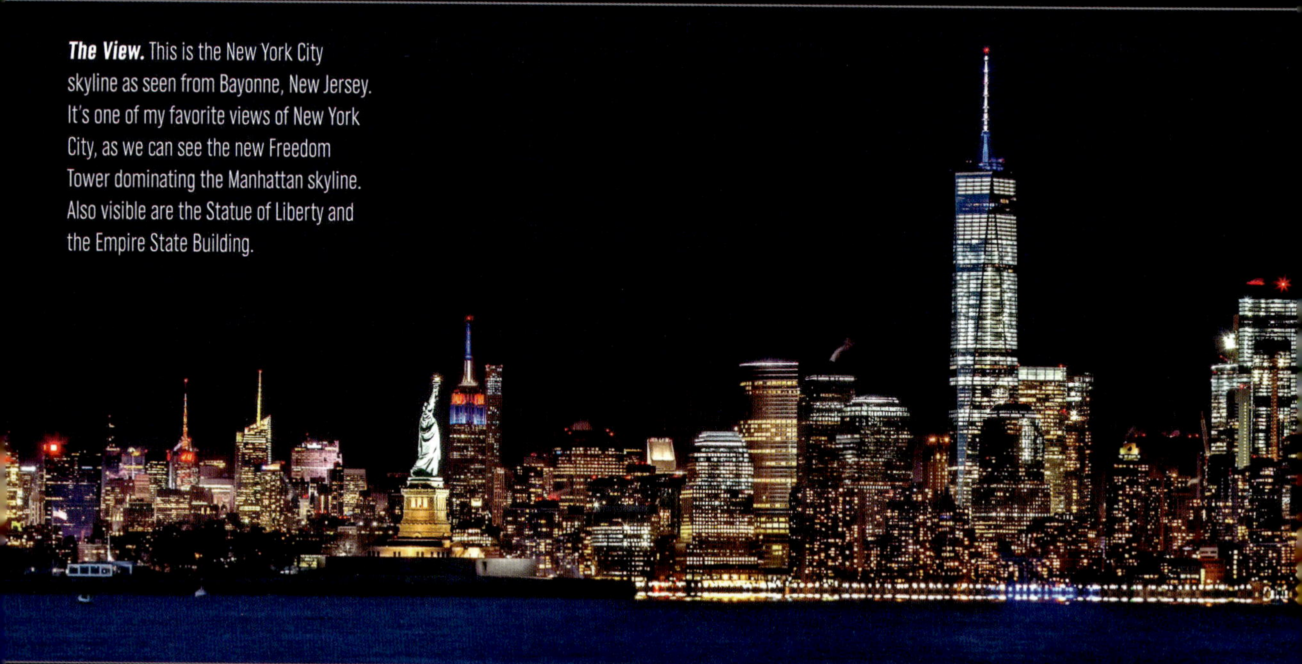

***The View.*** This is the New York City skyline as seen from Bayonne, New Jersey. It's one of my favorite views of New York City, as we can see the new Freedom Tower dominating the Manhattan skyline. Also visible are the Statue of Liberty and the Empire State Building.

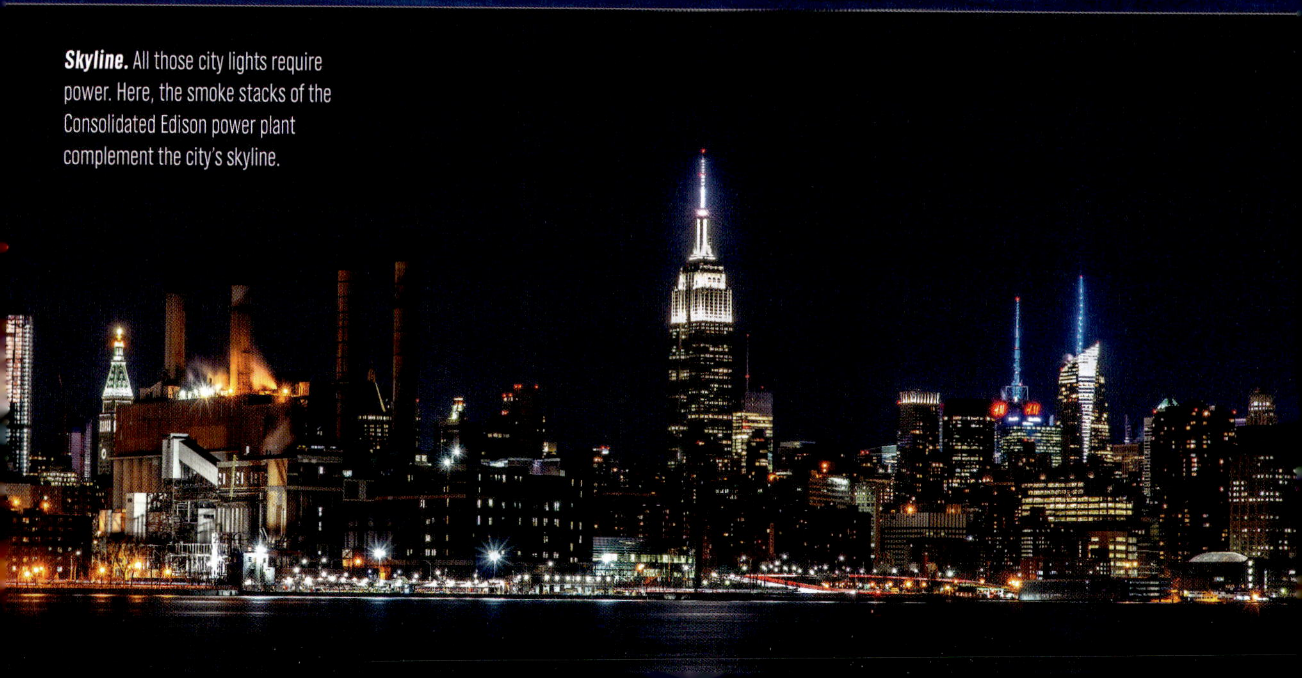

***Skyline.*** All those city lights require power. Here, the smoke stacks of the Consolidated Edison power plant complement the city's skyline.

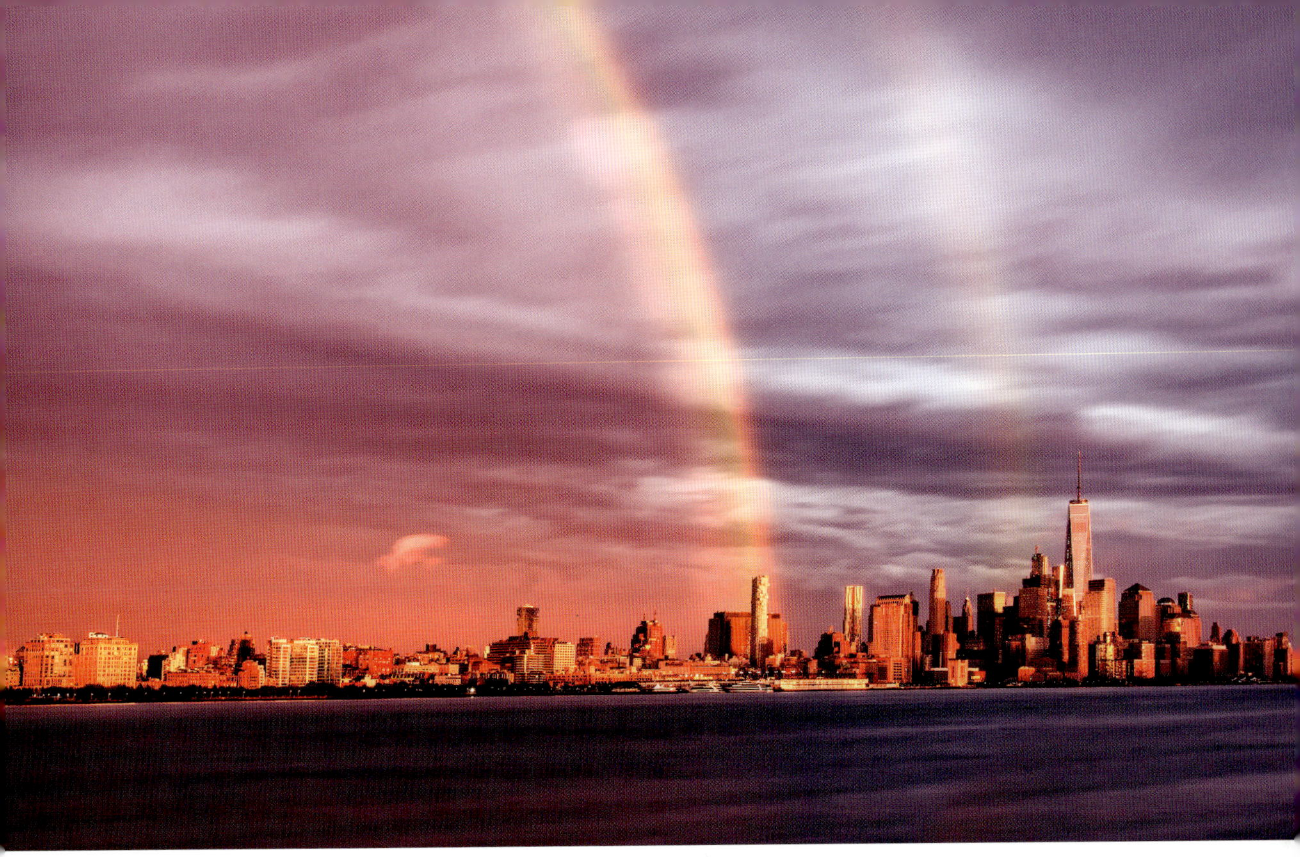

**Double Rainbow.** *(above)* Afternoon thunderstorms often give rise to rainbows over New York City. This particular day, a massive storm produced an equally massive double rainbow that arched over the entire city.

**Lower Manhattan During Blue Hour.** *(below)* During a long exposure, anything that is moving (clouds, water, traffic) blurs and takes on a surrealistic look. Here, the exposure was 30 seconds. I love the way you can see the motion of the clouds and the smoothness of the water.

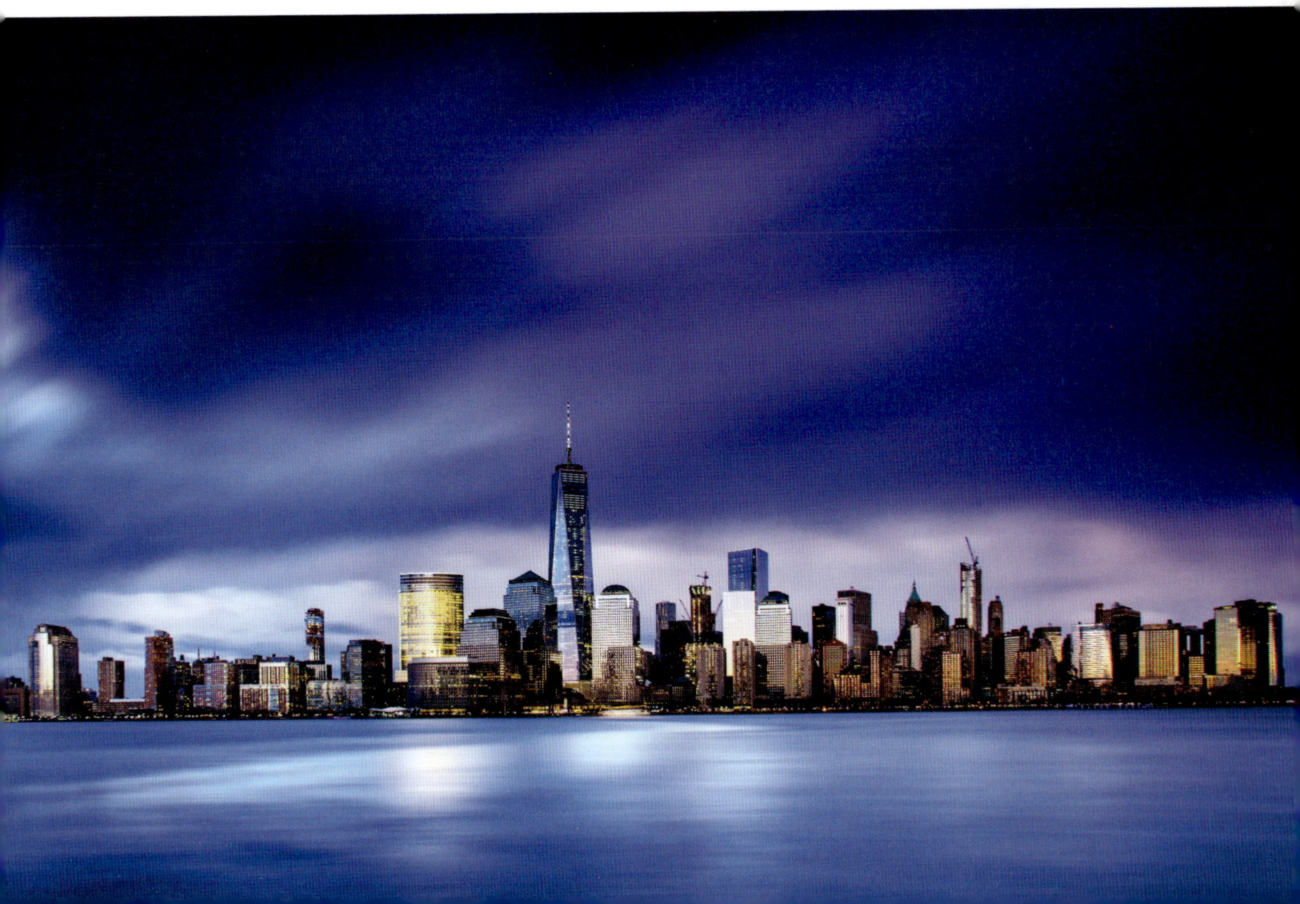

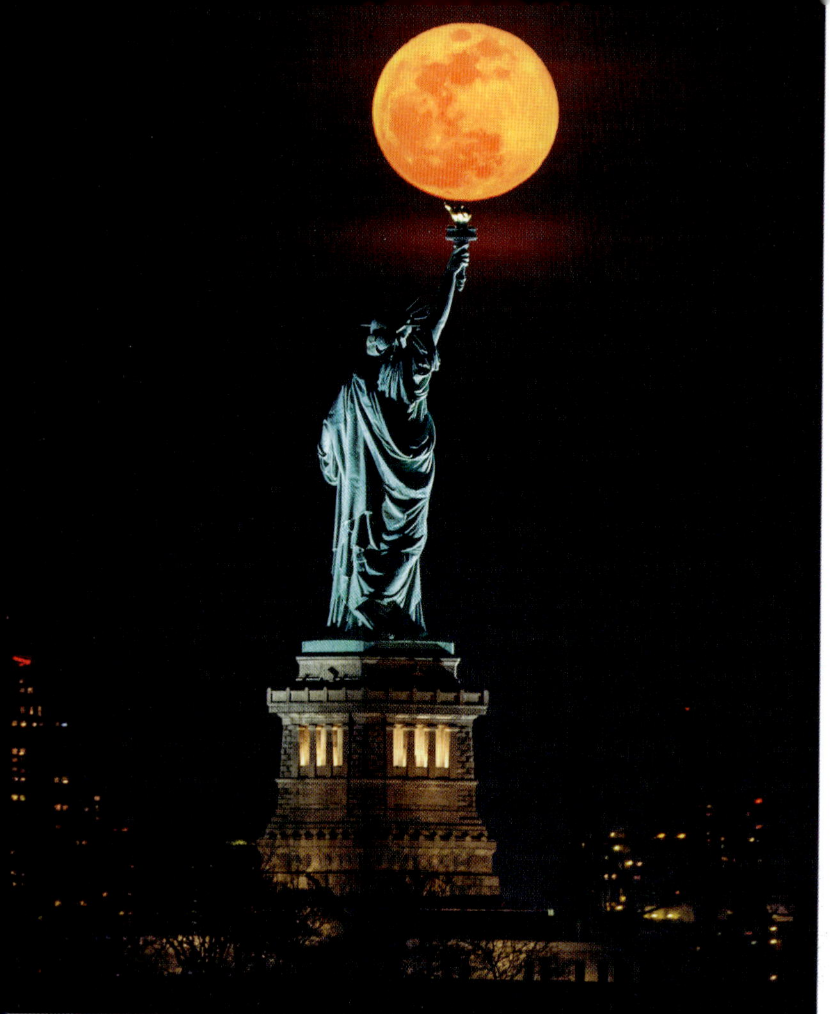

**Lunar Lady.** *(left)* Ongoing objects of my affection, the Statue of Liberty and full moon are best when photographed together. In this shot, the full moon is rising behind Lady Liberty, as seen from Jersey City, New Jersey. People often ask why the moon looks so big and colorful in my photos. There are three reasons. First, I use a long telephoto lens, which has the effect of making distant objects look larger. Second, I usually try to get as far away from my landmark as possible, meaning it looks smaller in comparison to the moon. Third, I usually shoot the moon when it is very low on the horizon. This has the dual effect of making it look larger, since the atmosphere has a magnifying effect, and also giving it the orange glow. The orange color is caused by dust, pollution, and moisture blocking all but the longer red wavelengths of light.

**GWB #1.** *(below)* This panoramic long exposure features the George Washington Bridge (GWB) in all its glory. Spanning more than 3,500 feet across the Hudson River and connecting New York and New Jersey, this was once the world's longest bridge. Today it's not the longest, but it is the busiest–with more than 330,000 vehicle crossings every day. You can see the Manhattan skyline contained nicely underneath the bridge's massive center span.

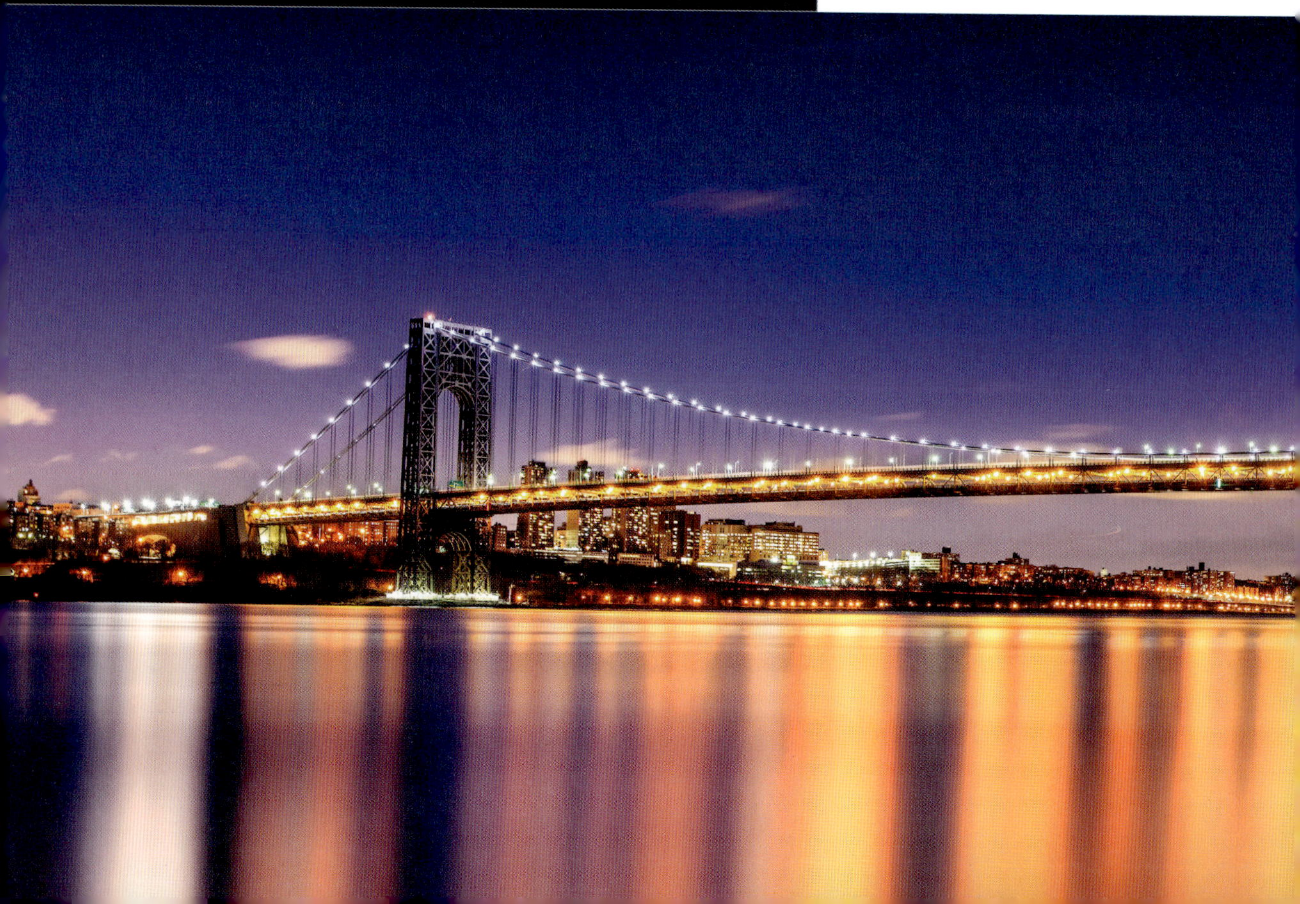

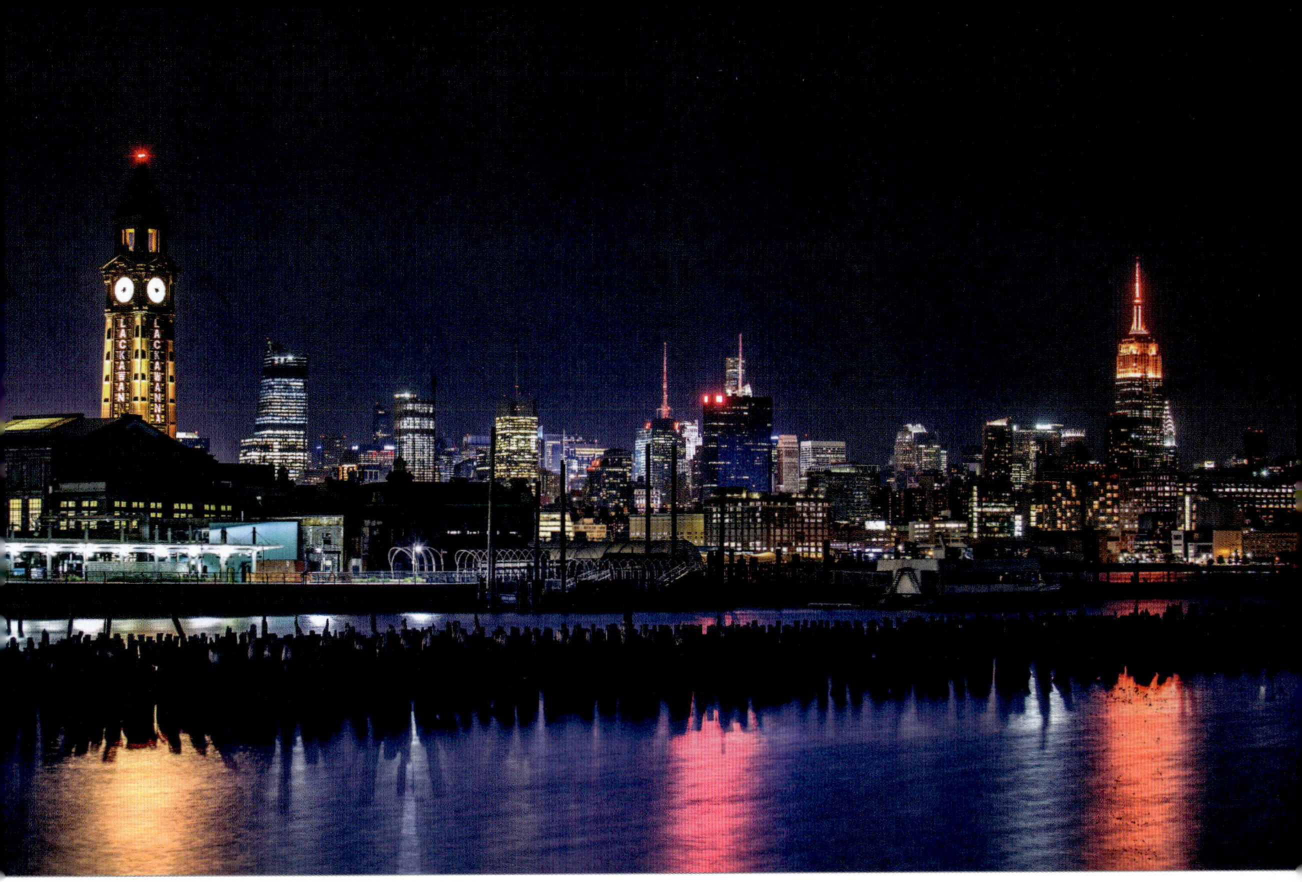

***Twin Peaks.*** *(above)* This is the New York City skyline as seen from Newport, New Jersey. To the left is the Lackawanna Clock Tower (actually in Hoboken). Across the Hudson River, at the center, are the spires of the H&M, Bank of America, and the *New York Times* buildings. To the right is the Empire State Building. In the foreground, we see remnants of an old wooden pier that used to greet day-tripping New Yorkers who crossed the river to the suburbs of New Jersey.

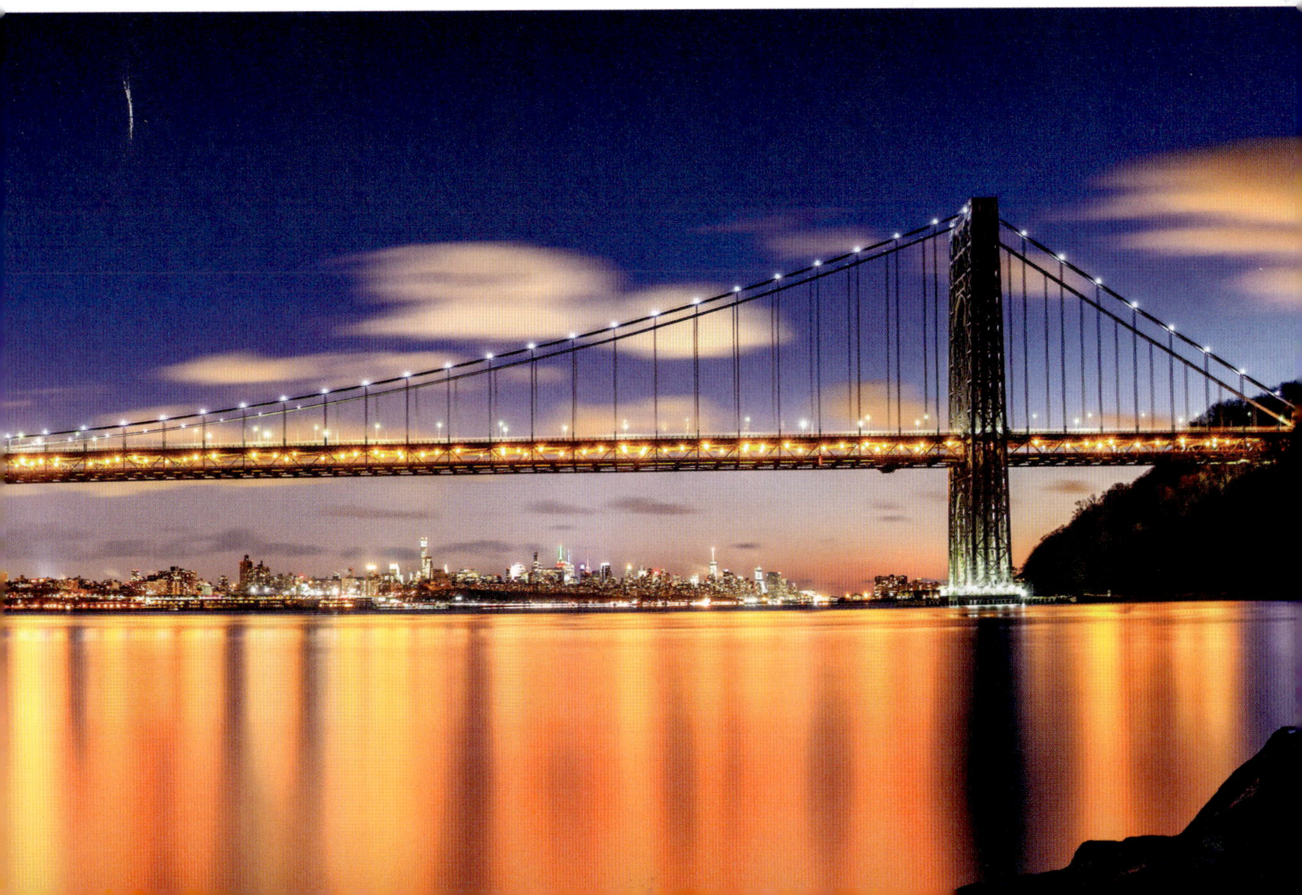

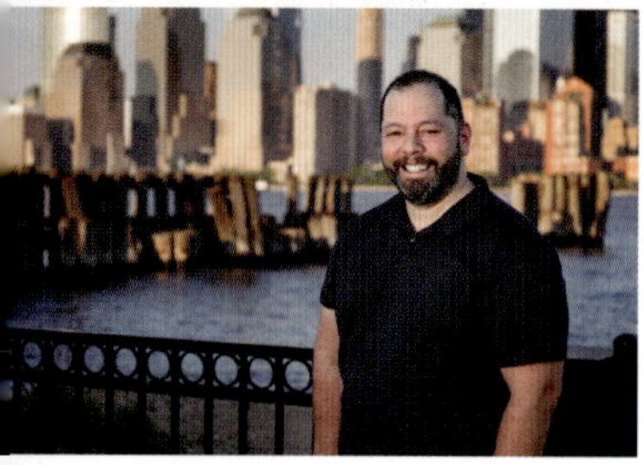

CHAPTER 2

# Bill Bernal

Instagram: @nycfotofun ■ Instagram: @myfotophun

As a kid, growing up in Plainfield, New Jersey, I dabbled in photography with a Kodak 110 camera and flash bulbs. Good thing I didn't know what I didn't know or I might have stop shooting then. I loved looking at the pictures in *National Geographic* and naively thought I could get shots like that too. What I actually learned was how to take really bad photos. Thankfully, through years of trial and error, and at times much heartache, I began to steadily improve on my craft. Because film was the only game at the time, those pennies added up. So my only choices were to get better—or to find a new hobby!

After Dunellen High School, I attended Kean University in New Jersey where I graduated with a bachelor's degree in psychology. At the time, this seemed like a pretty solid bet, given I had no clue what I wanted to do with my professional life. So after several jobs, I finally decided to grow up and landed a pretty neat opportunity at Union Square Hospitality Group as a Food & Beverage Director in New York City, where I still remain. While my work schedule can be intense, including long hours and travel, the photography bug is always there.

Over the years, as life led me down different paths, I put the camera down for a while. Then, as I got a little bit older and saw what was happening with technology and photography and especially with Instagram, I decided it was time to try it again and see what I could learn. With everything being all digital, shooting some bad photos from time to time was not quite so expensive this time around.

In the last three years, with the growth of Instagram and the ease of technology, I have renewed

**An Inspiring Skyline.** *(below)* The New York City skyline is always inspiring to see in person, regardless of how long you have lived in the area.

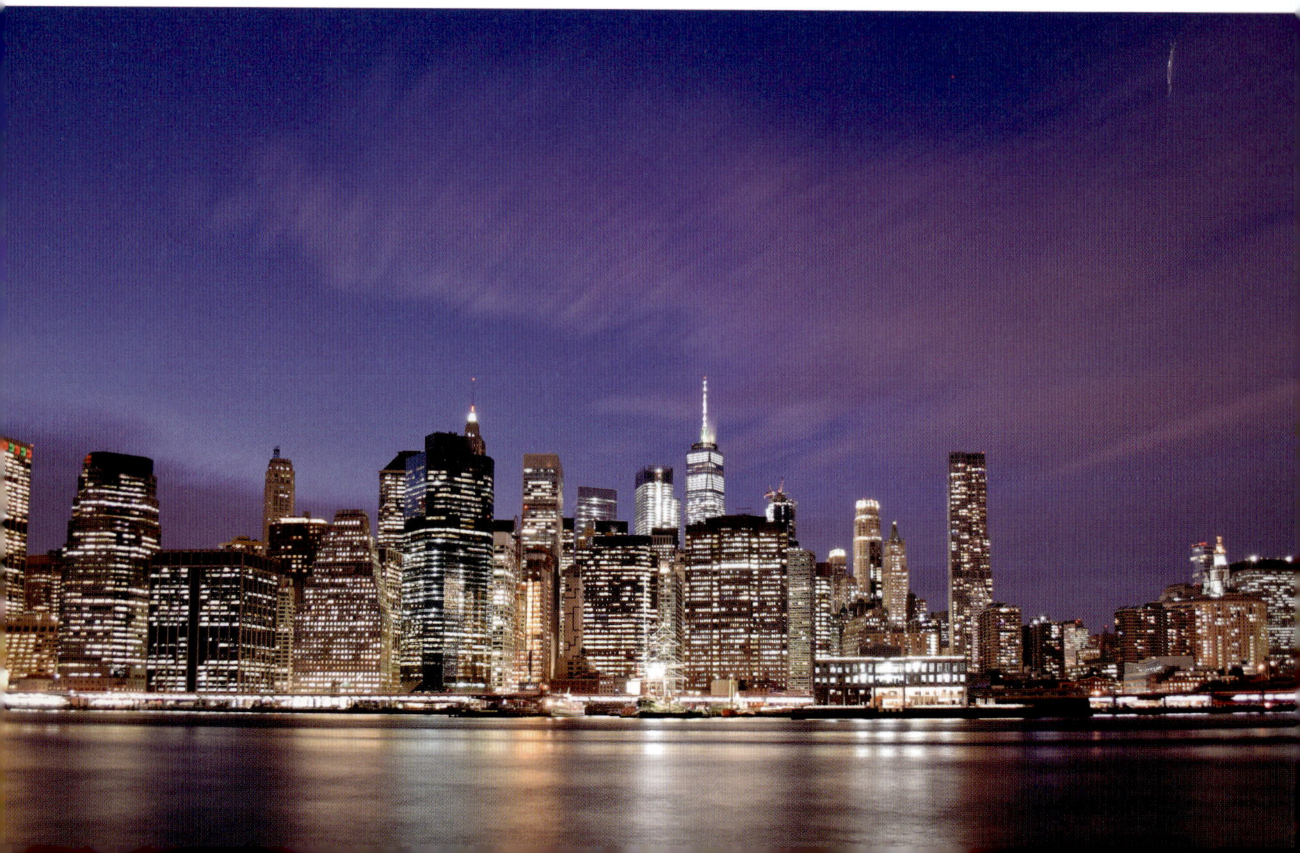

my passion for photography—and particularly New York City's skyline and architecture. My motivation has to do with nature—the ever-changing positions of the sun or moon along with the varying cloud formations. All of this offers frequent chances to capture unique views of the city.

When I'm not working or out shooting I am a dad to three wonderful kids, Christian, Hunter, and Charlotte. I also have a wonderfully patient wife, Corrie! Often, after some cajoling and even bribery, my family will accompany me on photography jaunts in and around the city. This way, we all get to experience the wonders of New York together—and pretty cheaply, too (with the exception of my bribes!). So it's a win for everyone.

I most often shoot sunrises, not only because of their breathtaking beauty and calm, but also because they never eat into family time. (When you have a full-time job, a wife, and three kids, it's all about balance.)

My work has been featured on a variety of social media channels as well as ABC and FOX TV in New York. Early in my Instagram ventures, I was featured in a 2016 FOX 5 segment; most recently, I was selected as a finalist in the 2017 Empire State Building photo contest. I am proud to say my image, along with those of about thirty other talented photographers, was on display in the lobby of this amazing building for over a month.

I am not sure what my style would be described as, but I do enjoy shooting long-exposure shots and I also have fun with editing my photos. I find the golden light of sunrise and sunset really can enhance a landscape. Getting into a helicopter and shooting from an aerial point of view can also be quite the adventure. Even though many of my fellow New York City photographers end up shooting

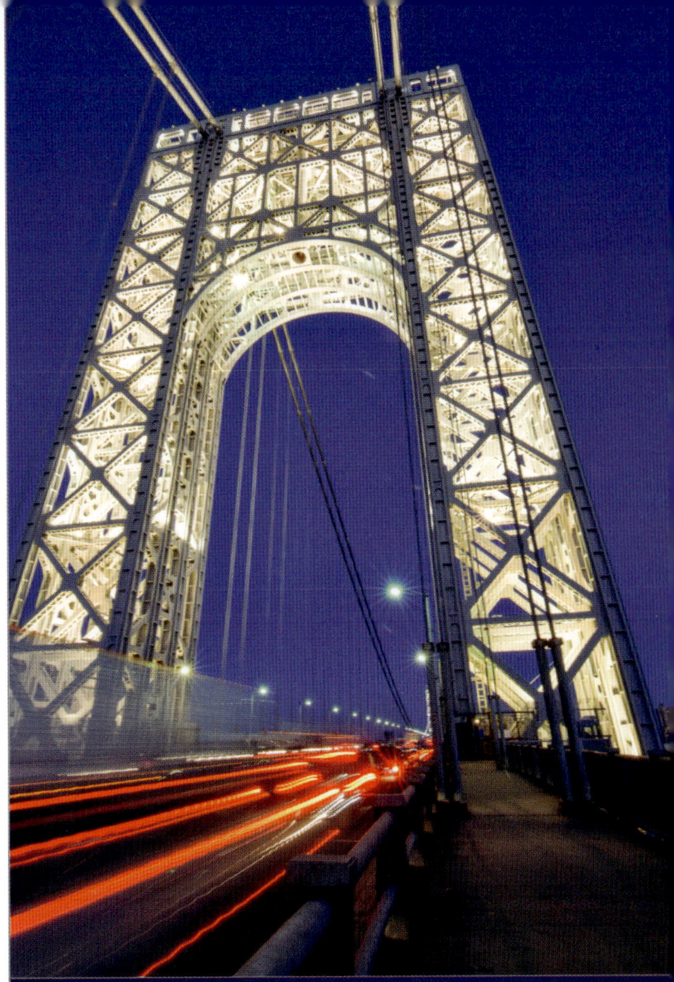

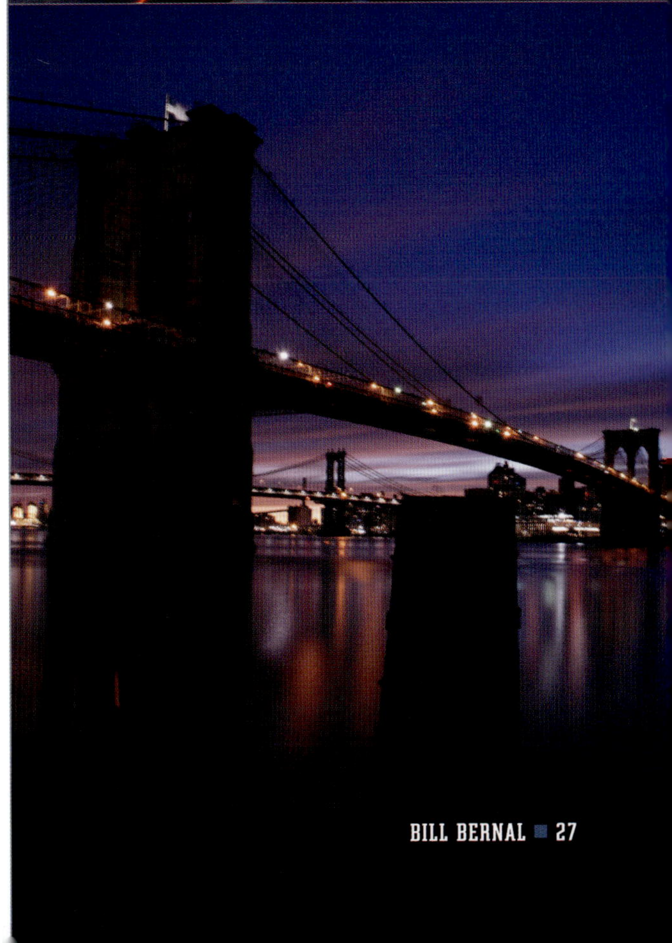

**George Washington Bridge.** *(top right)* Long exposure shots on the George Washington Bridge while it vibrates when an 18 wheeler goes by can be quite the challenge. But it does give it that magical feeling of traffic actually moving on this congested bridge.

**Brooklyn Bridge.** *(bottom right)* Morning sunrises at the Brooklyn Bridge make for a great gift especially when shot on Christmas Eve morning. I had the opportunity to shoot with a dozen or so talented photographers this day.

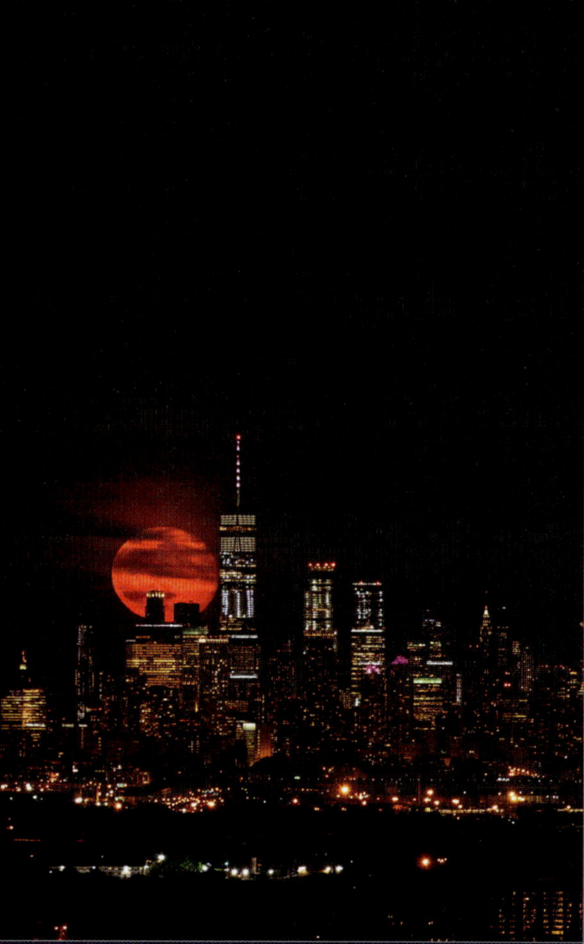

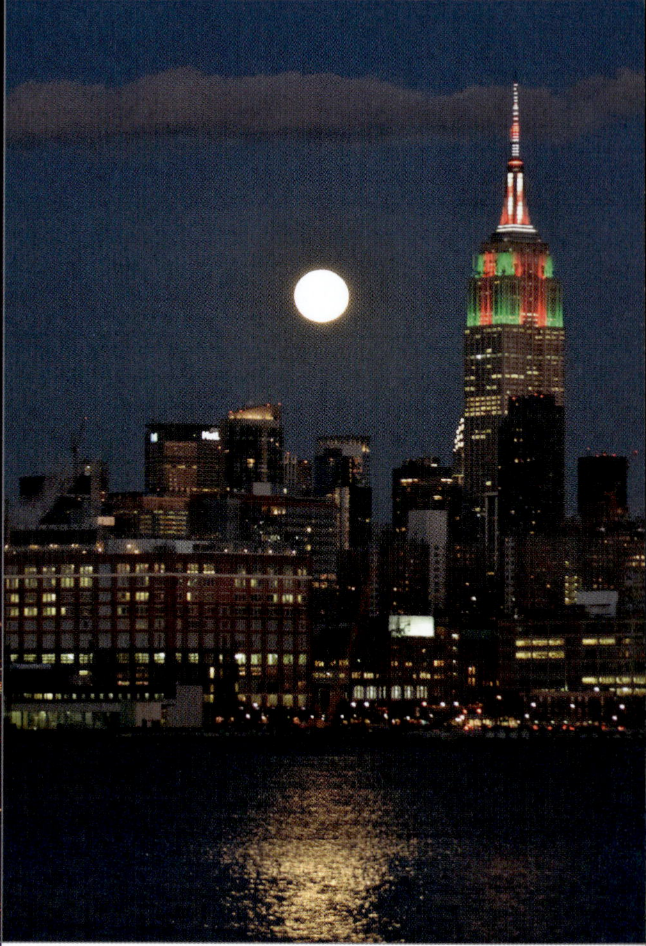

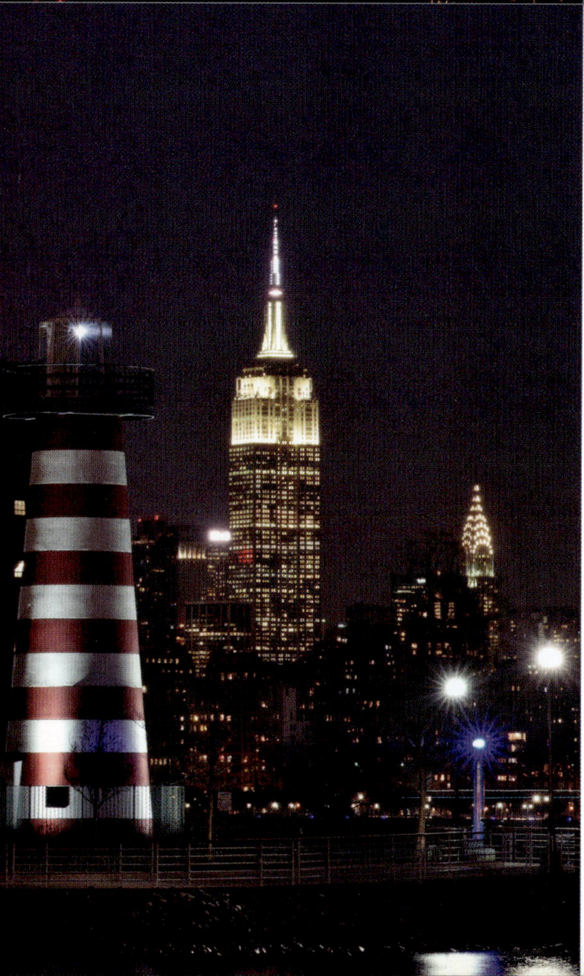

**Full Moon.** *(top left)* The full moon rising behind the New York City skyline. This view can be seen from Eagle Rock Reservation in New Jersey and is a popular destination for photographers for both sunrise and sunset shots, too.

**Moon Over Empire State Building.** *(above)* The moon makes its way over to the Empire State Building in another image captured during the supermoon of 2017. Looking for moonrise and moonset locations has been greatly aided by technology; there are now plenty of apps to help with that.

**A Classic View.** *(bottom left)* A classic line-up view of the LeFrak Lighthouse, Empire State Building, and Chrysler Building as seen from the Hoboken waterfront.

some of the same locations, it's always interesting to see the different interpretations each one brings.

Through photography and Instagram, I have had the pleasure of meeting other talented photographers, which inspires me to continue to capture the ever-changing city. As I continue to refine my techniques, I am always seeking to take my work to the next level. I accept work for family portraits and engagement shoots, but my passion is documenting landscapes in and out of the New York area. I hope to start selling prints of my landscape work.

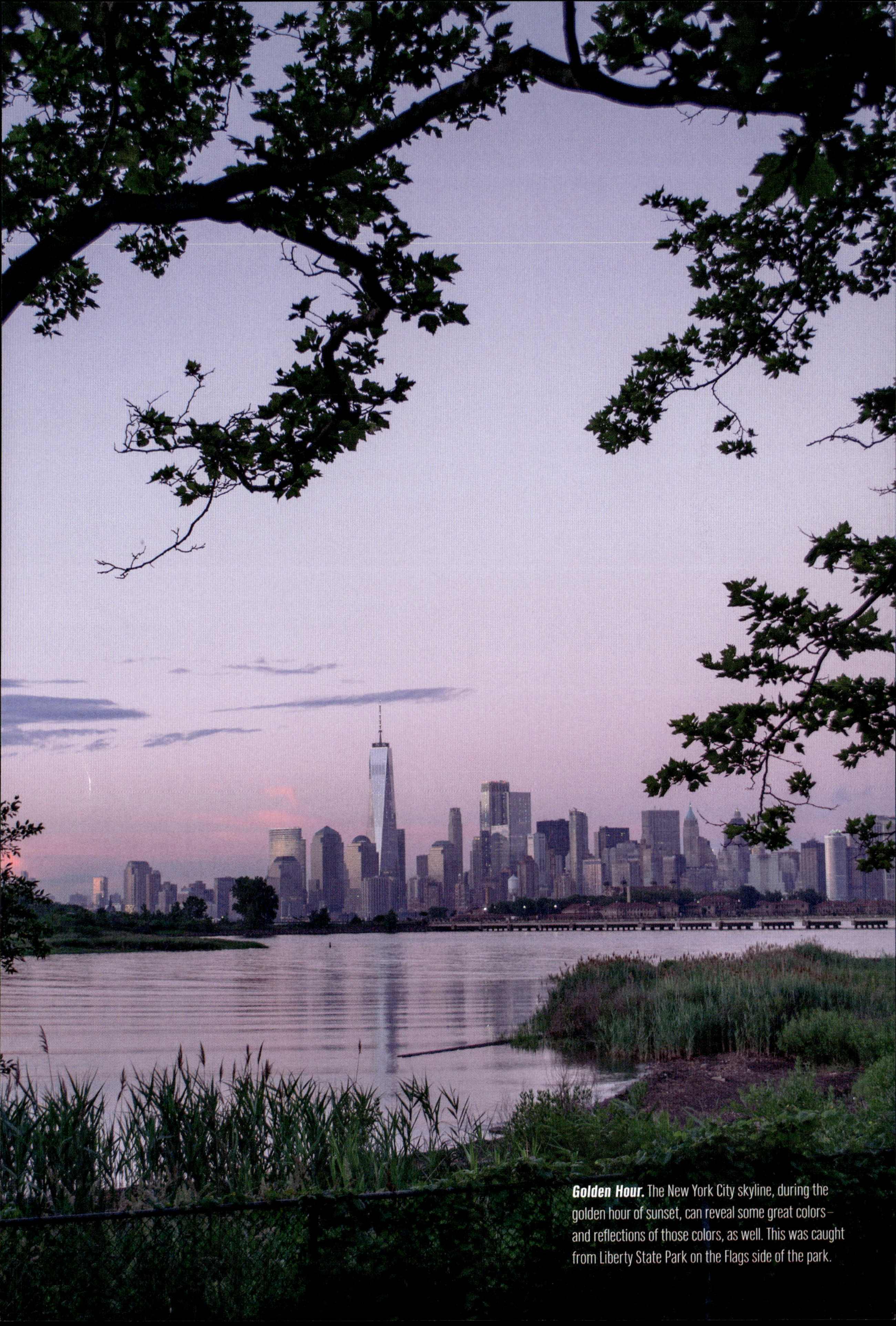

**Golden Hour.** The New York City skyline, during the golden hour of sunset, can reveal some great colors – and reflections of those colors, as well. This was caught from Liberty State Park on the Flags side of the park.

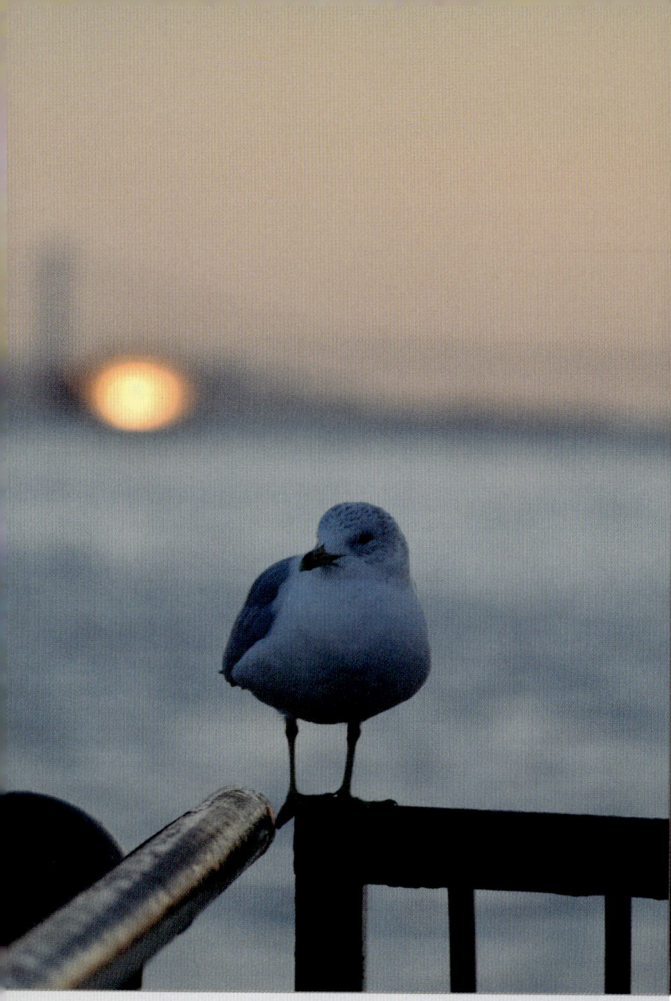

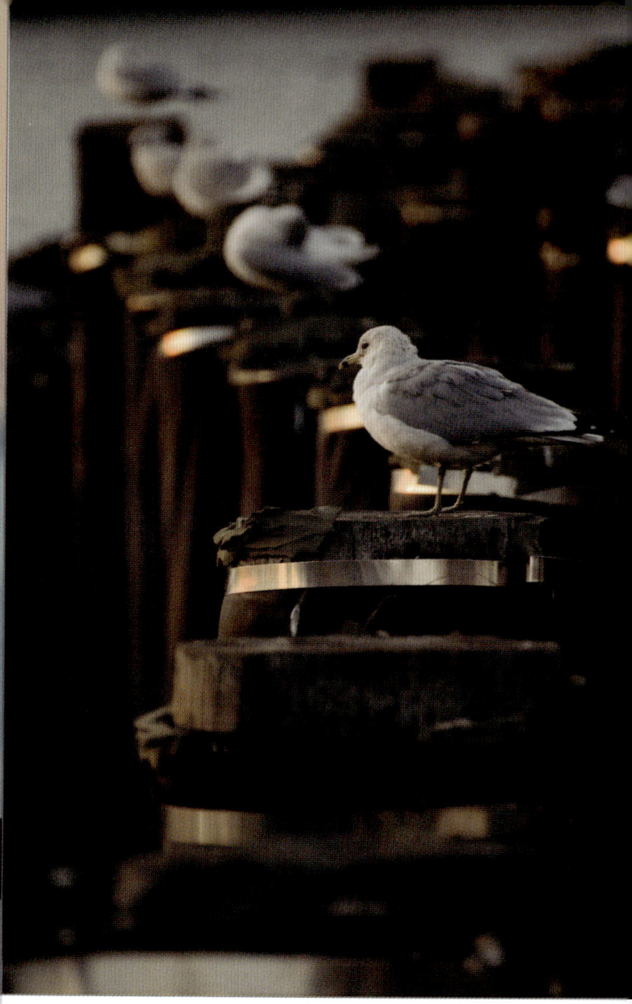

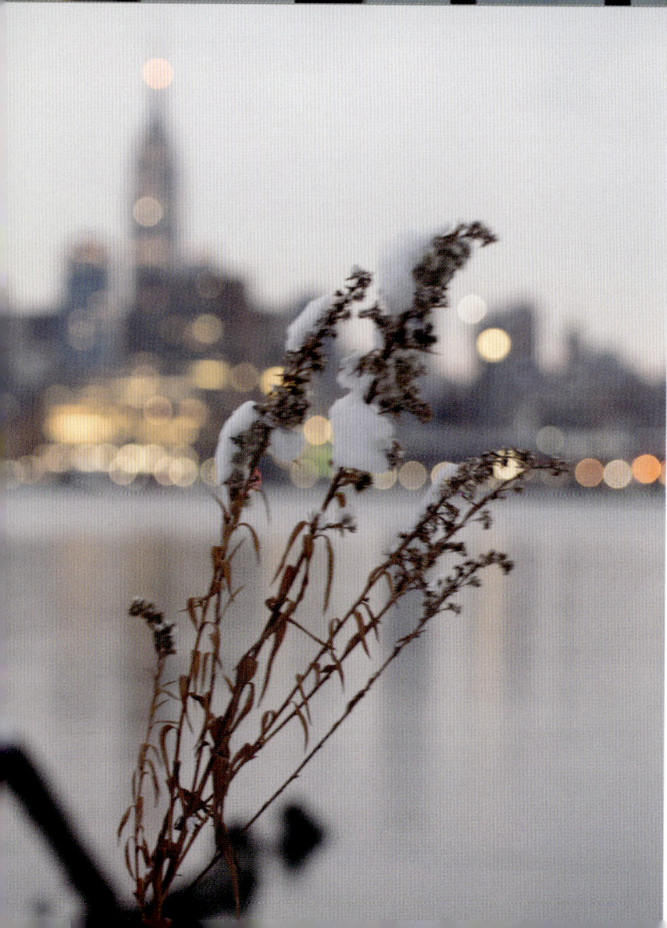

***A Sight to See.*** *(top left)* Even the seagulls like to take in views of the New York City skyline as seen from Liberty State Park on the day after a recent snowstorm.

***Birds of a Feather.*** *(top right)* These birds of a feather were taking in the New York City skyline views from Liberty State Park. This is a popular location for the birds to take in some sun—and it provides some nice photo ops for us photographers.

***City Lights with Bokeh.*** *(bottom left)* The Empire State Building makes for a great backdrop anywhere—and the bokeh effect adds to the overall composition. It is a great way to make one aspect of the picture (like this snow-covered plant) stand out.

***Lady Liberty.*** *(facing page)* Lady Liberty, lined up with the Empire State Building and 432 Park Avenue makes for a wonderfully iconic shot of these New York City landmarks. Adding a nice foreground (as on the facing page) can increase the drama. The soft bokeh effect of the branches enhances the image.

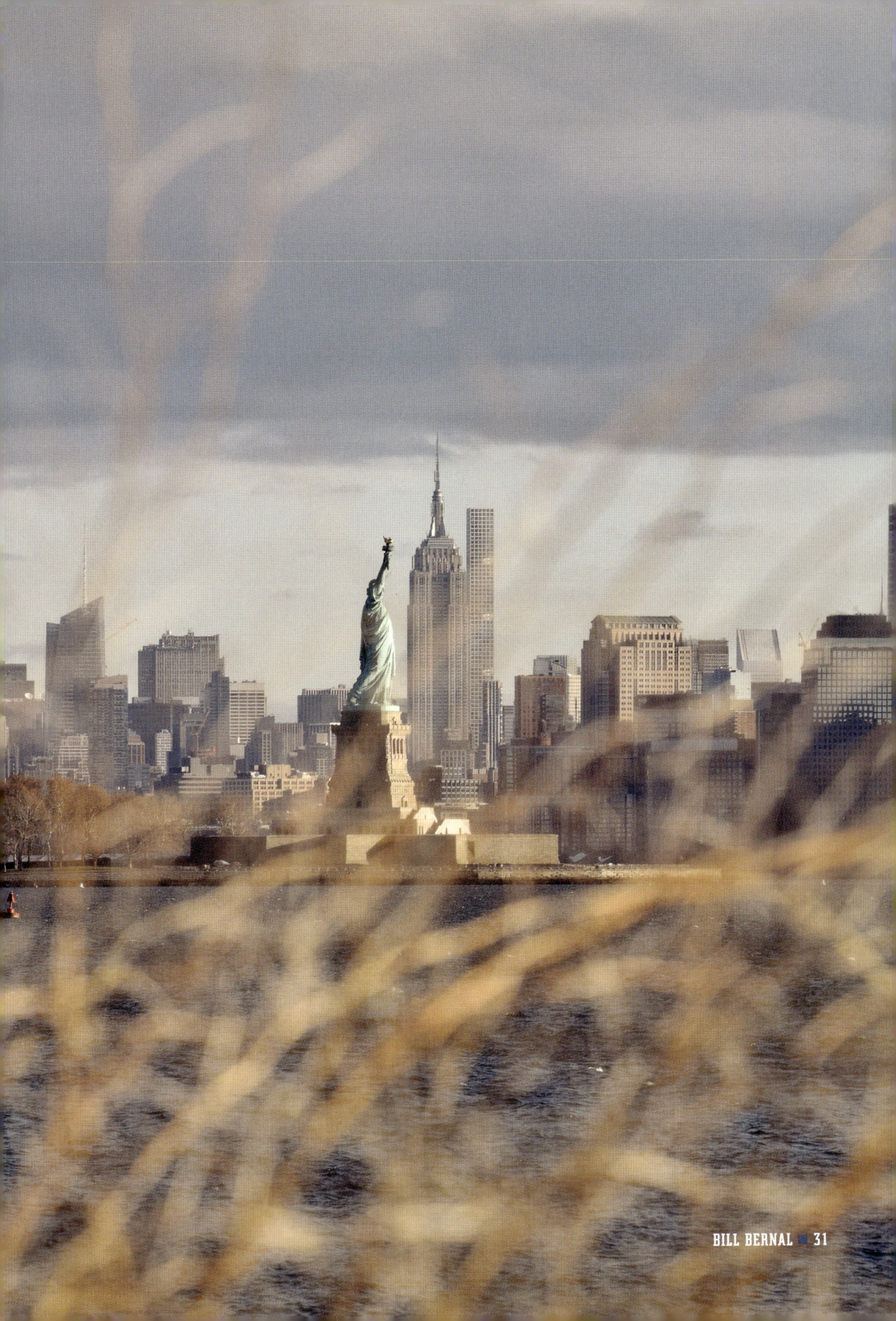

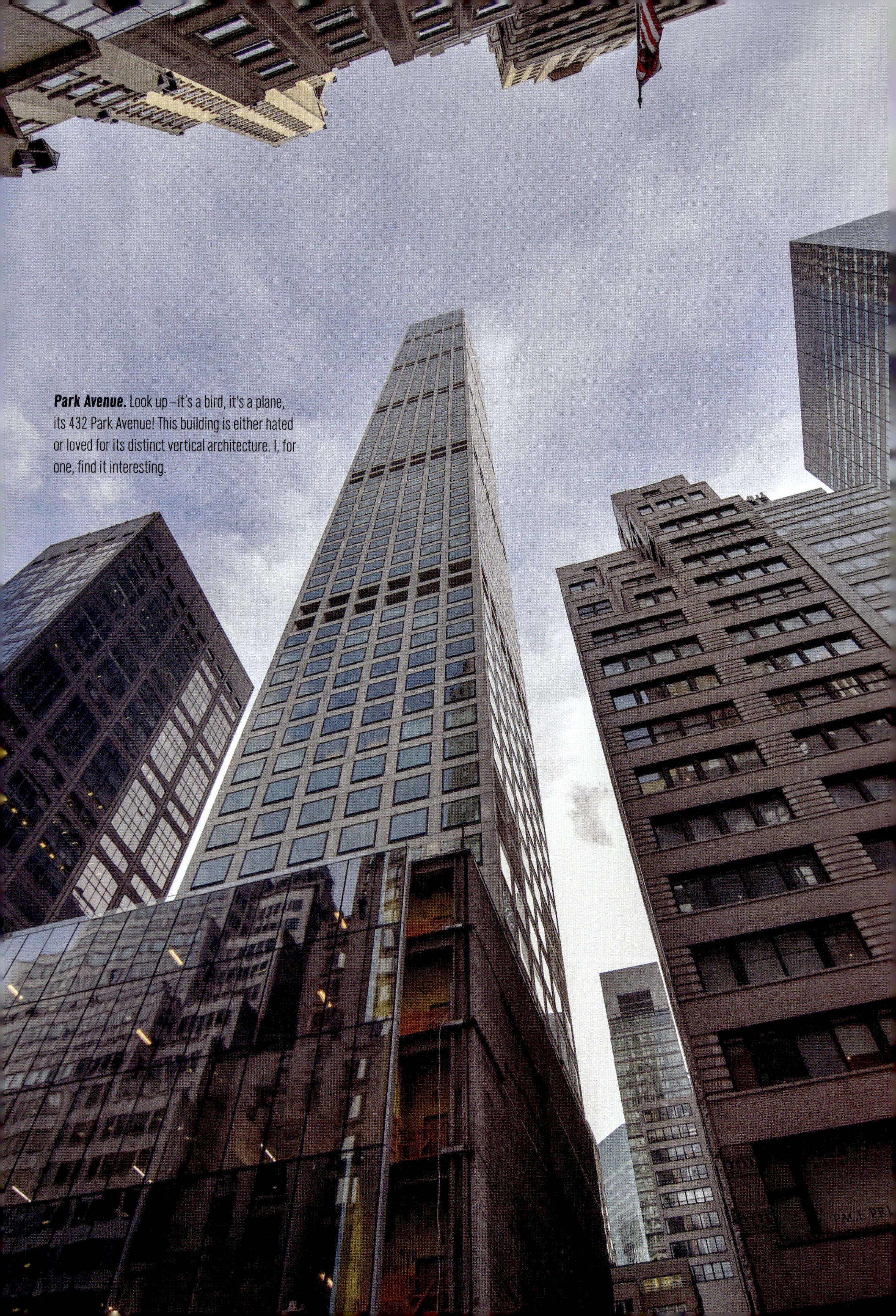


***Park Avenue.*** Look up – it's a bird, it's a plane, its 432 Park Avenue! This building is either hated or loved for its distinct vertical architecture. I, for one, find it interesting.

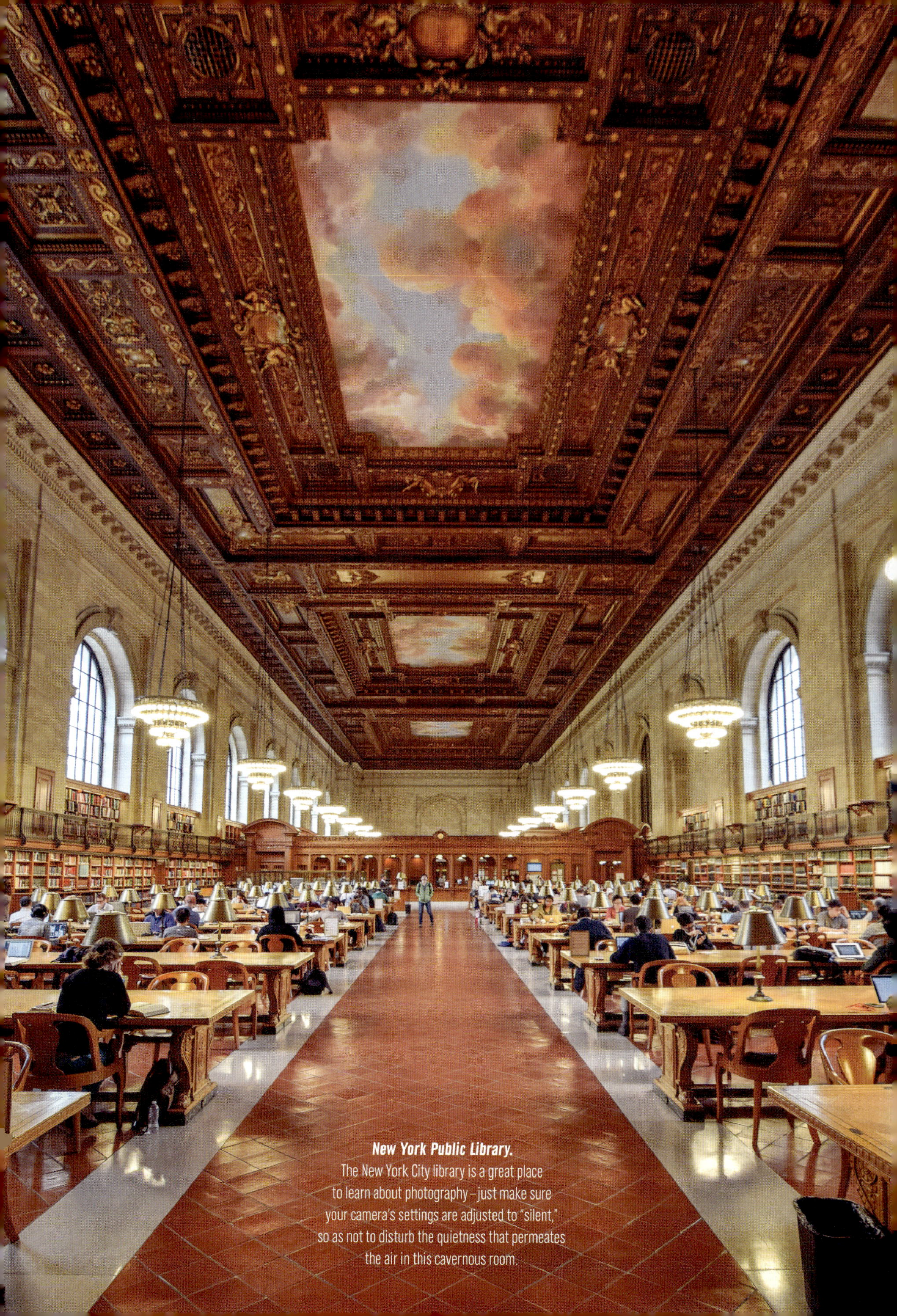

**New York Public Library.**
The New York City library is a great place to learn about photography – just make sure your camera's settings are adjusted to "silent," so as not to disturb the quietness that permeates the air in this cavernous room.

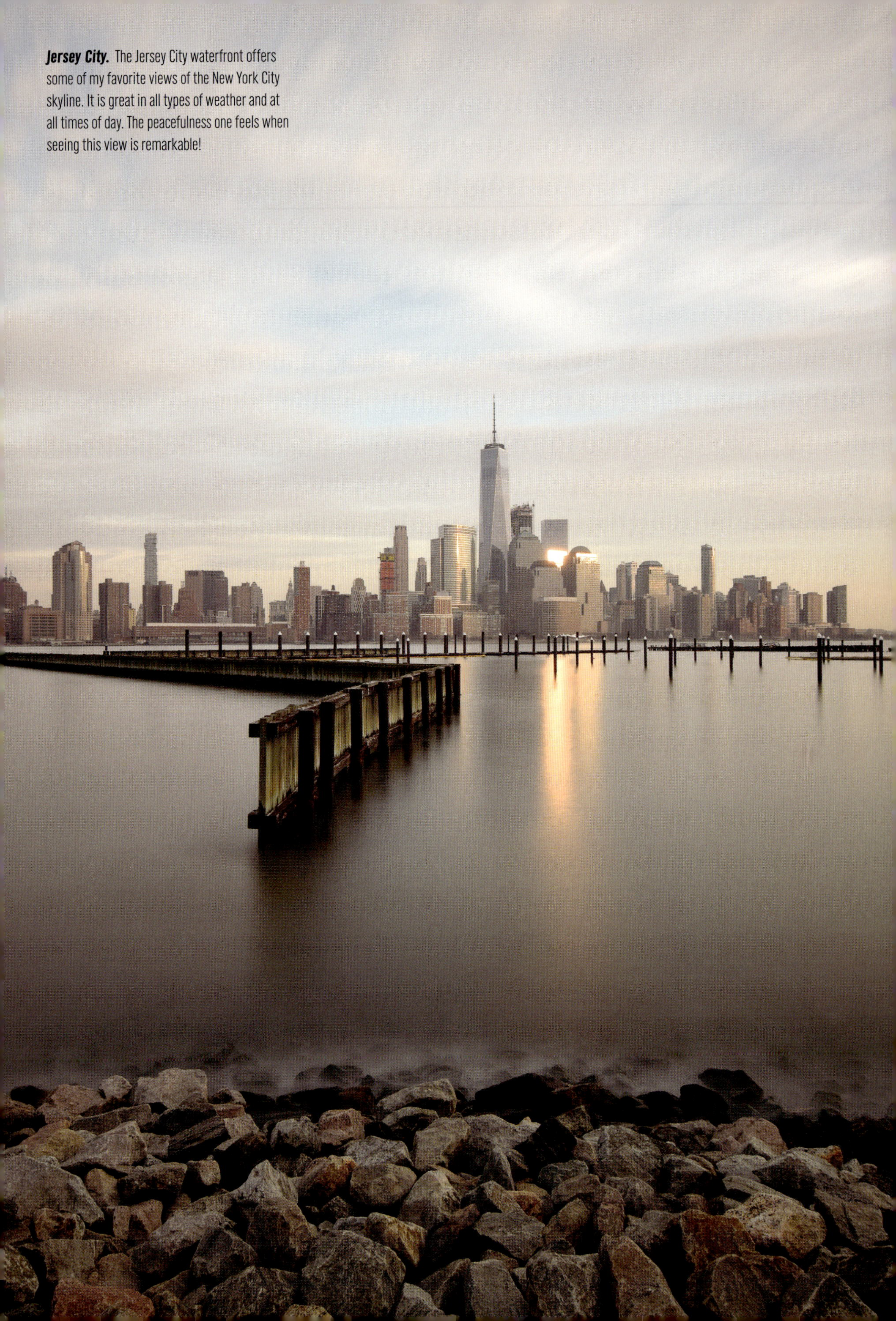

***Jersey City.*** The Jersey City waterfront offers some of my favorite views of the New York City skyline. It is great in all types of weather and at all times of day. The peacefulness one feels when seeing this view is remarkable!

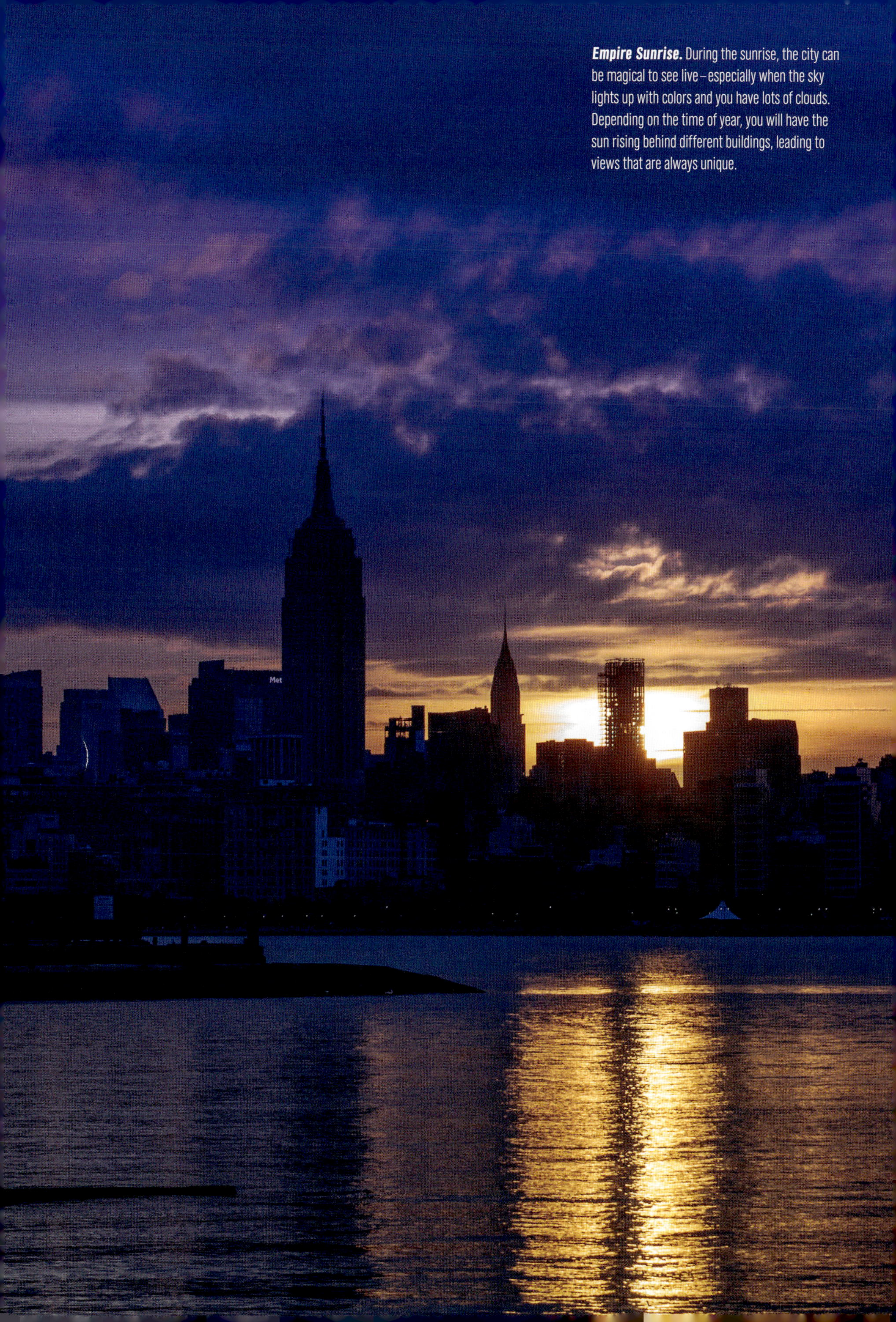


***Empire Sunrise.*** During the sunrise, the city can be magical to see live – especially when the sky lights up with colors and you have lots of clouds. Depending on the time of year, you will have the sun rising behind different buildings, leading to views that are always unique.

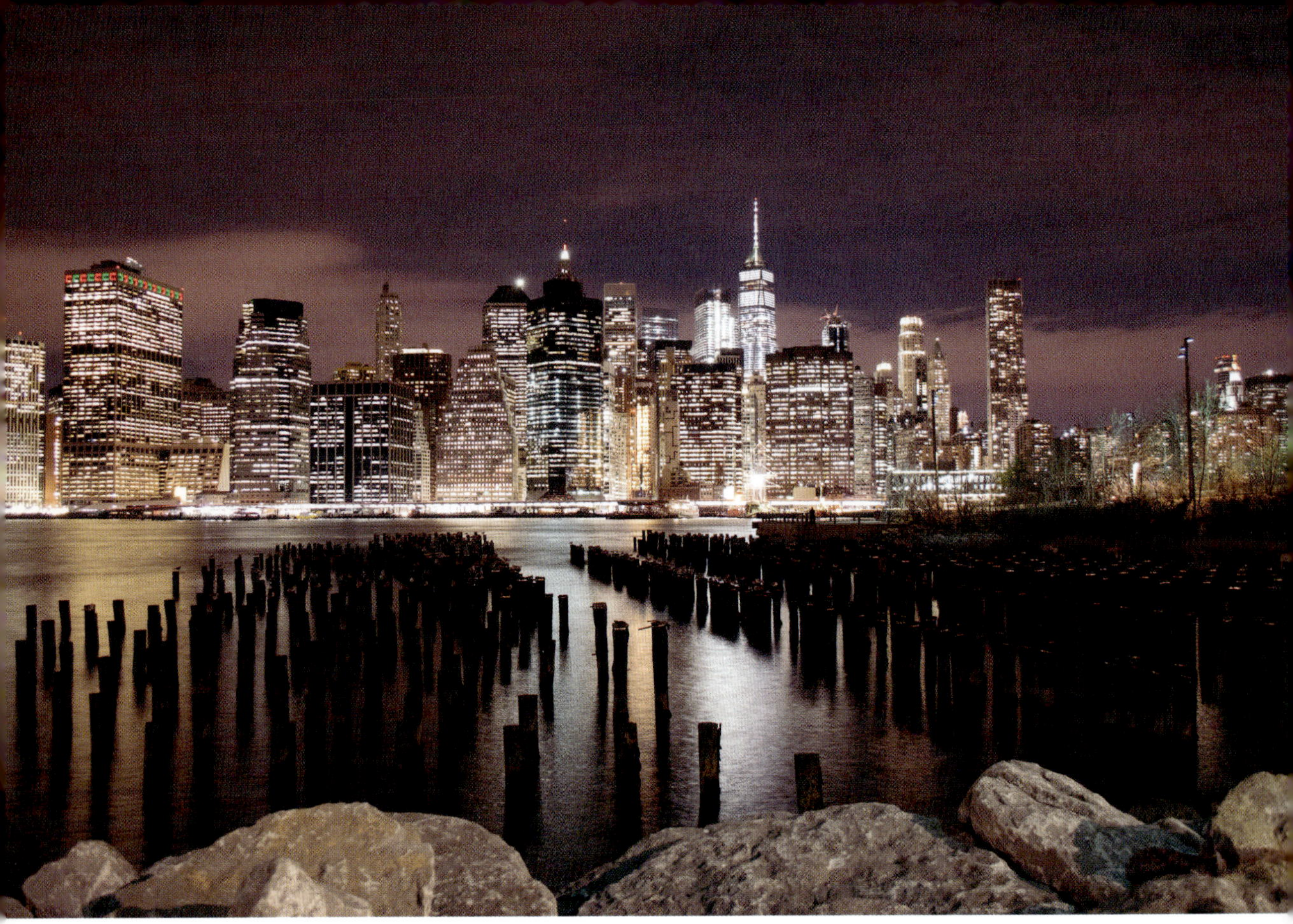

***A Sight to See.*** *(above)* This view of the New York City skyline is a sight to see–and one that might not be available for long, due to new construction. A telephoto lens helped compress the perspective.

***George Washington Bridge.*** *(below)* If only driving on the George Washington Bridge was as peaceful as photographing it! I think all New Yorkers can relate to the dreadful feeling of being stuck in bumper-to-bumper traffic on this bridge–especially when going to a Yankees game.

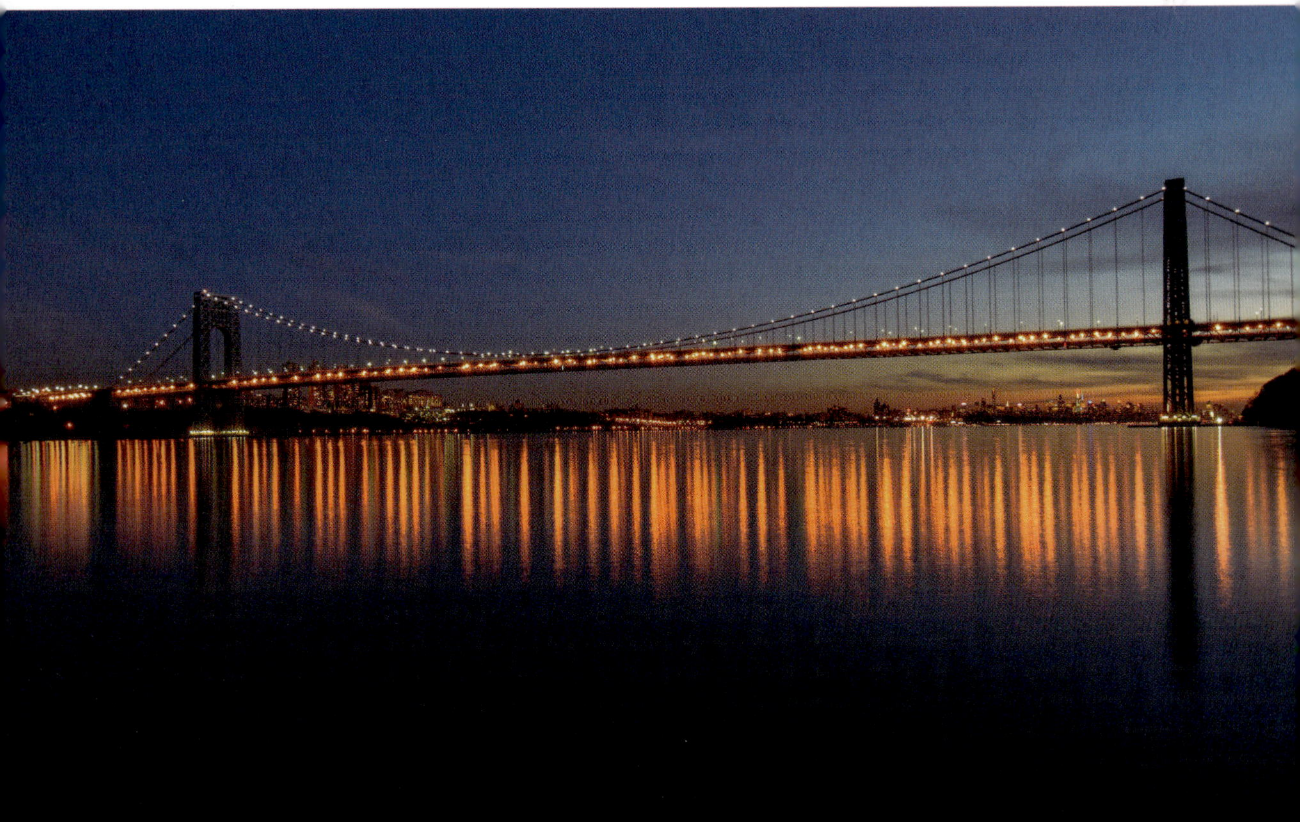

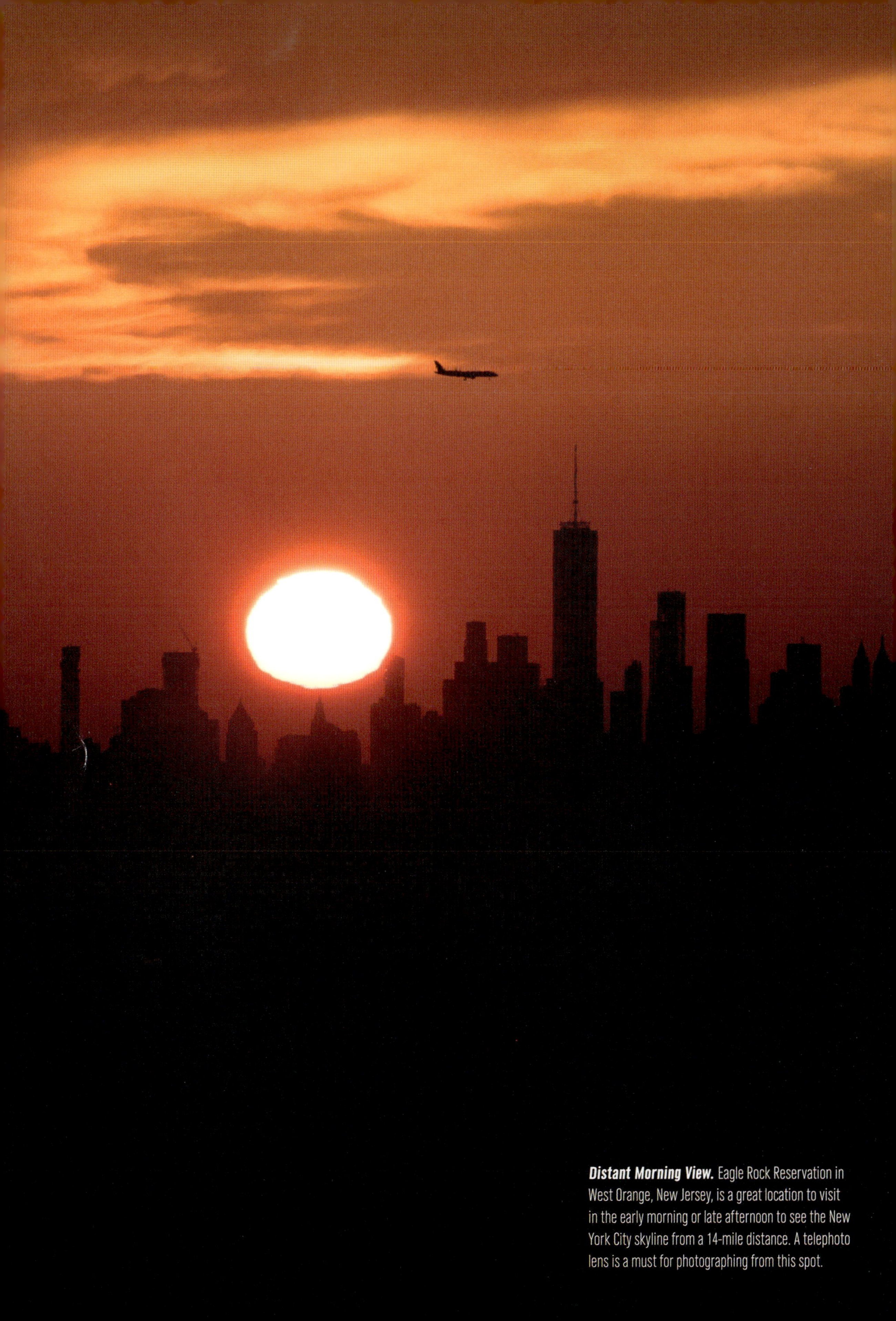

***Distant Morning View.*** Eagle Rock Reservation in West Orange, New Jersey, is a great location to visit in the early morning or late afternoon to see the New York City skyline from a 14-mile distance. A telephoto lens is a must for photographing from this spot.

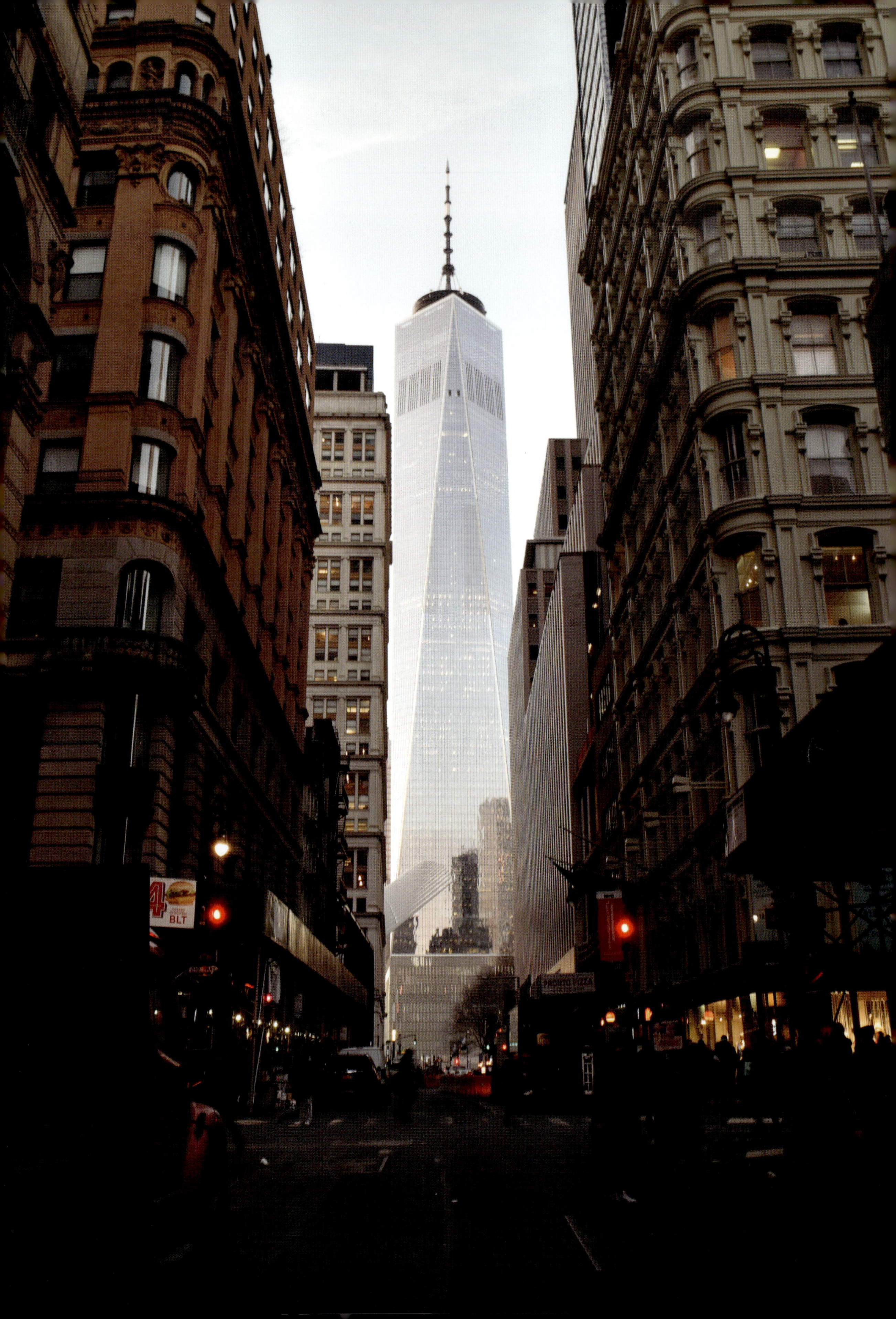
BLT
PRONTO PIZZA

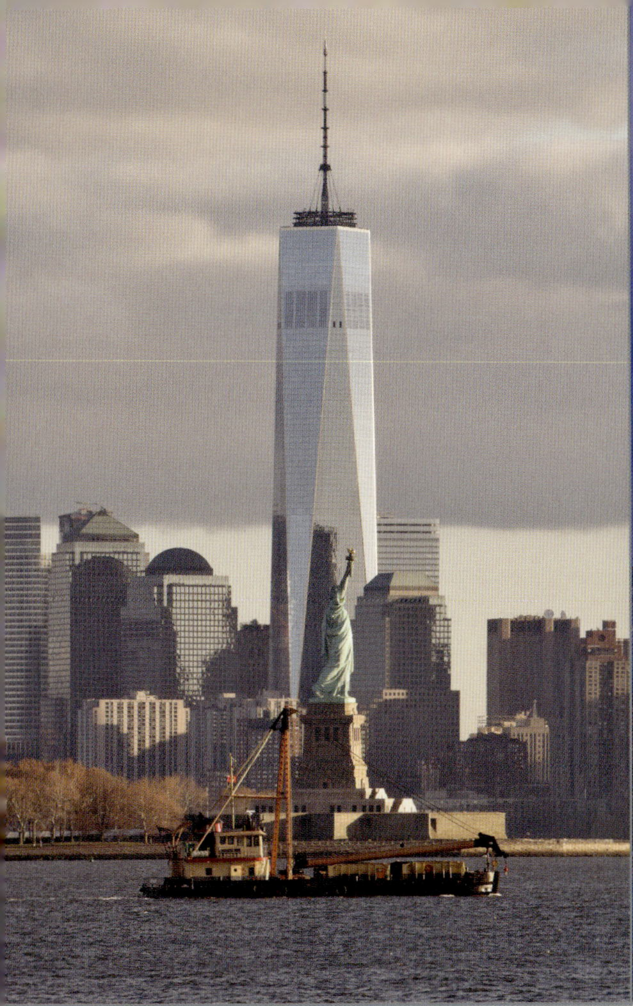

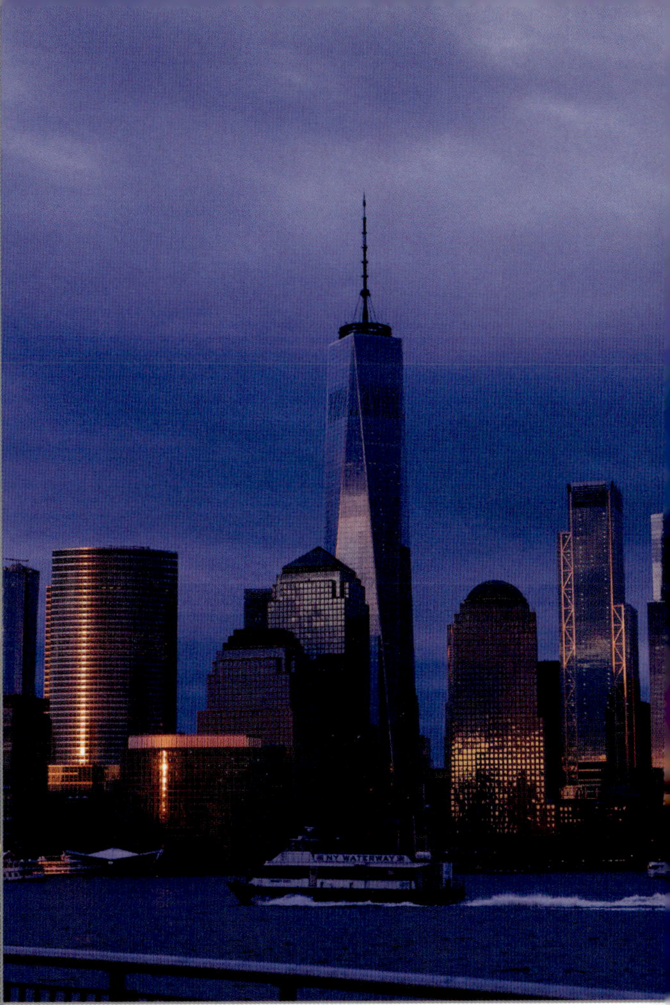

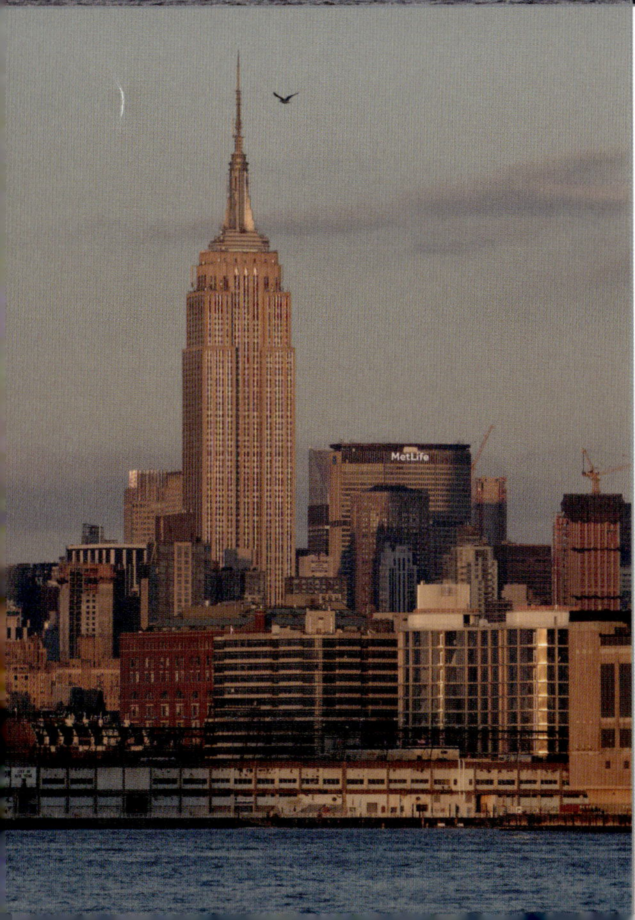


**Fulton Street View.** *(facing page)* One World Trade Center stands tall above the city streets. This view from Fulton Street makes for a wonderful composition and is a very popular shot.

**Lady Liberty and One World Trade Center.** *(top left)* Views of New York City from the New Jersey side are an easy way to capture its beauty while avoiding the crazy traffic of driving into the city. Here, Lady Liberty is lined up with One World Trade Center. This location in Bayonne, New Jersey, offers dramatic views. With a telephoto lens, you can get some wonderful compositions.

**The Hudson.** *(top right)* Want to see New York City from a different perspective? Take one of the many water cruise's that are offered along the Hudson River for some amazing skyline views and New York City closeups on some of the bridges.

**Empire State from New Jersey.** *(bottom left)* The Empire State Building is a sight to see in the late afternoon light. With a telephoto lens you can capture it nicely from the New Jersey side.

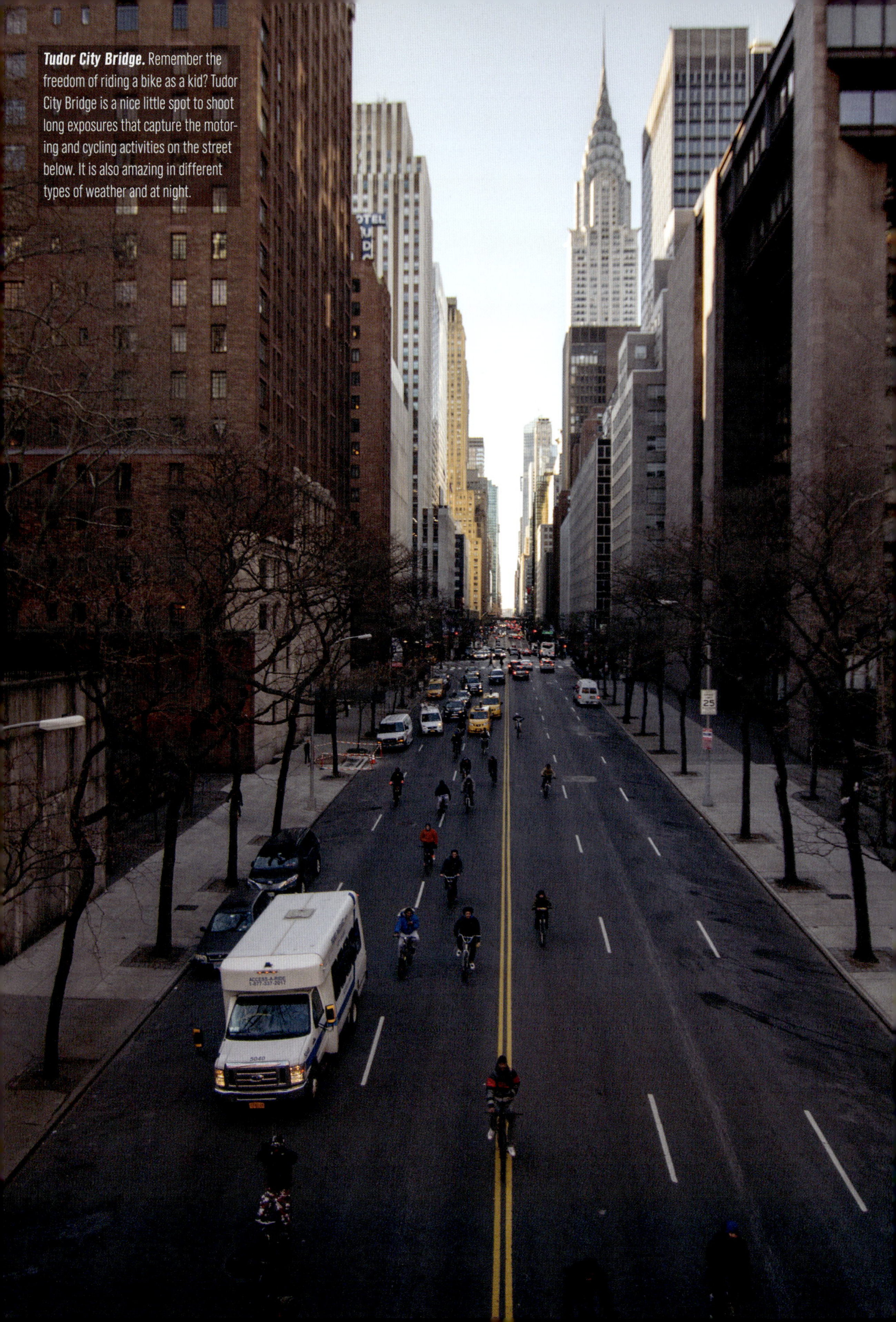

***Tudor City Bridge.*** Remember the freedom of riding a bike as a kid? Tudor City Bridge is a nice little spot to shoot long exposures that capture the motoring and cycling activities on the street below. It is also amazing in different types of weather and at night.

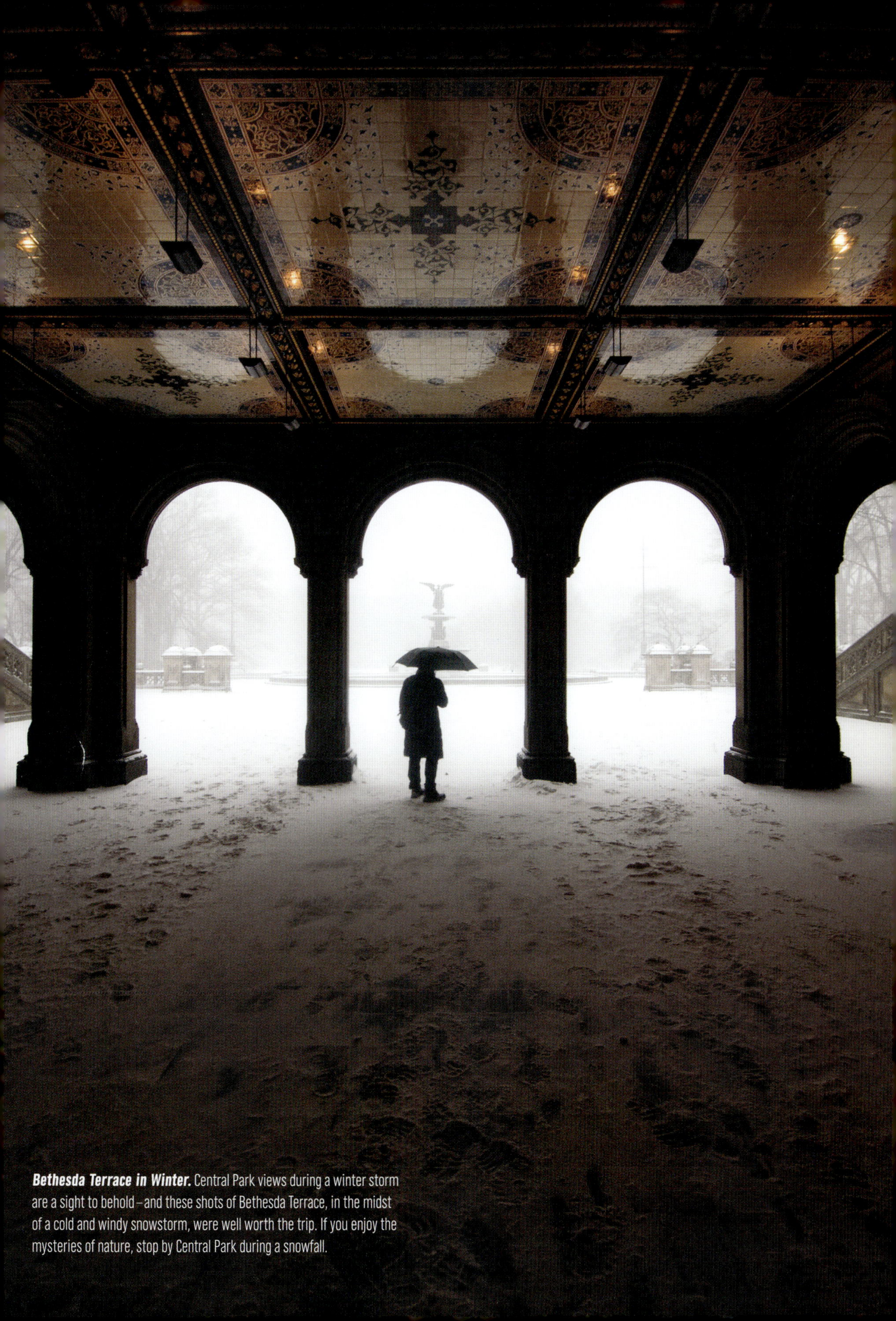

***Bethesda Terrace in Winter.*** Central Park views during a winter storm are a sight to behold—and these shots of Bethesda Terrace, in the midst of a cold and windy snowstorm, were well worth the trip. If you enjoy the mysteries of nature, stop by Central Park during a snowfall.

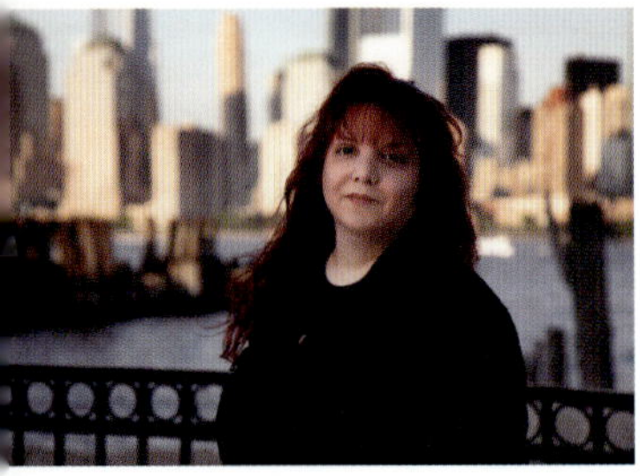

CHAPTER 3

# Gina Brake

Instagram: @gina_brake_photography_nyc ■ www.facebook.com/streetphotographynyc

I was born in Brooklyn, New York, so I grew up looking at and learning about the city. My grandparents lived in the historic Park Slope district of Brooklyn and, as far back as I can remember, I was obsessed with the brownstones and other architecture around their house. I remember sitting at my grandparents' window, staring in amazement at these lovely old buildings. I believe this is where my love of photography first took shape; I wanted to capture every detail of what I saw. Years later, I was able to do that through my photography.

Growing up in the 1980s, my first camera was a Canon SureShot. I had no idea what I was doing with it. I would buy film at any speed, as long as it was cheap. Sometimes I would be using 400 speed film in sunlight and 100 speed film in the dark (it should have been the opposite!). I had no knowledge of those things back then and would just photograph everything I saw. I especially loved the graffiti in New York's subways. I soon had a collection of hundreds of pictures of the New York City subways and city streets. I am sad to say that, over the years, most of those photos were lost. They must have been discarded in moves or clean-outs. It makes me deeply sad to think of the loss.

In 2004, I rediscovered my love for photography at the Metropolitan Museum of Art. Every weekend, I would take my new Canon Digital Rebel to the museum and take photos of everything and anything inside. I eventually moved to taking photos outside of the museum as well. This is where my passion for street photography grew.

I partner with my husband, Paul Brake, on many of my photography adventures. Since we share all of it together, we are more than husband and wife; we are shooting partners and colleagues in our art. To be honest, he is the artist and has taught me almost

**Diversity Row.** *(below)* This striking scene was taken from the Manhattan Bridge. It shows how diverse this great city is. Everything from graffiti, to high-rise office buildings, to tenements, to luxury apartment buildings all live together in the same great place. I love New York City and am so happy to have been born here. I will stay until my dying day.

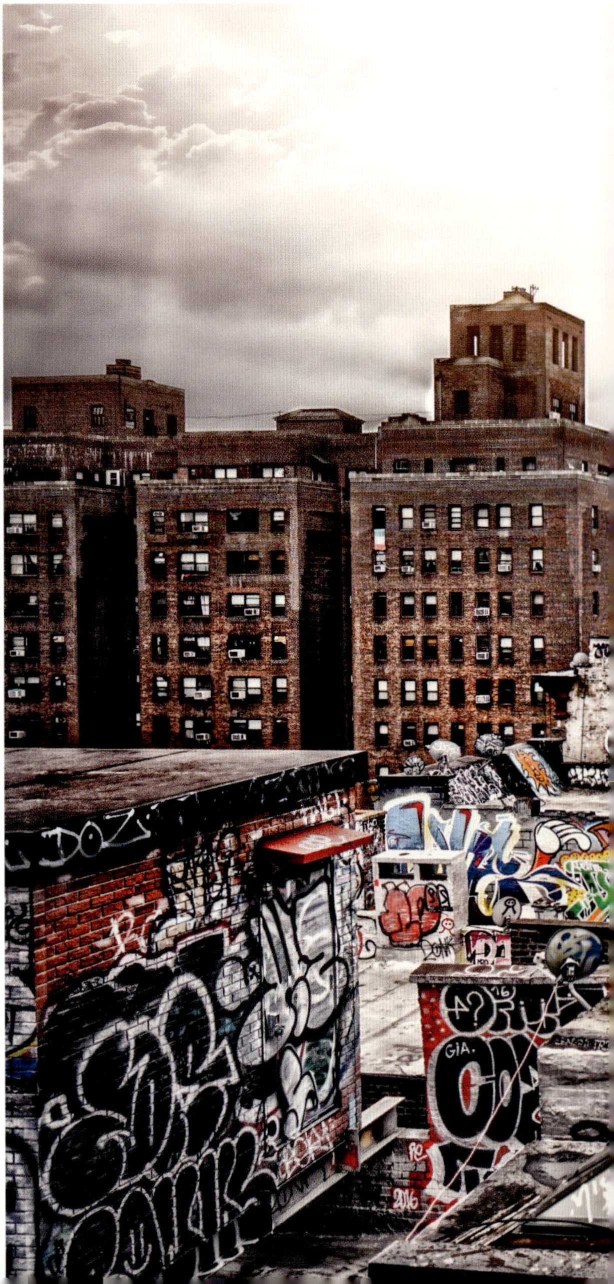

everything I know. I admire him greatly. Without his help, I would likely still be using the wrong speed films in old cameras!

Today, I can say I am in love with photography, whether it's planned photo shoots or the unpredictability of street photography. I enjoy capturing every moment I can. In addition, I am also an avid New York City history buff and enjoy collecting old photos of the city. I'm always wondering if someday someone will be collecting *my* photos, calling them "old New York City photos."

To me, photography is a way to share my thoughts and ideas. I may photograph something that makes me happy or sad with the hope that my photo can invoke some emotion in the viewer when they look at it.

My current camera system is the Sony A7RII, a mirrorless, full-frame 35mm digital camera, which I adopted after changing from Canon back in 2012. Initially, I wanted to change because of the much smaller size and weight, but I soon discovered that the mirrorless system was much better in low-light situations. The images were so much sharper at lower ISOs; often, I can take almost impossible shots in near complete darkness.

When it comes to lenses, I stick to fast prime lenses rather than zooms. In addition to either a

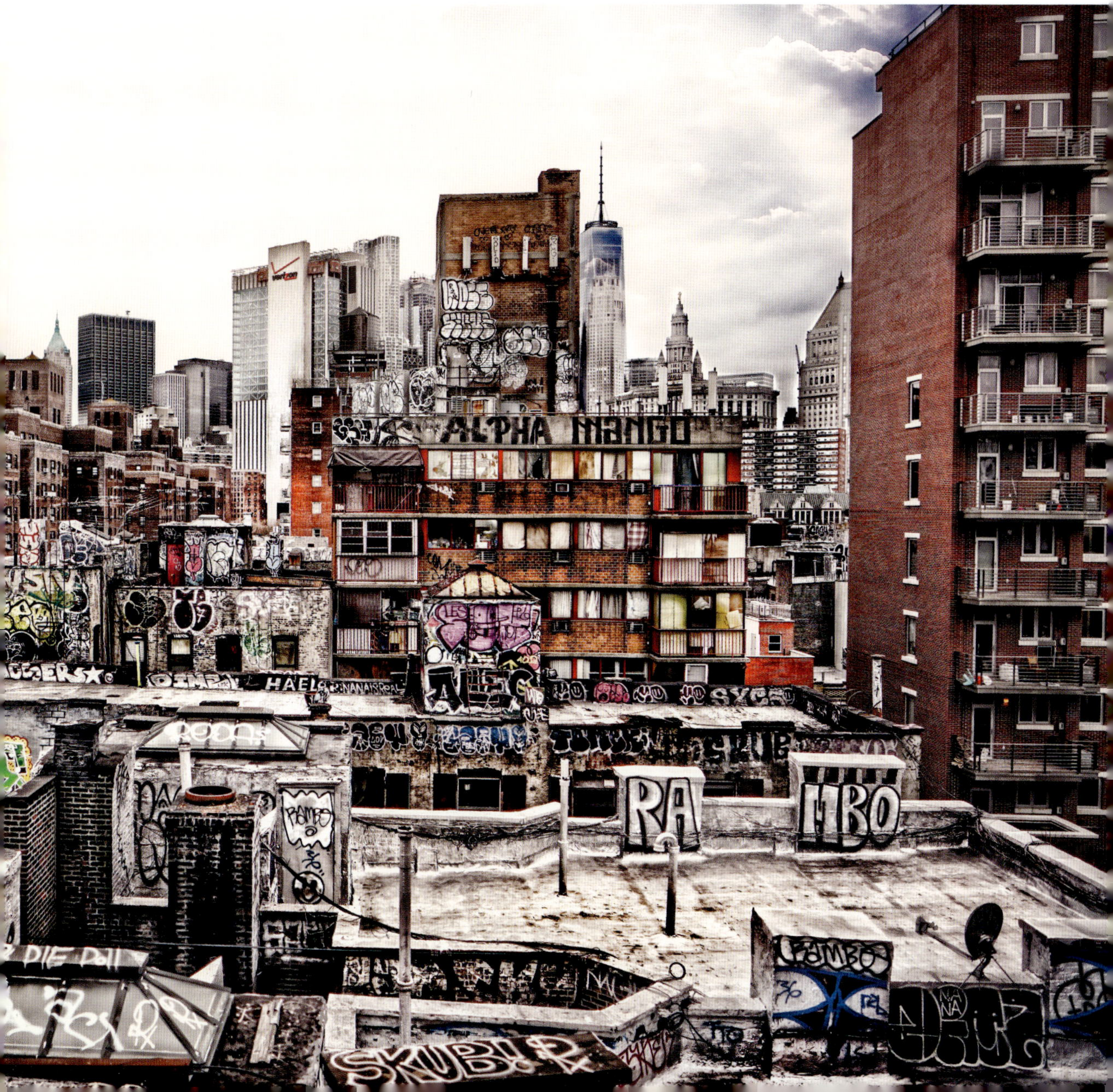

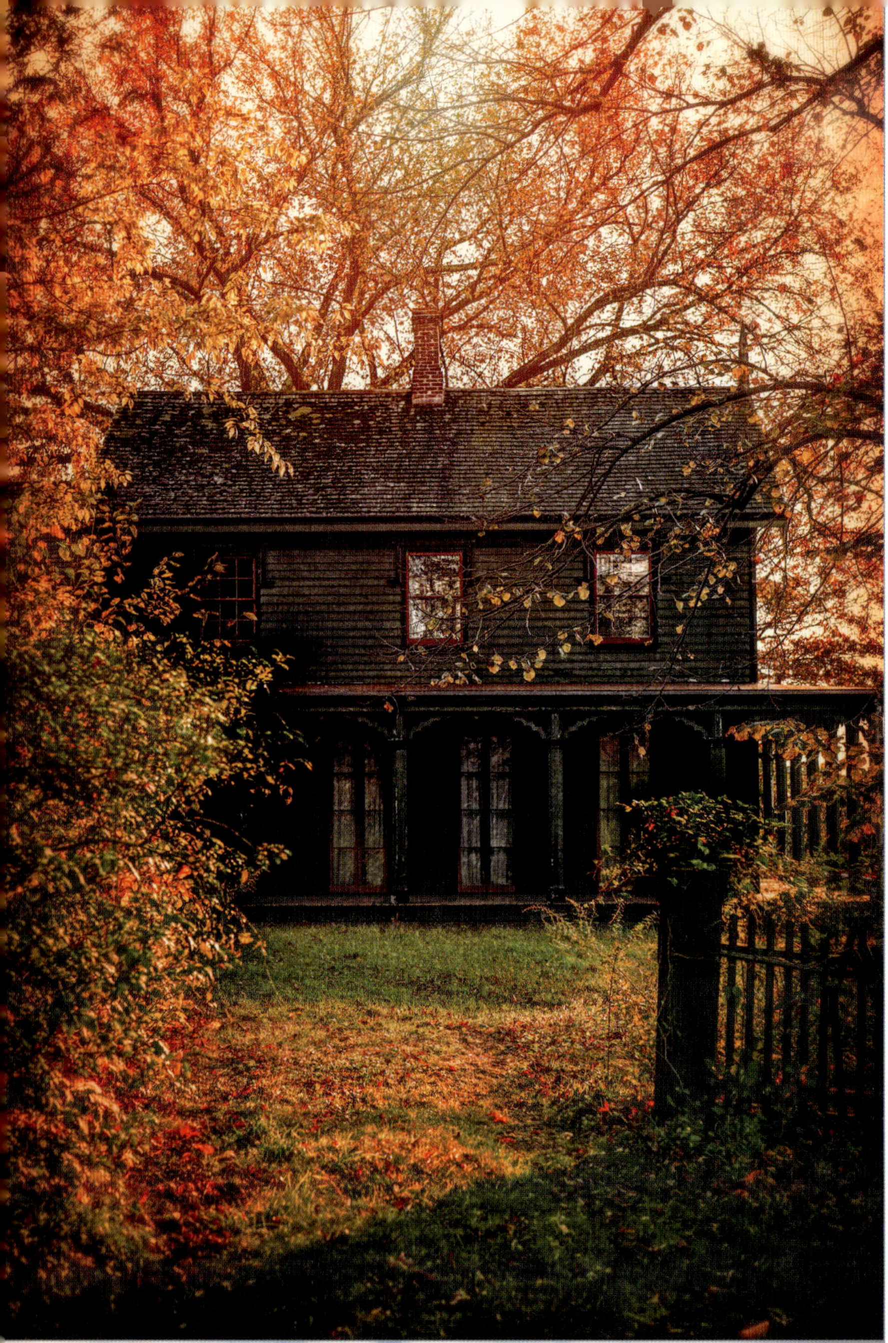

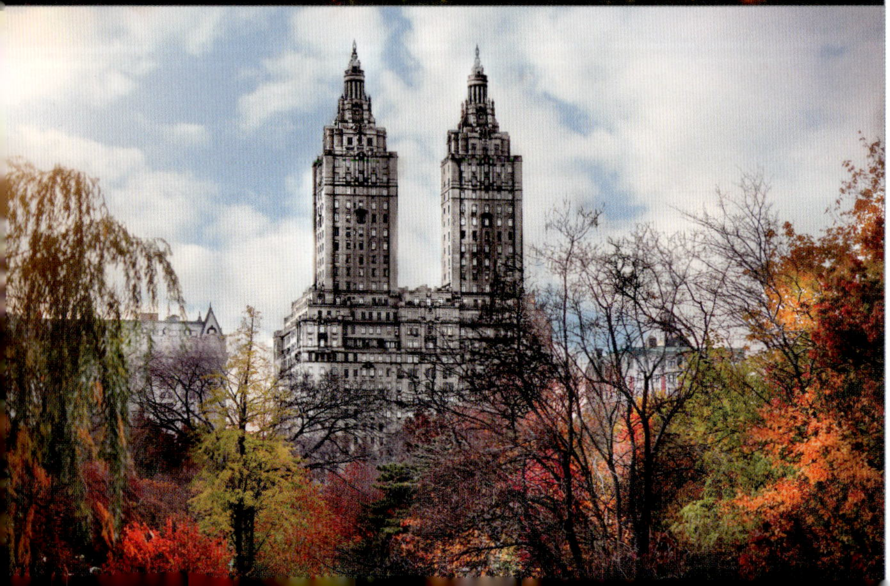

25mm or 35mm lens on my camera, I usually take a wide angle 14mm lens and another lens of 90mm or above. This way, I'm prepared for every situation.

I also refrain from using heavy tripods, sticking to light, anti-vibration materials such as carbon fiber. Since I often cover many miles walking around, weight is extremely important. Sometimes I do not even carry a tripod and take handheld shots at night using a unique camera feature that combines multiple burst shots to provide a noise-free image. (Digital noise appears as graininess in the photo and is more prominent at night or in other low-light situations.)

That said, when doing street photography at night, concerns about noise become secondary to maintaining an in-focus subject. Plus, a grainy

***The Parsonage.*** *(top left)* Being in New York City doesn't always mean concrete and traffic. In Staten Island there is a place called Historic Richmond Town where you will be transported into another time. The building in this photo, called The Parsonage, was built in 1855 as home for the Pastor of the Dutch Reformed Church. It is an example of Gothic Revival style architecture.

***Castle in the Sky.*** *(bottom left)* The San Reno rises behind the Central Park fall foliage like a mighty urban castle. Styled in Beaux-Arts architecture, this 27-floor luxury apartment building has housed some famous residents through the years – Demi Moore, Aaron Spelling, Tony Randall, and Rita Hayworth, just to name a few.

**The Ramble Stone Arch.** *(top right)* This image was taken in Central Park's most rural area, The Ramble. Here, you can find species upon species of birds and other urban wildlife. The Ramble Stone Arch is considered one of the most picturesque bridges in Central Park. It even holds a secret: a hidden cave underneath it, which was boarded up in the 1920s.

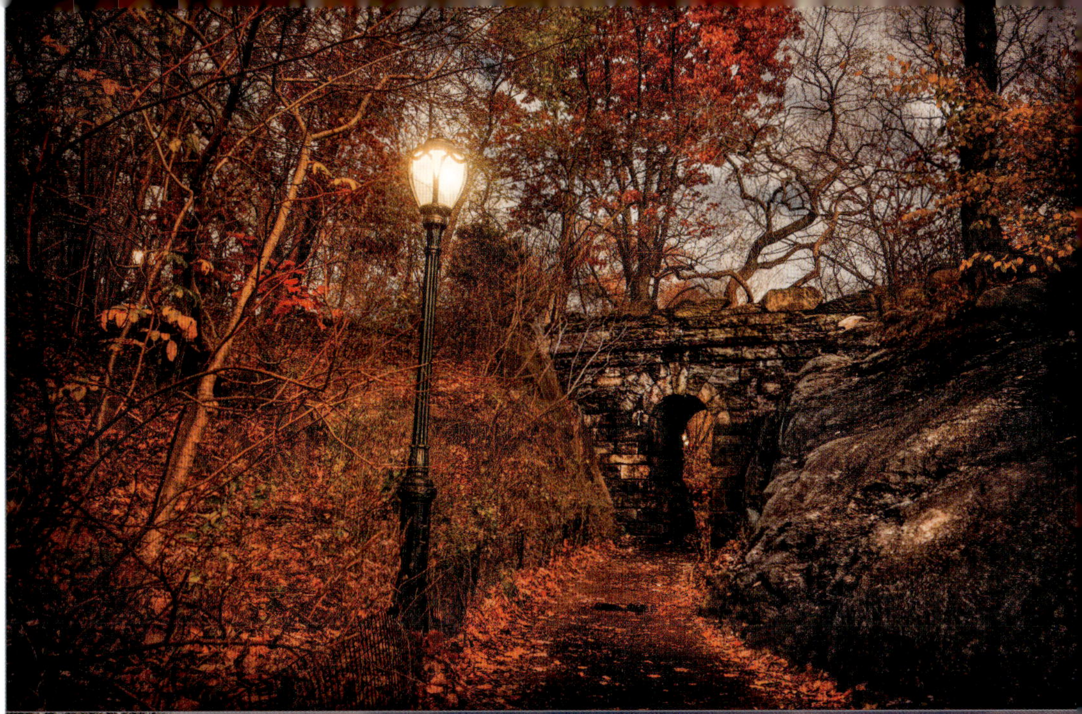

**Verazzano Bridge and Civil War-Era Tunnel.** *(bottom right)* Morning light illuminated the Verrazano Bridge and a military tunnel that was built after the Civil War. This tunnel was unknown until 2012, when Hurricane Sandy revealed it.

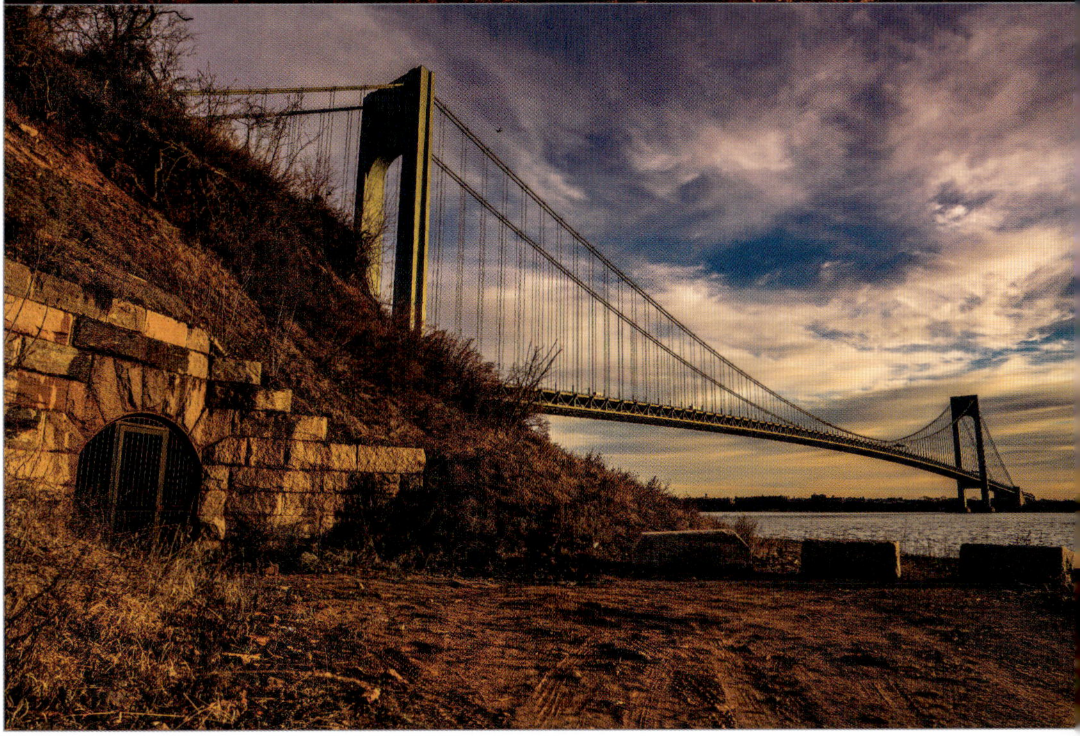

look can give my black & white photos a sense of drama as well as that classic New York City grungy feel—which can really make a photo stand out.

My advice to anyone starting out: do not aim for total perfection. If you do, you will never be satisfied with your work. Also, never delete your shots. Go back at a later date and look at them again. I can assure that you will see things you missed the first time. You may even pull out some of your best work from things you wanted to throw away! I am often unsatisfied when I first upload my day's photos. But when I look at them the next day, my eye has a whole new perspective.

I hope to continue my photography for years to come as it has become more than just my little hobby—it's my passion.

**The Hitcher.** *(top right)* The Statue of Liberty seems to be hitching a ride on the Staten Island Ferry. This shot was taken on a summer afternoon from Governors Island.

**Freedom Shines On.** *(center right)* Lady Liberty stands proudly as the sun sets behind her. Photographing her has become one of my passions. I try to catch her immersed in a good sunset, storm, moonrise, or just a beautifully cloudy day. She always seems to make the photo look just perfect. She is the symbol of freedom and my photos of her gain lots of attention.

**Freedom Will Never Be Eclipsed.** *(bottom right)* Notice the sun in this shot. It was taken on Liberty Island during "The Great American Eclipse" on August 21, 2017. We started to get a lot of cloud cover in New York City, but thankfully it cleared a bit and the eclipse was able to be viewed and enjoyed.

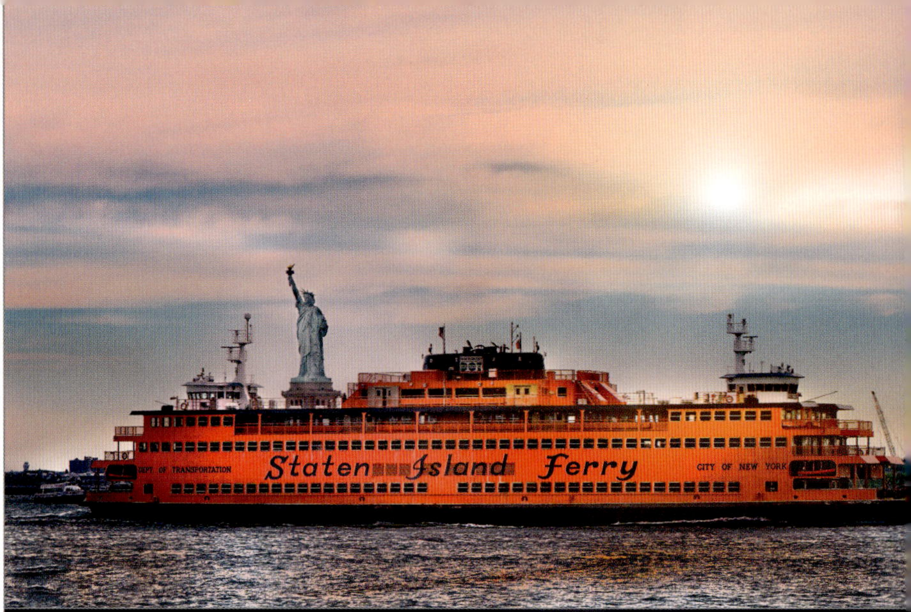


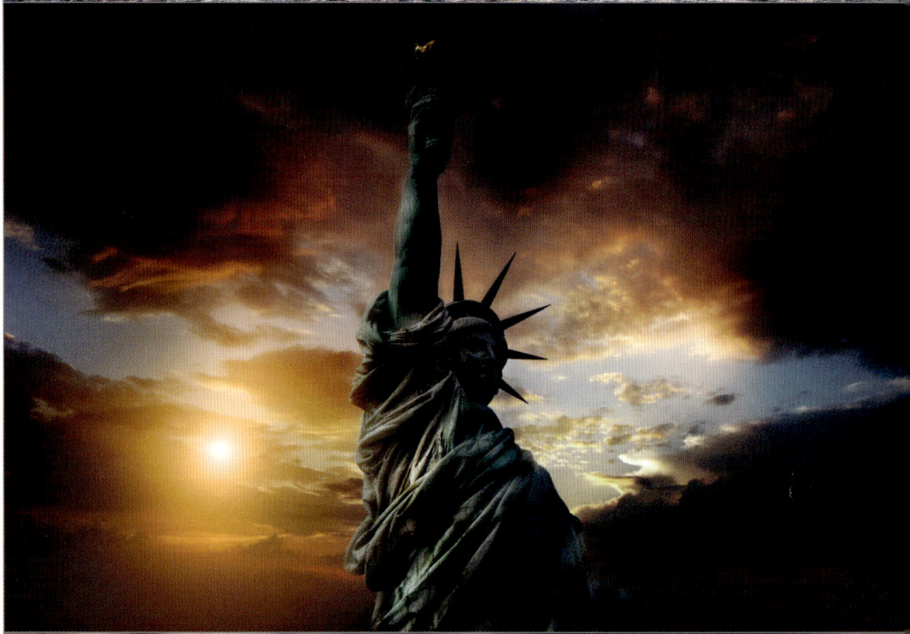

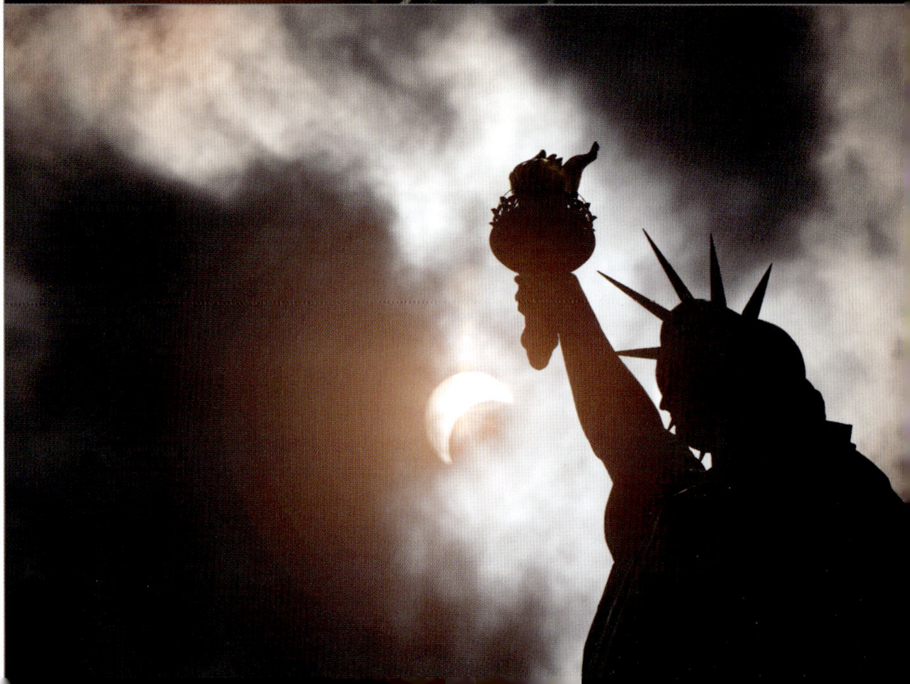

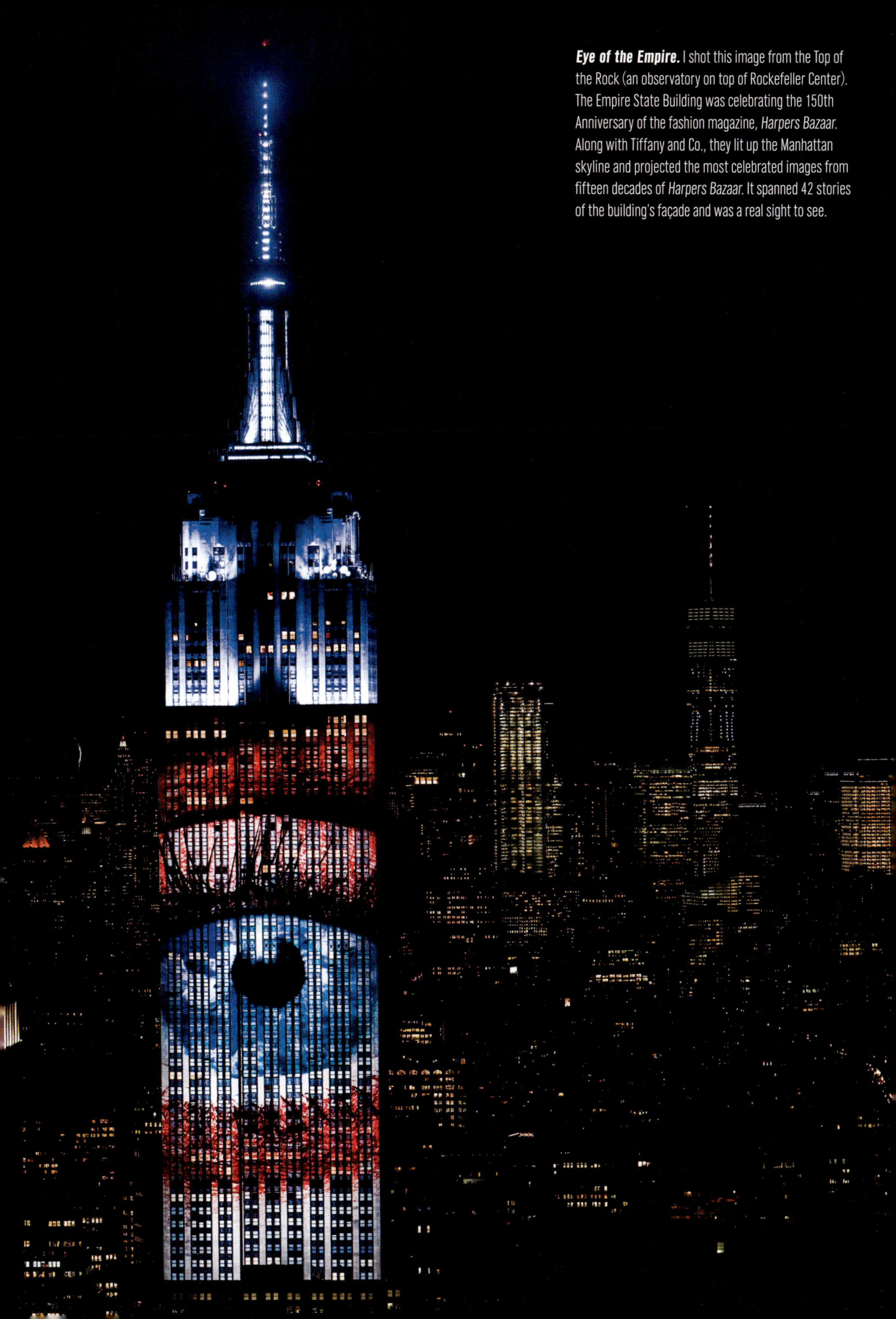

***Eye of the Empire.*** I shot this image from the Top of the Rock (an observatory on top of Rockefeller Center). The Empire State Building was celebrating the 150th Anniversary of the fashion magazine, *Harpers Bazaar.* Along with Tiffany and Co., they lit up the Manhattan skyline and projected the most celebrated images from fifteen decades of *Harpers Bazaar.* It spanned 42 stories of the building's façade and was a real sight to see.

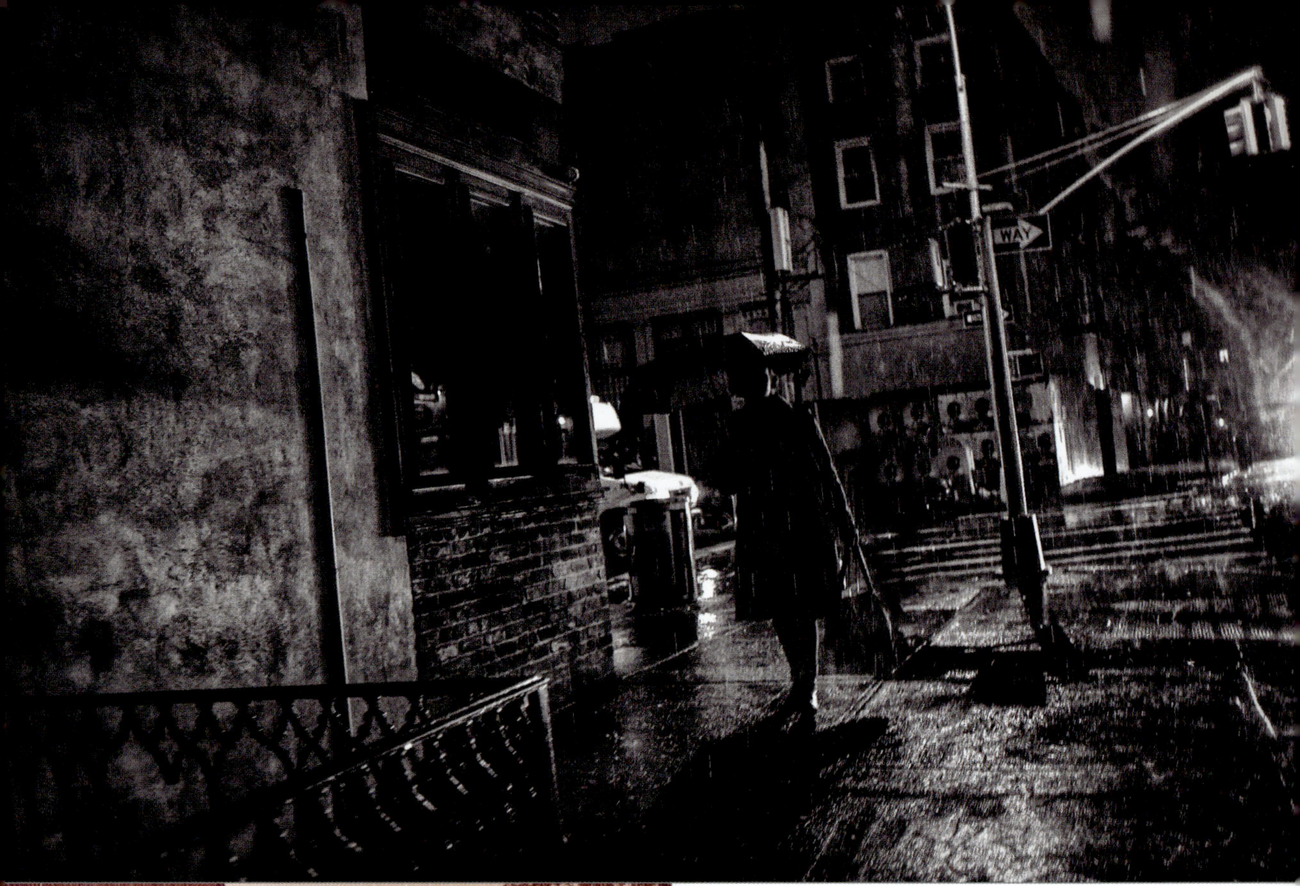


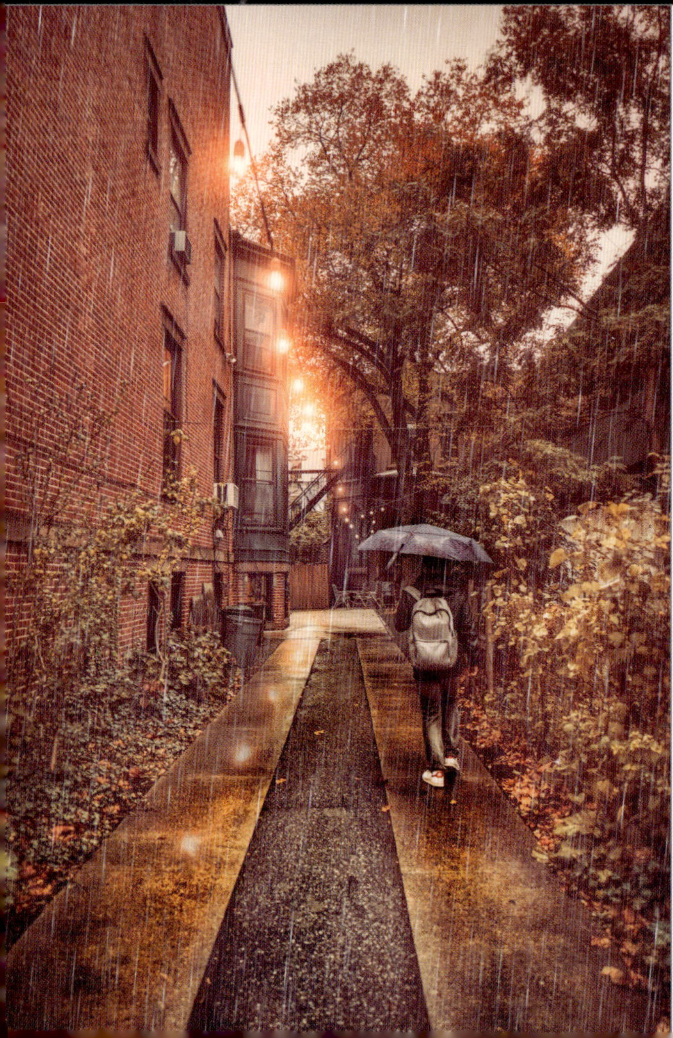

**Black Rain.** *(above)* Sometimes, I photograph mysterious subjects in the rain and process them for a black & white "film noir" tone. I search for mystery and bleakness to achieve these results. In this case, I don't worry about sharpness; grain helps achieve the desired mood.

**Rain Walker.** *(left)* Rain is also one of my favorite subjects in the daytime. Here, the wet ground and dismal, achromatic sky brought out the tones of the bricks and brownstones in the Cobble Hill section of Brooklyn. The entire area took on a gothic semblance, which I love.

**Reflections of a City Night.** *(facing page, top left)* People often ask me why I shoot in Central Park at night and if I'm afraid. I'm not–in fact, I find the park very peaceful at night. I think Hollywood movies give the park a bad rap, so people who aren't from here think you are instantly mugged or attacked once night falls. I thoroughly enjoy evening walks in Central Park.

**Freeman Alley.** *(facing page, top right)* One of my favorite streets is Freeman Alley, a hidden gem in the Lower East Side. This long alley is a haven for street art and leads to a restaurant at the end of the alley. When I am in the neighborhood, I stop for some photos. It is irresistible.

**A Secret in Brooklyn.** *(facing page, bottom)* My favorite part about walking the streets, looking to photograph something, is the discovery of hidden gems. This is one of Brooklyn's more charming finds. Located in the Cobble Hill section of Brooklyn, you will find Warren Place. The classical fountain in the middle of this bricked cottage street makes you feel as though you have been transported back to 18th century England. It's just mind-blowing. Walk out the gate, and the Brooklyn-Queens Expressway is practically in your face. Talk about one extreme to another.

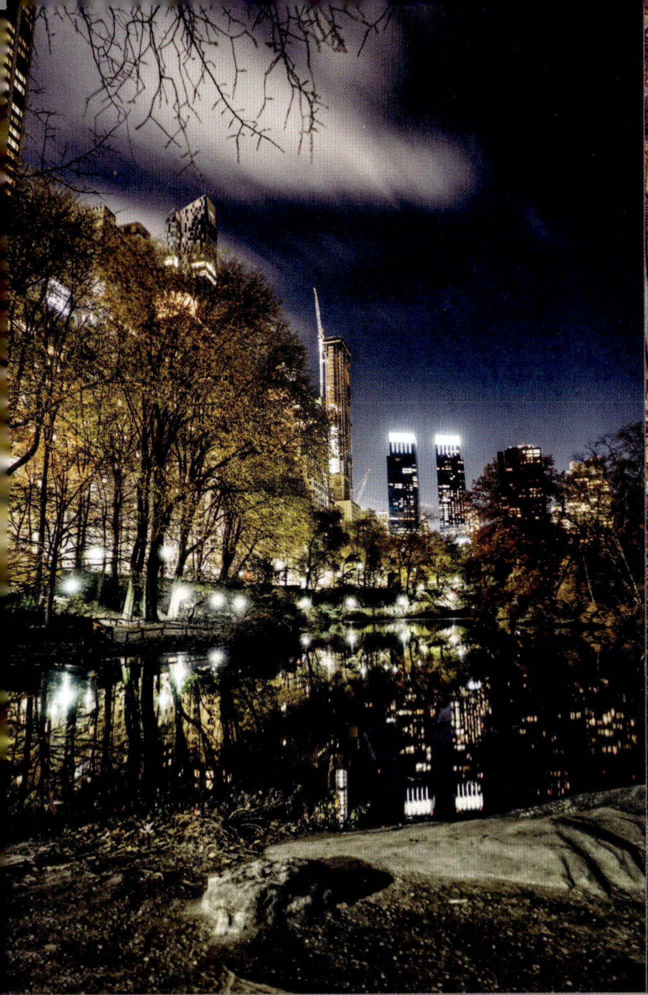
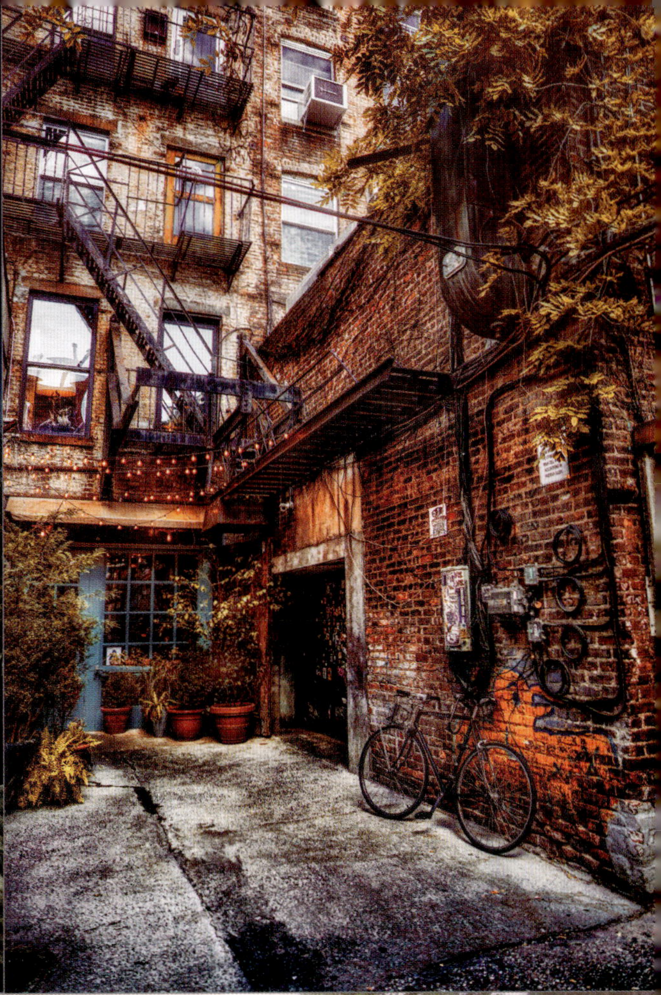
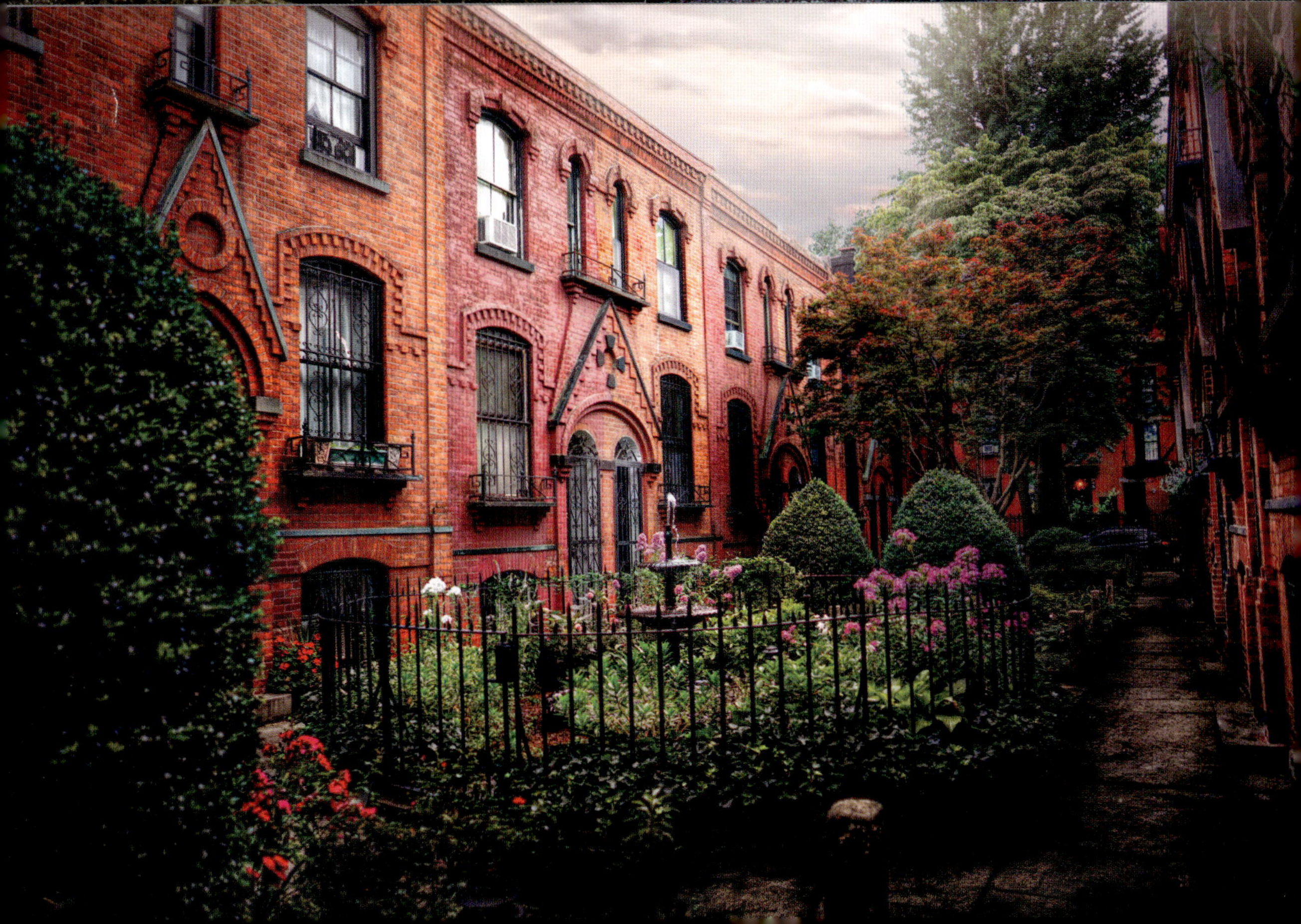

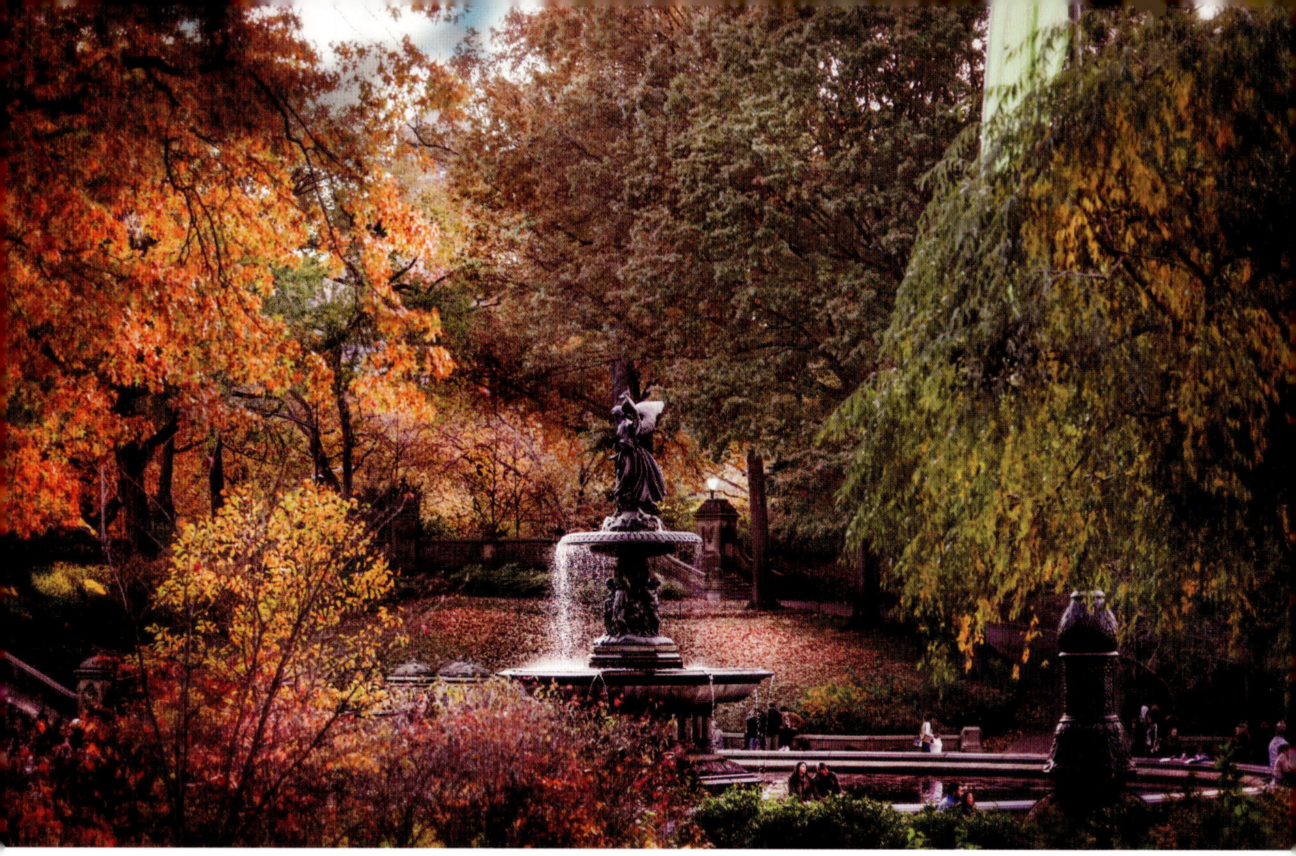

**Angelic Autumn Fantasy.** *(above)* The Angel of the Waters, one of Central Park's most iconic fountains, is surrounded by autumnal color. Created in 1864, she stands high above Bethesda Fountain and is a sight that everyone, from near and far, goes to see.

**Autumn Twist.** *(below)* For this image, I used a special art lens that twists the sides of the photo and gives it a dreamy look. (Why? I dropped and broke my other lens and had this little art lens with me!) This was after nightfall, and the colors of the leaves along the Mall in Central Park glowed above me.

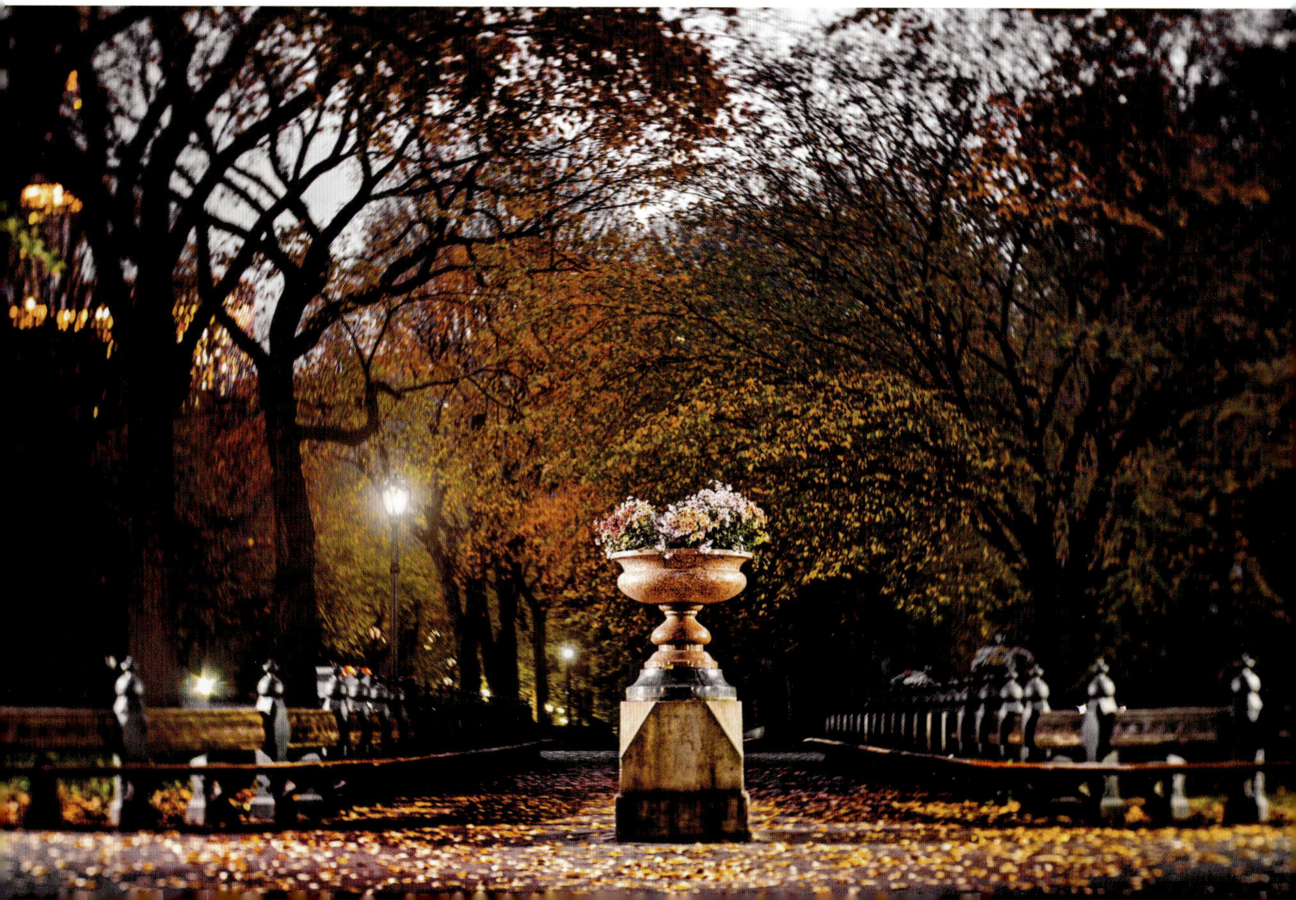

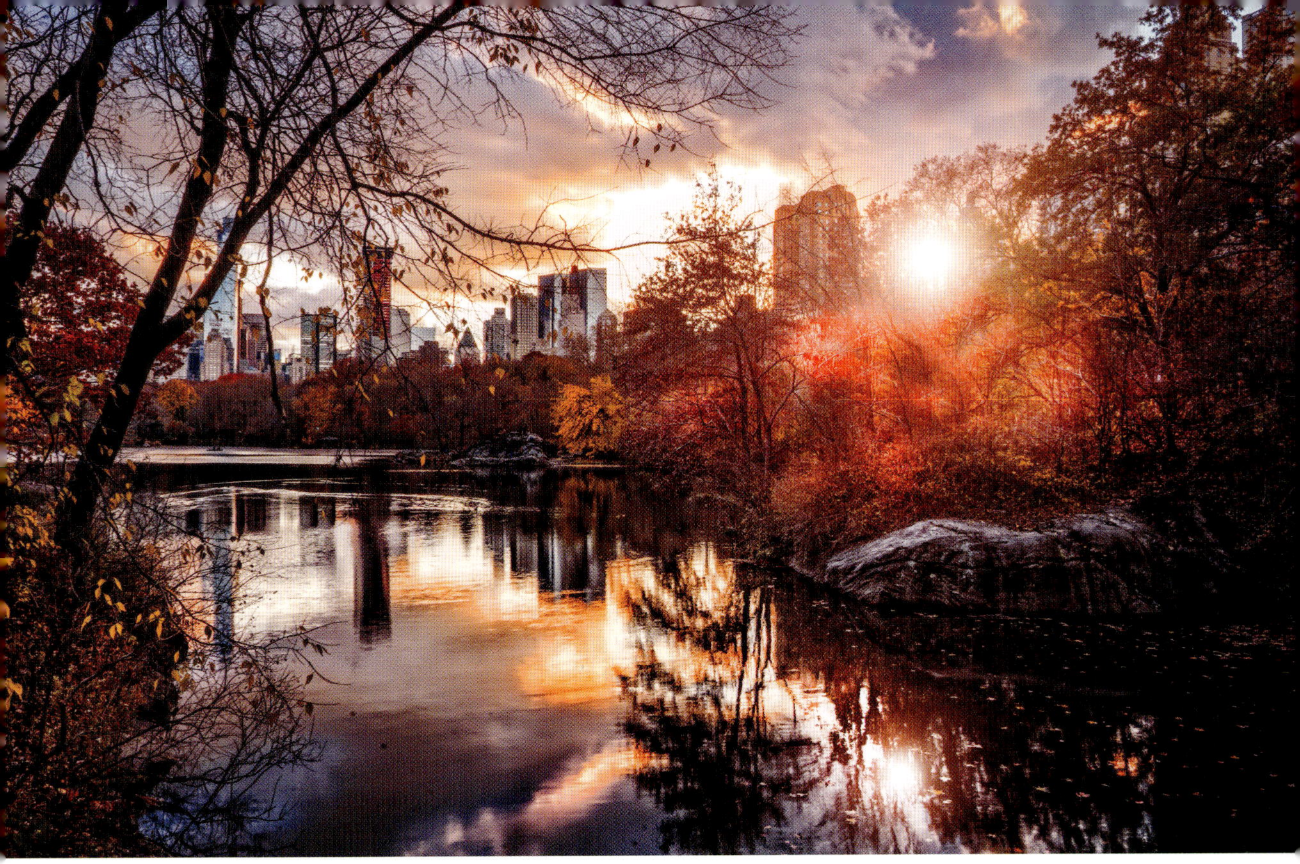

***Late Fall Sunset.*** *(above)* This was taken from Bank Rock Bridge, originally known as Oak Bridge, which was built in 1860. This bridge gives you a spectacular view of the lake. In the distance, urban towers rise high above the foliage. It's one of the most picturesque spots in Central Park.

***Little Japan in Brooklyn.*** *(below)* Infrared photography is one of the most surreal forms of taking photos and I had one of my cameras converted to take these images. This one is the Hill-and-Pond Garden in the Brooklyn Botanic Garden. Some of the foliage was hand painted to enhance the color.

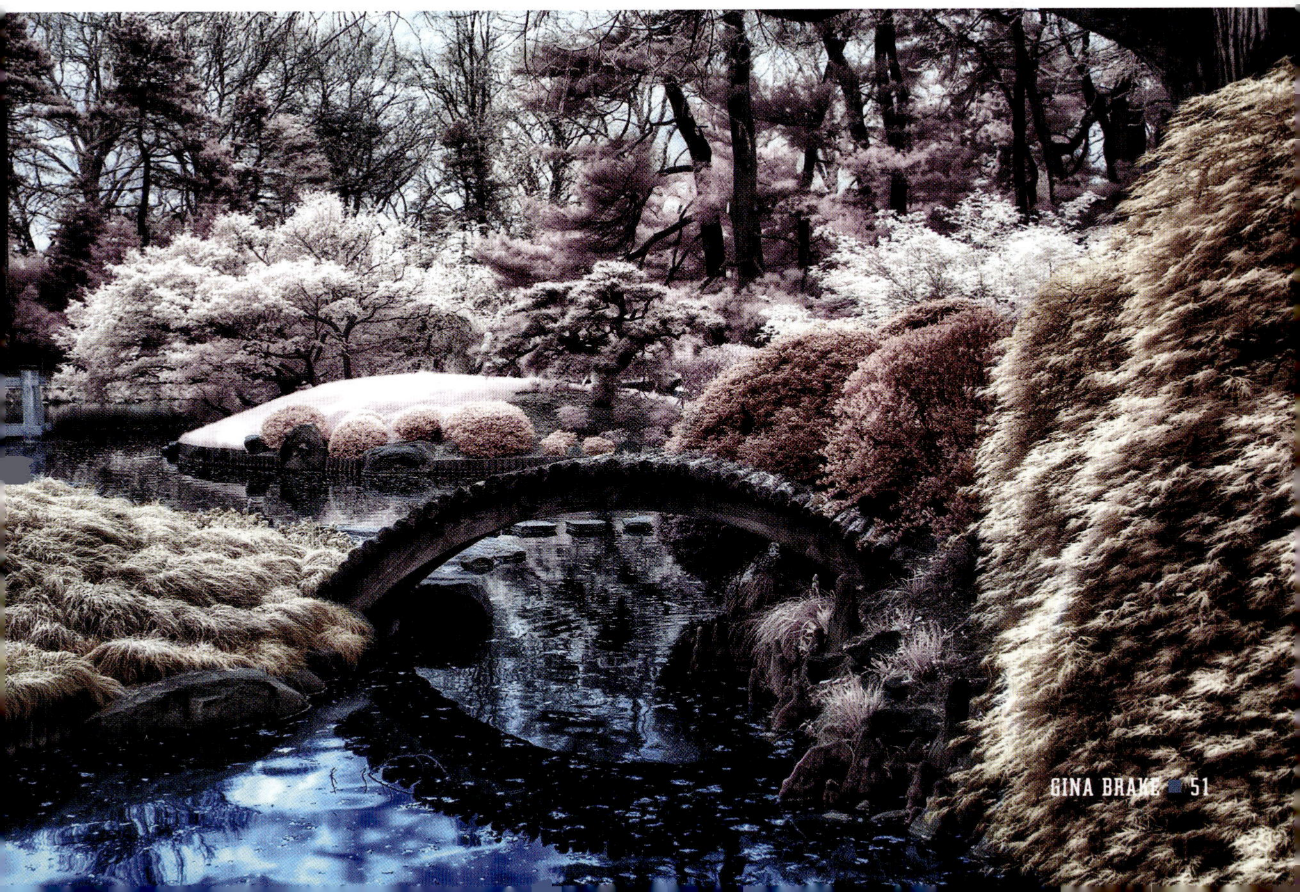

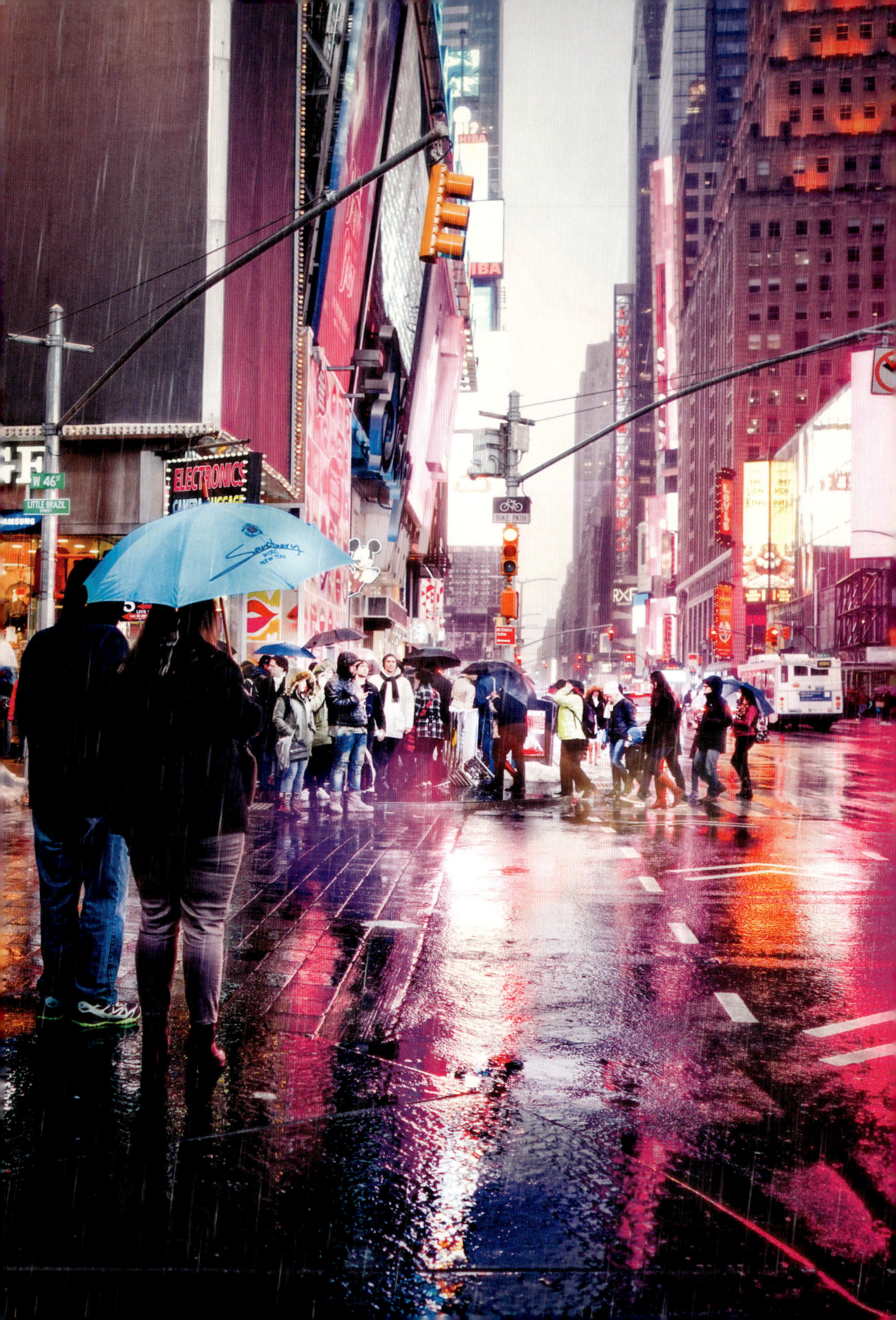
W 46ST
LITTLE BRAZIL
ELECTRONICS
BIKE PATH

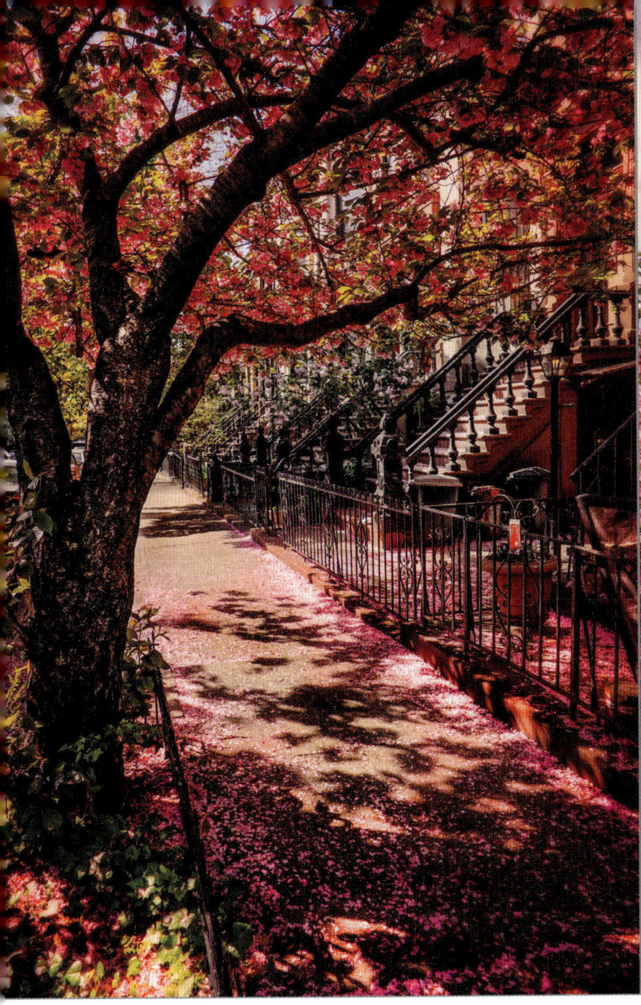

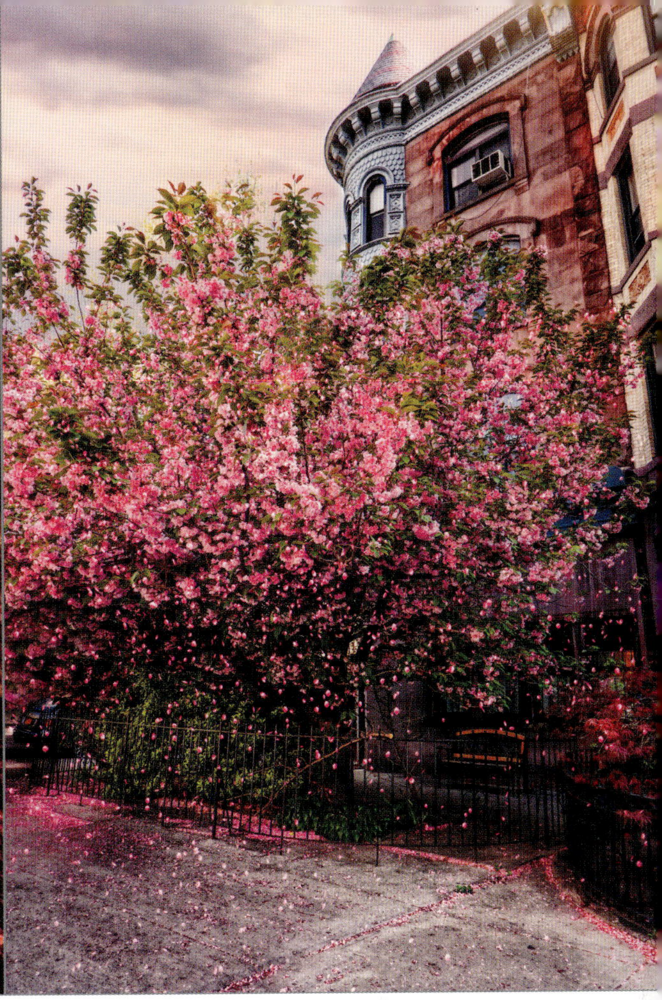

**The Color of Spring.** *(top left)* This photo was taken in the Park Slope Historic District of Brooklyn. The blocks are lined with brownstones and the pink tones of the cherry blossoms glow against the terra-cotta colored residences. Late April is the best time to experience this sea of color.

**Pink Storm.** *(top right)* Cherry blossoms and brownstones, what could be better? In the Park Slope Historic District of Brooklyn, the cherry blossoms leave a carpet of color fit for royalty. I personally think that seasonal changes make for some of the best photos in New York City streets.

**Purple Rain.** *(facing page)* There is no better time to experience the lights and shine of Times Square than in the rain. The rain turns the ground into a vibrant, glowing path.

**Garden of Urban Dreams.** *(right)* The High Line is an urban utopia, landscaped with beautiful flora. You can overlook the city streets and skyline while standing on it, surrounded with color—especially in the spring and summer months.

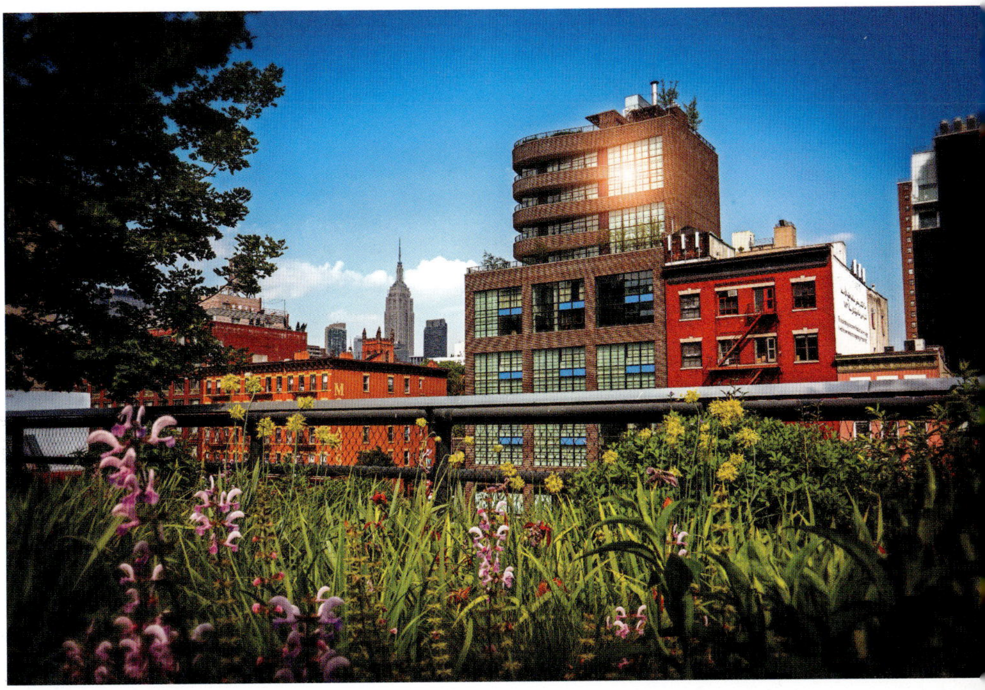

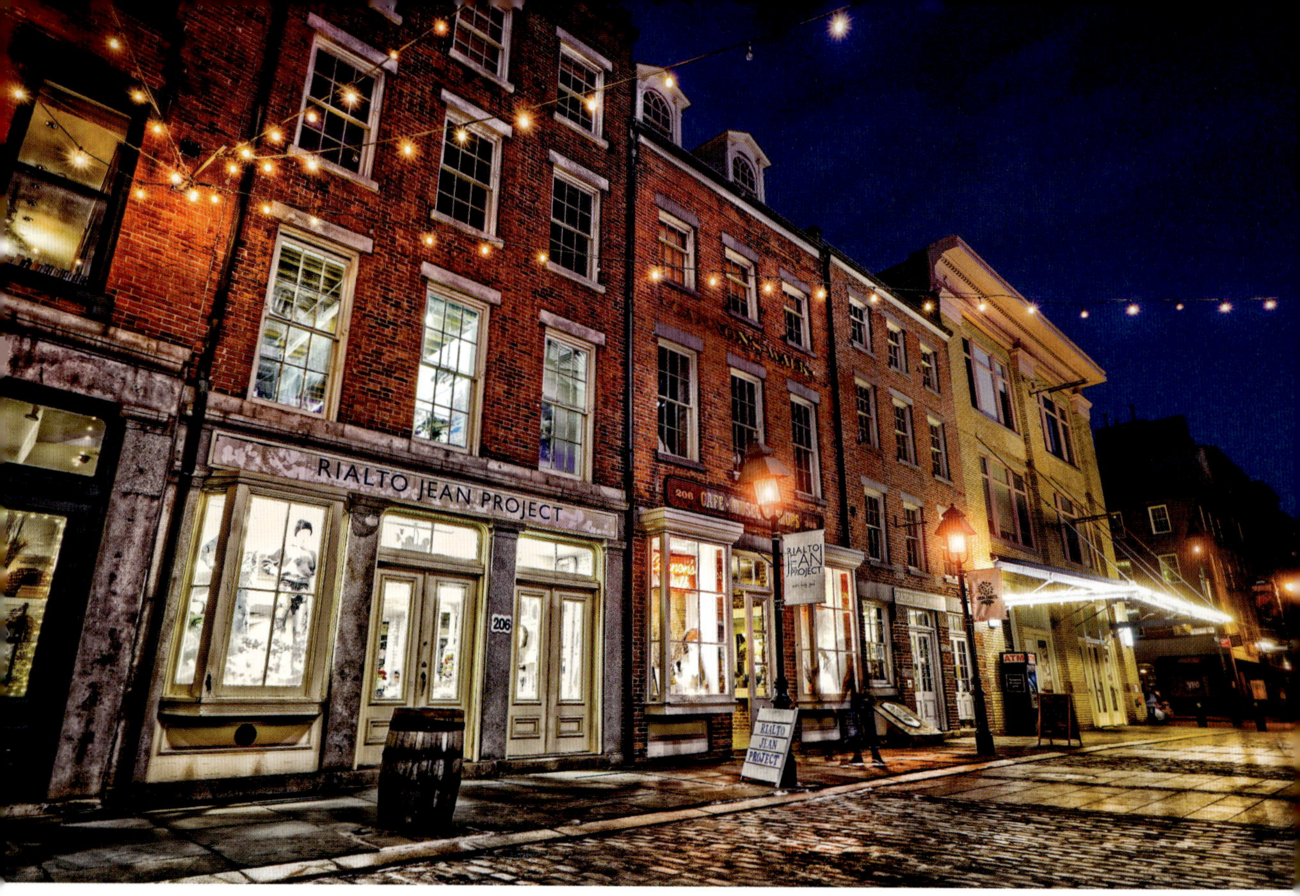


***Van Gogh Scene in NY.*** *(above)* In Manhattan's South Street Seaport, I came to a halt seeing the ultramarine blue sky paired with zinc yellow buildings and reflections. It hit me: I was looking at the colors of Vincent Van Gogh's palette. This was a shot I could not resist as I am a huge Van Gogh fan.

***Wall Street Gold.*** *(below)* Wall Street seems to be paved with gold in this photo shot on a warm summer night. The statue of George Washington stands on the steps of Federal Hall National Memorial. Federal Hall is rich with American history.

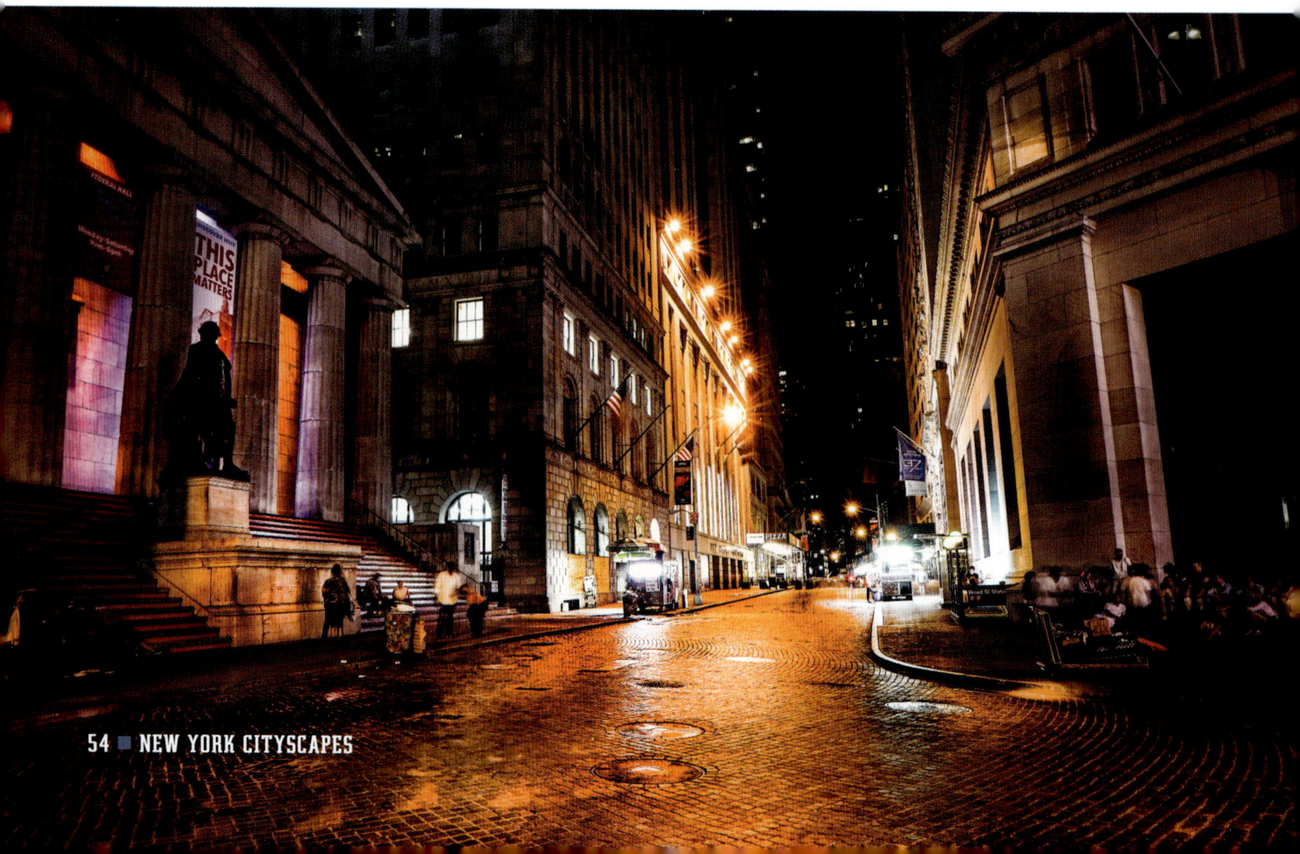

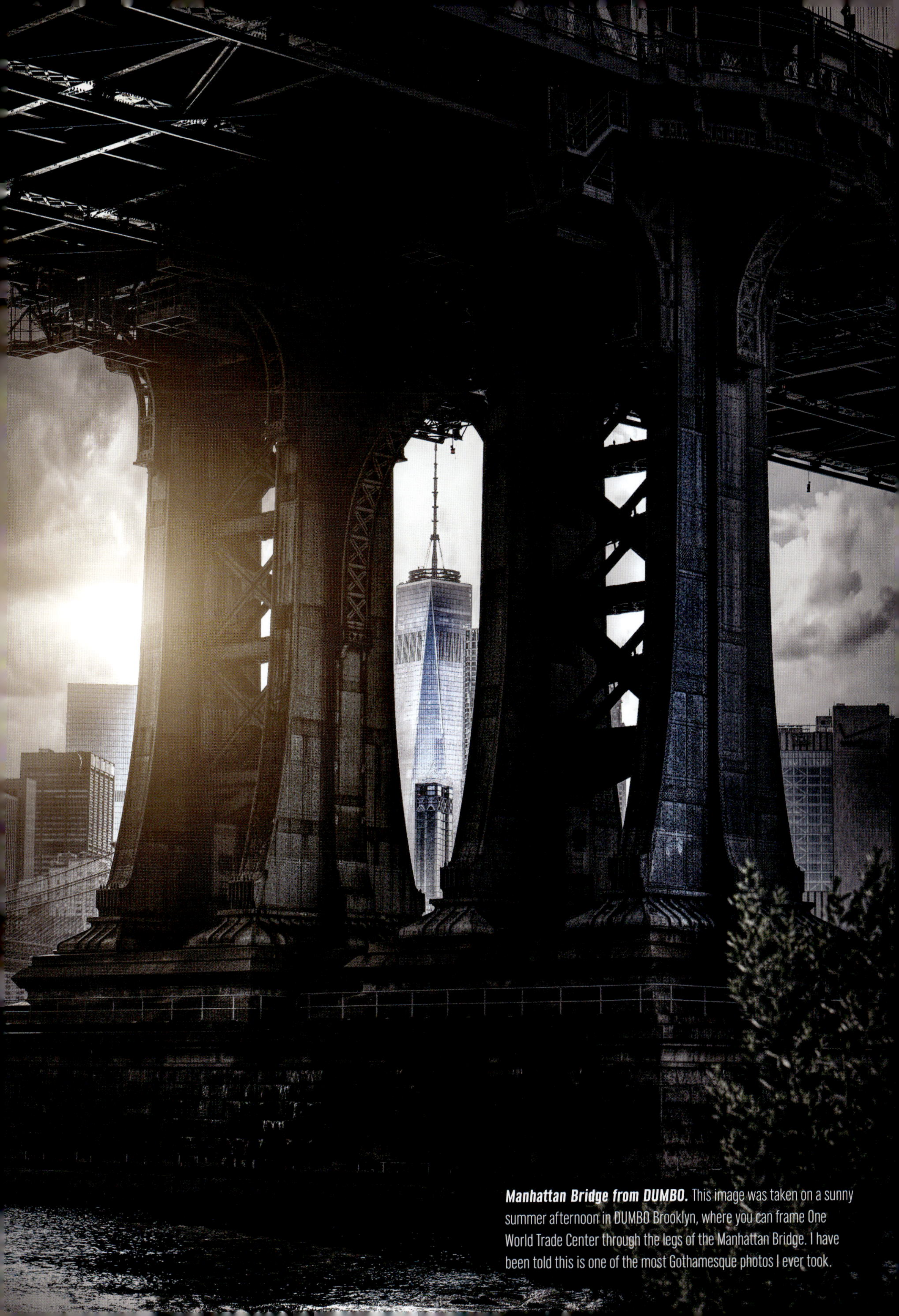

***Manhattan Bridge from DUMBO.*** This image was taken on a sunny summer afternoon in DUMBO Brooklyn, where you can frame One World Trade Center through the legs of the Manhattan Bridge. I have been told this is one of the most Gothamesque photos I ever took.

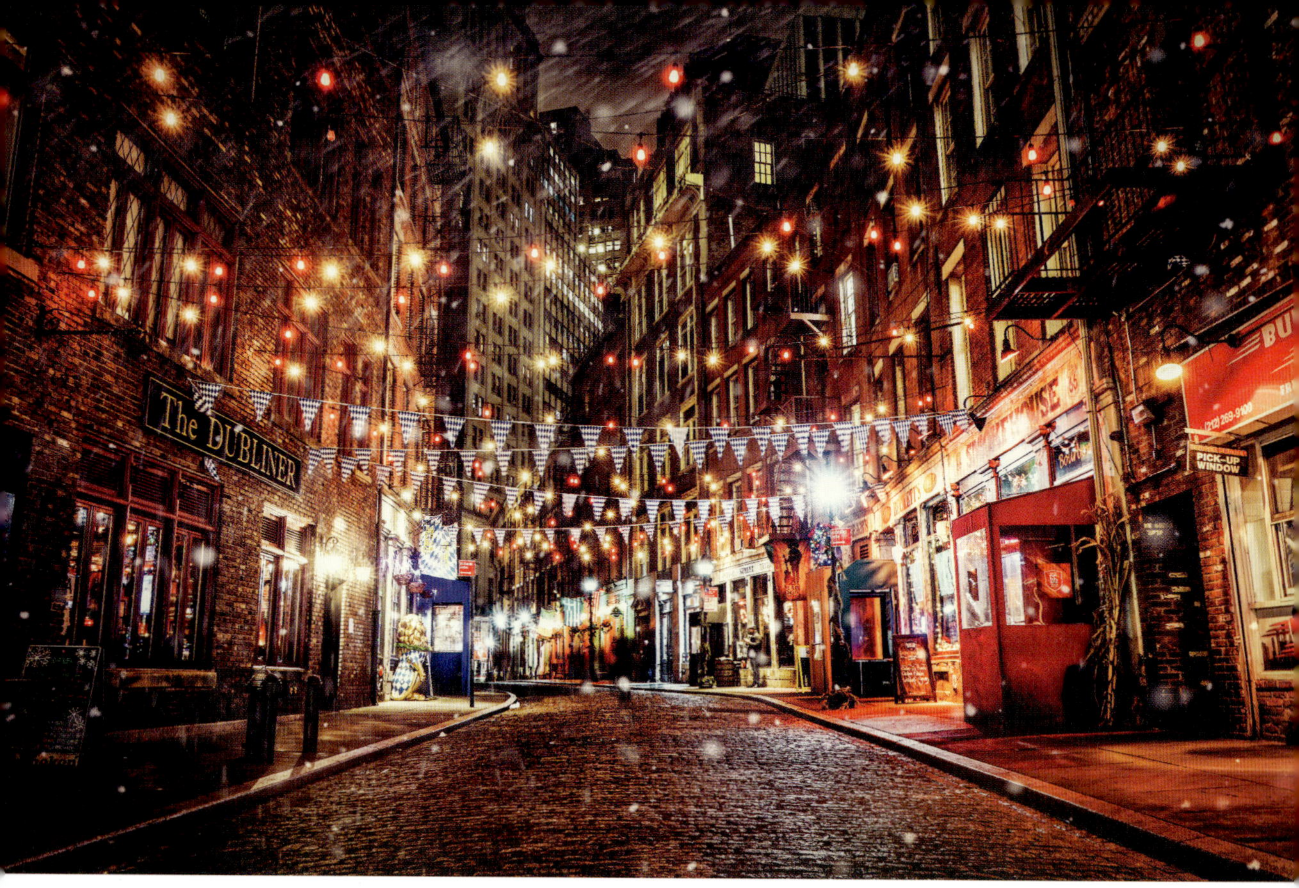


**A Flurry on Stone Street.** *(above)* Located in downtown Manhattan, Stone Street is one of the city's oldest cobblestone streets. It has gone from a derelict alley to one of New York City's most happening spots, lined with pubs and restaurants that offer European charm right here in the city of New York.

***Doyers Street in Snow.*** *(below)* Doyers Street in Chinatown is one block long and has a sharp bend in the middle. To me, the water tank above the end of the street makes the whole block. This is one of my favorite streets in Manhattan.

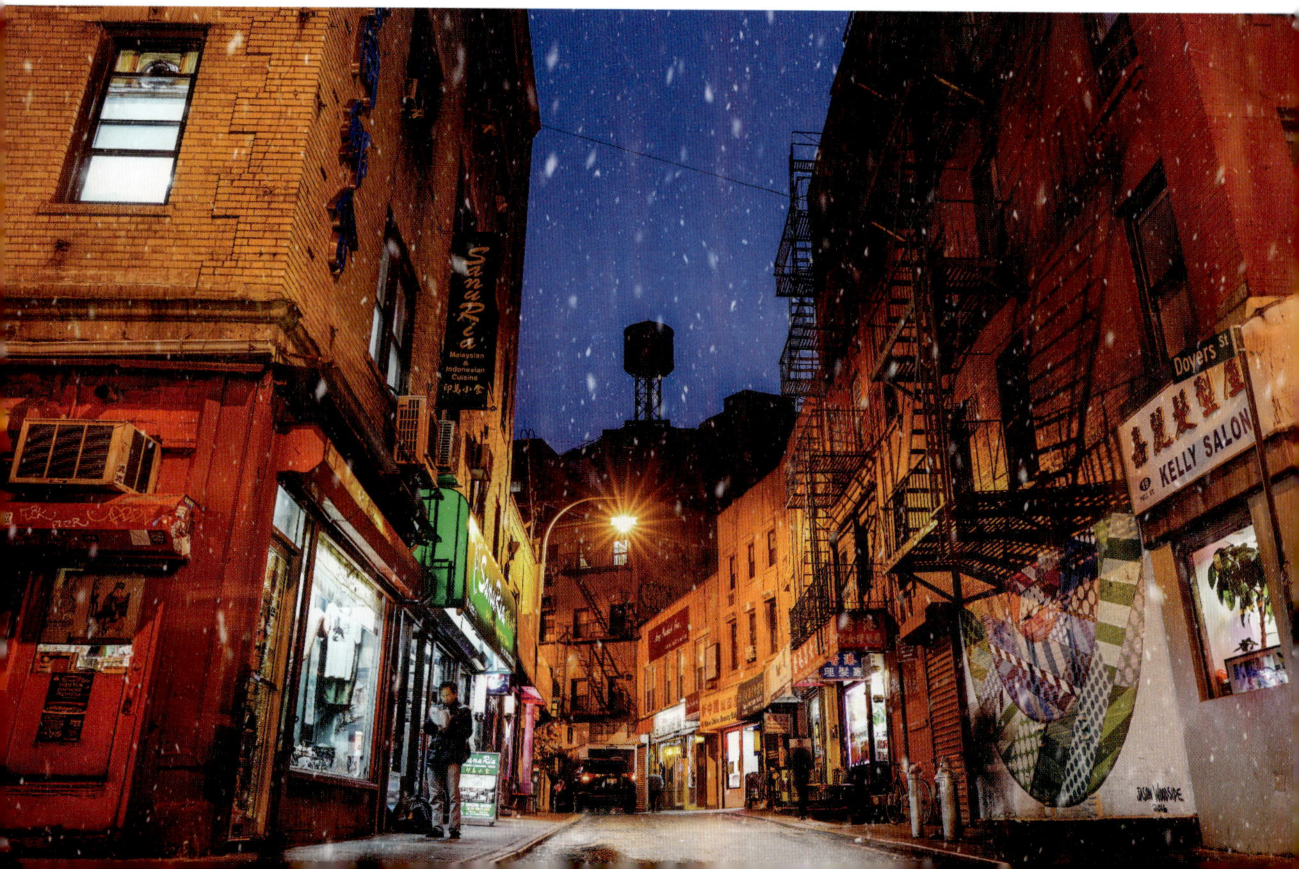

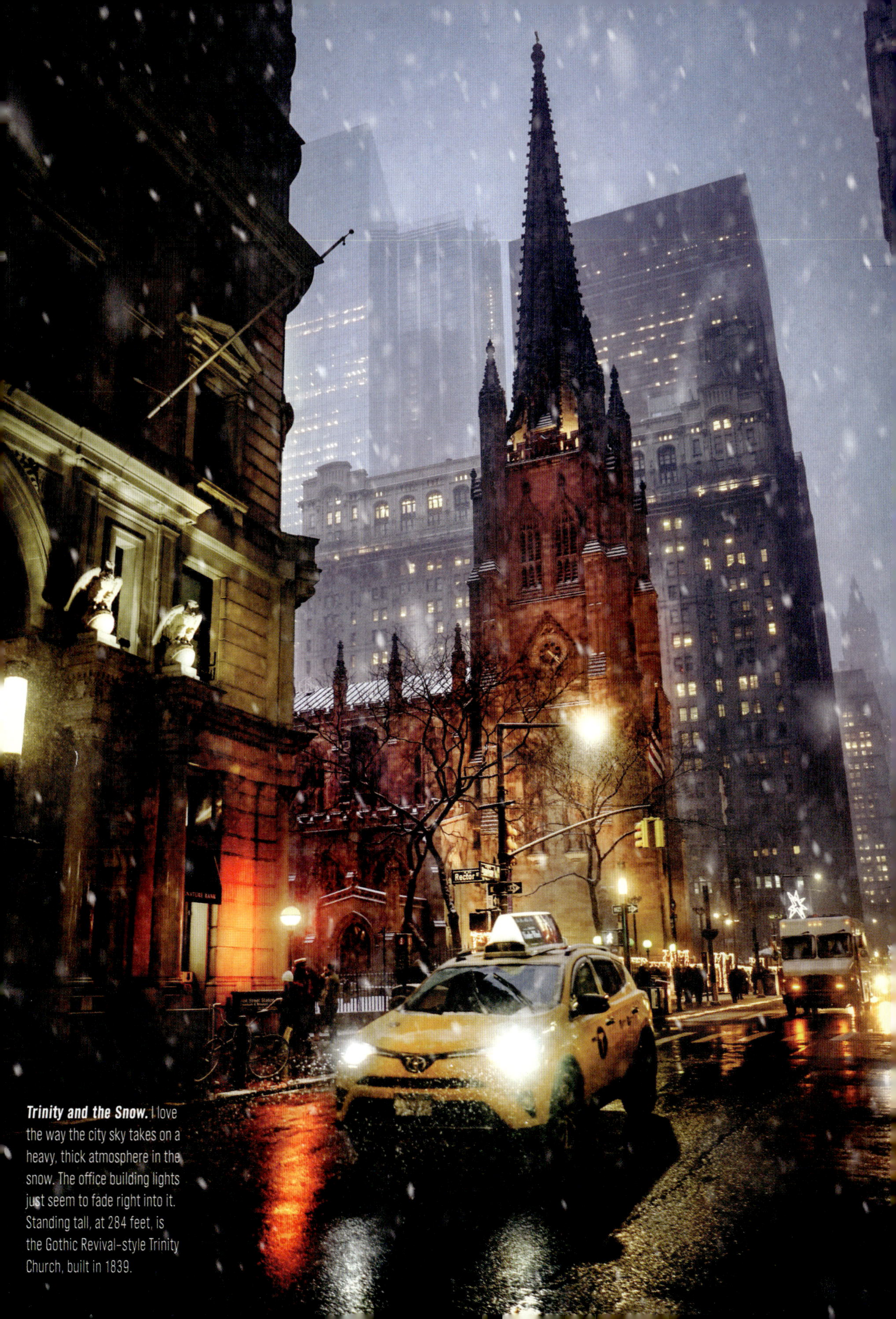


***Trinity and the Snow.*** I love the way the city sky takes on a heavy, thick atmosphere in the snow. The office building lights just seem to fade right into it. Standing tall, at 284 feet, is the Gothic Revival–style Trinity Church, built in 1839.

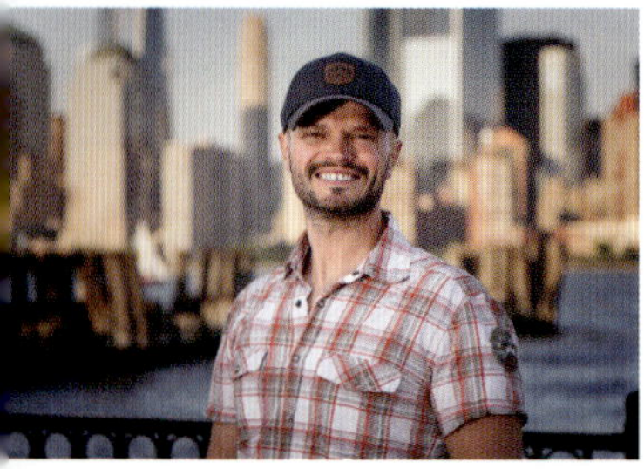

CHAPTER 4

# Viktor Buriak

Instagram: @vikvik7 ■ www.vikburiakphotography.com

I'm not going to sit here and tell you that I was born with a camera in my hand or that I have always wanted to be a photographer. To be honest, I never knew my life would lead me down this road. Who knew I would fall in love with something as simple as a click? I certainly didn't. When I think back on the fact that I have always loved art, I suppose it's not that hard to imagine why I became a photographer. As a child, I was always drawing something. For me, it was more than just drawing a picture for fun—it was a genuine way for me to express myself.

Thirty-five years ago, I was born in the historic city of Rivne, Ukraine. While most of my immediate family lived in the city, my other relatives didn't live far away on their farms. Throughout my childhood, it was very common for my family and I to be out at the farm, helping with the always challenging workload. Coming from a farming background, my family continuously instilled in me the value of hard work and the importance of persevering through whatever challenges life may throw at me. Those lessons have stayed with me throughout my life. We lived in Rivne until my early teenage years, when we left to pursue the American dream.

I first discovered my passion for photography in high school when I took a photography class. This was by far my coolest class to date. I learned how to line up my camera to capture a good picture and how to develop film in a darkroom. To be honest, I was probably a little bit *too* comfortable in the

***Top of the Rock.*** *(below)* I learned the hard way that tripods are not allowed at this overlook. Tripod or not, I was determined to capture the view.

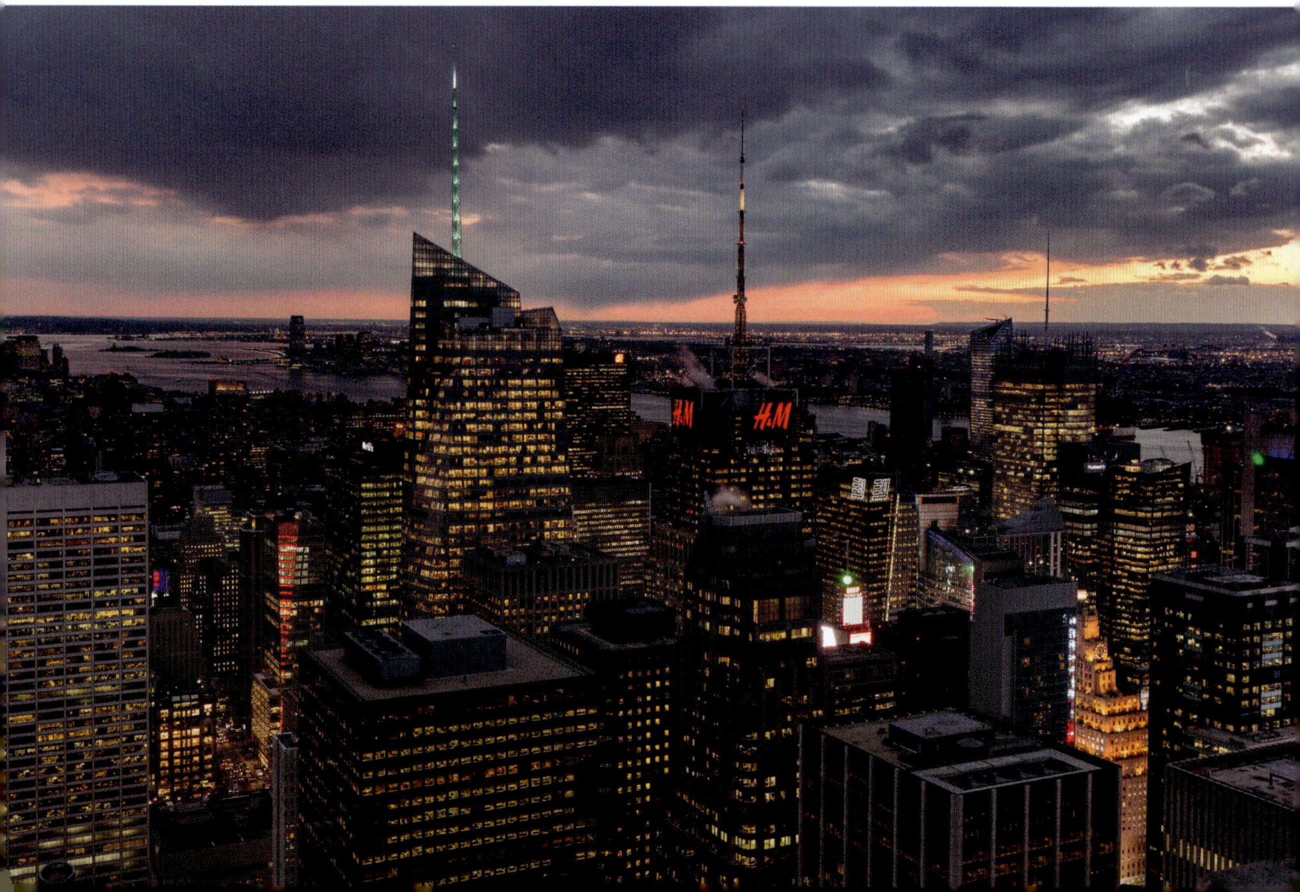

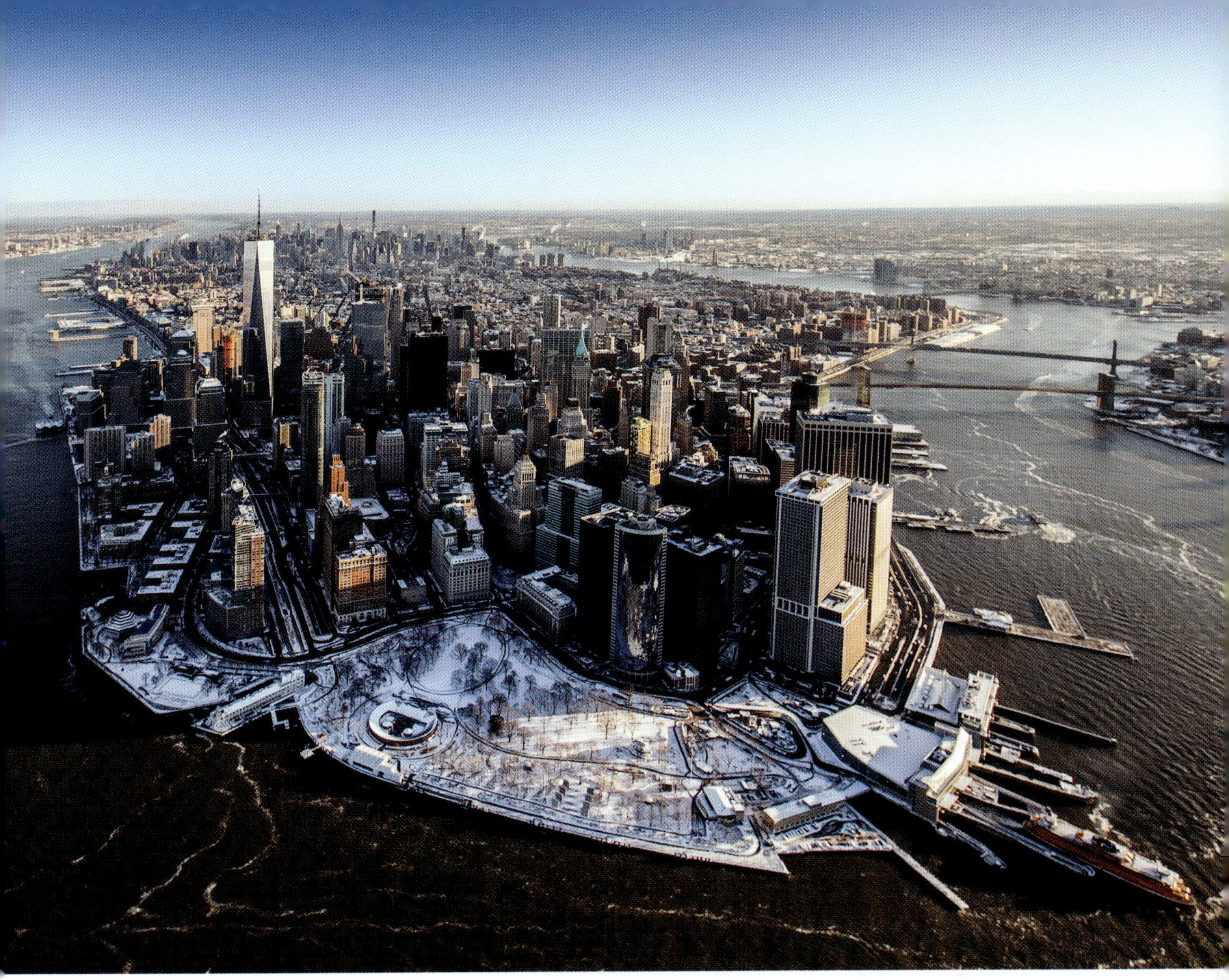

darkroom—as I literally need light in order to communicate. You see, I'm deaf.

I have been deaf since I was a toddler. At the age of two, I became seriously ill with meningitis. While this sickness could have killed me, luckily it did not. It did however leave me forever changed. Because I was so young, it was quite some time before my family realized just what the disease had done to my ability to hear. Please do not feel sorry that I have never heard the birds sing on a nice spring morning or that I've never heard the beautiful music you so much enjoy. I am absolutely proud to be deaf. I am grateful for the experiences and relationships I have because of it. Without my deafness, I wouldn't be who I am today. I wouldn't want it any other way. I was blessed to learn four languages because of my deafness. While living in Ukraine, I attended a school for the deaf. I learned to read and write in Ukrainian, and I also learned

**Manhattan Look Down.** *(above)* It sure was freezing when I took this from way up in the sky. I was in a helicopter with the doors off—but the view made it worth the icy temperatures.

Ukrainian Sign Language. After my family and I moved to the States, I learned written English and American Sign Language. I'm sure some of you reading this probably thought sign language was universal. Fortunately, it is not; there are many countries with their own beautiful variations of sign language.

Experiencing life in silence has given me many blessings, but not without many challenges. No matter what it is, I never let my deafness define me. I persevere because I have the grit to do it. Quitting has never been an option.

One thing I have in common with my camera is that I, too, view the world through a lens. Being deaf, I have only my visual perception. This means

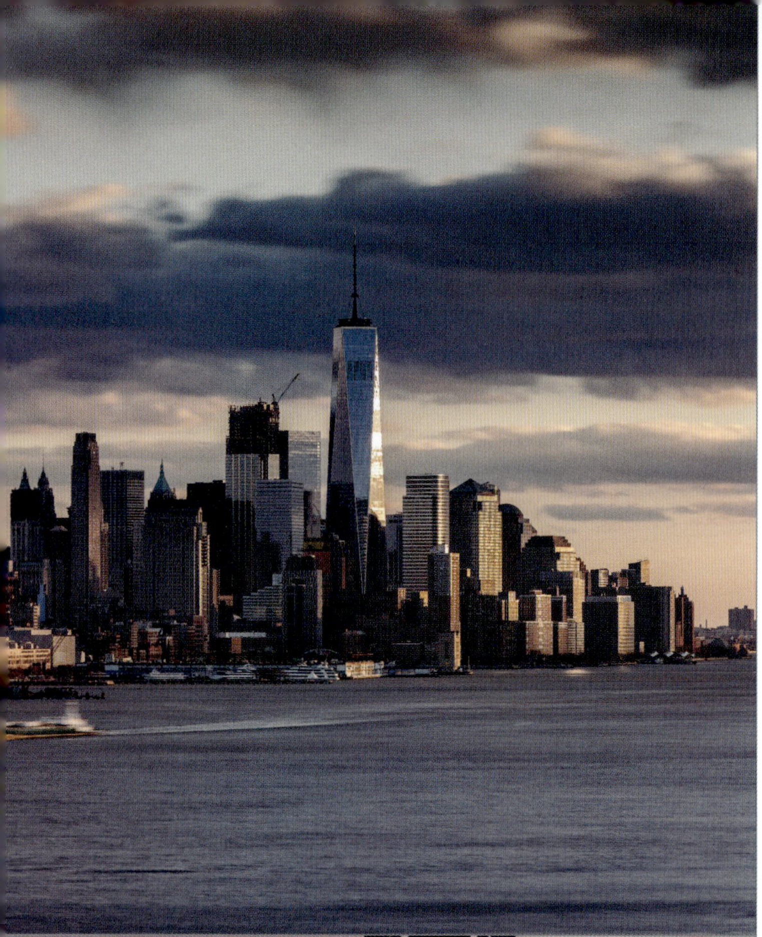

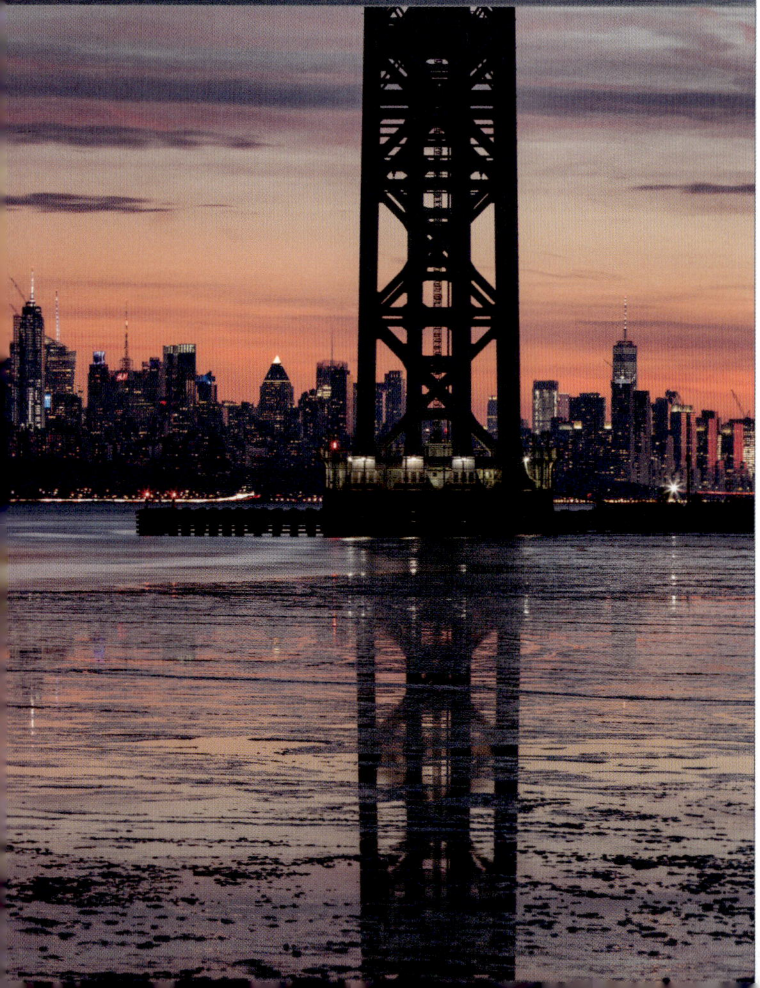

that my perspective is different from that of those who view the world using all of their senses. This is one of the many blessings I have gained. I am able to see the beauty in the world all around me and truly appreciate it, which drives me to take that perfect shot.

Moving to the suburbs of New York City has also shaped my life. Being a sports fan, I quickly became a NY Yankees and Jets fan. It was effortless to fall in love with The Big Apple. It's no wonder that I would start snapping shots of this amazing city. I can honestly say New York City is as much responsible for my love of photography as my passion for art. I have also enjoyed meeting many talented photographers at local shooting spots, as well as through Instagram, and have made some great friends.

Most of my photography is of various prominent landmarks the city has to offer, from street to aerial views. I have spent the last ten years honing my skills while taking shots of New York City. However, over the past couple of years, I have been expanding my focus and started venturing into photographing portraits and wildlife. Being deaf while shooting wildlife can present its own challenges. This is especially true when photographing birds. It's not exactly easy to track a bird in silence. Nevertheless, I push through and it has turned out to become a favorite of mine. The bigger the challenge, the greater amount of gratitude I have for the opportunity. I have

***One World Trade Center Skyline.*** *(top left)* People who don't photograph don't truly know how frustrating the clouds can be. Often, I spot great clouds and decide to go see what I can capture – but by the time I arrive, the clouds have vanished. I really appreciate the clouds in this picture.

***Sunset at the George Washington Bridge.*** *(bottom left)* Without the icy waters and the amazing sky, this picture wouldn't have been so cool. I like the sky's reflection on the icy water. To me, the extra texture adds to the reflection.

had so much fun and enjoyment from all of my photography experiences. I am forever grateful for those I've met and those who have helped me along the way.

Many people aspire to be something world changing, like being rich and famous. I just want to live my life making people happy. I want to spend my life doing what I love, taking great pictures of the many beautiful things the world offers us every day. I want to have the opportunity to take pictures of people while they are experiencing their milestones, enabling them to look at those photos years later and perhaps escape daily stresses while they reflect back to those precious moments. I want to capture the emotions of the event and the love that is so effortlessly displayed.

**Brooklyn Bridge.** *(below)* It doesn't get much better than the beauty of the Brooklyn Bridge. I absolutely love a good sunrise to start the day.

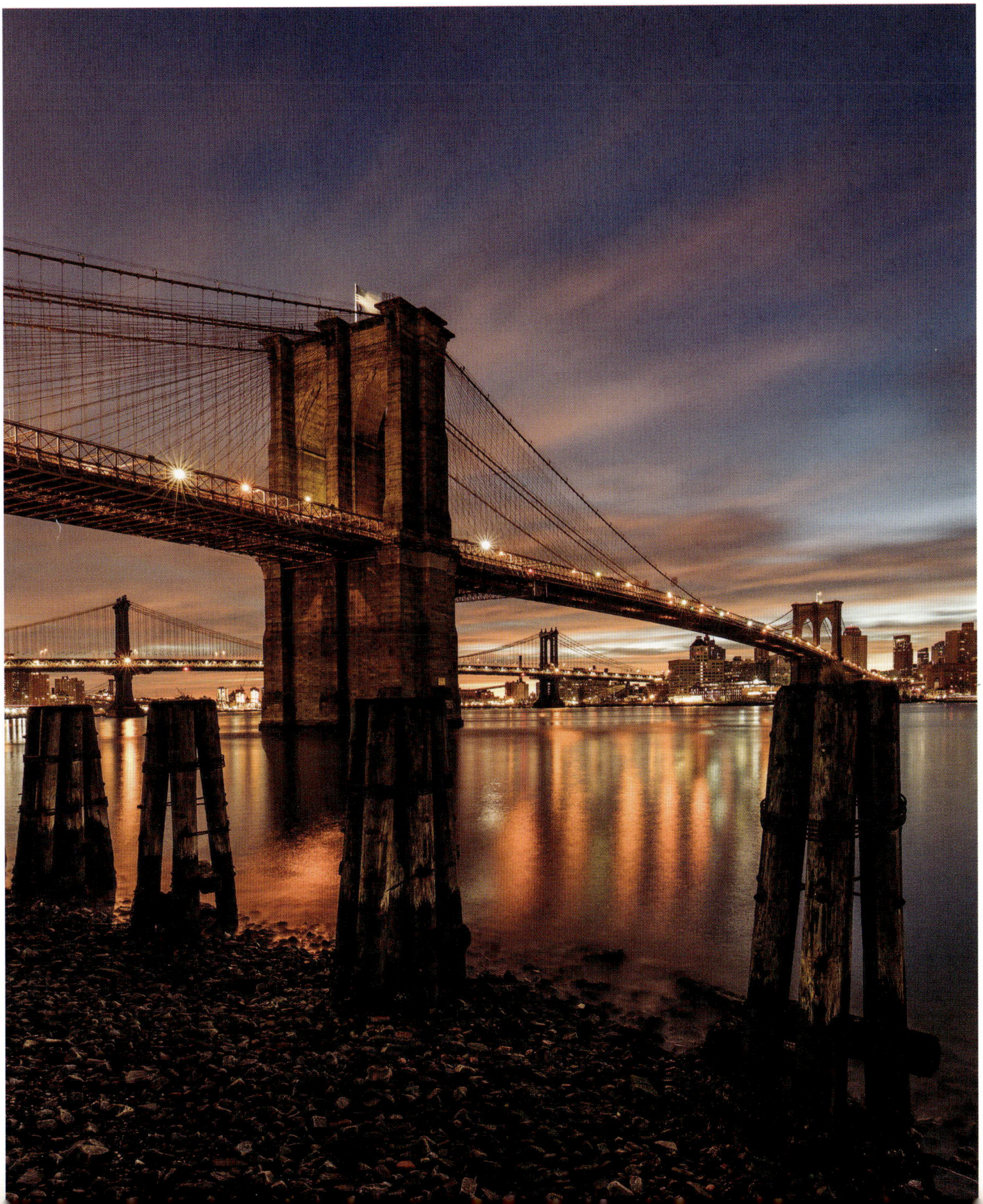

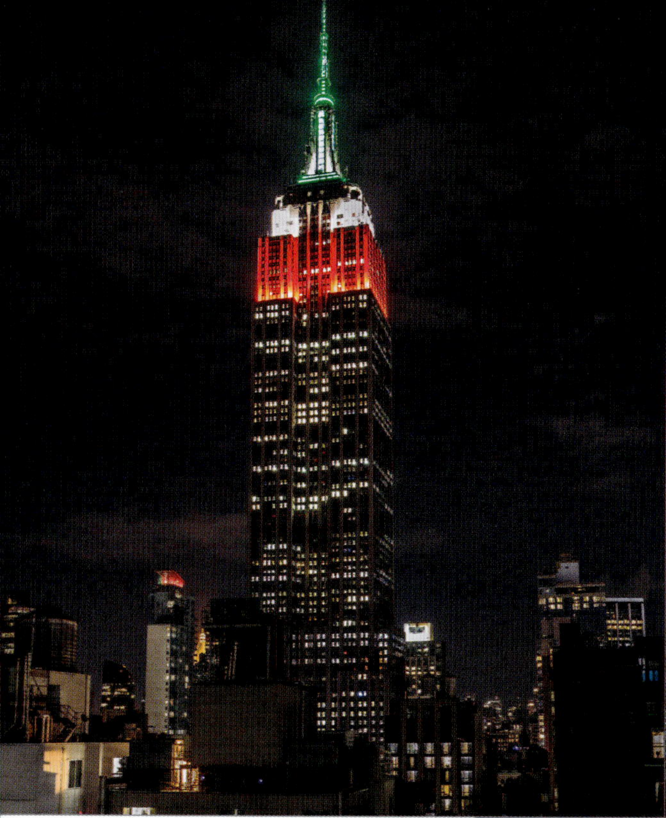

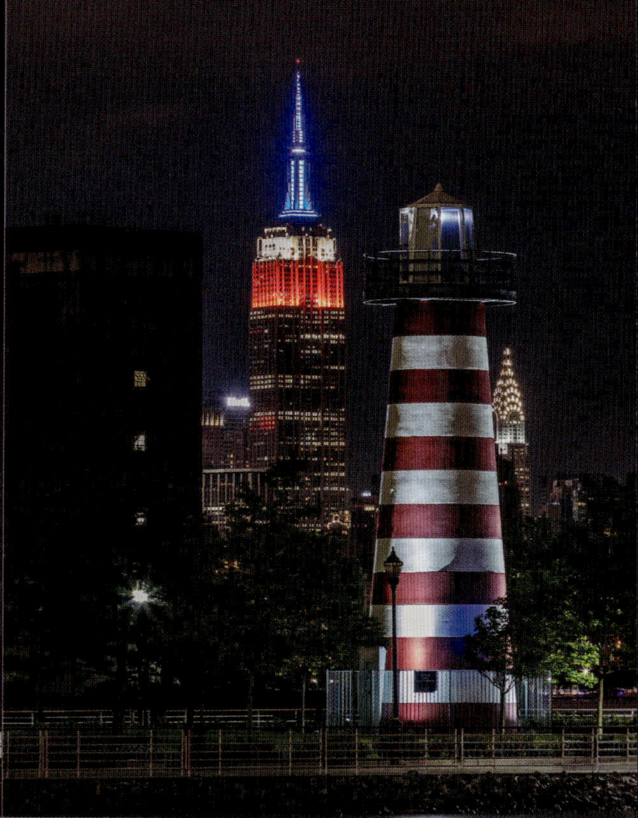

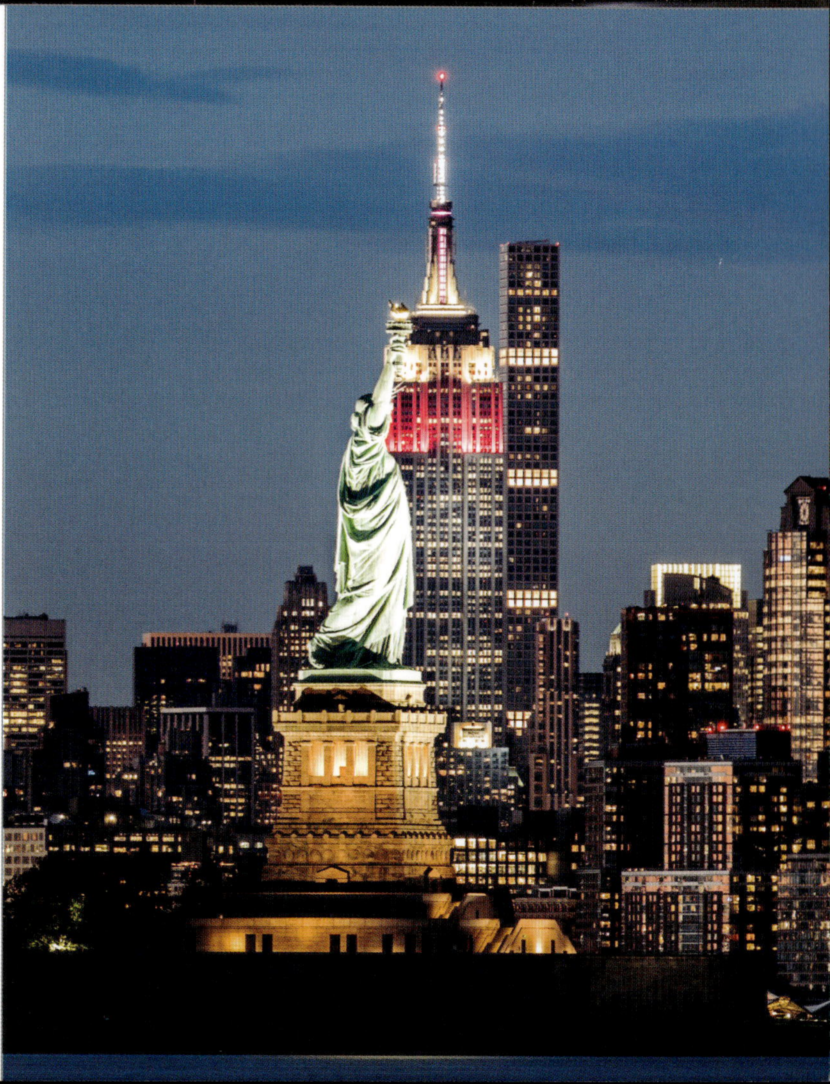

***Empire State Building.*** *(top left)* In September, the Empire State building was illuminated in red, white, and green to honor Mexican Independence Day.

***Lefrak Point Lighthouse and Empire State Building.*** *(top right)* I couldn't resist stopping in Jersey City to capture the Lefrak Point Lighthouse with red, white, and blue glowing from the Empire State Building in the background.

***Pink and White Empire State Building.*** *(right)* The Empire State Building was lit up in pink and white to honor the tenth anniversary of Qatar Airways flying in the United States.

***Celebrating Love.*** *(facing page)* The Empire State building was lit up red on Valentine's Day to celebrate love.

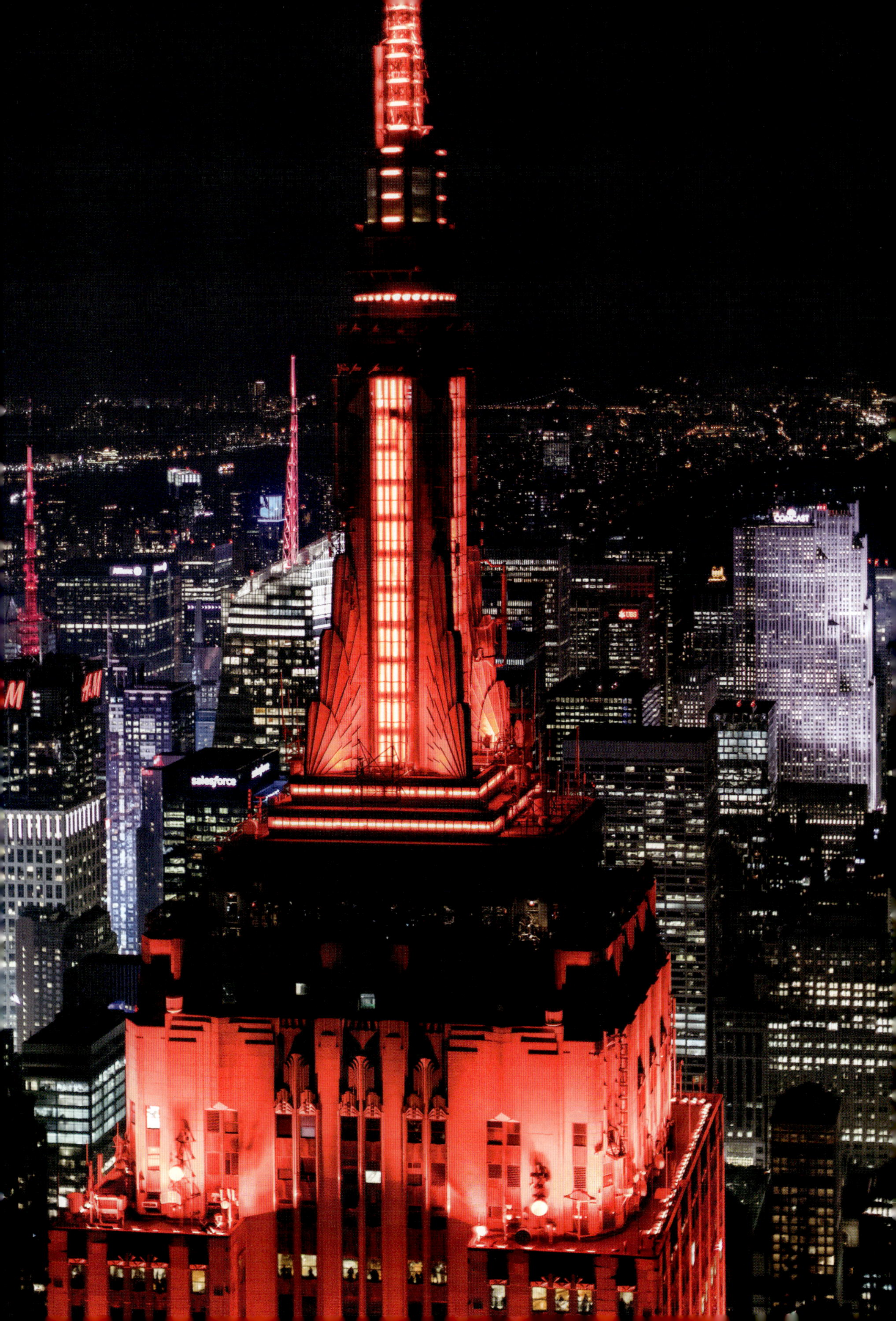
H&M
H&M
salesforce
COMCAST
UBS

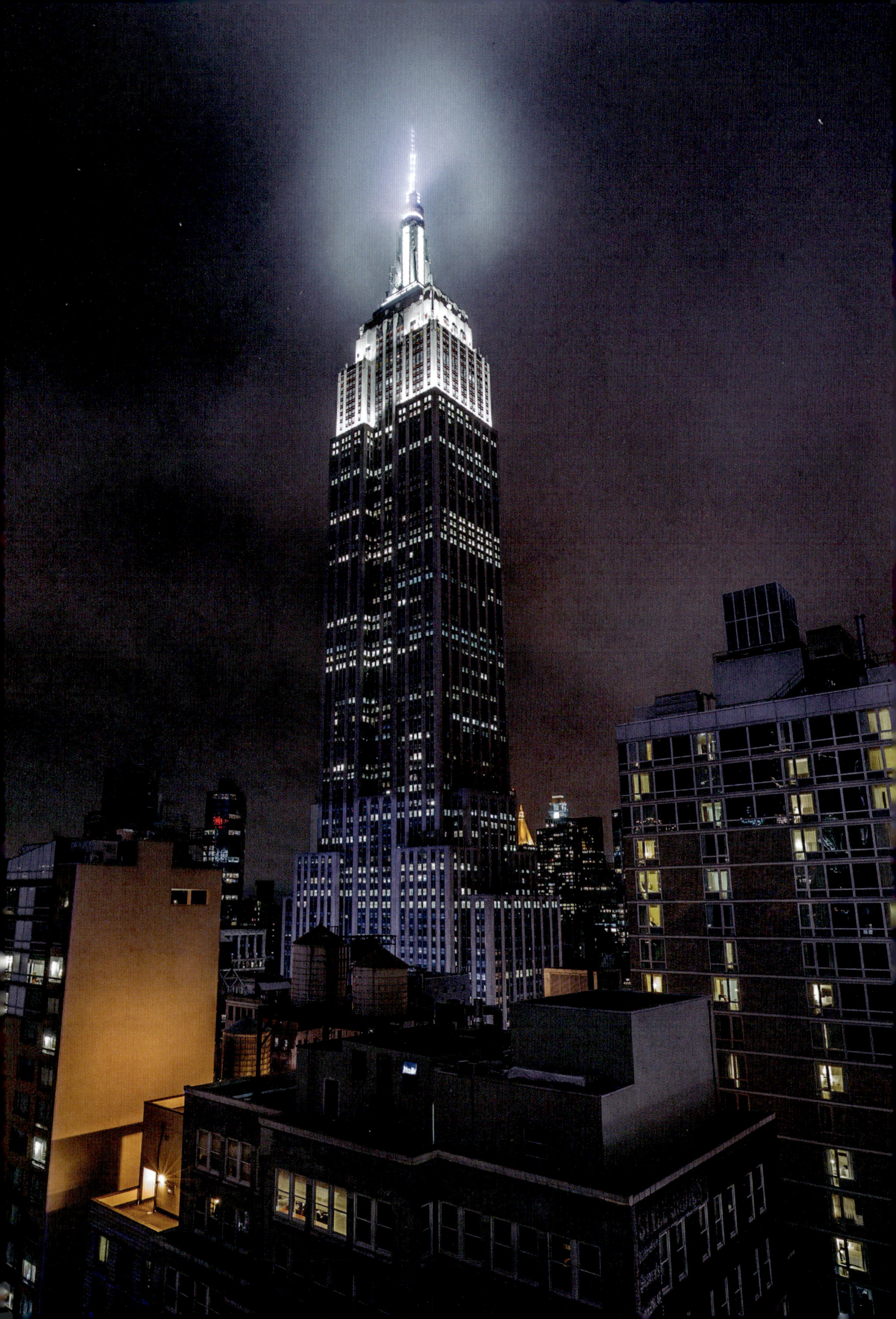

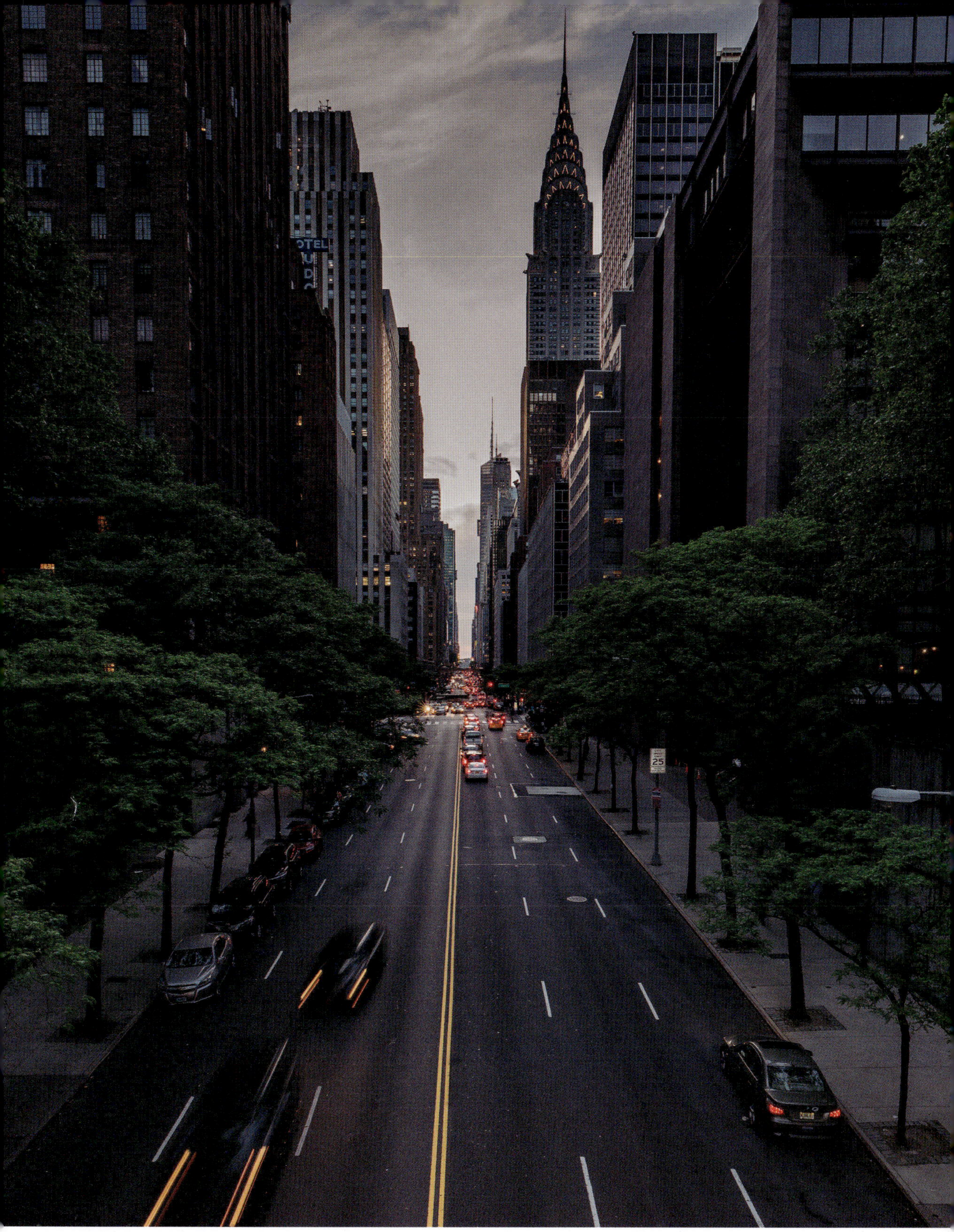

***Foggy Empire State.*** *(facing page)* I just love to watch when clouds meet skyscrapers. It's even cooler when the Empire State Building is lit up.

***Tudor City.*** *(above)* This is a great street view in Tudor City. I took this picture from the 42nd Street Bridge at Tudor Place.

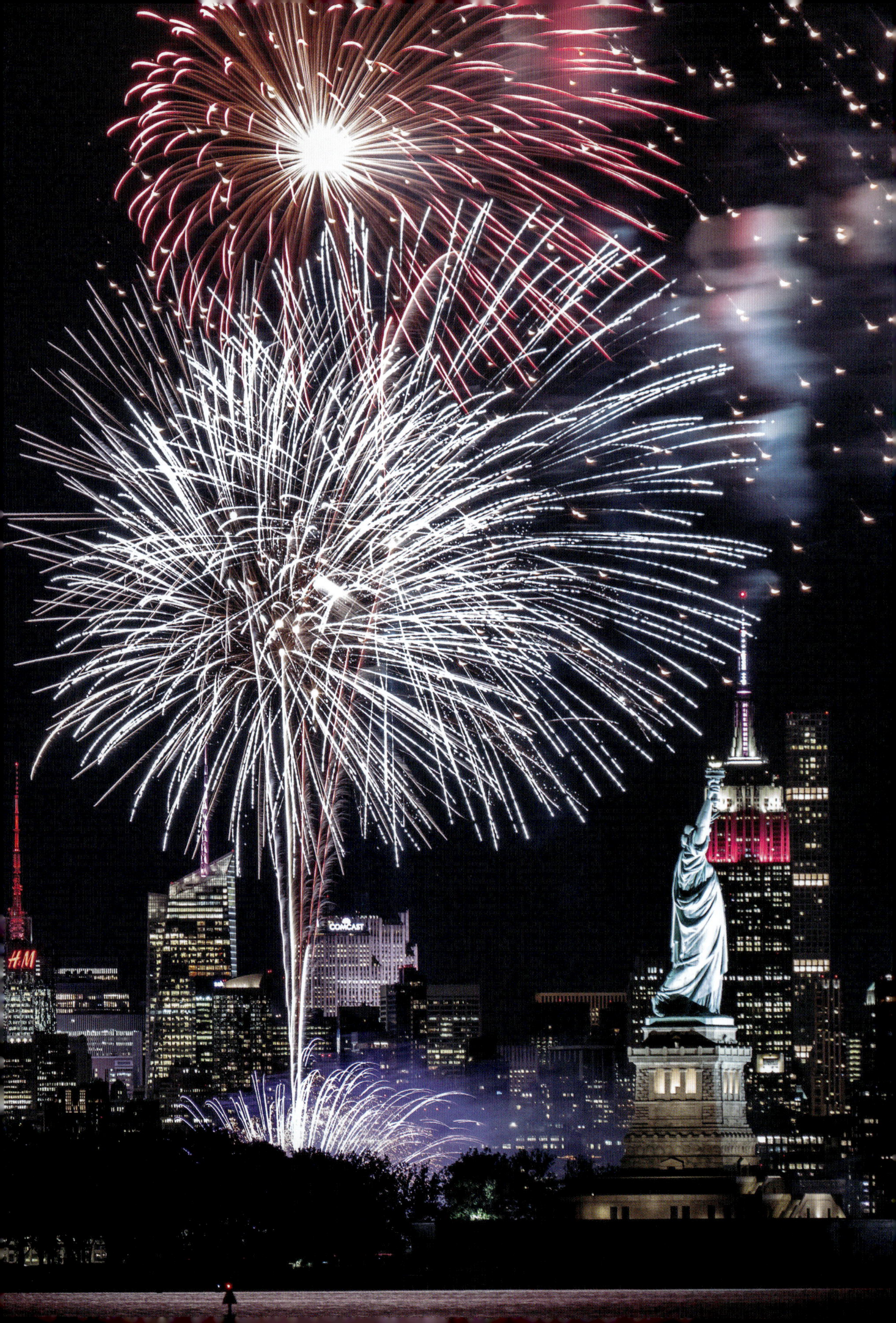
H&M
COMCAST

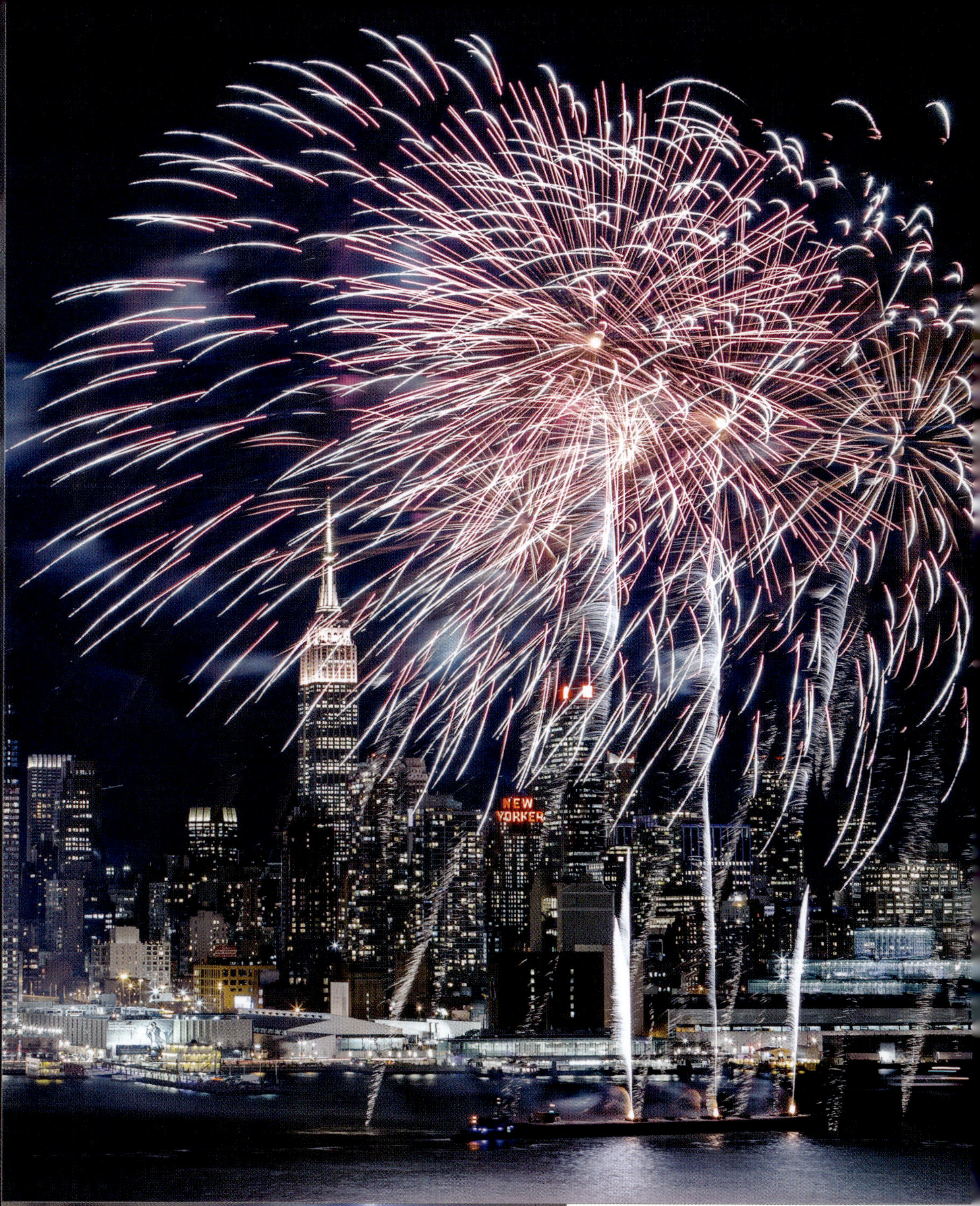


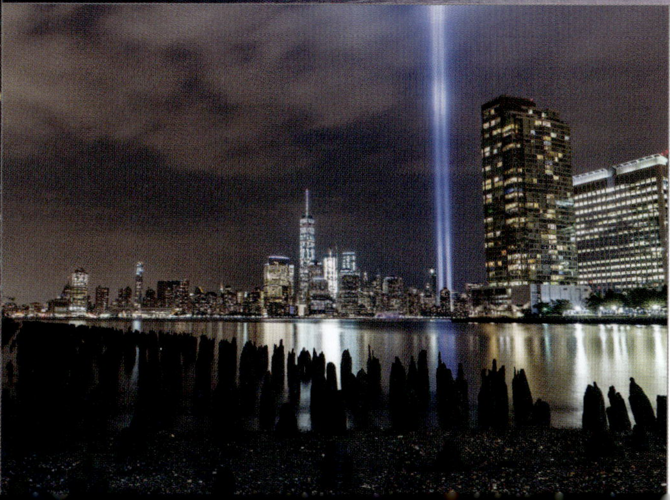

***Fireworks Over the Statue of Liberty.*** *(facing page)* When I look at this picture, I can't help but be a proud American!

***Chinese New Year.*** *(above)* Photographing fireworks is always a challenge and adventure. When this photo was taken in 2017, we were wishing for a great Year of the Dog!

***Never Forget 9/11.*** *(left)* The sadness of this tragic day has never faded in my heart. Thank you for all of those who stepped up and sacrificed to help others. I am forever grateful.

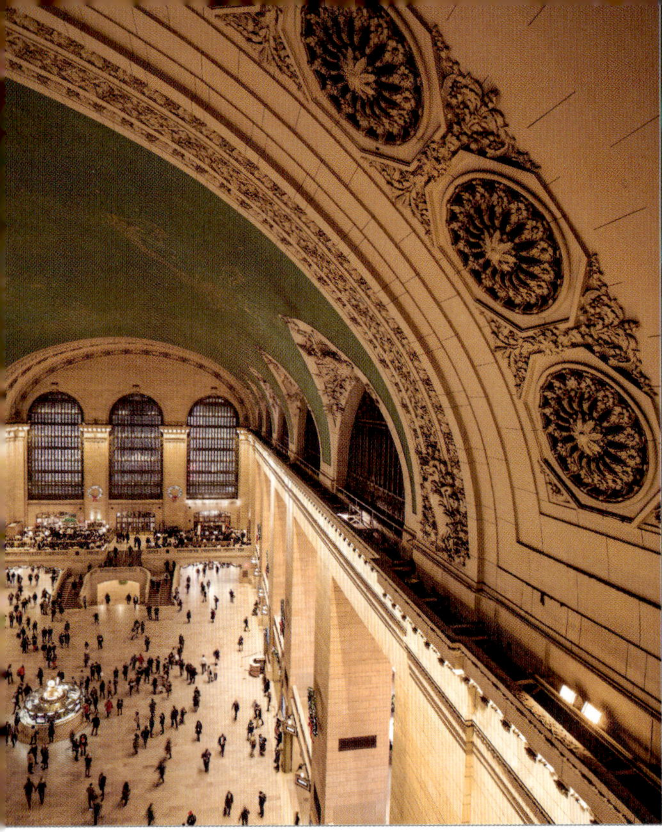

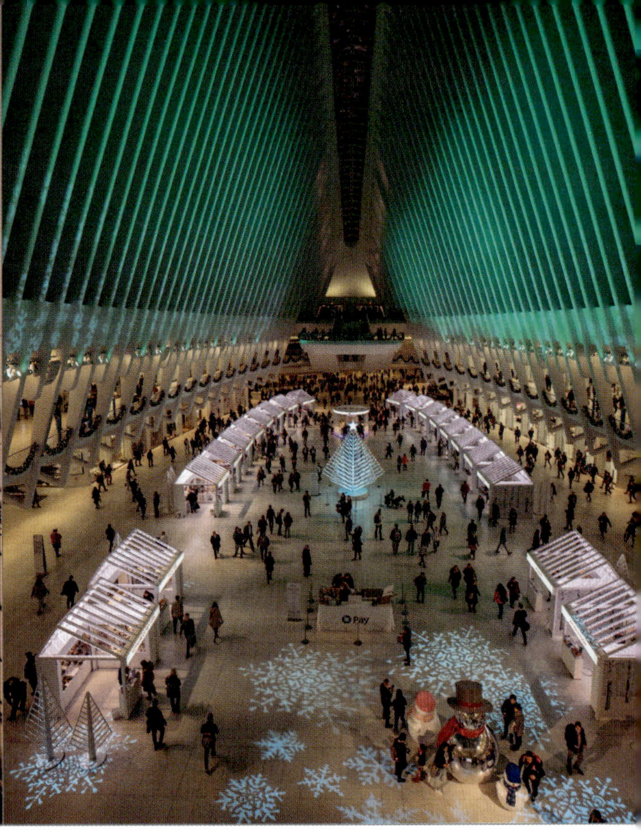

***Grand Central Terminal.*** *(top left)* New York City has unbelievably amazing architecture – and Grand Central Terminal is filled with it. Its design is so incredibly beautiful that it is honestly hard *not* to get a stunning shot.

***Christmas at the Oculus.*** *(top right)* The Christmas season at the Oculus is just stunning. Green lights illuminate the one-of-a-kind ceiling and white snowflakes dance on the floor.

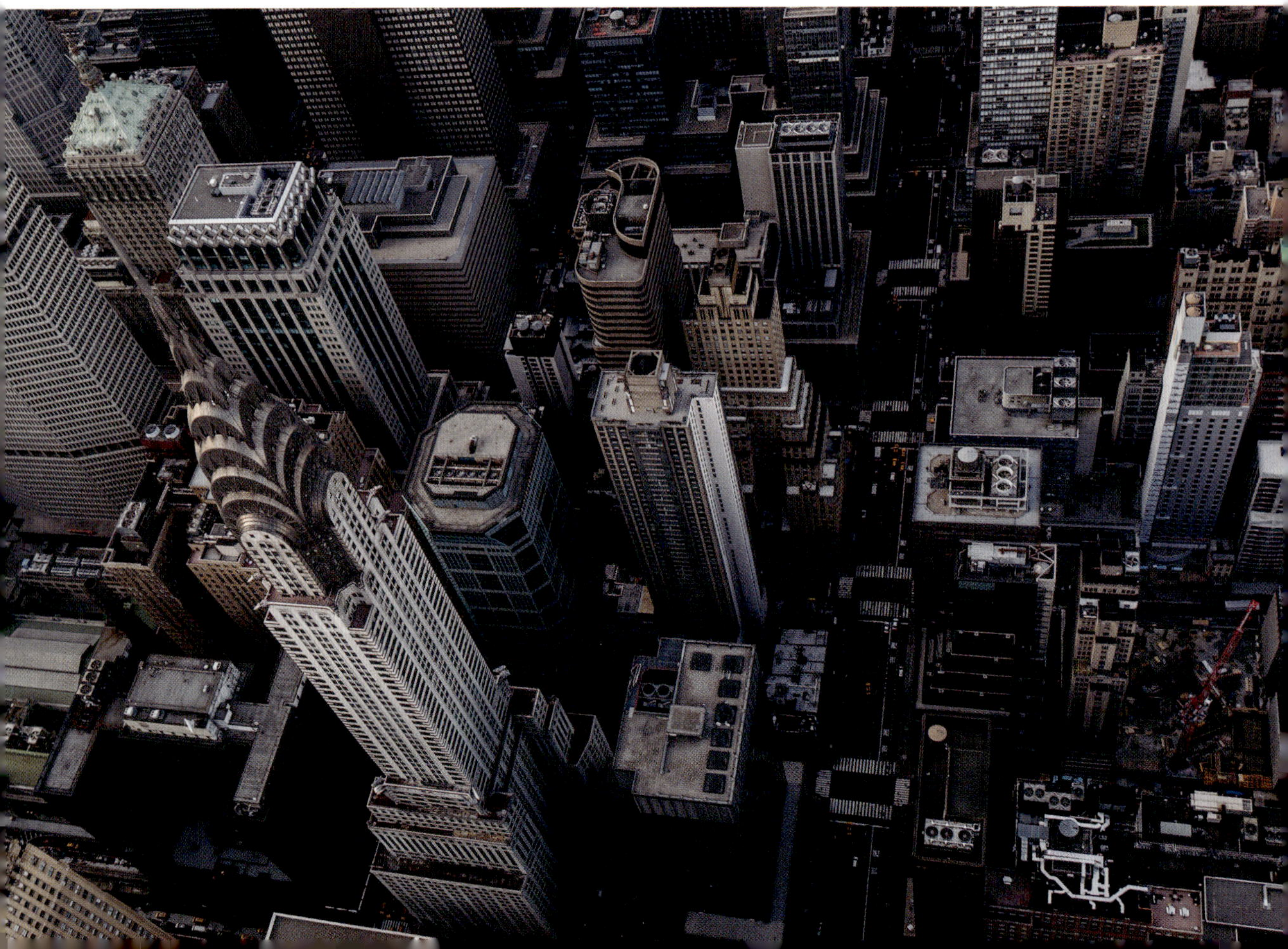

**Chrysler Building from the Air.** *(facing page, bottom)* I had an absolute blast capturing this aerial view of the Chrysler Building. I took this picture during a flight with a very adventurous pilot. I just love the feeling and challenge of being up in a helicopter with the doors off. Quite the thrill!

**Aerial Street Shot.** *(below)* I can't help but think of Legos when I look at this picture with all of the rectangular shapes and various building heights. This is another capture from one of my helicopter rides–with the doors off because, for me, that's the only way to ride.

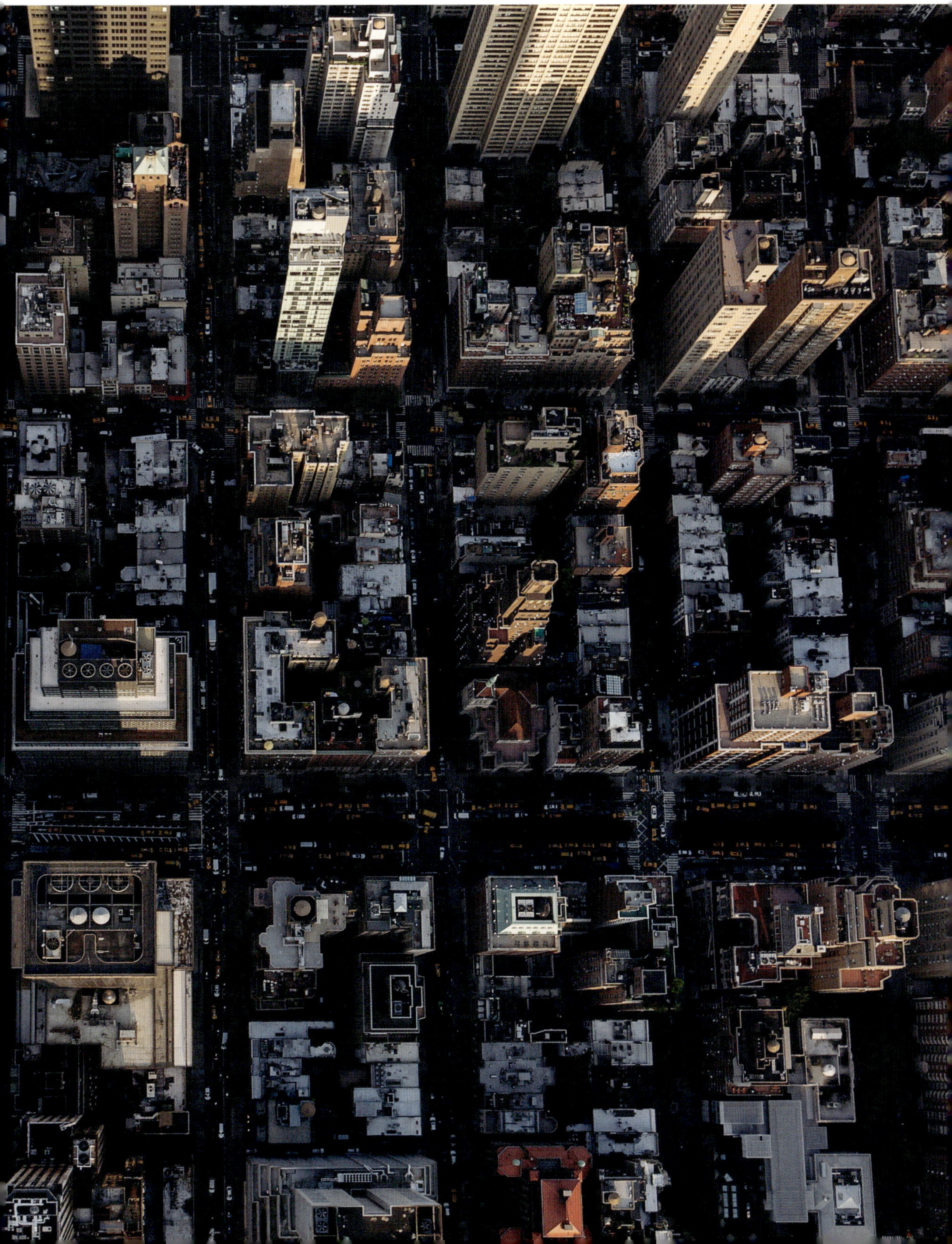

***Snow Time in the City.*** *(top right)* I purposely went into the city prior to a strong snowstorm just to meet up with my friends and spend the night taking pictures of the fresh snowfall.

***Times Square.*** *(bottom right)* I'm thankful for all of the men and women who put on the uniform, no matter the weather, to keep people like myself safe.

***Winter Skyline.*** *(facing page)* I took this shot from Newport, New Jersey, on a freezing cold morning in January. I really like how the water is different on each side of the wooden barrier. The right side is partially frozen while the left doesn't seem to be frozen at all.

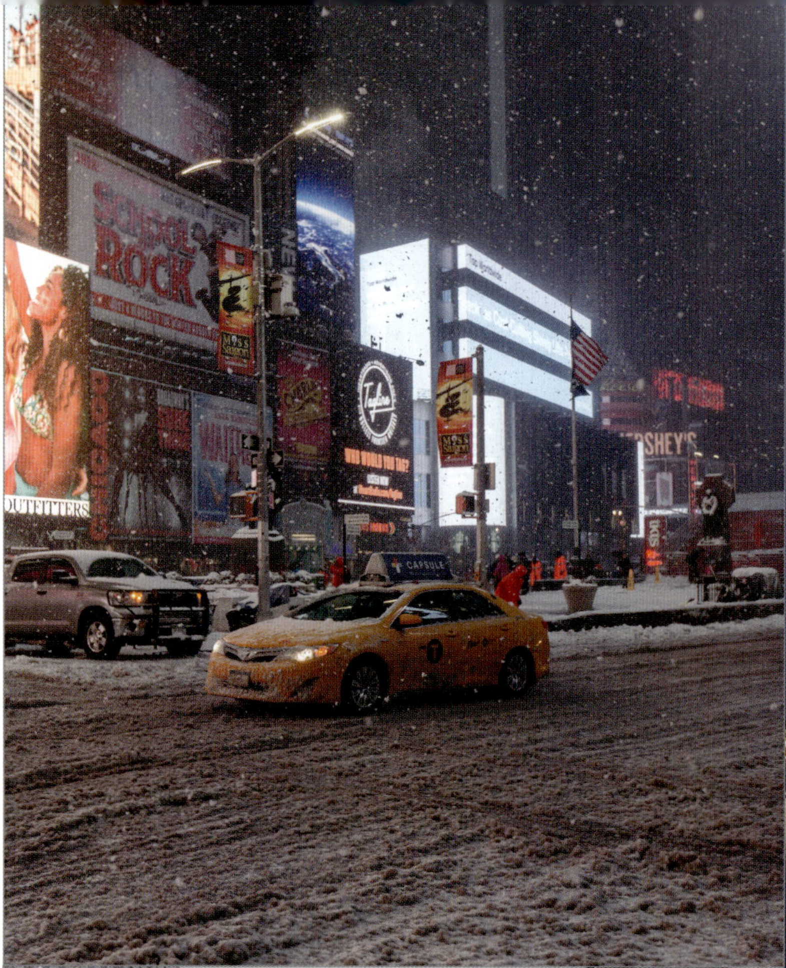


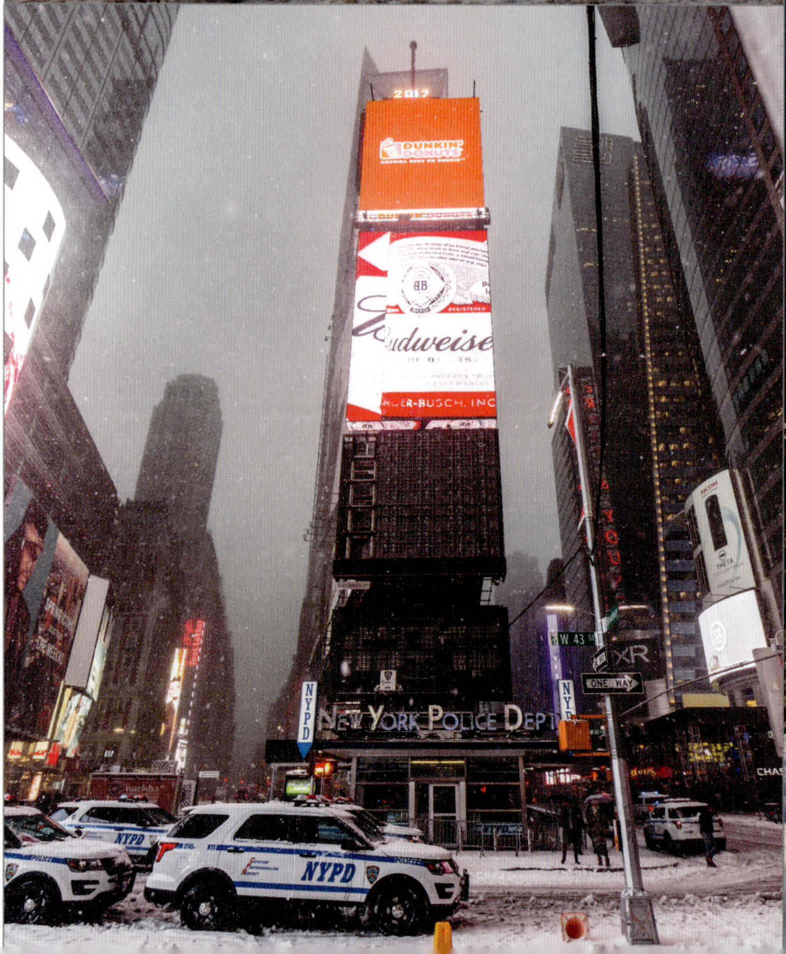

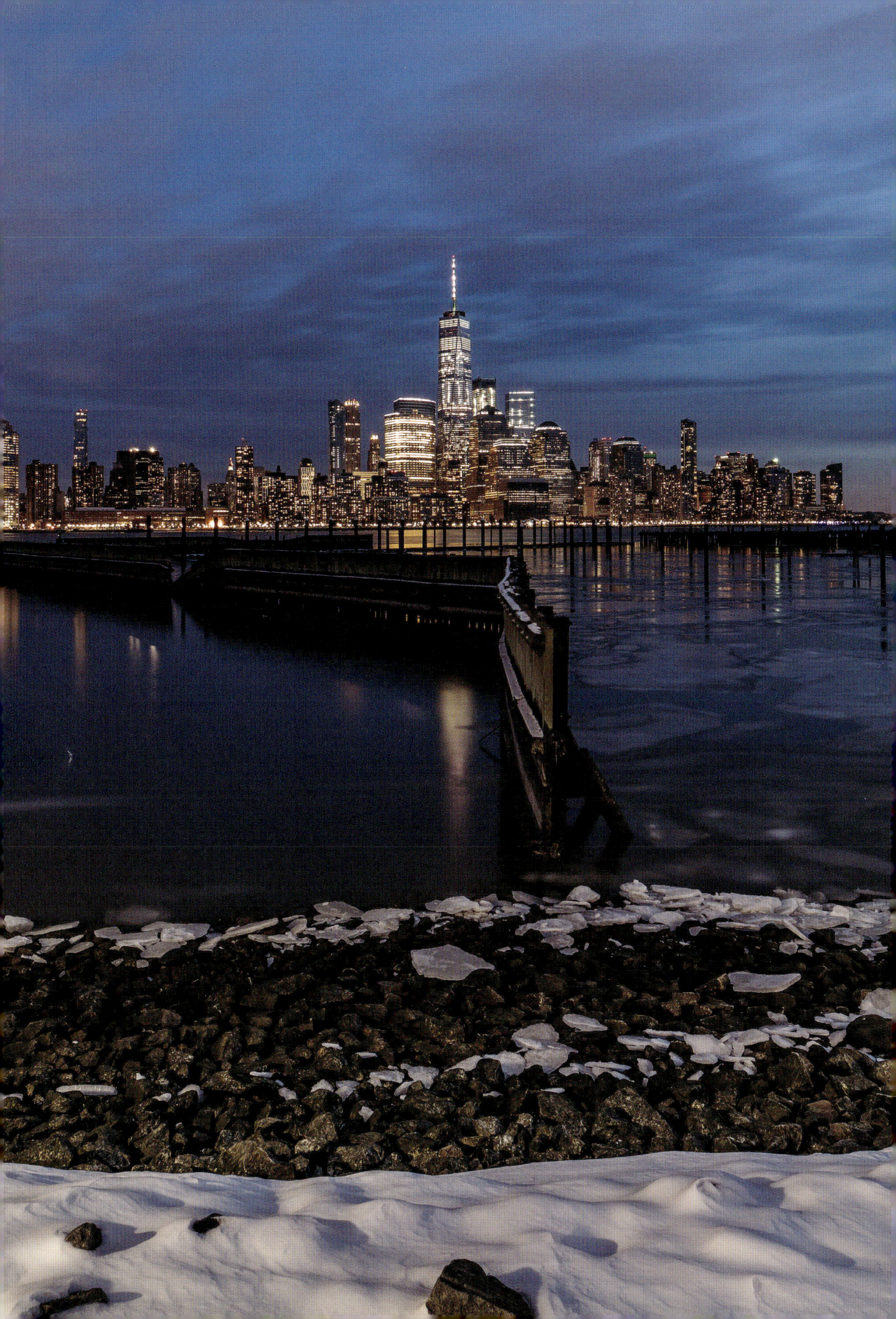

***City Sunright.*** *(below)* Hoboken, New Jersey, is a special place located across the Hudson River. There are many great places to capture New York City skyline views.

***Newport, Jersey City.*** *(facing page, top)* The clouds are my favorite part of this photo, it looks like they are dancing as they move.

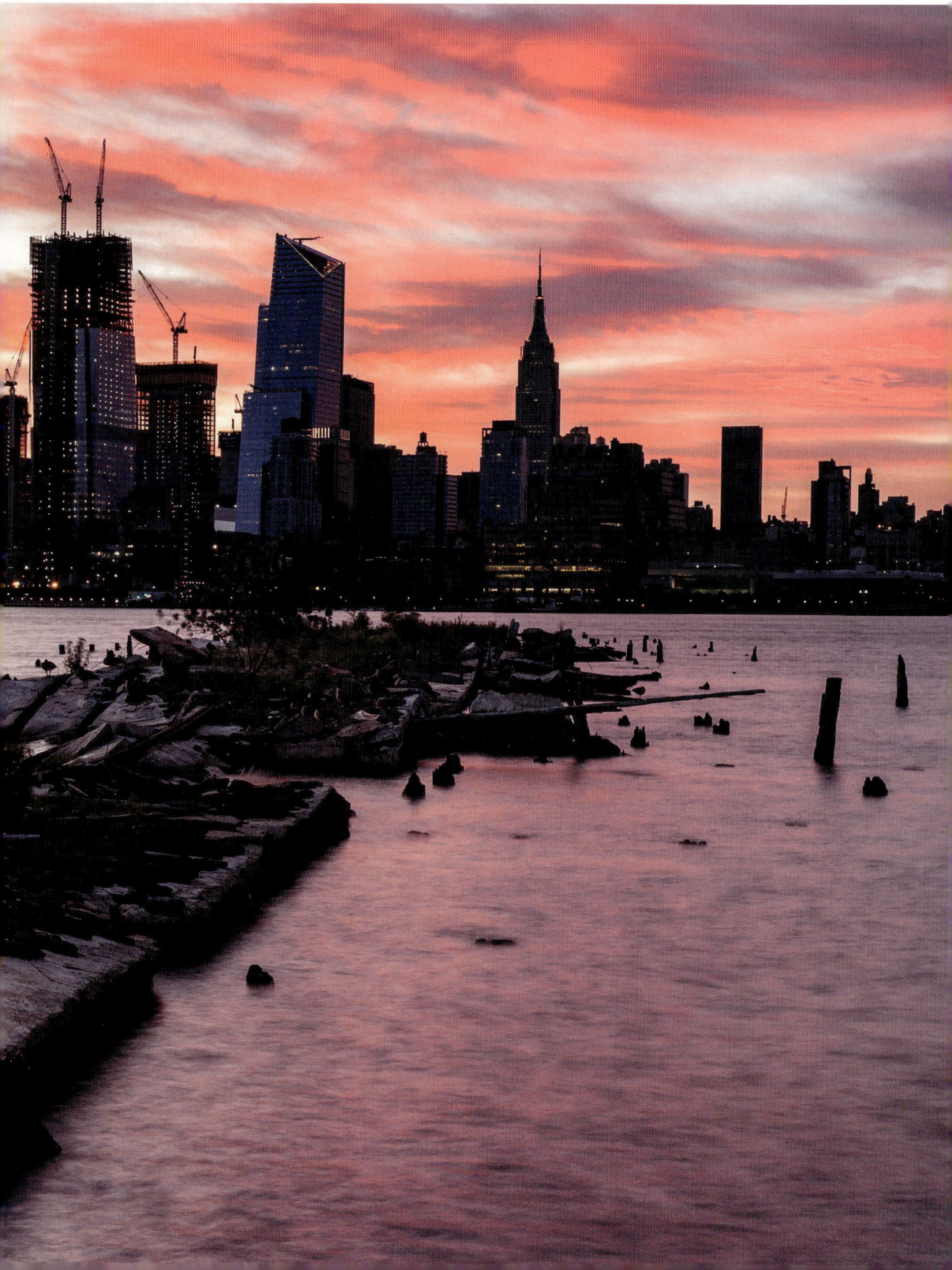

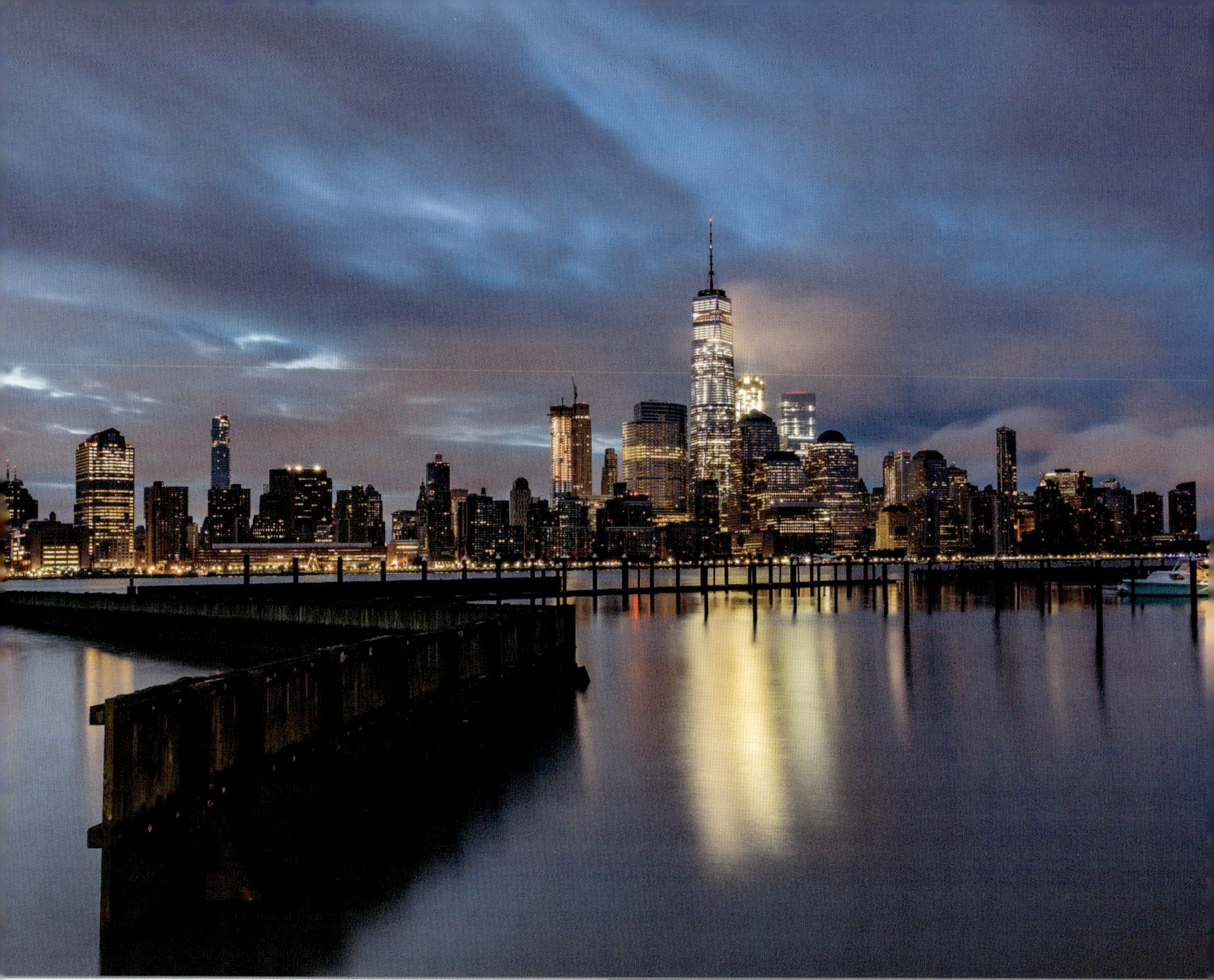

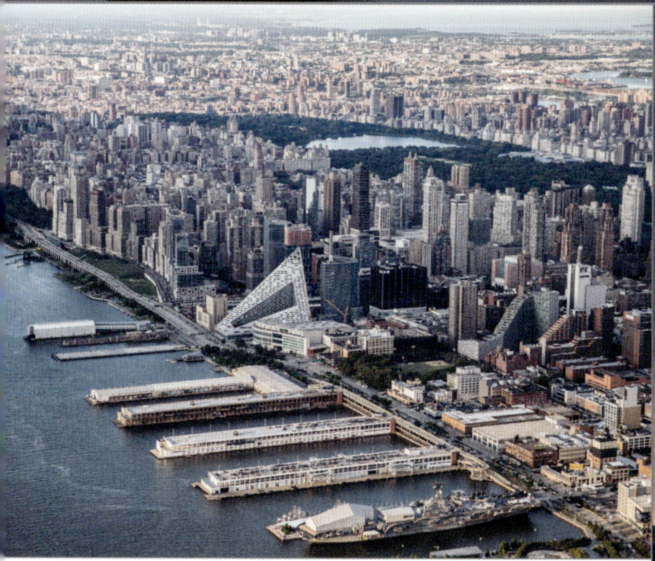

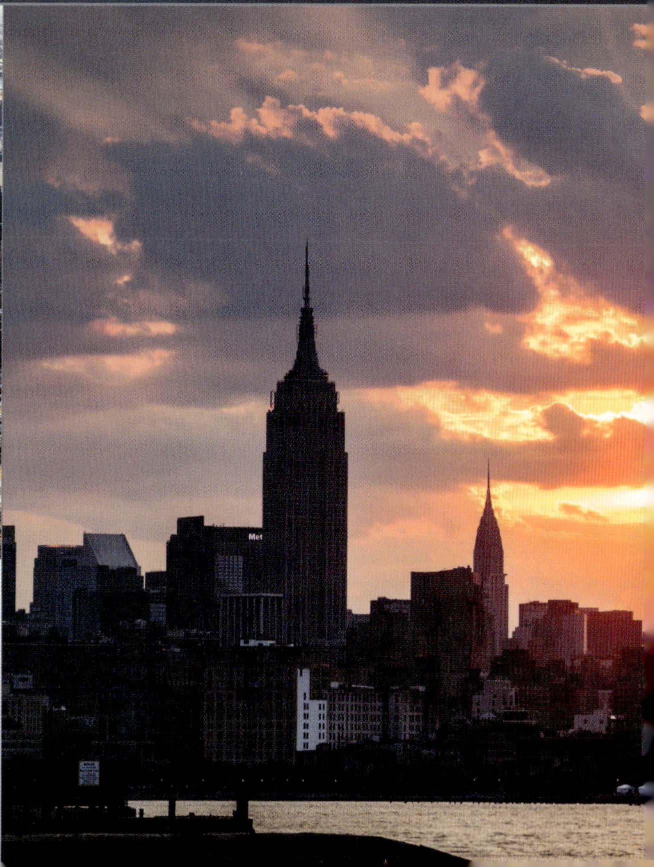

***VIA 57 West.*** *(above)* How could you not like this environmentally friendly apartment building? The triangular architecture is so unique it is impossible to miss. Notice that Central Park lies in the background.

***Empire State Building.*** *(right)* I was teaching a private lesson when I noticed the sun trying to come out from behind the clouds. I like this picture because of how the sunlight shines through the holes in the clouds.

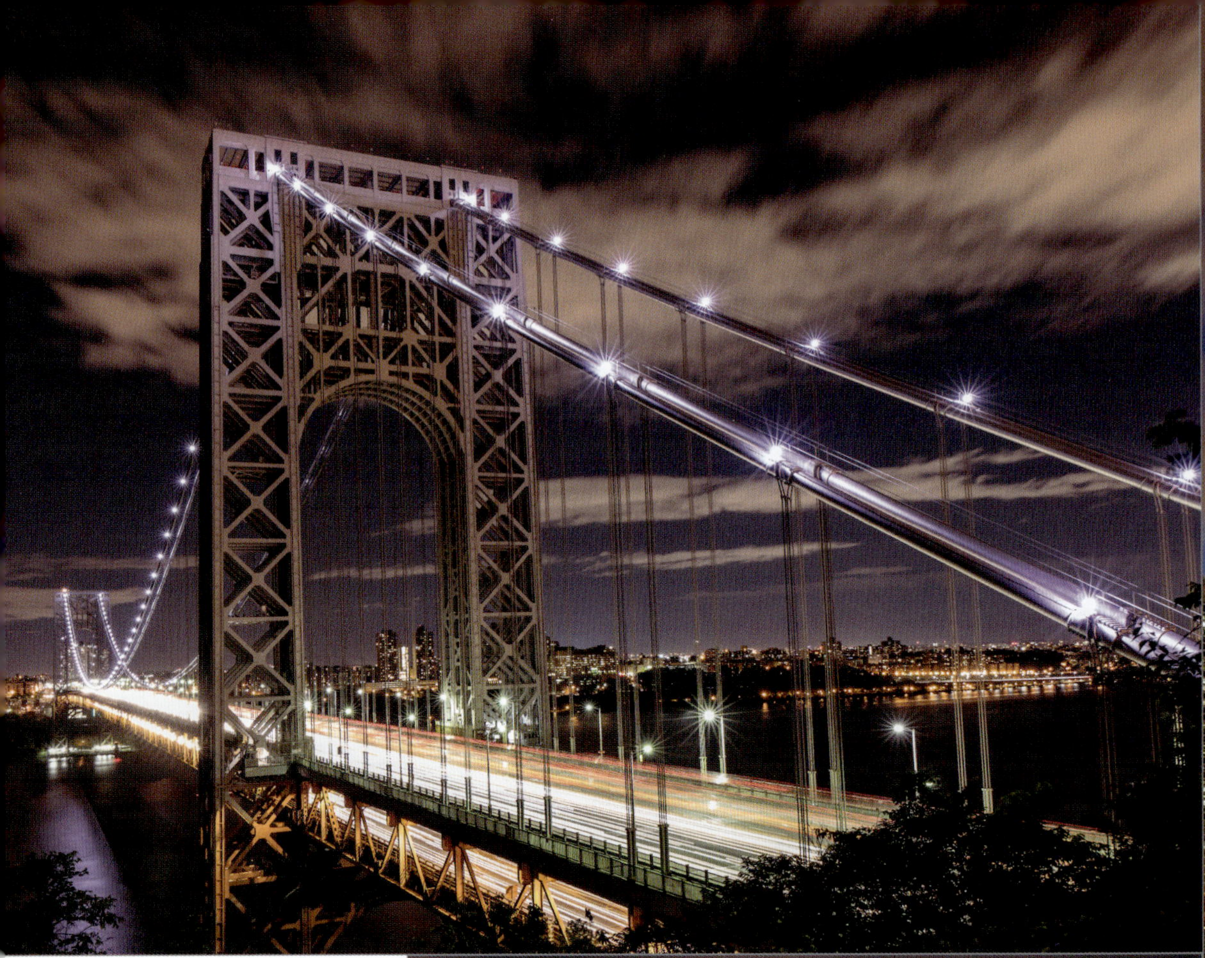

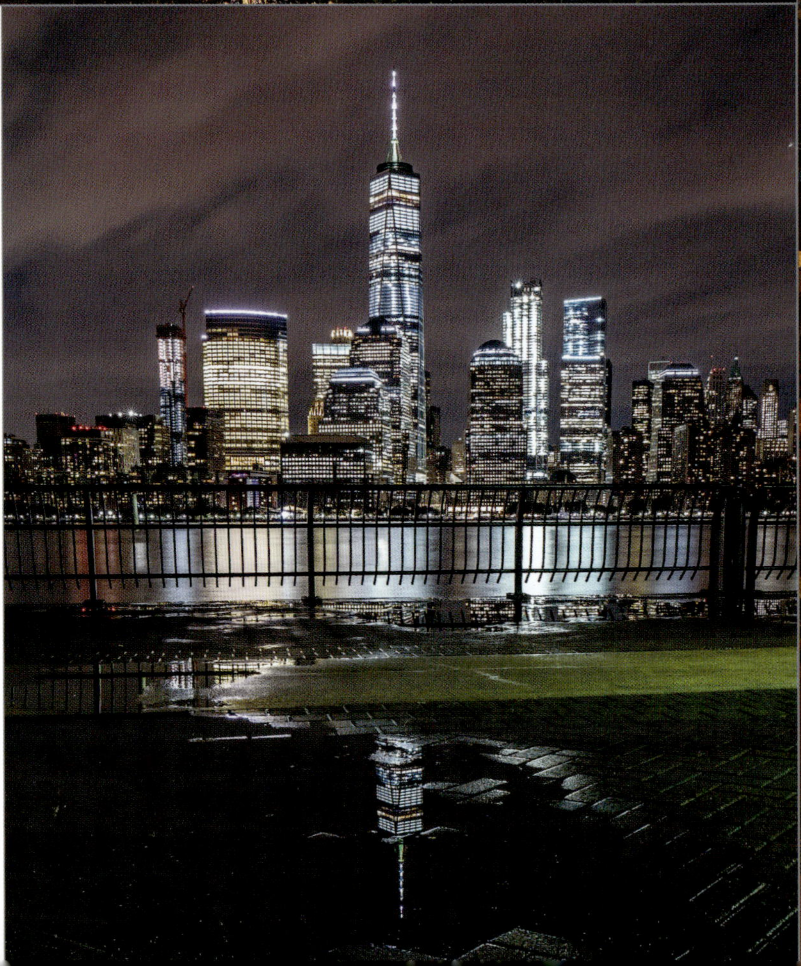

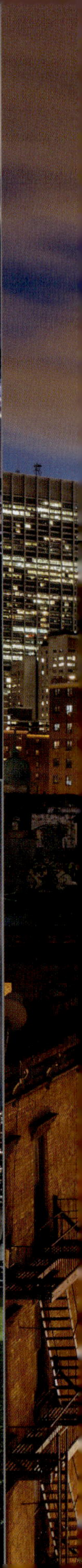

***George Washington Bridge.*** *(above)* This is a long exposure shot of the George Washington Bridge. Although it was not lit up, it is still a beautiful structure.

***One World Trade Center Reflection.*** *(right)* I sure enjoyed the shots I was able to get after this rainstorm. The rain pooled in just the right spots for me to capture a reflection of One World Trade Center in the puddle.

***Chinatown.*** *(facing page)* This long exposure picture of a local street in Chinatown was shot while standing on the Manhattan Bridge.

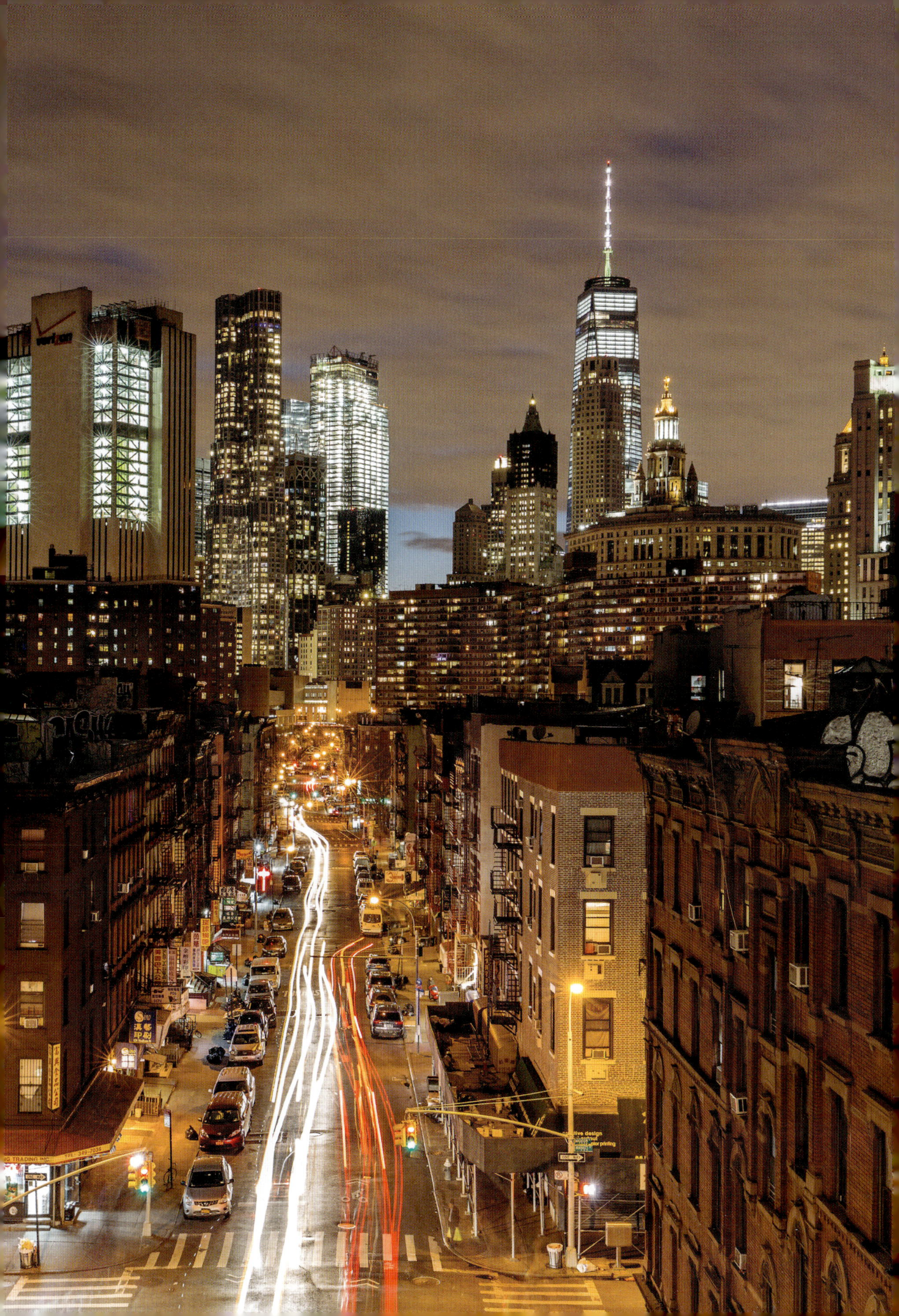

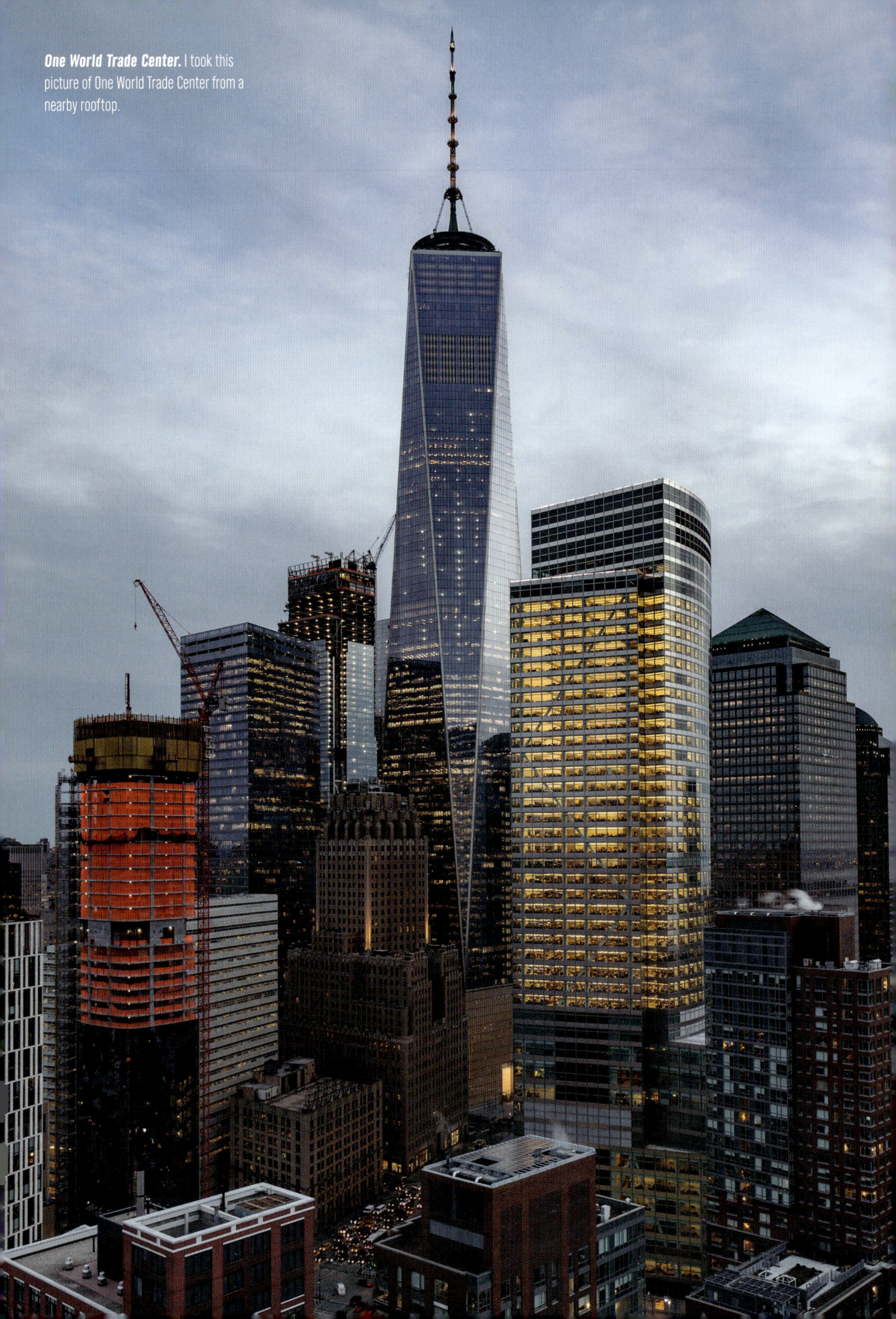

**One World Trade Center.** I took this picture of One World Trade Center from a nearby rooftop.

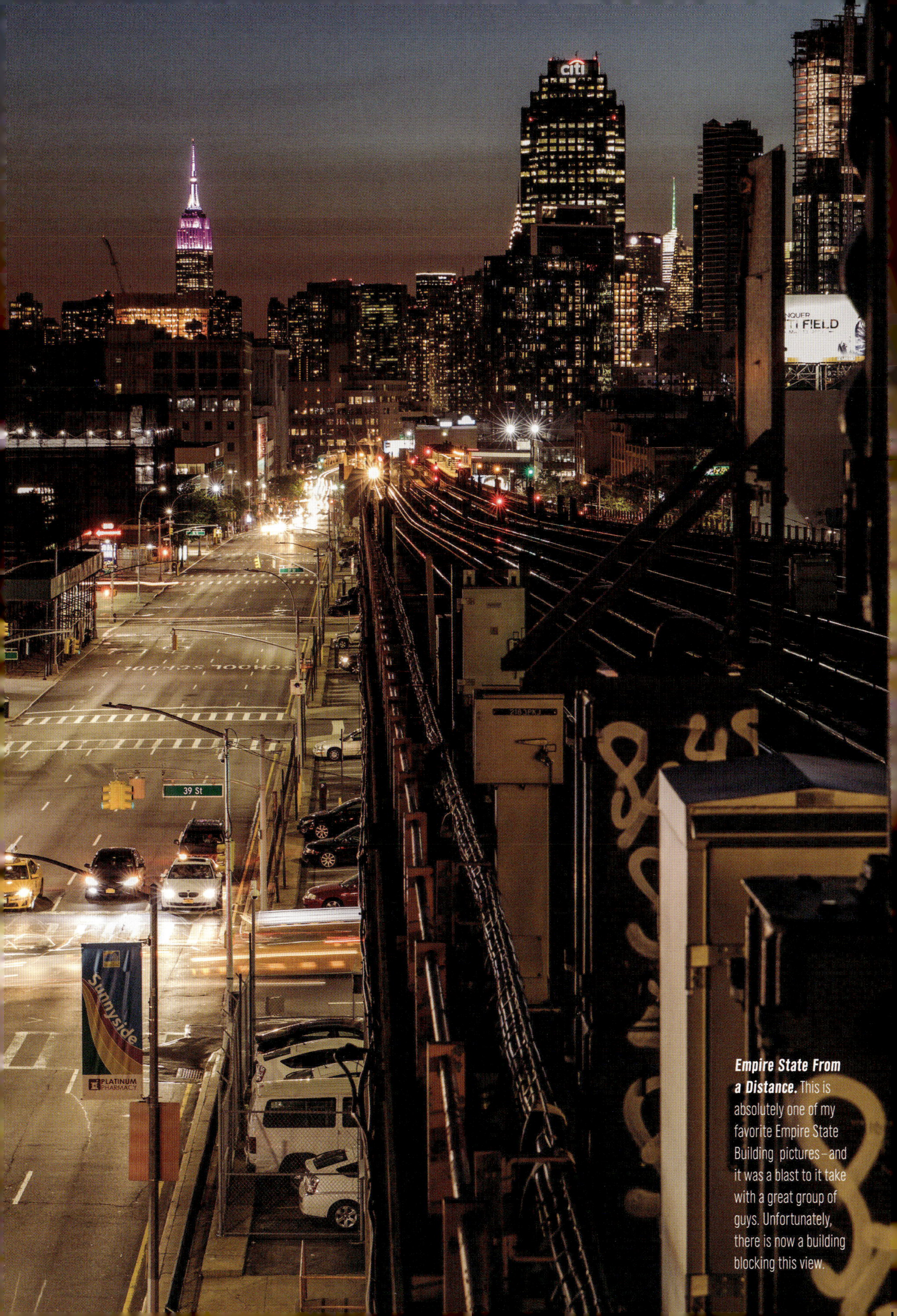


***Empire State From a Distance.*** This is absolutely one of my favorite Empire State Building pictures–and it was a blast to it take with a great group of guys. Unfortunately, there is now a building blocking this view.

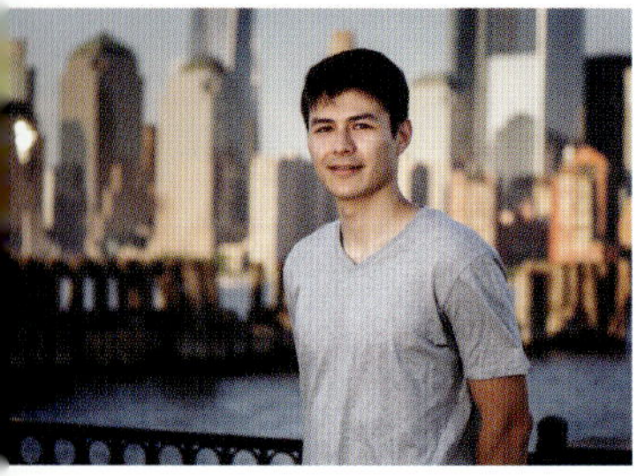

CHAPTER 5

# Max Guliani

Instagram: @maximusupinnyc ■ Twitter: @maximusupinNYc

I grew up in Manhattan's West Village, a culturally vibrant and diverse neighborhood within New York City. My home was a short walk from the Hudson River and West Side Highway, located on the western border of Manhattan. Throughout my youth, in the 1990s, the Hudson River Park waterfront was a dilapidated setting, consisting of a jagged walkway adjacent to crumbling piers strewn with old trash and forgotten auto parts on the edge of the highway. Despite its unpleasant appearance, the Hudson River Park was my backyard, where my love of sports and the outdoors was cultivated. As a child, I was committed to athletics, spending hours honing my skill in soccer with Downtown United Soccer Club, a premier athletics organization located in the West Village. My hard work and dedication was rewarded with an offer to play collegiate soccer for SUNY Oswego, as a varsity player. SUNY Oswego is located in upstate New York, on the shore of Lake Ontario, and widely renowned for its majestic sunsets. Despite my fondness for athletics, my passion for photography arose on the shores of Lake Ontario, while witnessing a breathtaking sunset over the horizon. The impact of that day was profound, and led me to consider photography as a career.

***Corner in Bloom.*** *(below)* The morning commute on a spring day in Washington Square Park, framed under a Kwanzan cherry tree in full bloom.

***Dragon Celebrations.*** *(facing page)* Lunar New Year Dragon celebrations march down East Broadway. This image was taken from the Manhattan Bridge pedestrian walkway.

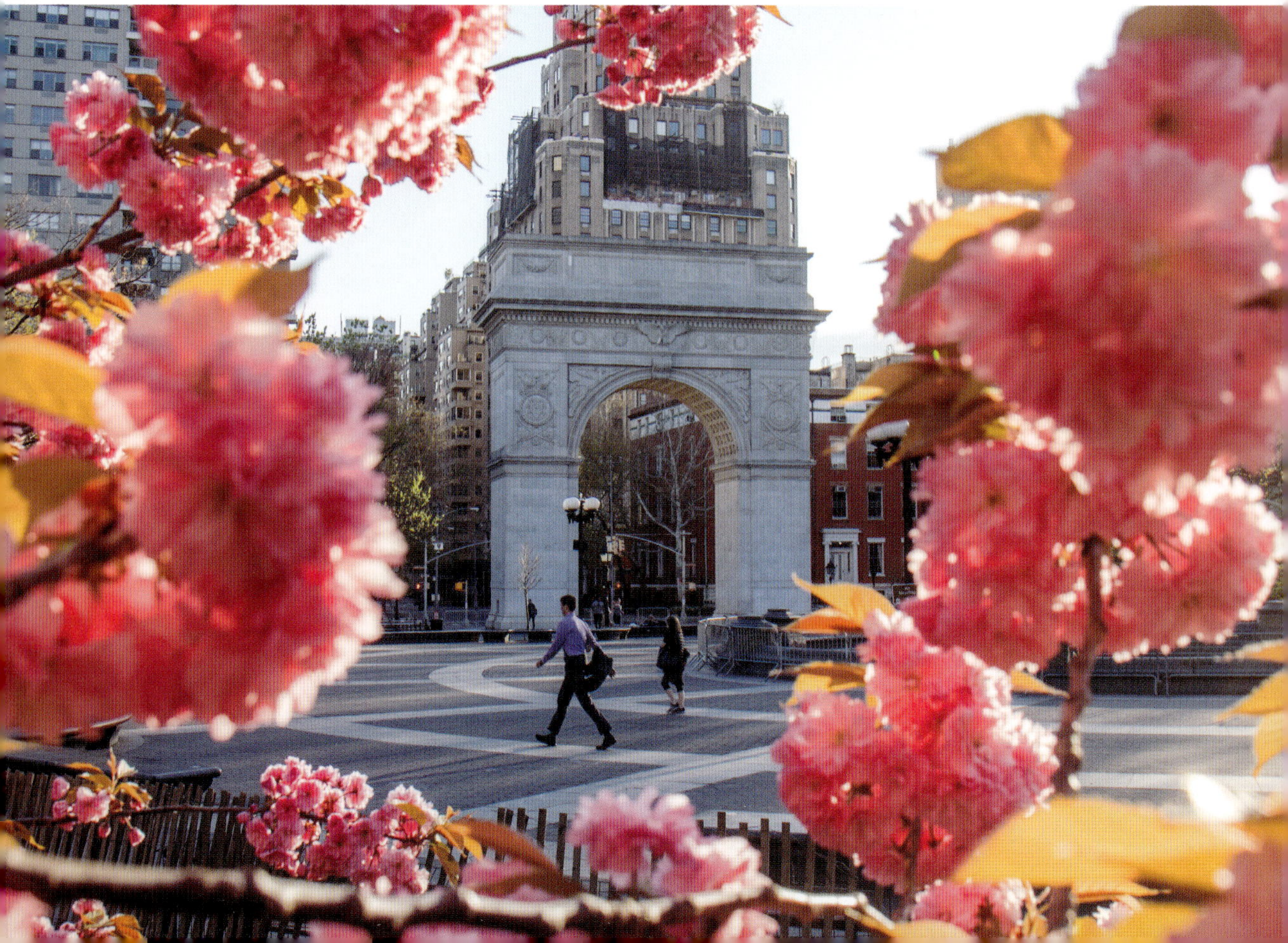

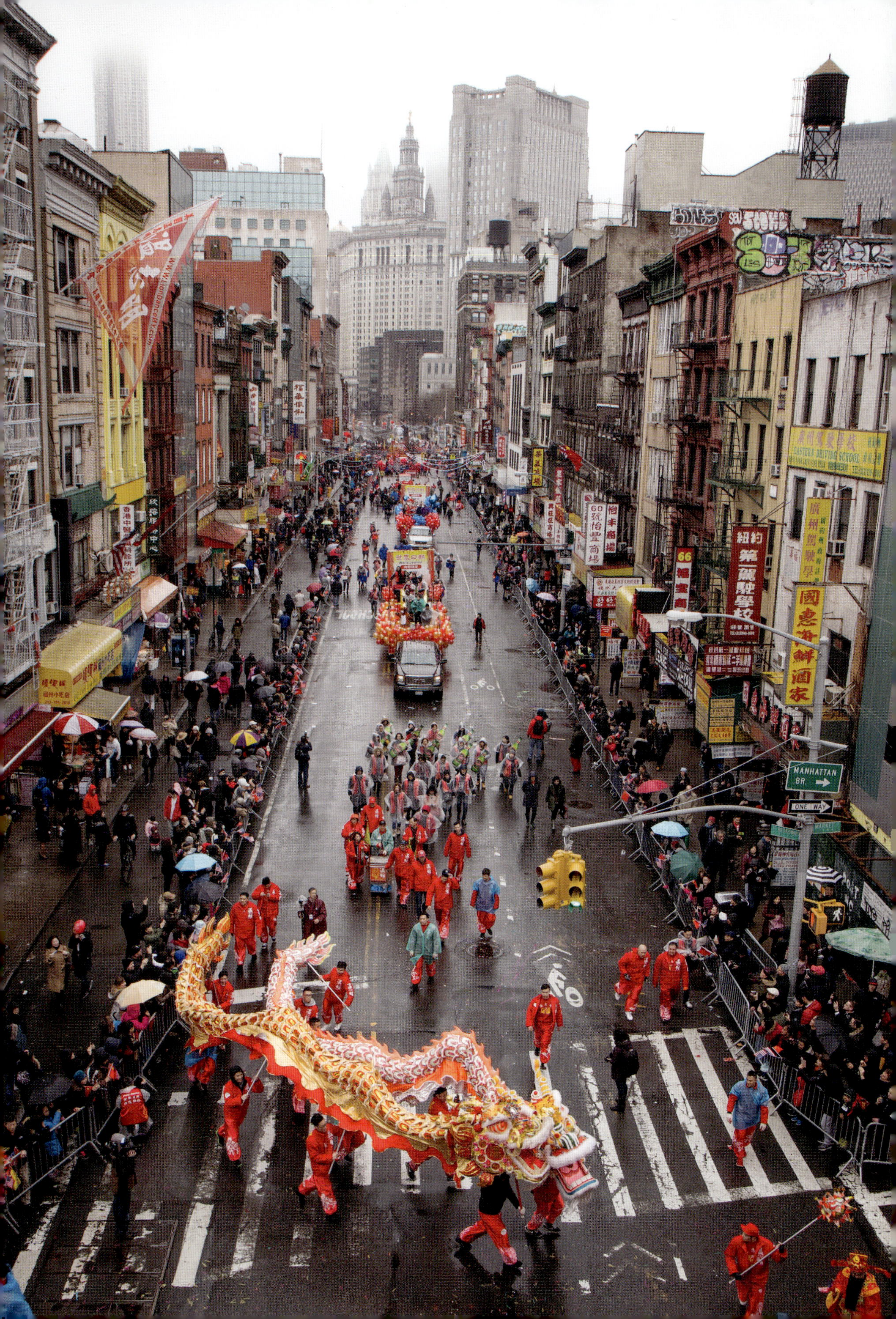
MANHATTAN BR.
ONE WAY

**Spider Lightning.** *(left)* Lightning illuminates Lower Manhattan, as seen from the West Village waterfront on Halloween eve.

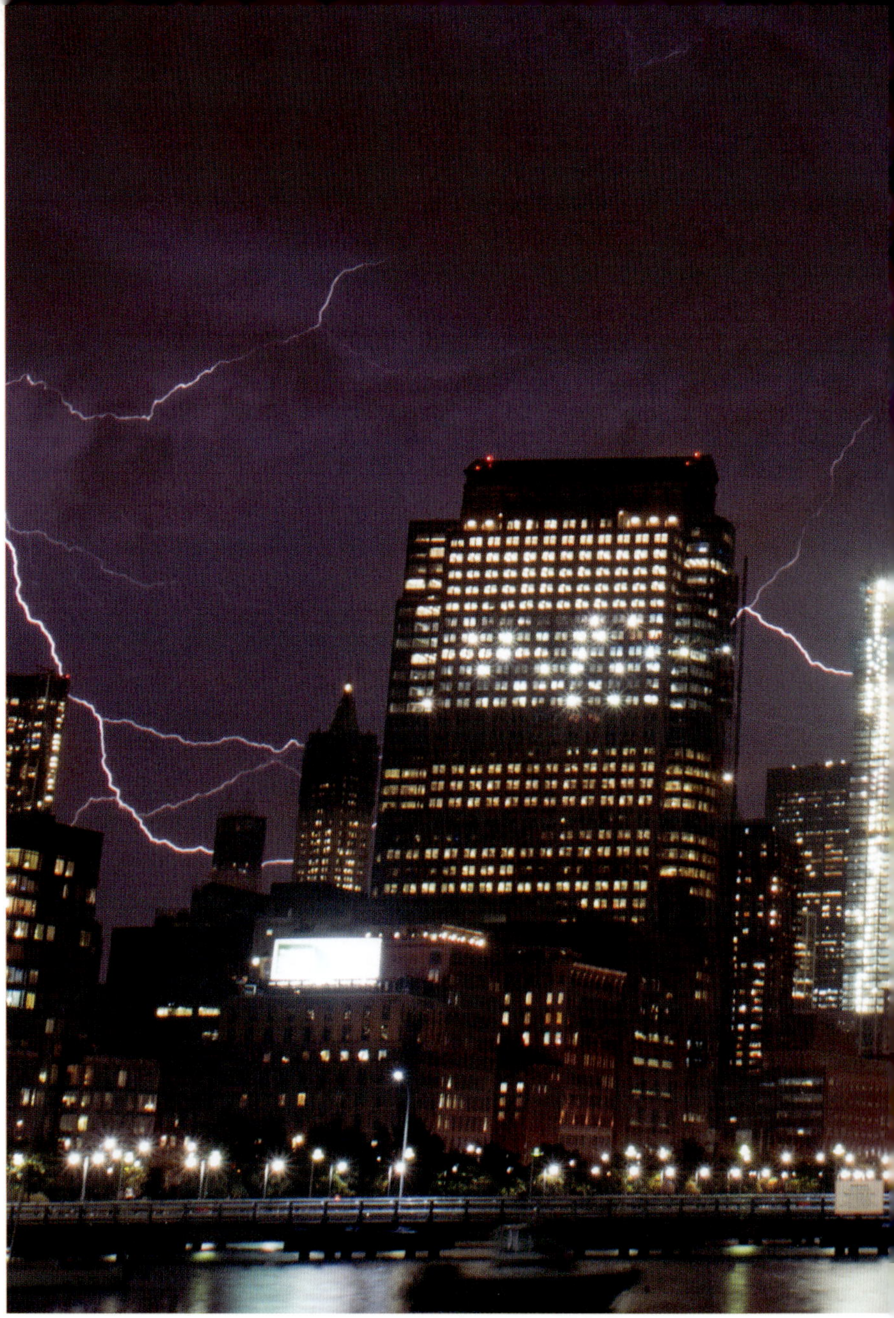

Currently, I am a social media strategist, event photographer, and content creator for the Hudson River Park Trust (HRPT). The HRPT is a not-for-profit organization which maintains the nation's longest riverfront park, extending from Chambers Street up to 59th Street, and offers a multitude of educational, cultural, and recreational events. Within the years since my youth, the park has blossomed into five miles of prime green-space, bike paths, piers, and cafes. My duty for the park is to capture and document its transformation into a multifaceted public space, where New York City residents can come to escape the rigors of everyday life. In the past three years, I have shot over seven hundred events, including dance, water sports, marine education, youth events, concerts, sports, and fitness.

As a photographer, I follow the sun, moon, and clouds through their daily phases as they cast ever-changing light over New York City. My essential tools for capturing nature's elements are my camera, tripod, and bicycle, which enable me to quickly traverse New York City's fast paced environment and photograph ephemeral moments within the city's landscape.

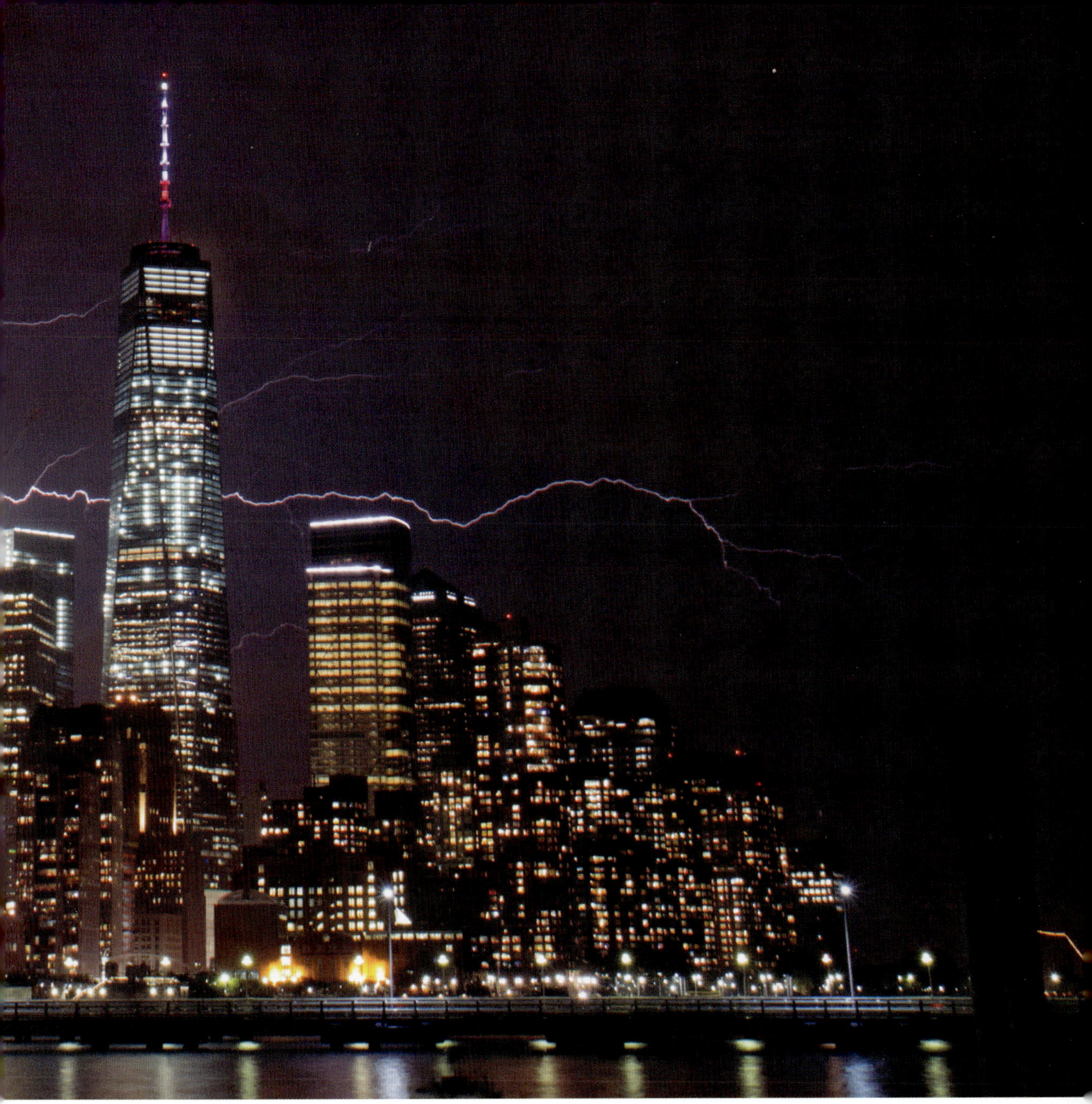

In addition to capturing the cityscape, I enjoy photographing extreme weather conditions in New York—the snow, thunderstorms, fog, Nor'easters, and even tropical storms. For example, while storm chasing on the river I captured thirteen consecutive lightning strikes to One World Trade in one night.

My lifelong residency in New York City has instilled a natural appeal of photographing its landscape. New York City's environment is in a state of perpetual change, so there is often something new to see. In the years since my youth, new buildings have risen, neighborhoods have expanded, street art has proliferated, and green-space has flourished. It is a pleasure to capture this change, whether at Hudson River Park, on a daunting rooftop overlooking the horizon, or from a soaring helicopter flight over the city. Landscape photography is my passion because it forces me to explore new places and share the city I love. One can always find me riding my bike, with tripod attached, and camera in hand, looking for new angles to view New York's iconic neighborhoods.

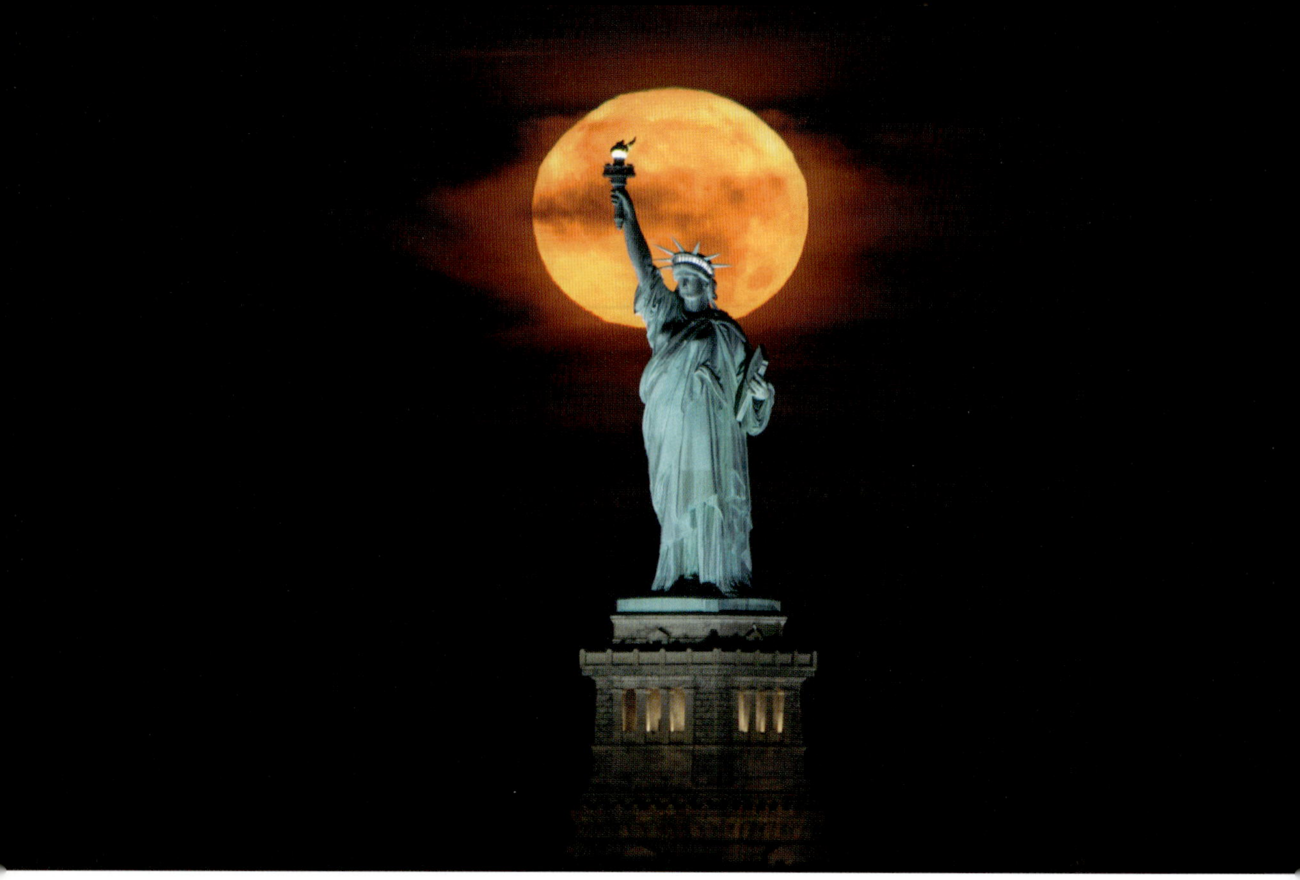

***Statue of Liberty Supermoon.*** *(above)* A supermoon setting on a December night. This was photographed just before dawn from Red Hook, Brooklyn.

***Crescent Moon.*** *(below)* This is a crescent moon setting between the Chrysler Building and The Empire State Building. To capture this placement, I was positioned adjacent to Socrates Sculpture Park in Astoria, Queens.

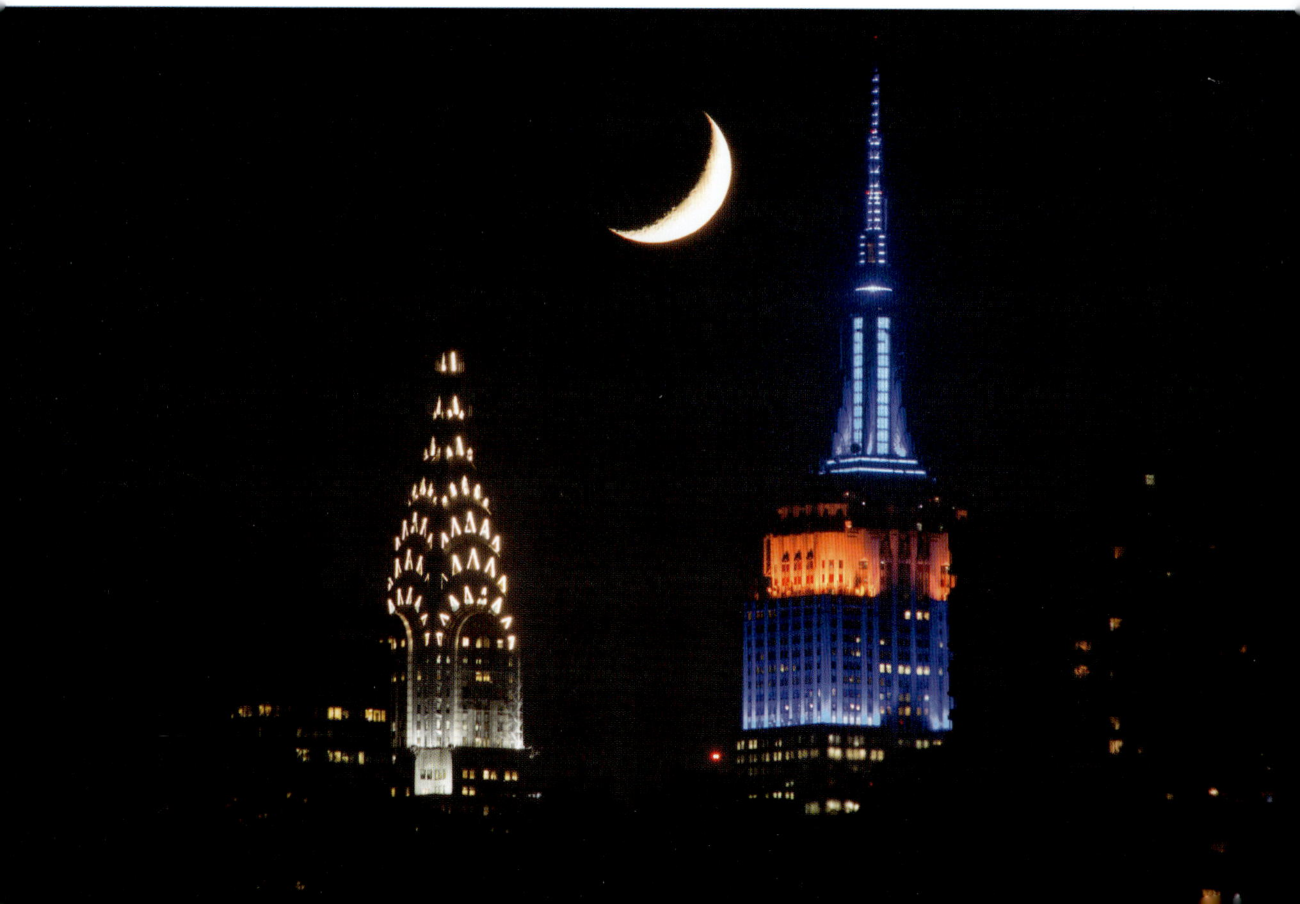

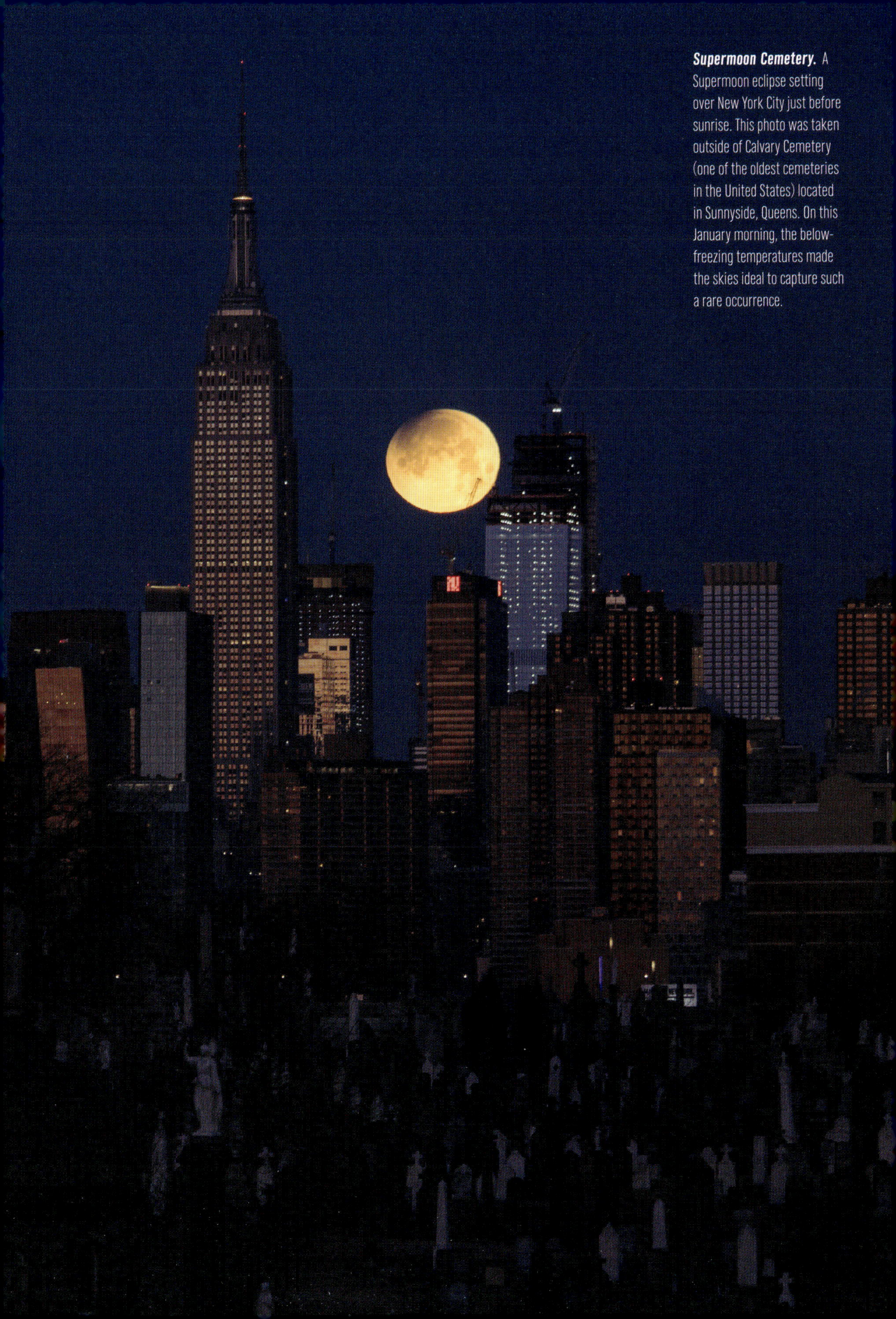

***Supermoon Cemetery.*** A Supermoon eclipse setting over New York City just before sunrise. This photo was taken outside of Calvary Cemetery (one of the oldest cemeteries in the United States) located in Sunnyside, Queens. On this January morning, the below-freezing temperatures made the skies ideal to capture such a rare occurrence.

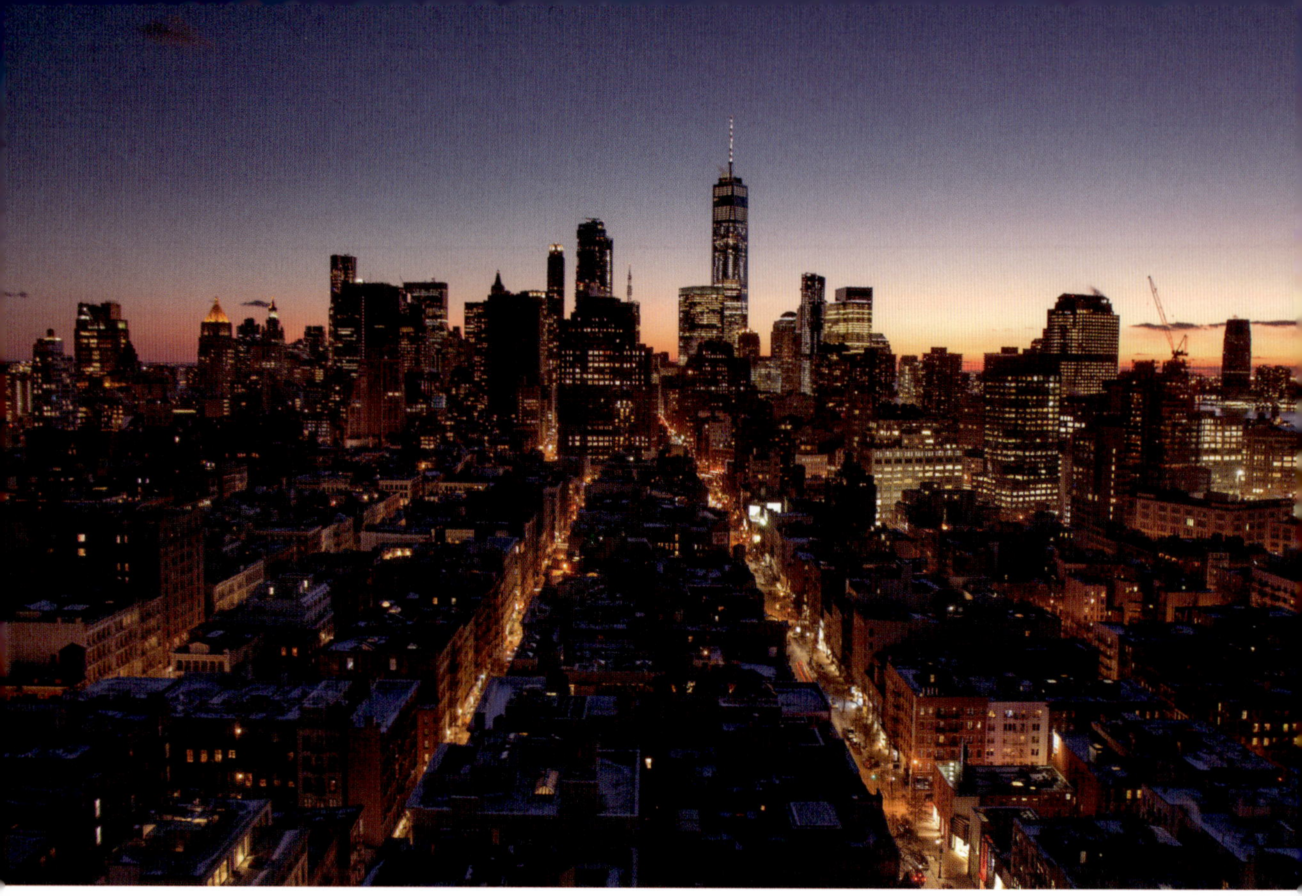

***New York at Sunset.*** *(above)* Overlooking SoHo and Lower Manhattan, a frozen slice of New York at sunset from a rooftop on the corner of West Houston and LaGuardia Place.

***Governors Island.*** *(below)* This was a spectacular finale to the last Governors Island "after hours" day of the season.

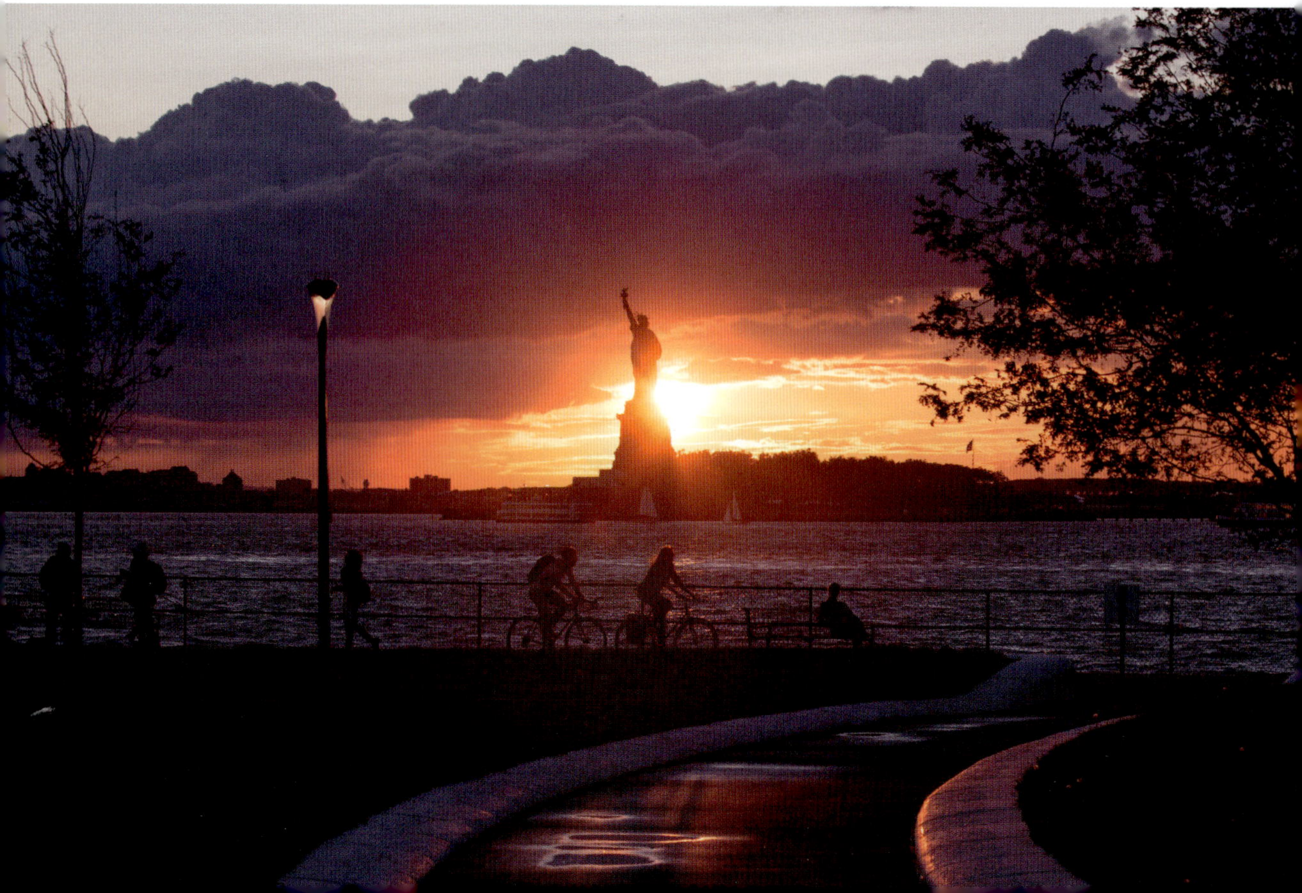

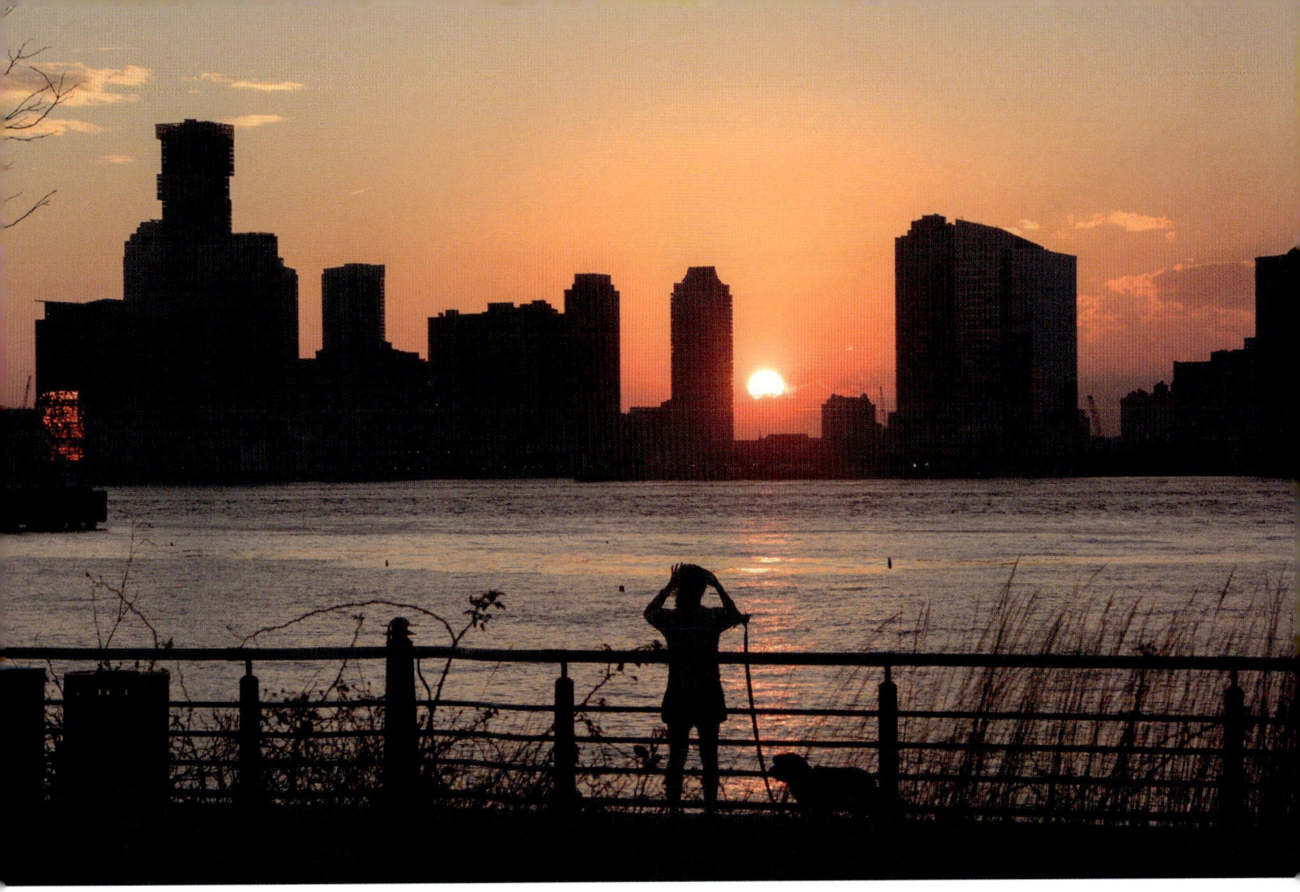

***Winter Heat Wave.*** *(above)* During an unusual February heat wave, I photographed the red sun setting over New Jersey, from just south of Pier 40 in Hudson River Park.

***Double Rainbow.*** *(below)* A double rainbow arched over lower Manhattan after a summer storm swept across the city.

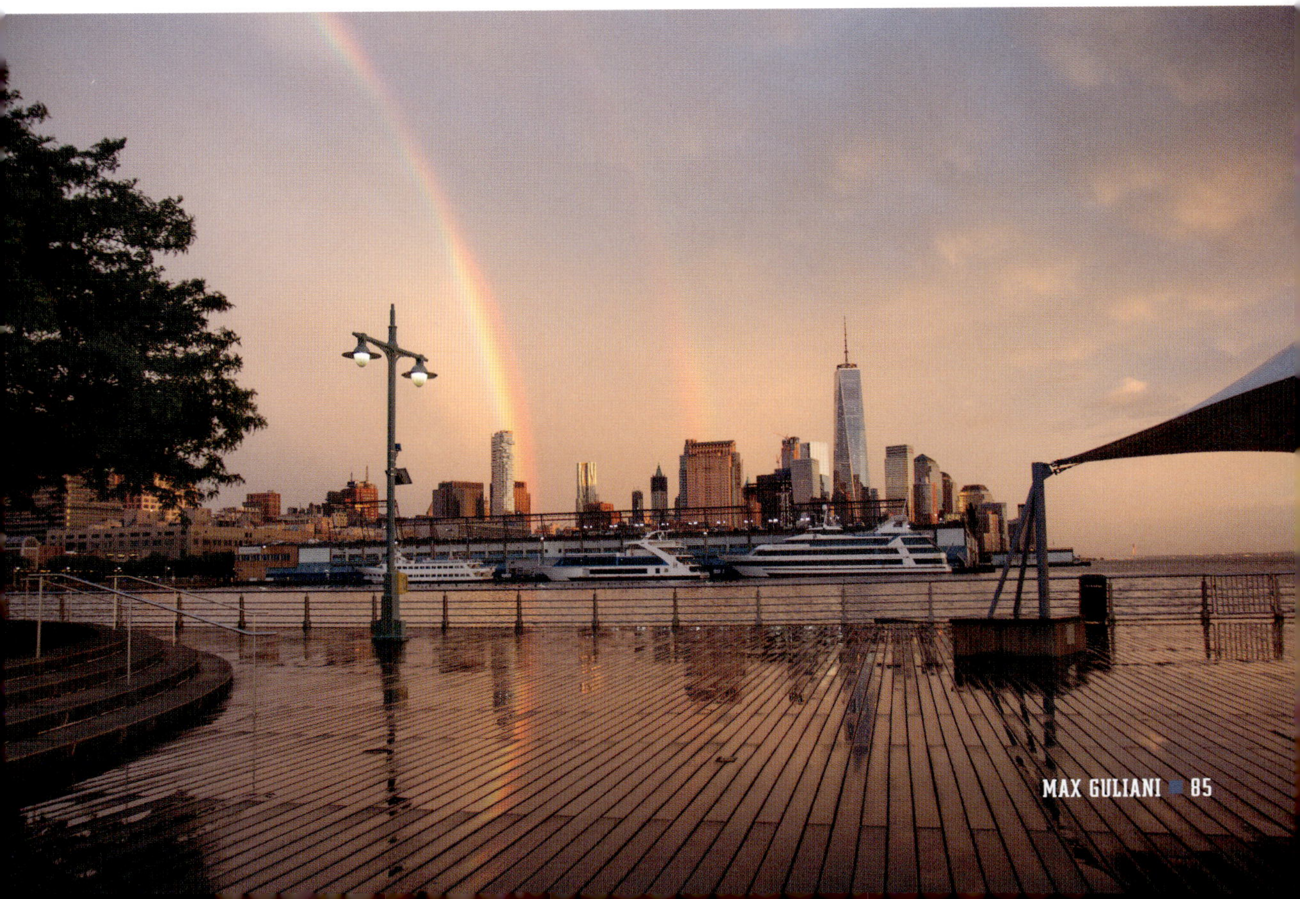

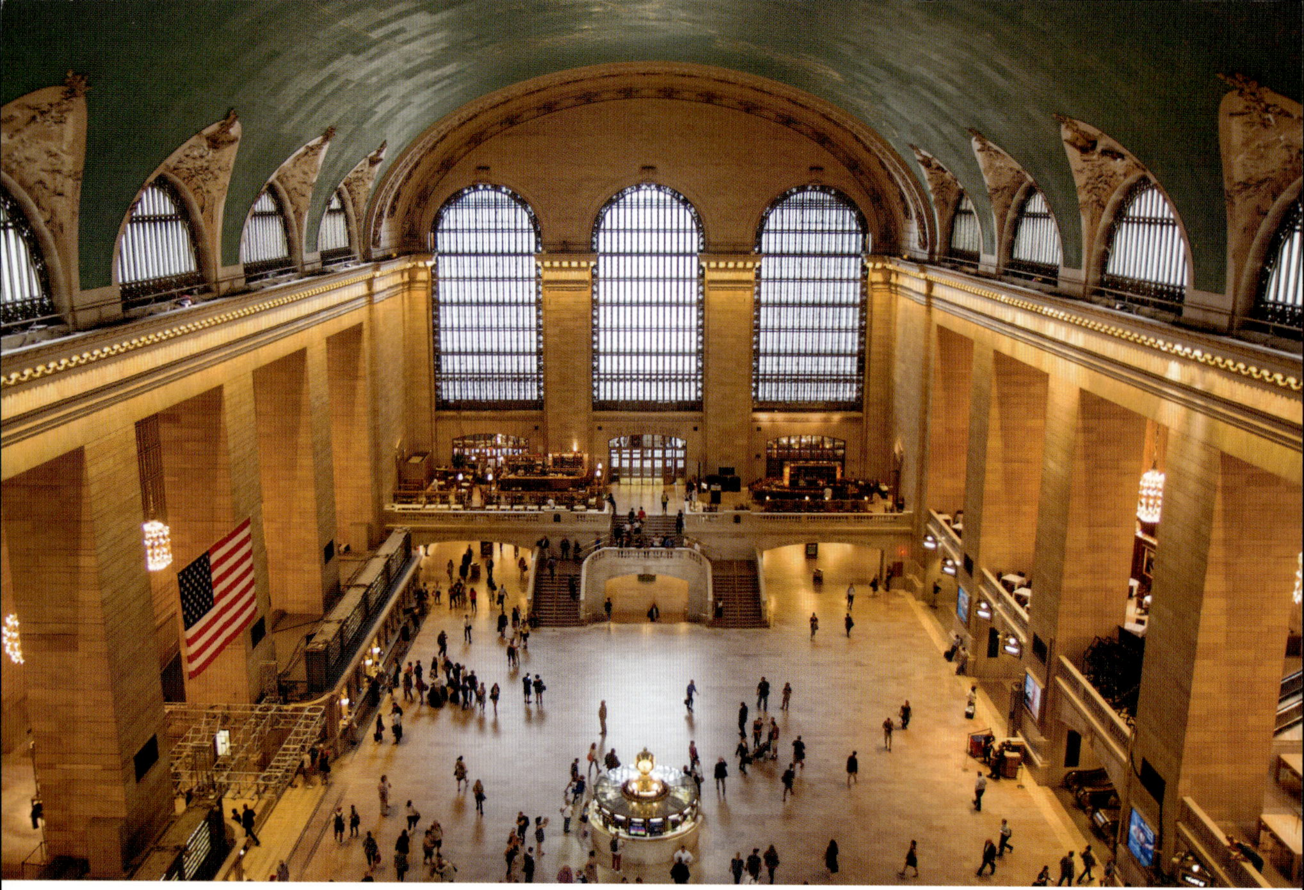

**Grand Central Terminal.** *(above)* Here's where the sky meets the city–at Grand Central Terminal. This photo was captured during a behind-the-scenes-tour of the station.

**Rush Hour.** *(below)* An aerial view of the Park Avenue rush hour, photographed from a rooftop in Greenwich Village.

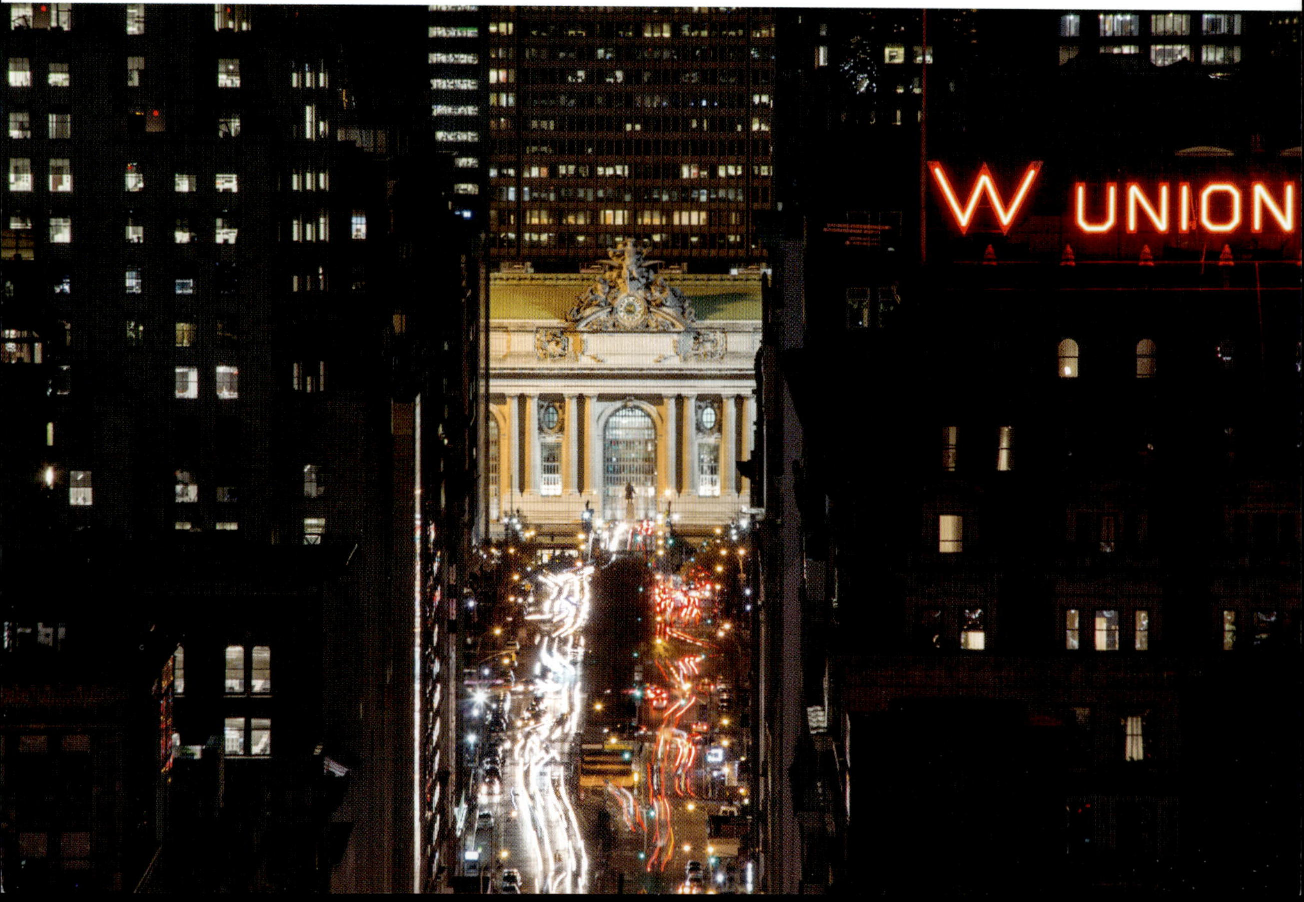

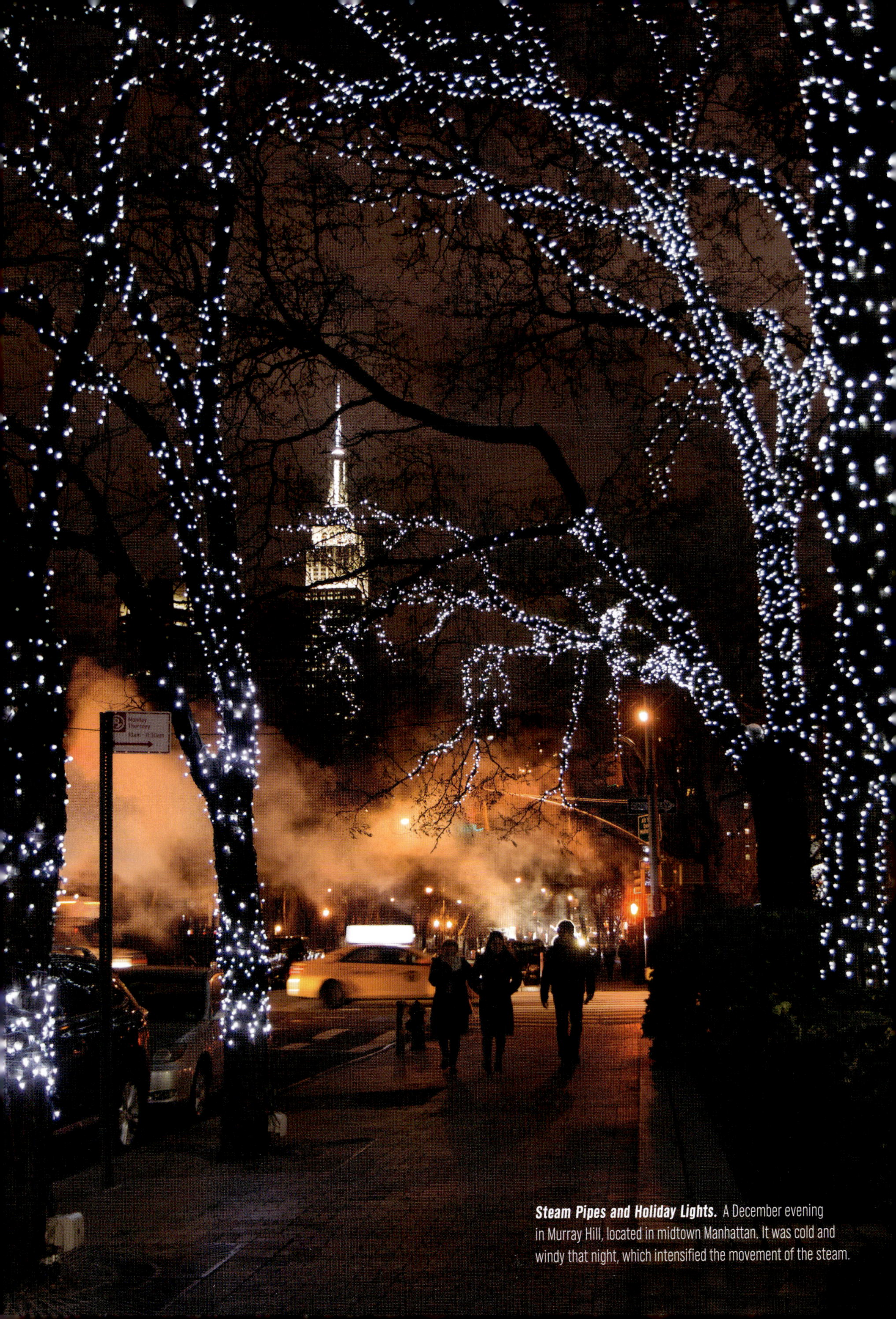


***Steam Pipes and Holiday Lights.*** A December evening in Murray Hill, located in midtown Manhattan. It was cold and windy that night, which intensified the movement of the steam.

***Sunset Skies.*** *(top right)* This beautiful sunset above One World Trade Center was photographed during a sightseeing helicopter ride.

***Harpers Bazaar Anniversary Celebration.*** *(center right)* A projection of model Linda Evangelista was part of the light show on the Empire State Building to mark the 150th anniversary of the fashion magazine *Harper's Bazaar*. It was displayed on the north side of the Empire State Building which made The Top Of The Rock (at Rockefeller Center) a perfect vantage point.

***Crescent Moon Over Manhattan.*** *(bottom right)* New York City has so many great public parks to explore. This scene was captured from Rainey Park, located along the East River in Astoria, Queens.

***East River Fourth of July.*** *(facing page, top)* The East River was jam packed for the Fourth of July fireworks extravaganza. It's one of my favorite images because of the way the lights illuminate the river.

***Brooklyn Bridge Fireworks.*** *(facing page, bottom)* This fireworks display appeared through the suspension cables of the Brooklyn Bridge, viewed from the pedestrian walkway on the Manhattan Bridge.

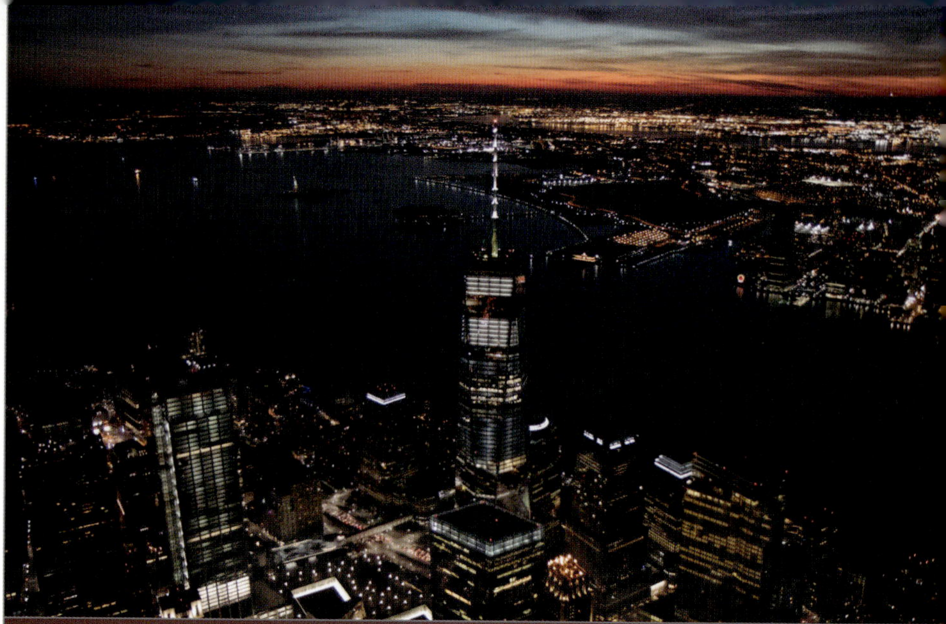

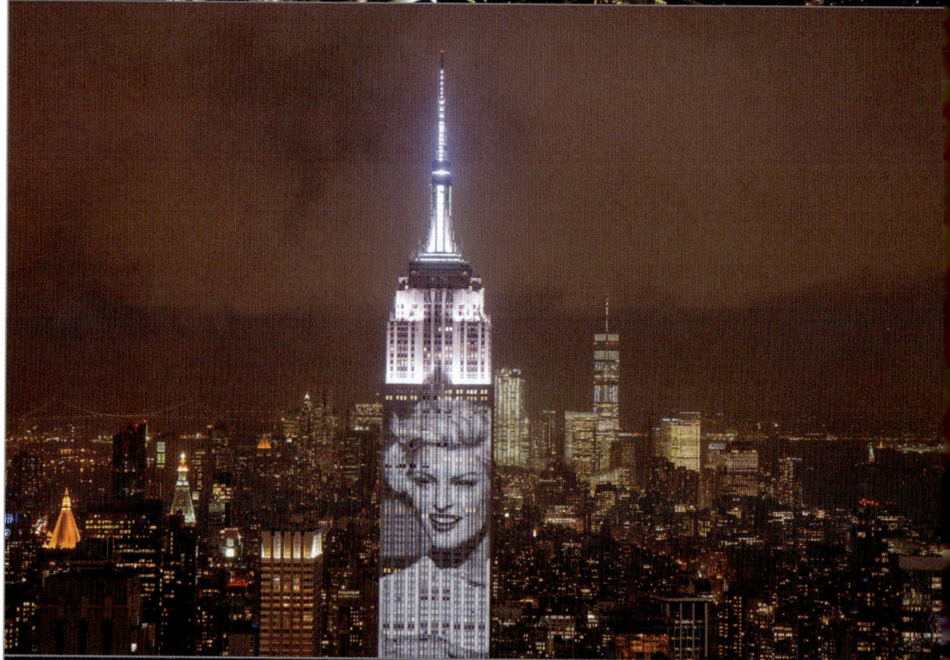

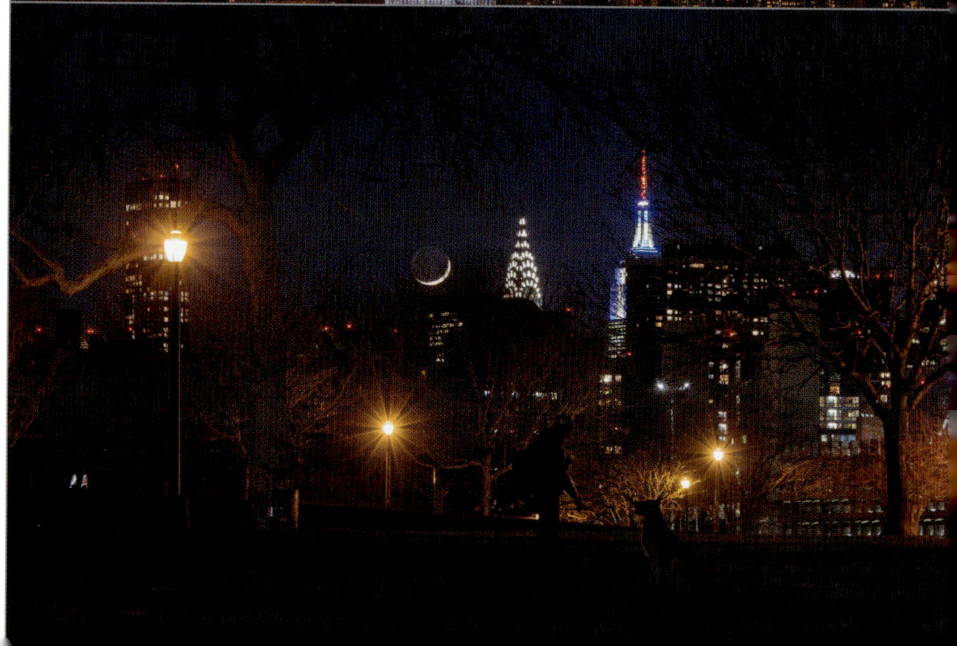

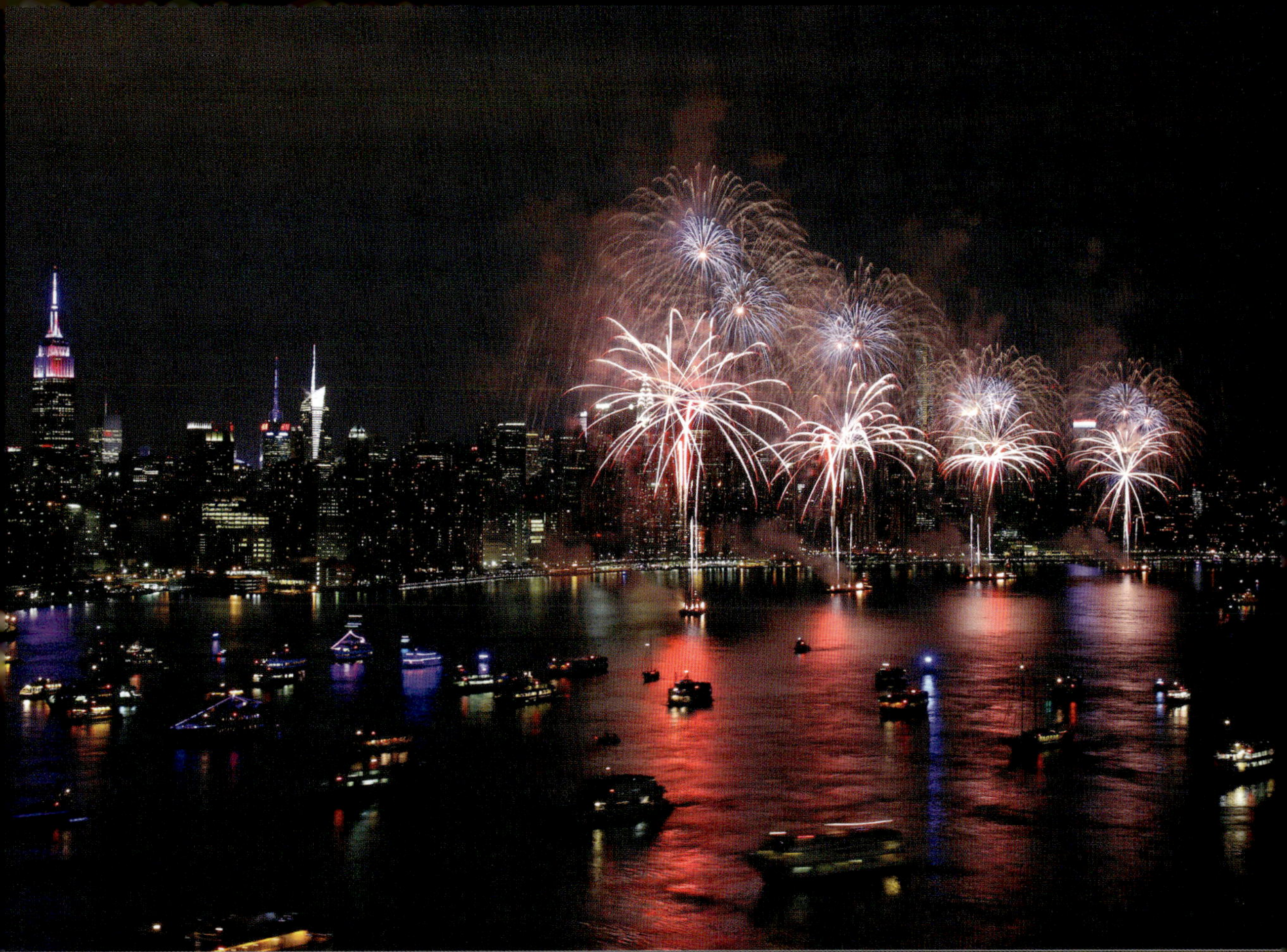

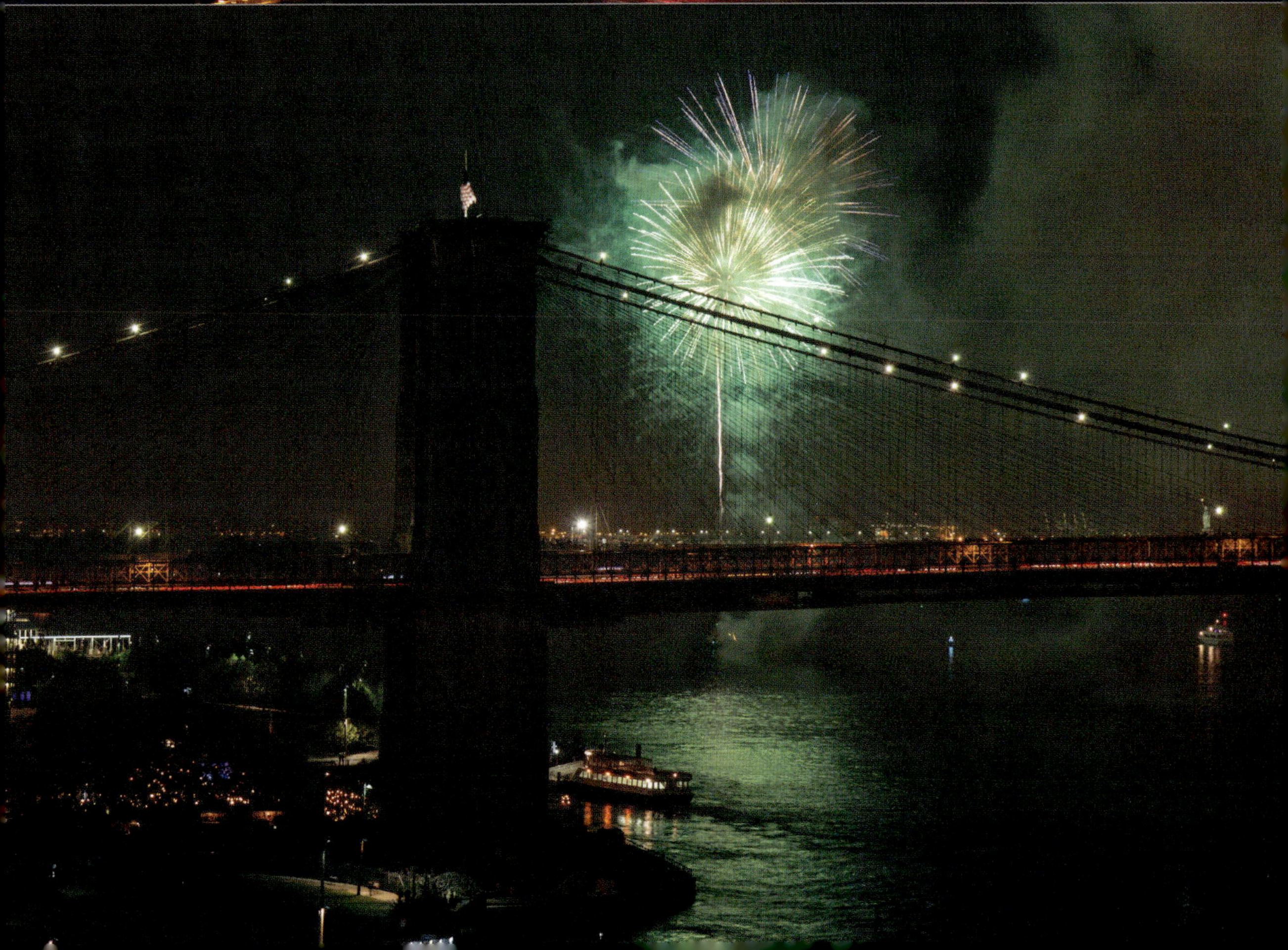

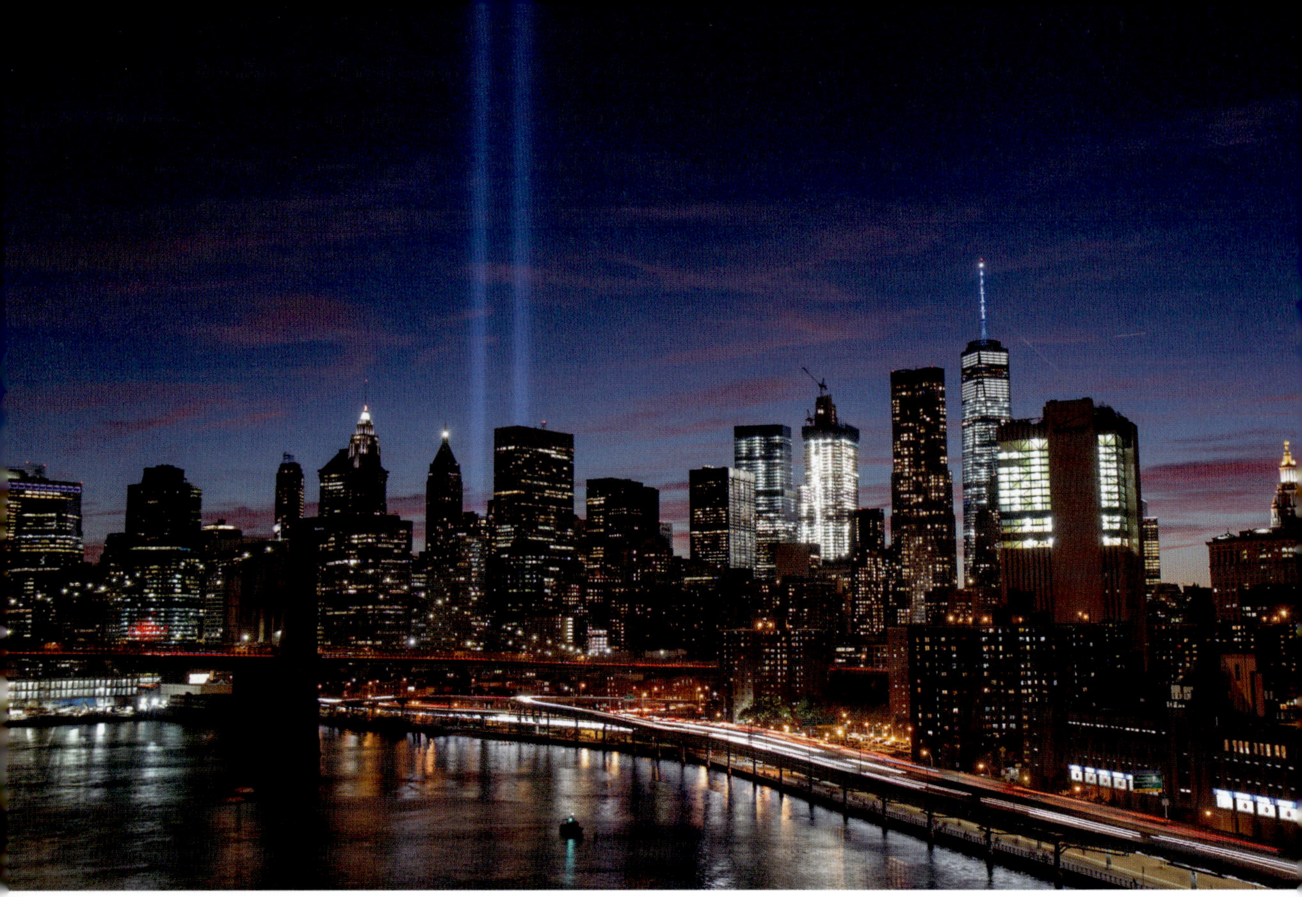

***Tribute in Light.*** *(above)* Captured at dusk over the East River, the Tribute in Light shining over Lower Manhattan honors the victims of 9/11. This was photographed on September 11, 2016, from the pedestrian walkway on the Manhattan Bridge.

***Ice Floe Sunset.*** *(below)* Occasionally, ice chunks are caught in the changing tides between the the old piers and pilings during the harsh winter months.

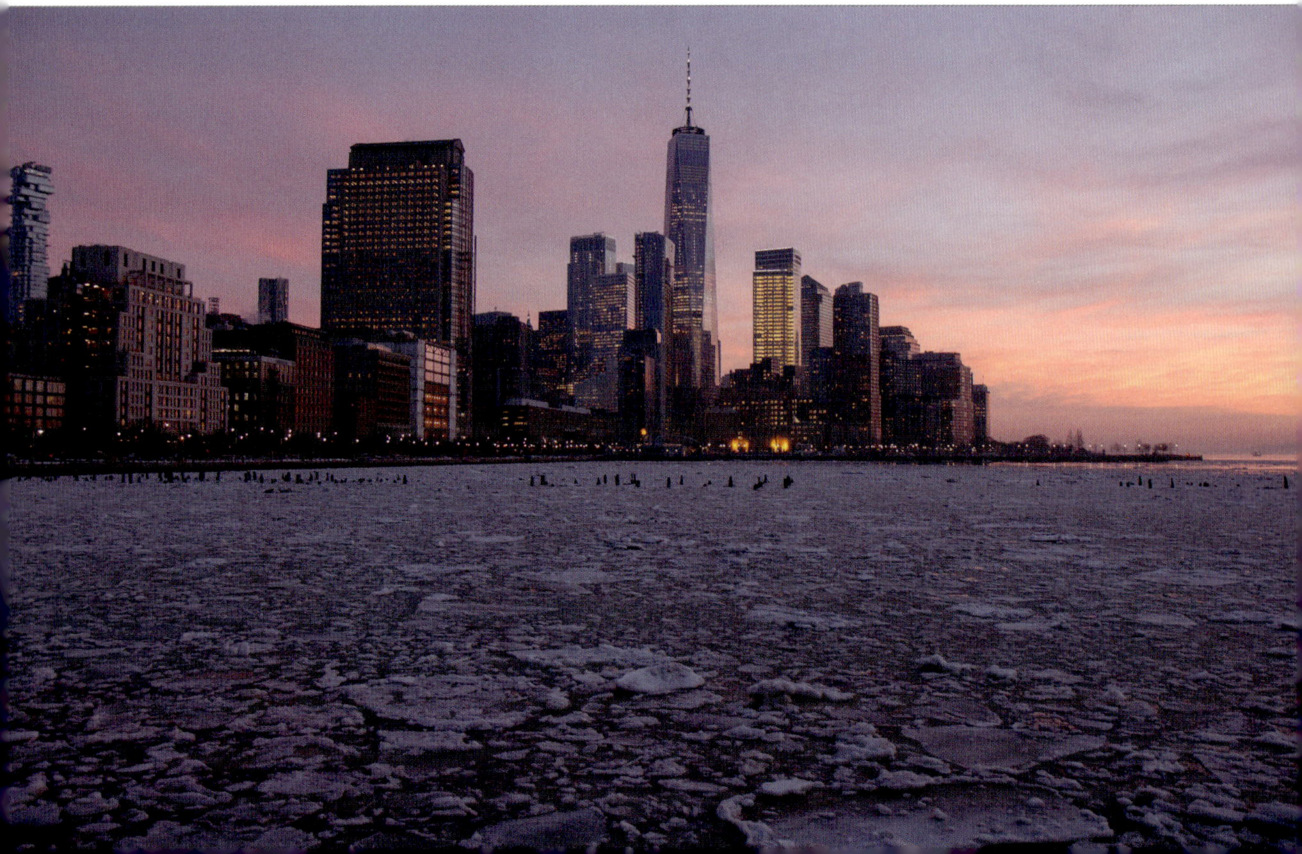

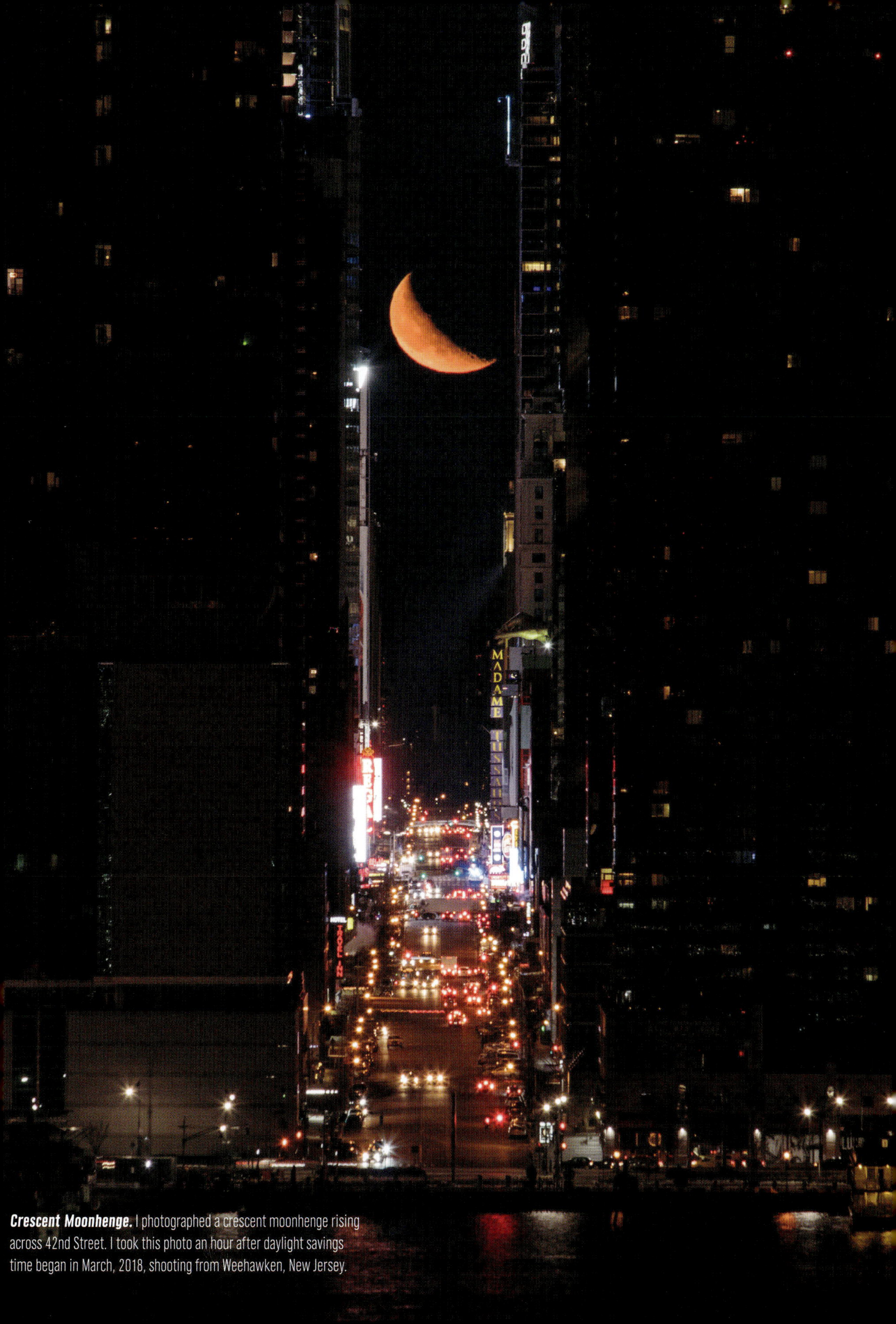


***Crescent Moonhenge.*** I photographed a crescent moonhenge rising across 42nd Street. I took this photo an hour after daylight savings time began in March, 2018, shooting from Weehawken, New Jersey.

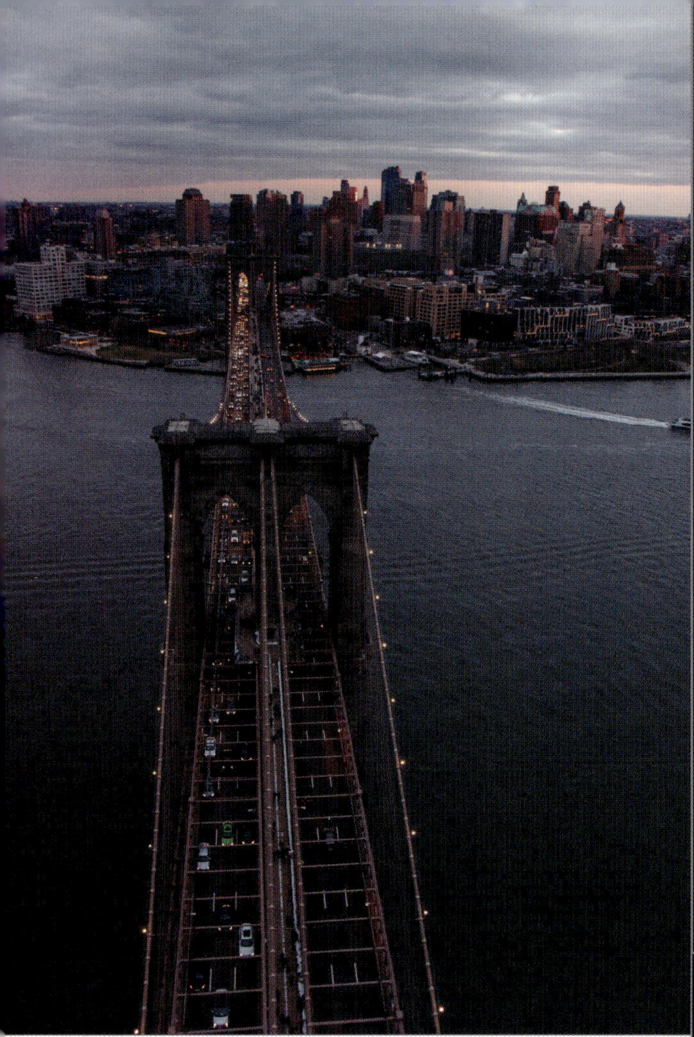

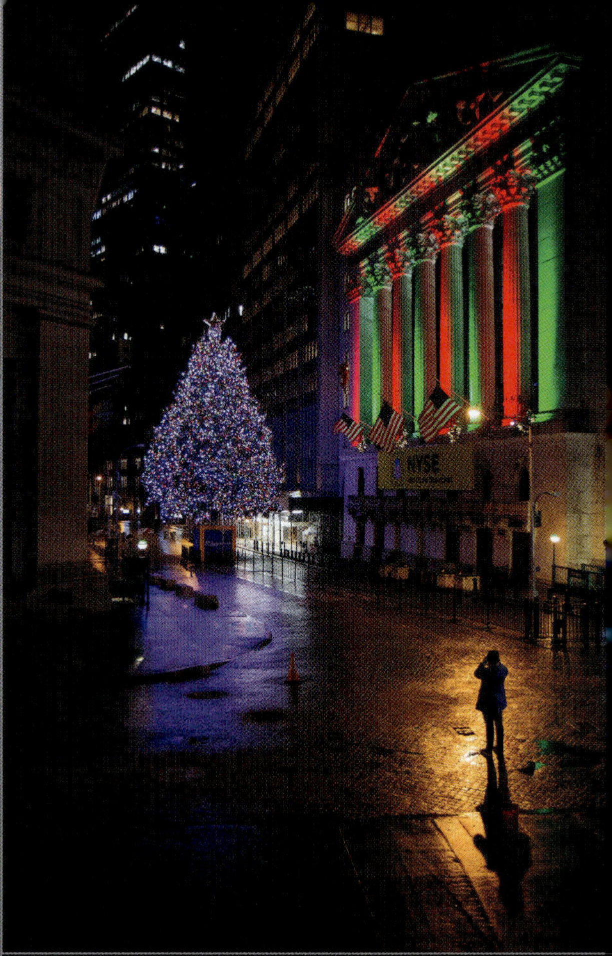

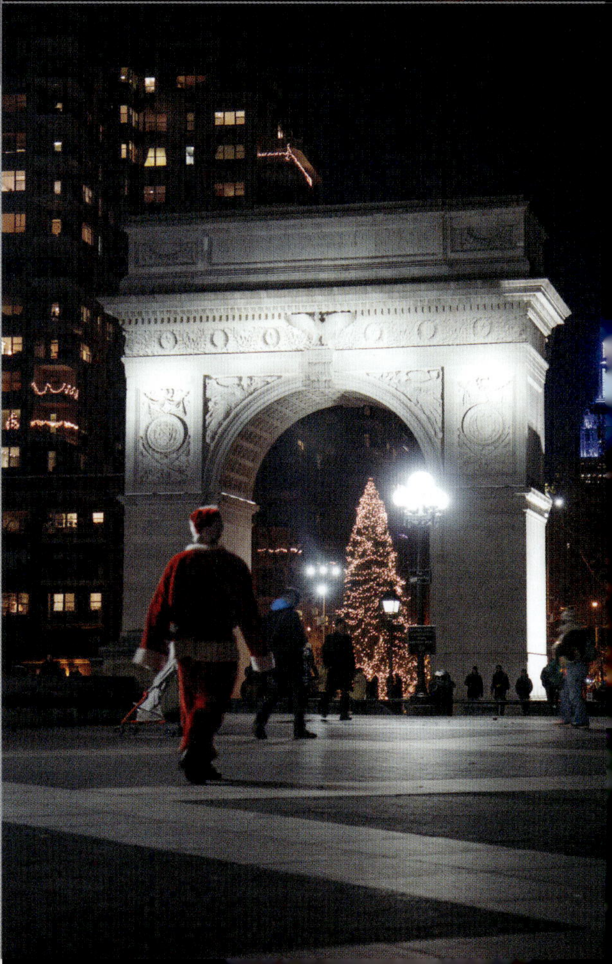

**Brooklyn Bridge Aerial.** *(above)* The Brooklyn Bridge is one of New York City's most iconic landmarks. Built in 1883, it carries more than 150,000 vehicles and pedestrians daily. The photo is an aerial view of the bridge, captured from a sightseeing helicopter tour of Lower Manhattan.

**Wall Street.** *(top right)* A classic holiday tree can be viewed outside the New York Stock Exchange, from the steps of Federal Hall National Memorial.

**Washington Square Park.** *(bottom right)* A lone Santa Claus crosses Washington Square Park on the night of the annual pub crawl called SantaCon.

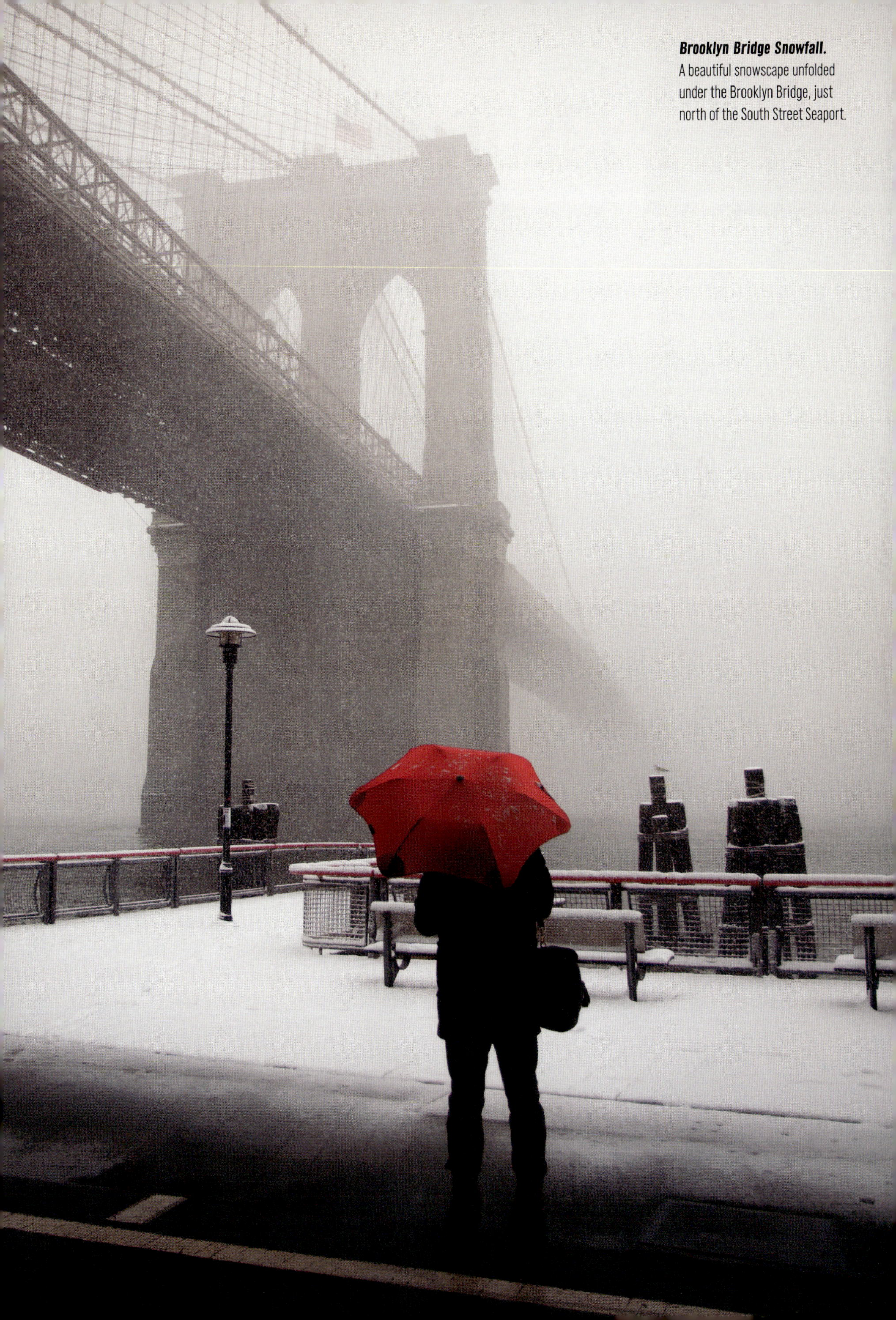

**Brooklyn Bridge Snowfall.** A beautiful snowscape unfolded under the Brooklyn Bridge, just north of the South Street Seaport.

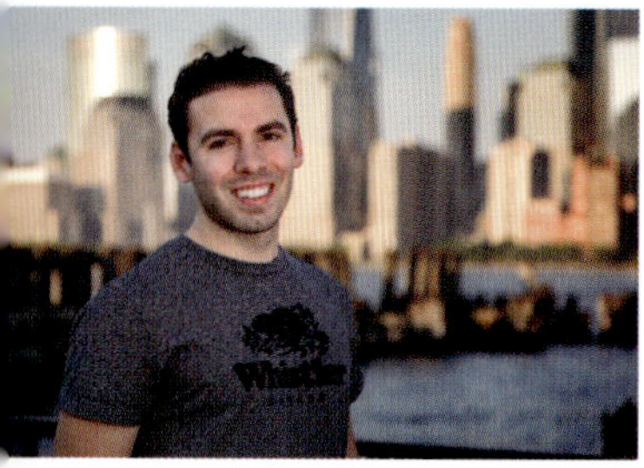

CHAPTER 6

# Jason Risorto

Instagram: @jrisorto ■ www.jasonrisorto.com

I grew up on Long Island in the shadows of this amazing city and have always been inspired by its grandeur, architecture, and the cadence of everyday life. As I developed a career in commercial real estate, I began to fall in love with New York City in a more intimate way. Taking residence first in Manhattan and now in Brooklyn, I've spent a lot of time admiring this amazing city and photography has become my creative outlet for sharing it.

My exploration into photography began in 2014 when I was interested in taking some higher quality photos during an international trip. My sister had always been the family photographer and I purchased my first DSLR from her with little to no understanding of the basics of exposure or composition. I found that I enjoyed the process of taking photos and, upon my return to New York City, I would discuss photography basics with two friends who are talented shooters. After walking away with more questions than answers, I set out to understand how to use my camera properly. Instagram was gaining in popularity at this time and it gave me a reason to want to improve as I could get immediate feedback on the images I shared.

My personal style took a long time to develop, and required a lot of self-evaluation and analysis.

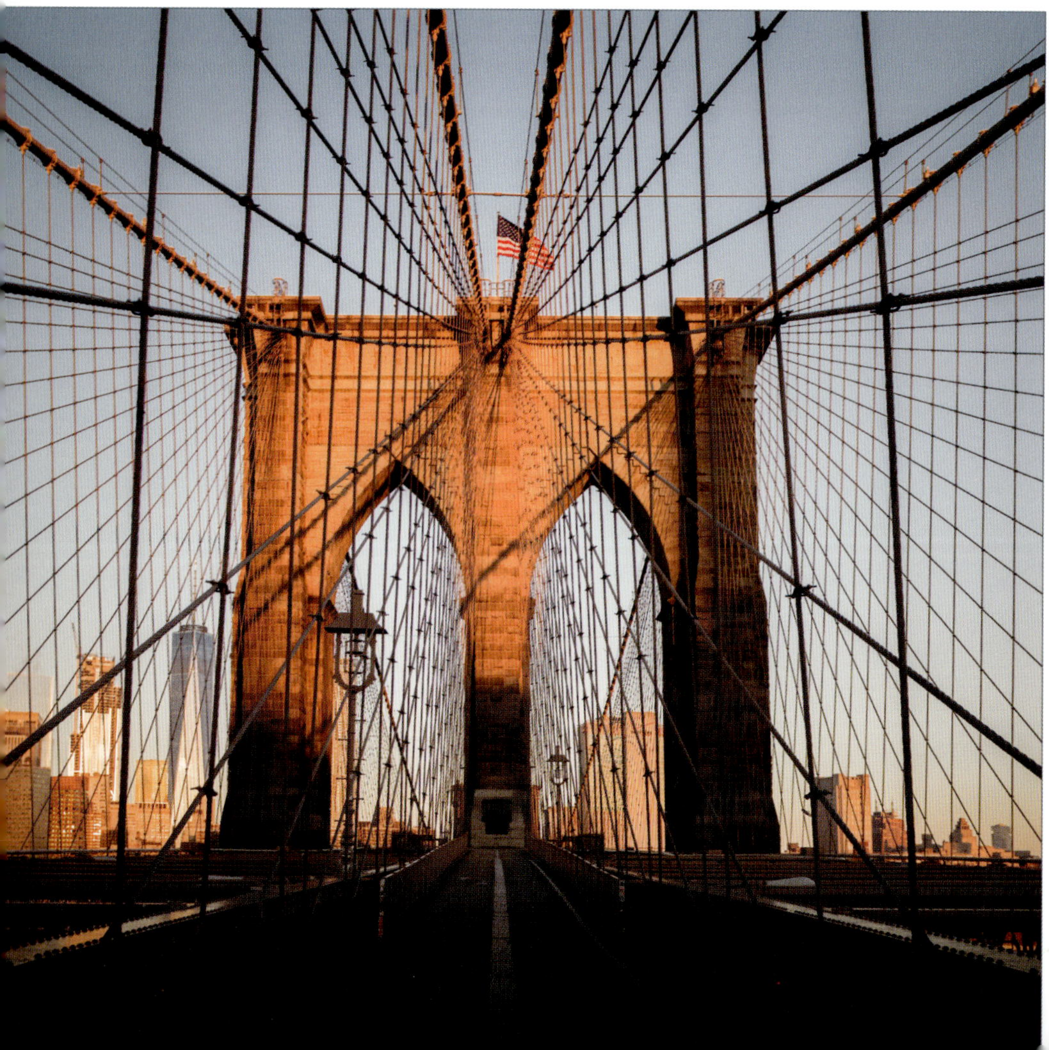

***All Alone on the Brooklyn Bridge.*** *(left)* Sunrise in New York City is my favorite. Not only is there warm light but you have the city to yourself while everyone else is still asleep.

***Bethesda Fountain.*** *(facing page)* Bethesda Fountain, with its famous *Angel of the Waters* statue, is located in Central Park. Most times, my photos are planned well in advance but this is a rare occasion where I stumbled upon something great and captured the view.

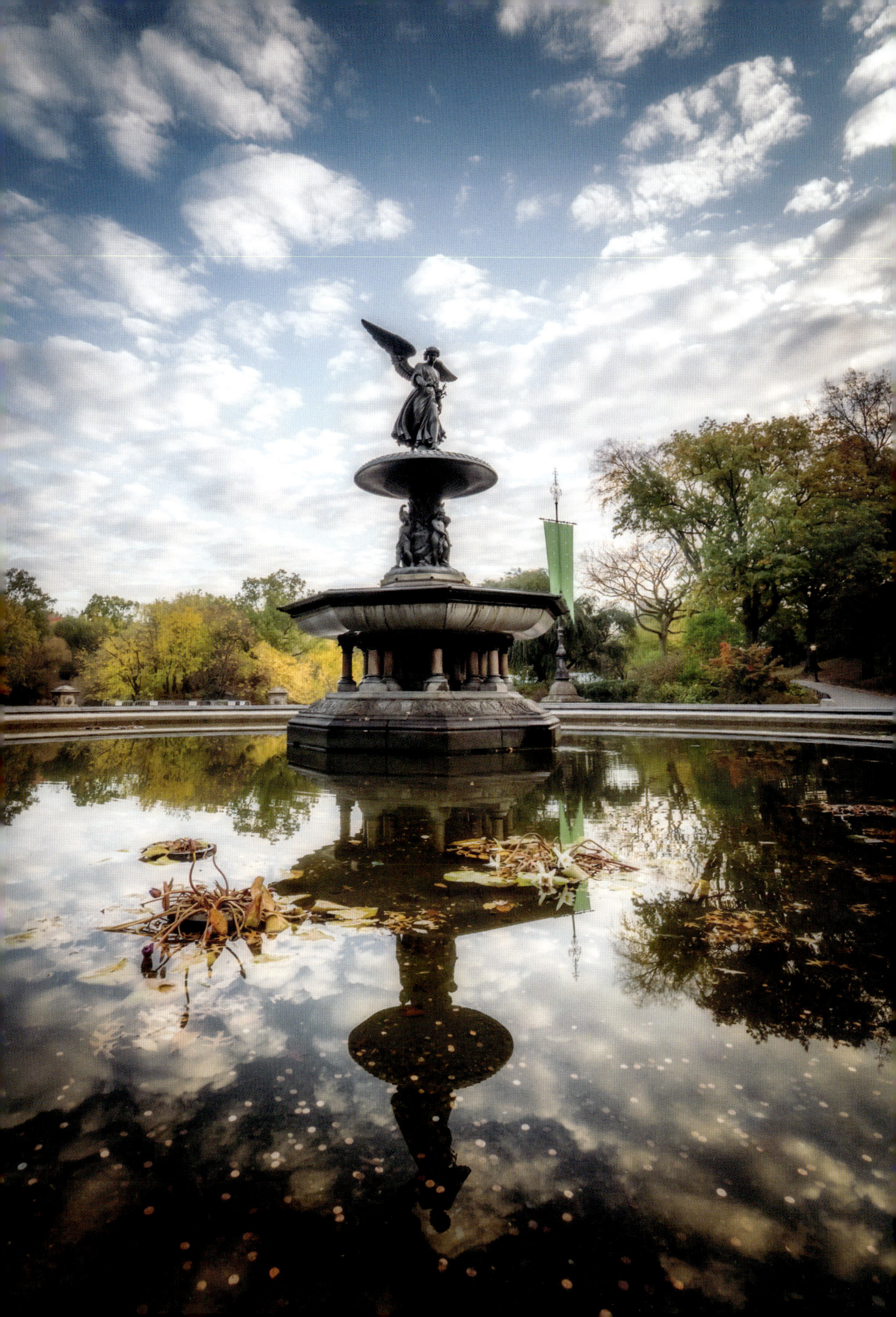

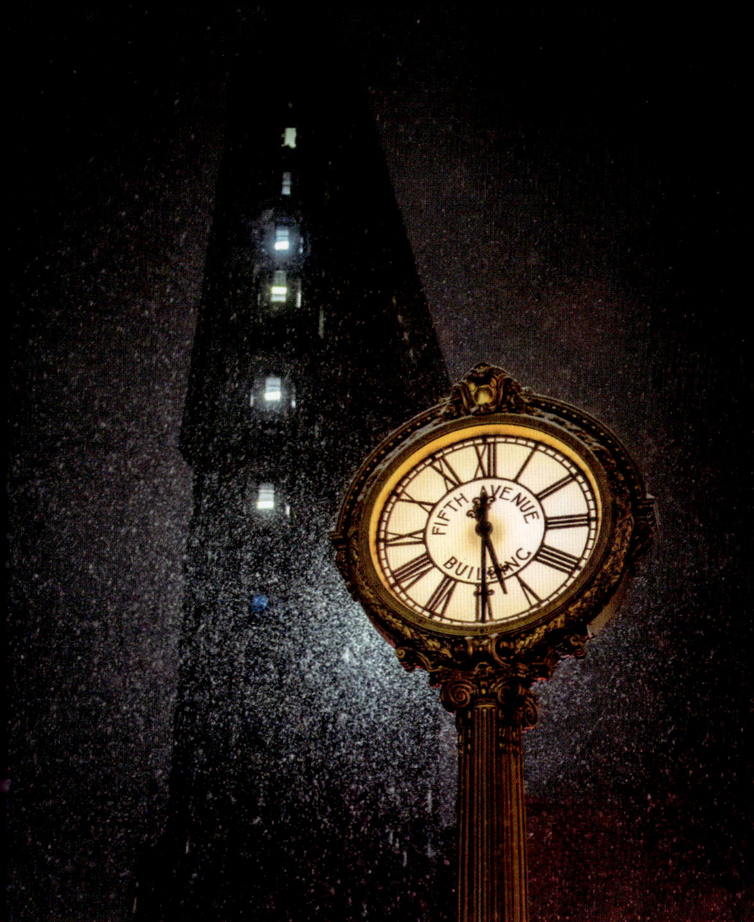

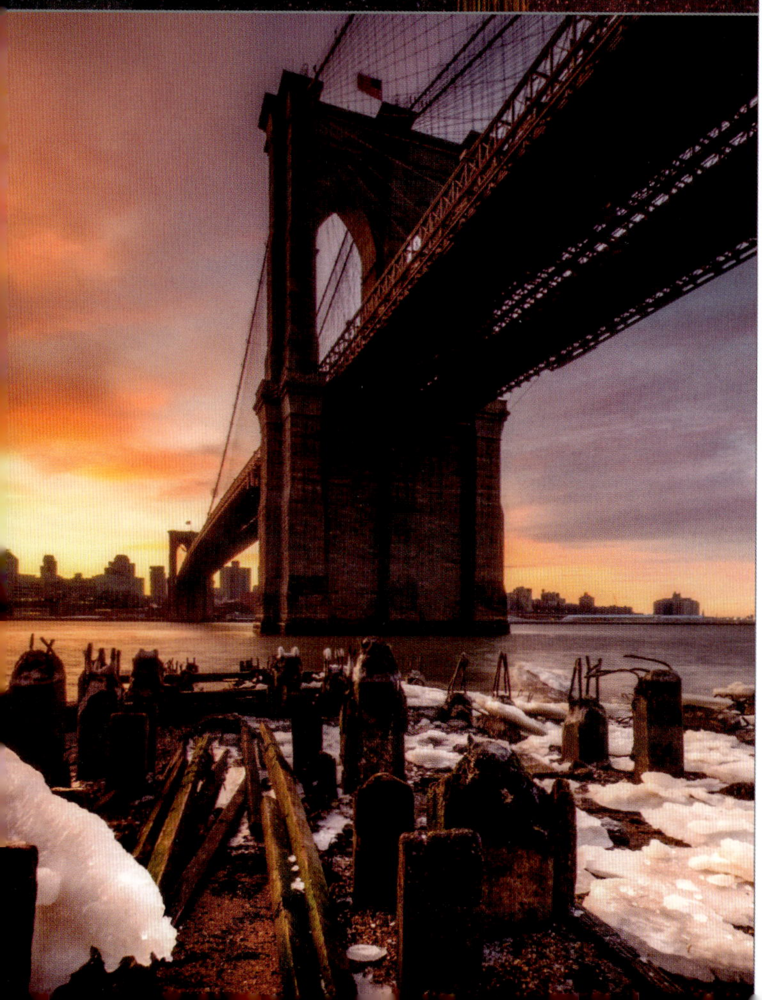

When I began sharing my images, it was mostly details of New York, some interesting angles, and more lifestyle-oriented photos. I was told on numerous occasions that I should work to develop a style, but it wasn't immediately clear to me what it should be or what message I wanted to convey. I was sharing images because I enjoyed taking them but over time I began to notice that my sunrise and sunset photos received the most praise. I then began the journey of learning how to increase my odds of taking great golden hour images. Today, I'm known for carefully composed images that showcase New York City with beautiful light and colors. Although I've now found comfort in my particular niche, it took a lot of time before I could confidently describe my aesthetic.

After qualifying a few of my early photos with phrases like "the picture doesn't do it justice," I knew I wanted to learn what I could do to change the result. I've never formally studied photography, but I've spent countless hours researching and practicing the art of it. It's not unusual for me to get fully engulfed in a topic and to read every article I can find on the subject and then go out and practice it until I have it mastered. Some of my best resources have been Internet articles and YouTube videos, where I've been able to learn from some of the world's best photographers. I've also learned a lot from simply trying and making mistakes.

**Flatiron in Snow.** *(top left)* Everything looks better with a fresh layer of snow. The famous Flatiron Building is getting a dusting of white powder as the street lights illuminate the scene. Although I much prefer warm summer nights, exploring the city in the snow is always a ton of fun.

**Low Tide at Brooklyn Bridge.** *(bottom left)* This shot is from a morning spent under the Brooklyn Bridge. Capturing this view properly required a lot of coordination. This beach is only accessible at low tide and it took a while before I was able to time a colorful sunrise to coordinate. Little details like that make the final product more rewarding.

That said, I'm still working to improve my photography every day. Today, images of amazing quality are available across social media platforms and other outlets, so I aspire to always learn something new and to publish images I'm proud to share.

As a result, I've found myself noticing things I had never paid attention to before. I now spend my days admiring the movement of clouds and watching the light and shadows move throughout the city. I've begun to think and view the city as a frame

**Radio City Christmas.** *(below)* Most days, rain means my photo plans are spoiled. On this night, though, I found myself getting drenched and photographing the light reflecting off the streets—and I couldn't have been happier.

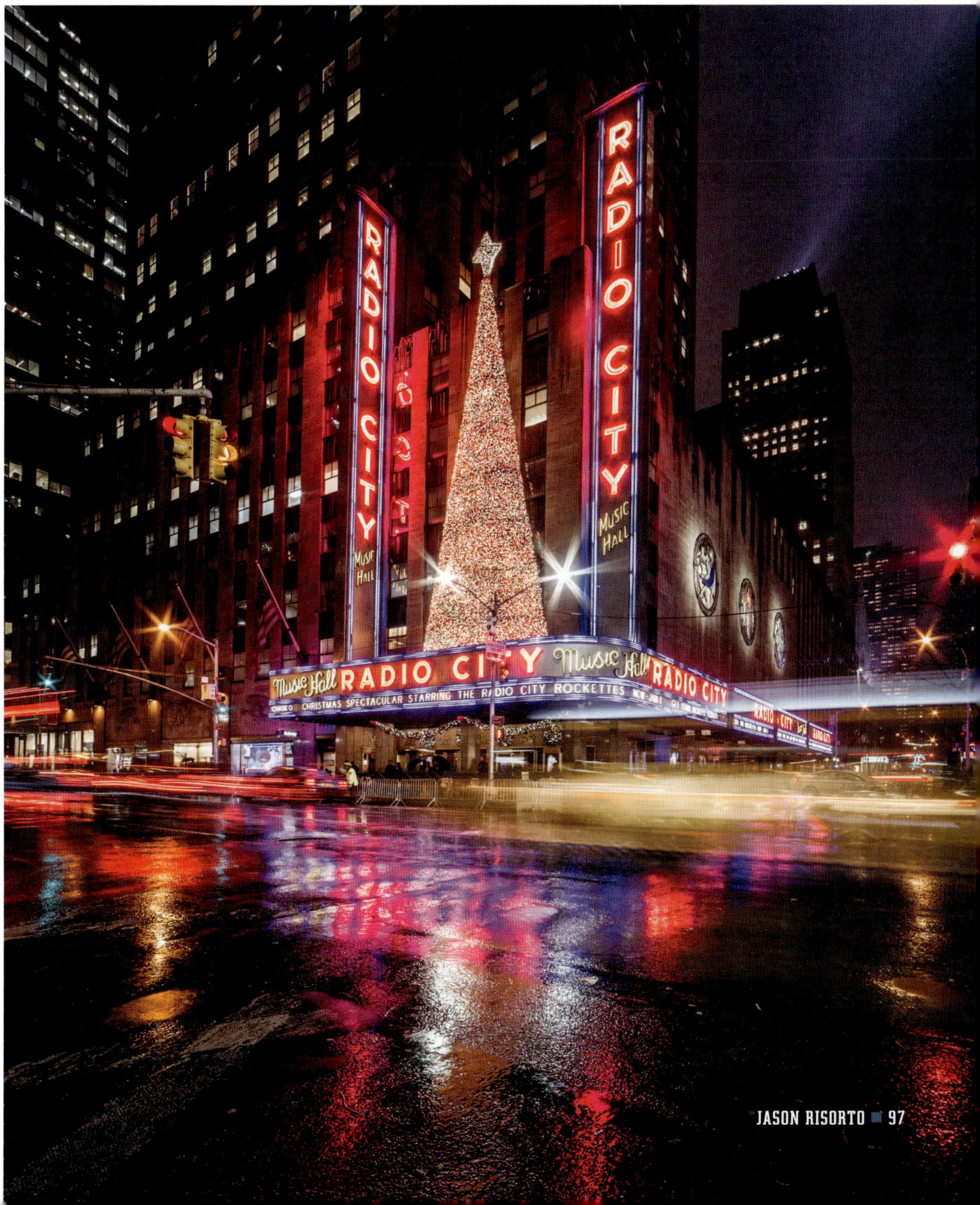

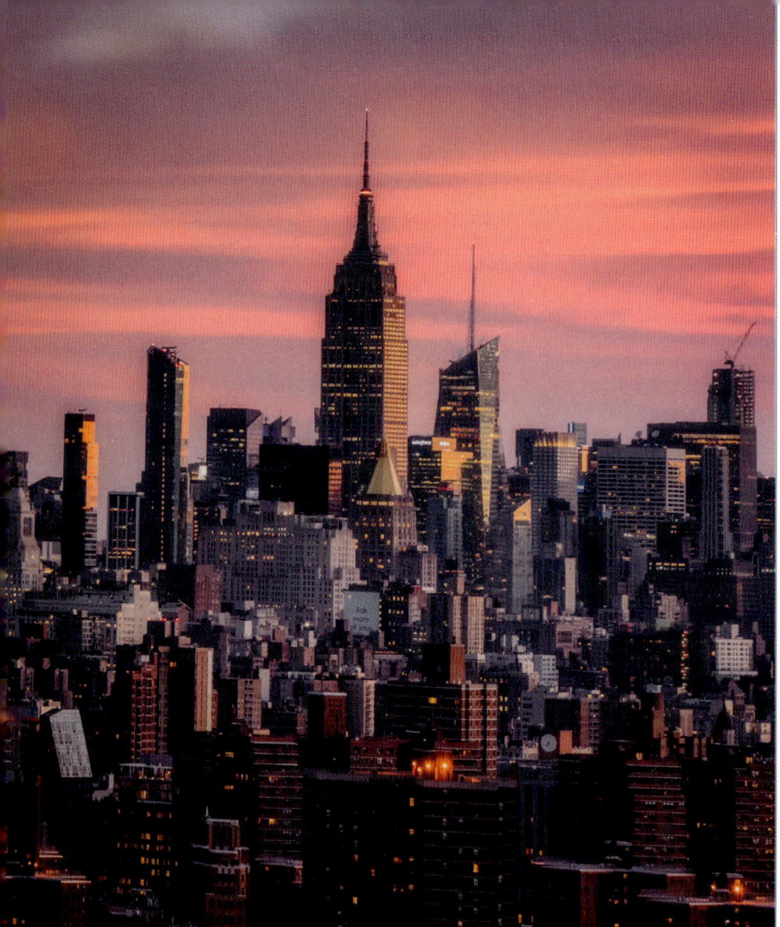

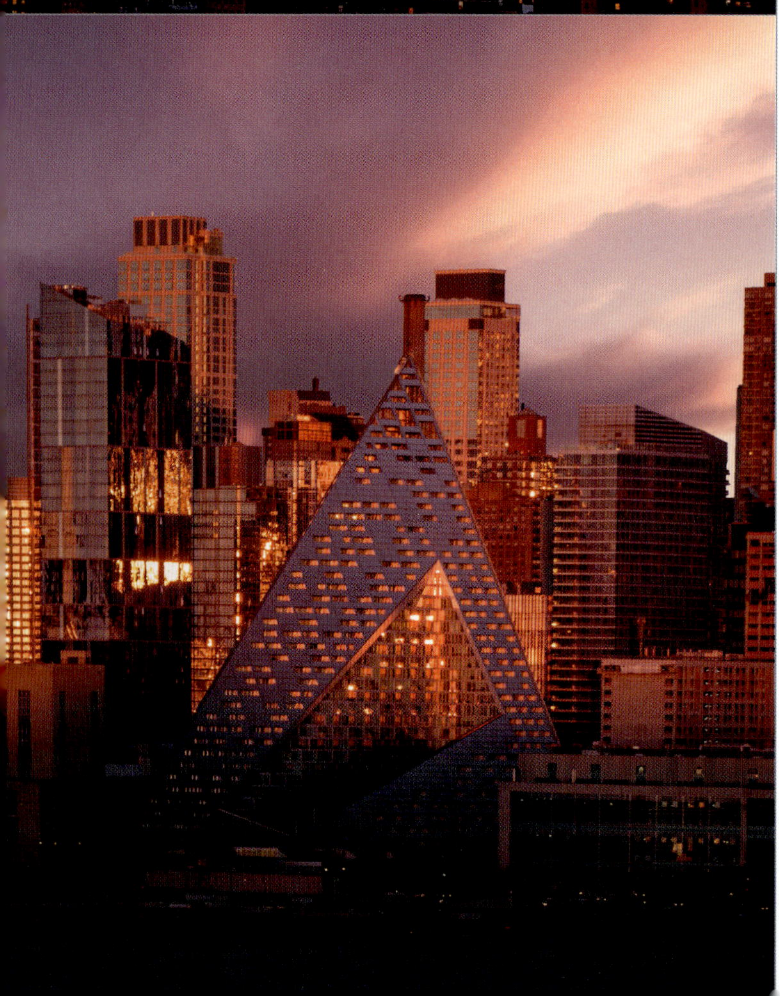

and less like a pedestrian. I began with a small notebook and would scribble down bits of information on a given day when I noticed a sunset was particularly colorful and dramatic. Over time, I noticed a few trends and now I try to make sure I have my camera in hand when the weather conditions are looking optimal. Through photography, I've explored wonderful places that I would otherwise never have seen and I have experienced New York City at its best moments.

I never would have imagined that I would be waking up at the crack of dawn to stand outside in freezing temperatures in order to take a photo. Sunrises are particularly special to me because of the intimacy I experience with the city. At that time of day, most people are still snoozing at home, so popular destinations that are usually packed with tourists and commuters stand totally empty. The process of taking photos is therapeutic and I enjoy having a creative outlet to balance my quantitative professional career. I've met some great photographers through Instagram and have been fortunate to explore and take photos with people I would not have met without this shared interest. Still, I very much enjoy having the moments alone with New York City, particularly along the waterfront.

**Daybreak.** *(top left)* At the first moment of daylight over midtown Manhattan – the colorful clouds, the warm glow reflecting off the buildings, and the building lights – everything came together in this image. These moments usually last for only about a minute, but they are truly magical.

**VIA 57 West.** *(bottom left)* I've always considered myself to be more of a landscape photographer and nothing reminds me more of a mountain than VIA 57 West. It took a few attempts but I was eventually able to capture the light of sunset reflecting off its facade.

**_Morning Commute on FDR Drive._** *(top right)* The warm colors of sunrise reflect off the buildings and clouds as cars race down Manhattan's FDR Drive

**_My Trophy Case._** *(bottom right)* I had wanted to take this photo for a while, but the logistics had always been tough. I arrived on a cold, dark morning with whipping winds. It was nearly too cold to operate my camera but thankfully, with a large zoom lens, I was able to capture this unique view.

One thing I love is that you can revisit the same place and have a different experience each time. While I have a few personal favorite photo locations (which might be evident when reviewing my work), the lighting, weather, and composition can change each time I visit, so I never feel bored or uninspired.

I watch for that magic moment when the building lights are still on and the clouds are highlighted in colorful tones. Usually, that one- to two-minute period is when I'm snapping away. I'm perfectly happy walking away with one image worth keeping. I really embrace the idea that a single image I'm proud of is much better than multiple mediocre photos. As a result, I don't share images as frequently as others but I take pride in the work do I share.

My current approach has shifted slightly from mostly taking photos with the purpose of sharing on social media, to focusing on larger format prints. I have a growing list of new places I'd like to explore and will be working to photograph those locations during ideal conditions.

One of the best things about New York City is that there are endless possibilities for photography and I'm looking forward to making further improvements and sharing work that inspires me to continue creating.

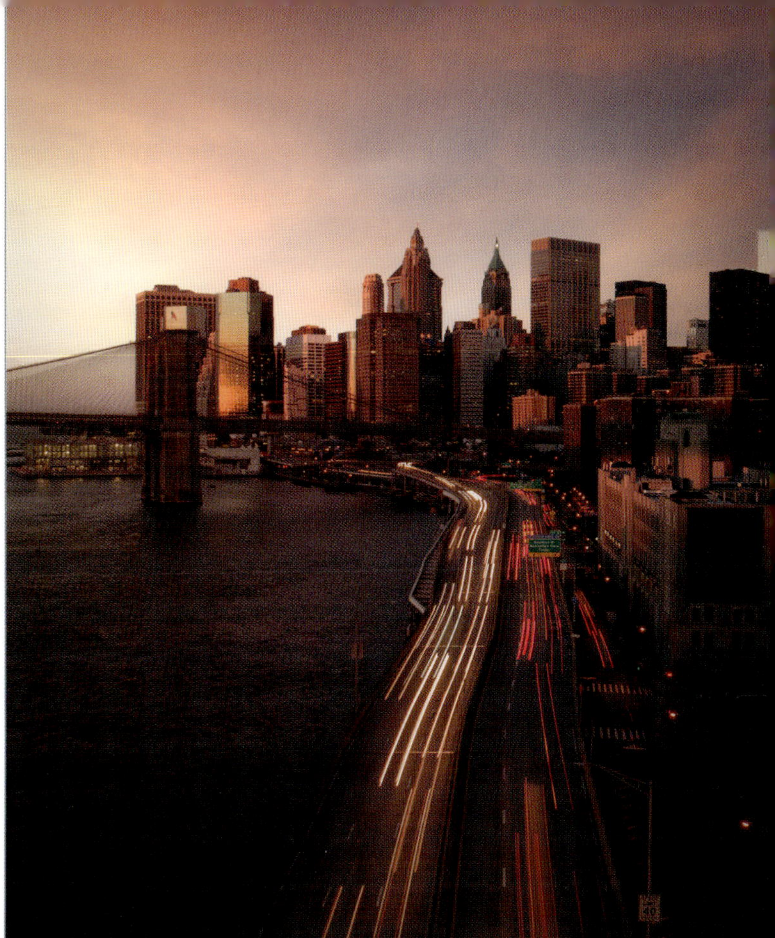

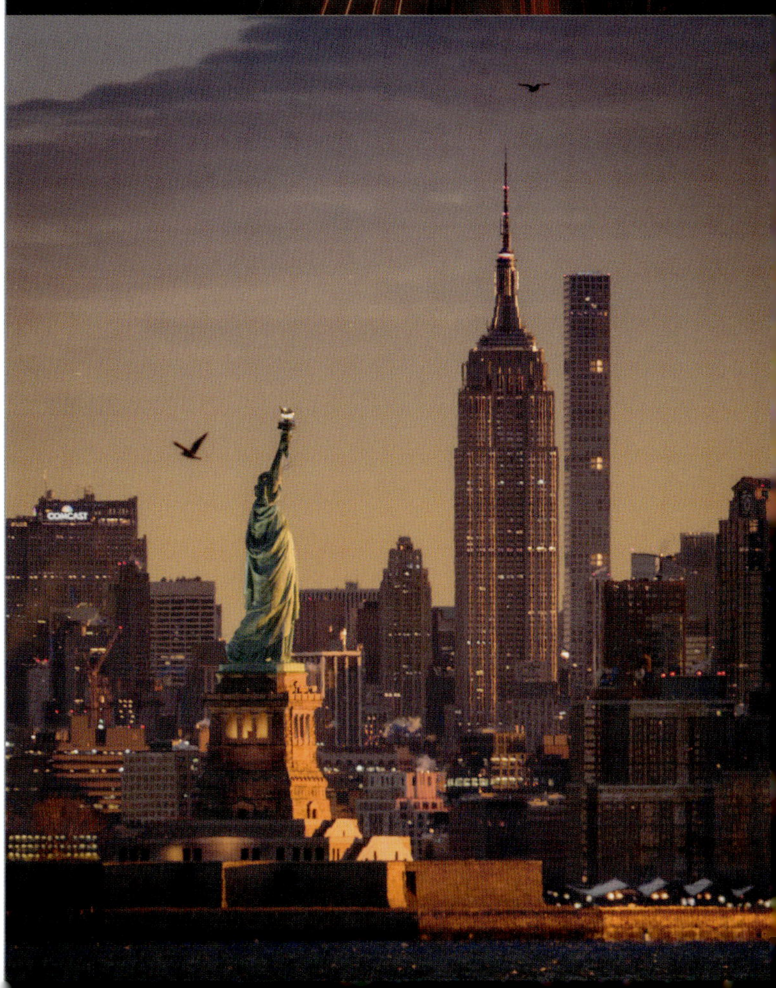

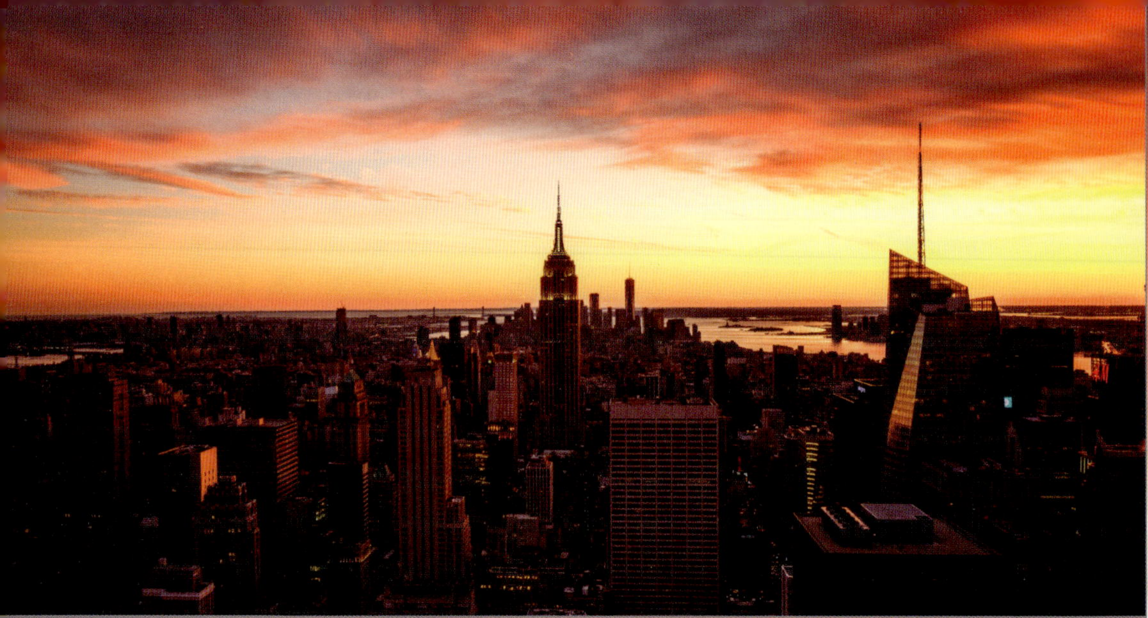

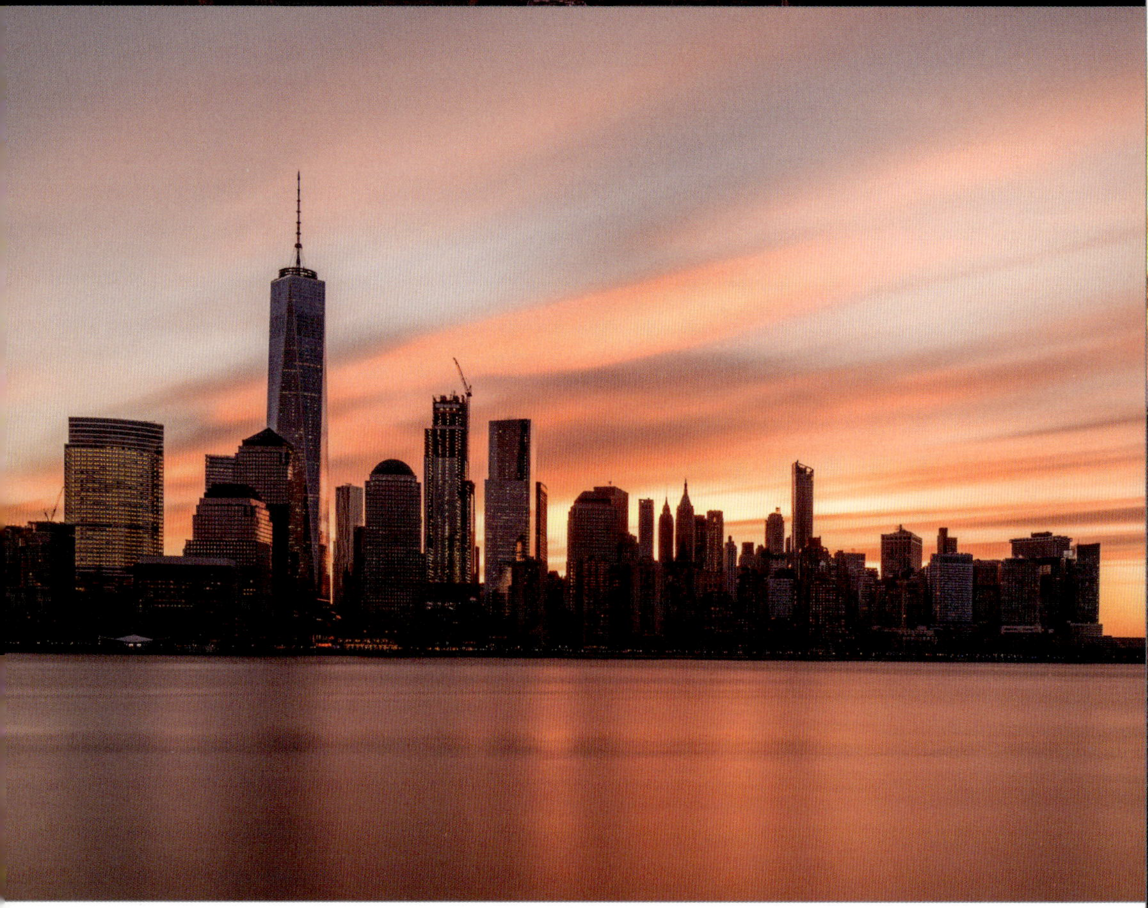

***Sunset Drama.*** *(top left)* I've spent a lot of time trying to figure out what weather conditions will make for the best sunrises and sunsets. This evening, I knew I was in for something special and I wanted to capture a dramatic view. I get lost in the small details of this image, including the Statue of Liberty in the distance and the multiple bridges.

***Peaceful Sunrise.*** *(bottom left)* Here's another peaceful sunrise over Lower Manhattan. My favorite time to take photos is that magic moment when the building lights are still on and the clouds are glowing with warm colors

***Across the Brooklyn Bridge.*** *(facing page)* This unique view is probably my favorite scene I've captured. It was amazing staring down the Brooklyn Bridge—and when the sky ignited with color, I began to cheer and jump for joy. Sometimes you get lucky; I consider this one of those times where everything worked out perfectly.

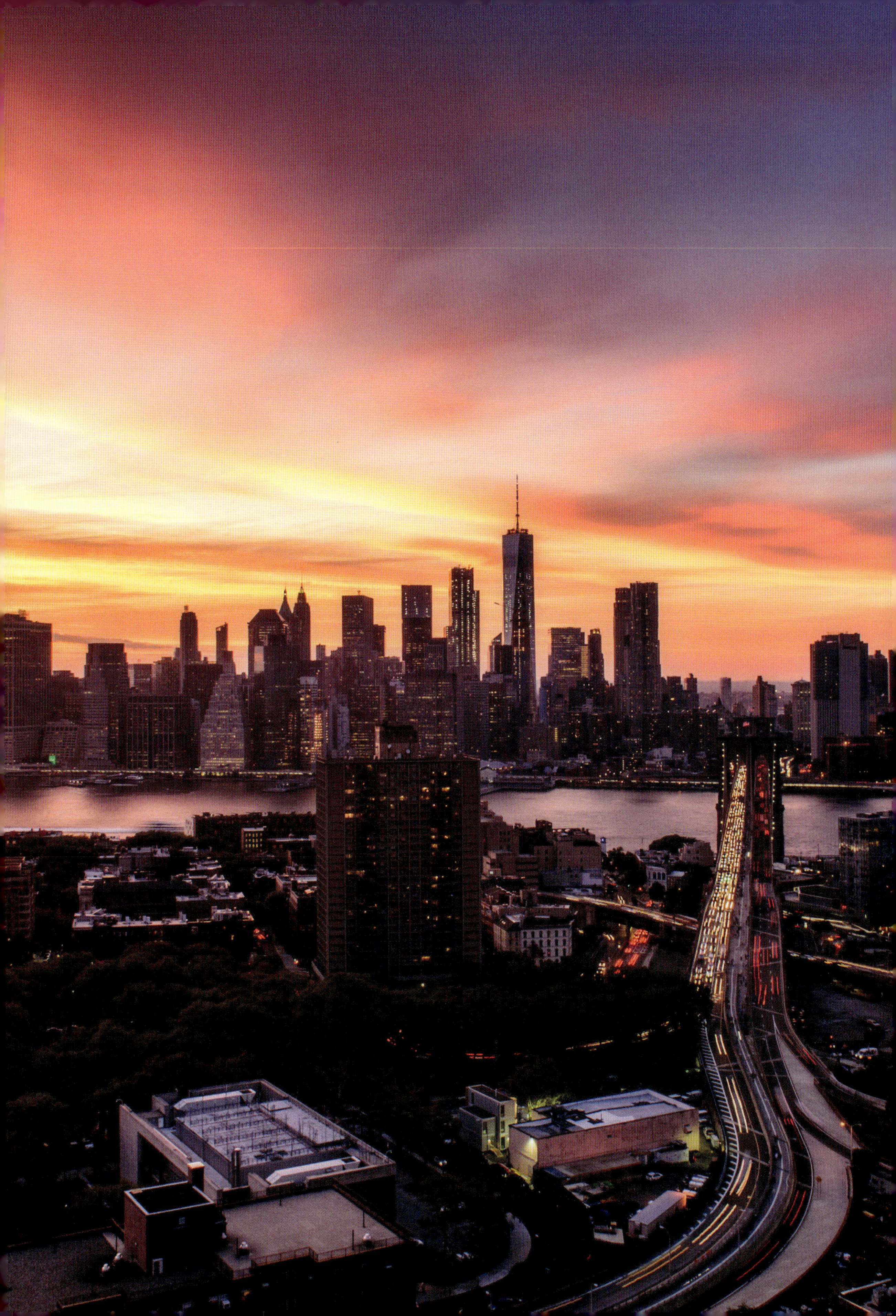

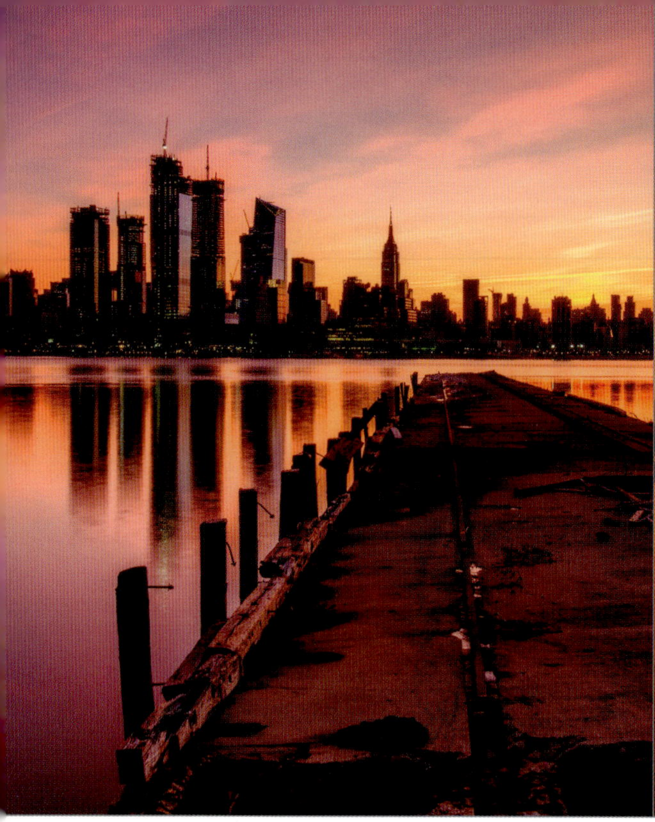

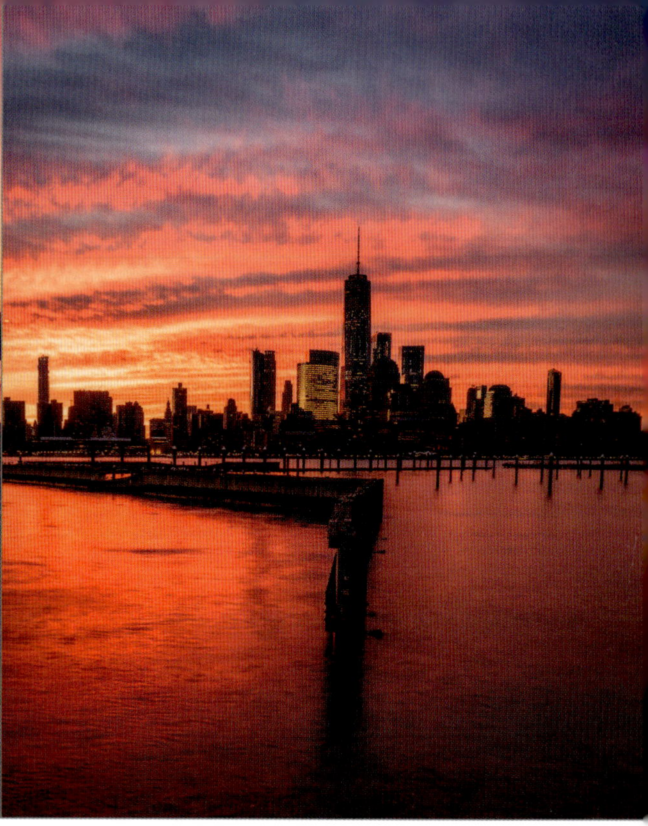

***Hudson Yards.*** *(top left)* This morning view from Hoboken, New Jersey, was truly special as the water of the Hudson River was particularly calm. It has been interesting watching Hudson Yards being built.

***A Favorite Scene.*** *(top right)* Some views are so special that you keep going back – but this was the best. I ran to take a photo while the sky was on fire.

***Fleeting Moments.*** *(below)* It was amazing watching things come together this evening. As the sun set, the light illuminated the buildings in a glow of red and the clouds moved into the perfect position to reflect the fleeting light.

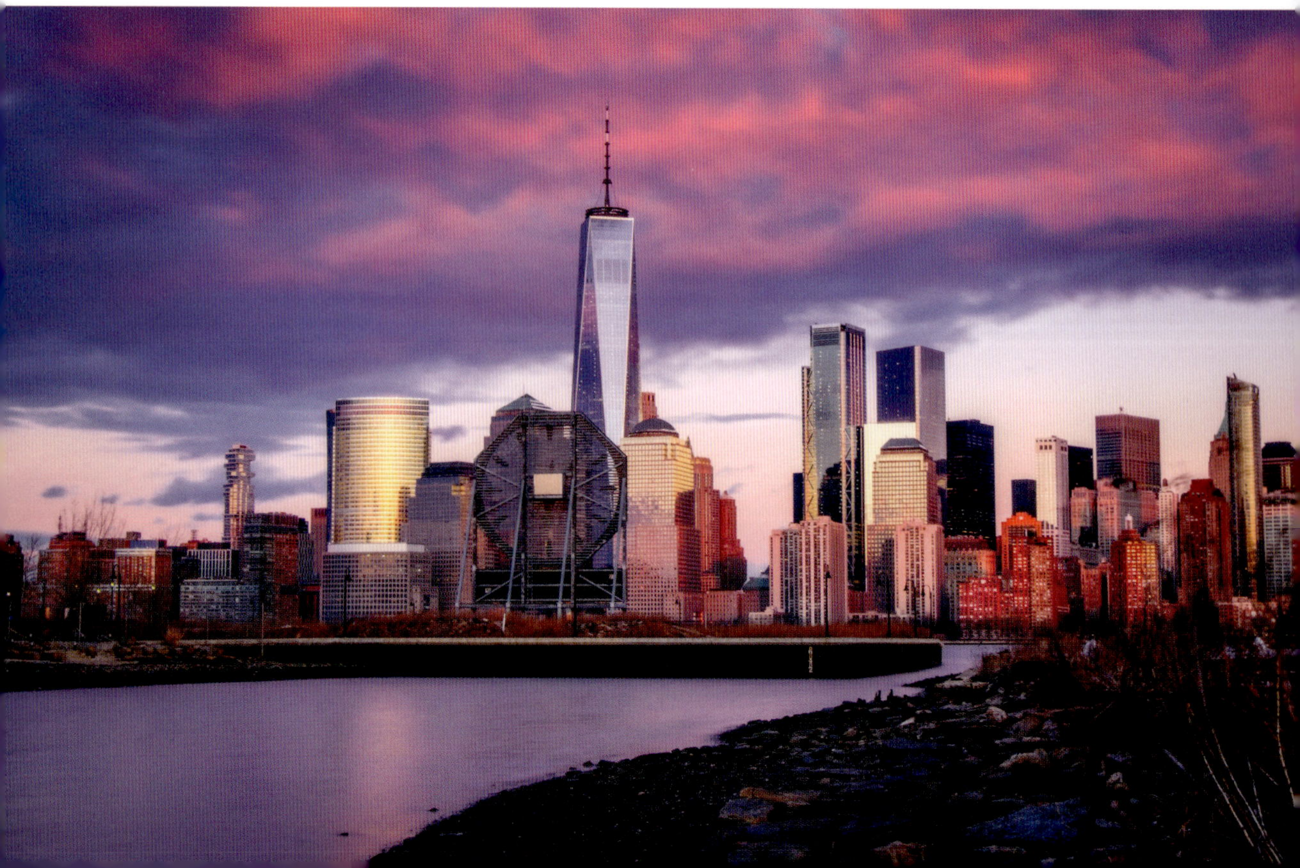

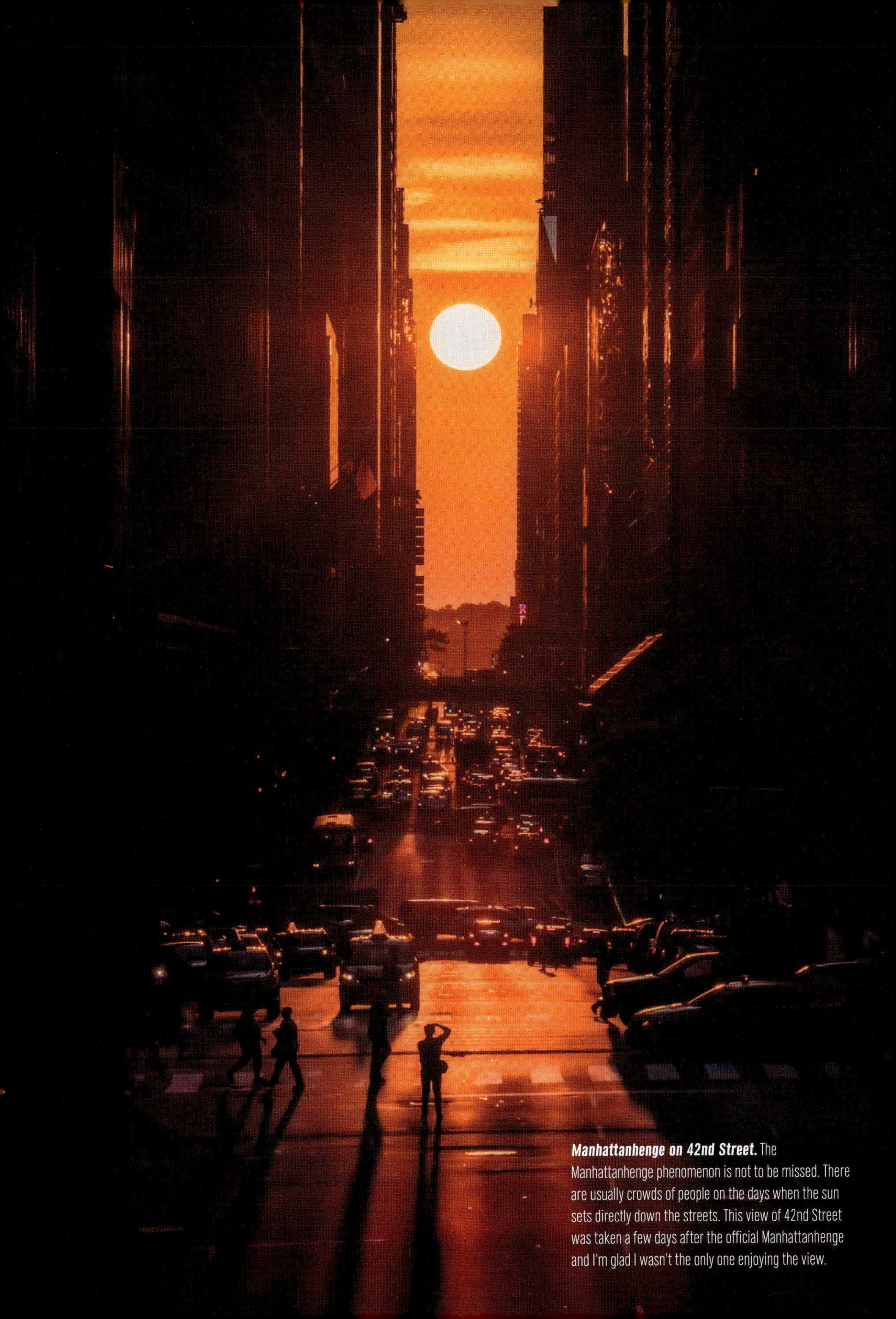

***Manhattanhenge on 42nd Street.*** The Manhattanhenge phenomenon is not to be missed. There are usually crowds of people on the days when the sun sets directly down the streets. This view of 42nd Street was taken a few days after the official Manhattanhenge and I'm glad I wasn't the only one enjoying the view.

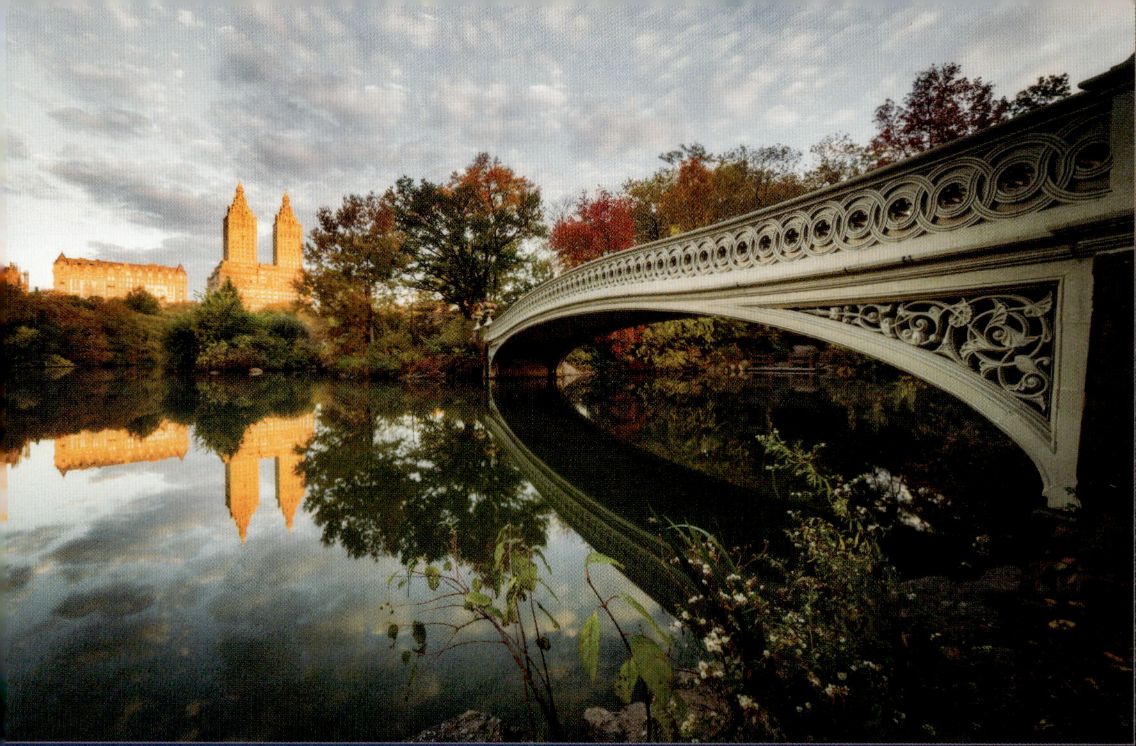

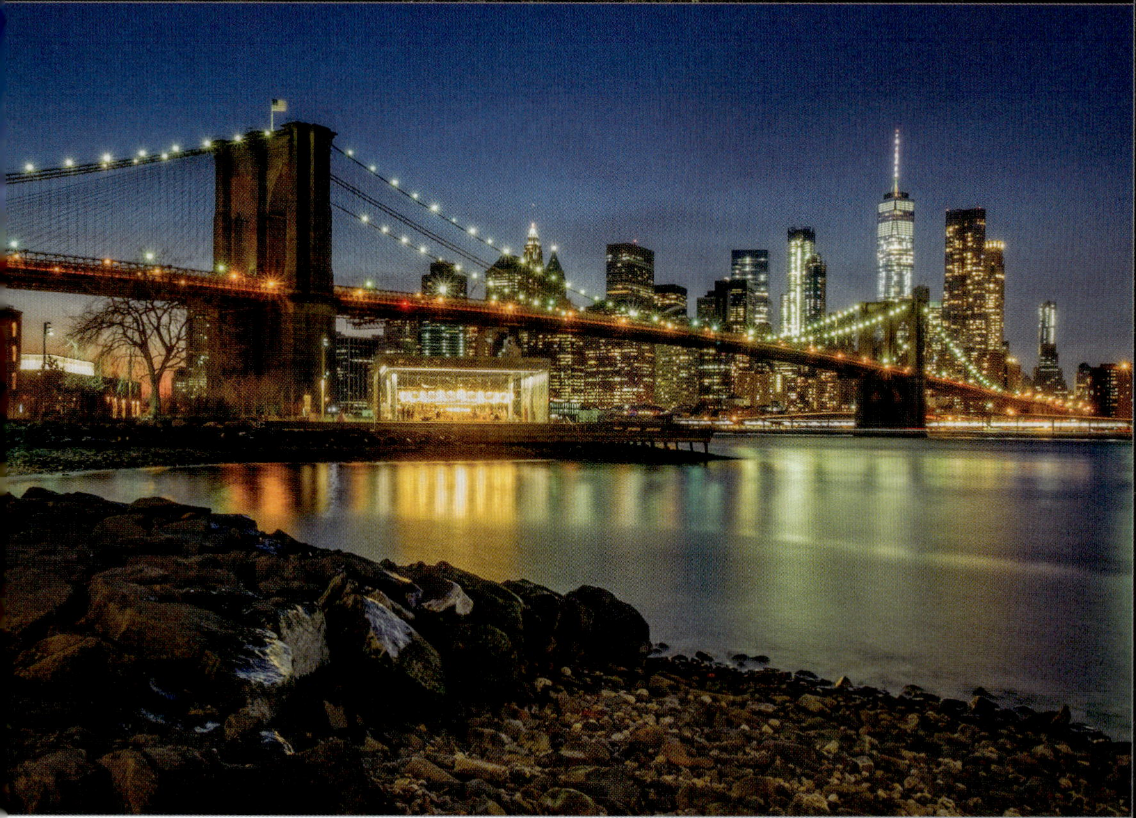

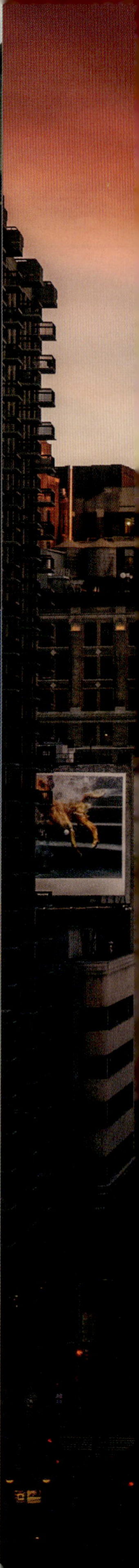

**Morning Reflection.** *(top left)* Here's another example of why sunrises are my favorite. Normally, this area is filled with people and the water is occupied by small boats. I wasn't treated to a colorful sunrise, but the combination of fall tones, warm light on the buildings, and the calm reflection made it special.

**Brooklyn Blues.** *(bottom left)* Brooklyn blues from a classic location. The DUMBO waterfront is a photographer's dream with iconic views of the city. Although some might pack up after sunset, I always stick around for the twinkle of lights along the skyline.

**Flatiron Sunset.** *(facing page)* It took me a long time to figure out the logistics for this photo and even longer to be at the iconic Flatiron Building for a colorful sunset. At one point, I considered this my "holy grail" photo, so I was particularly happy to cross it off my list!

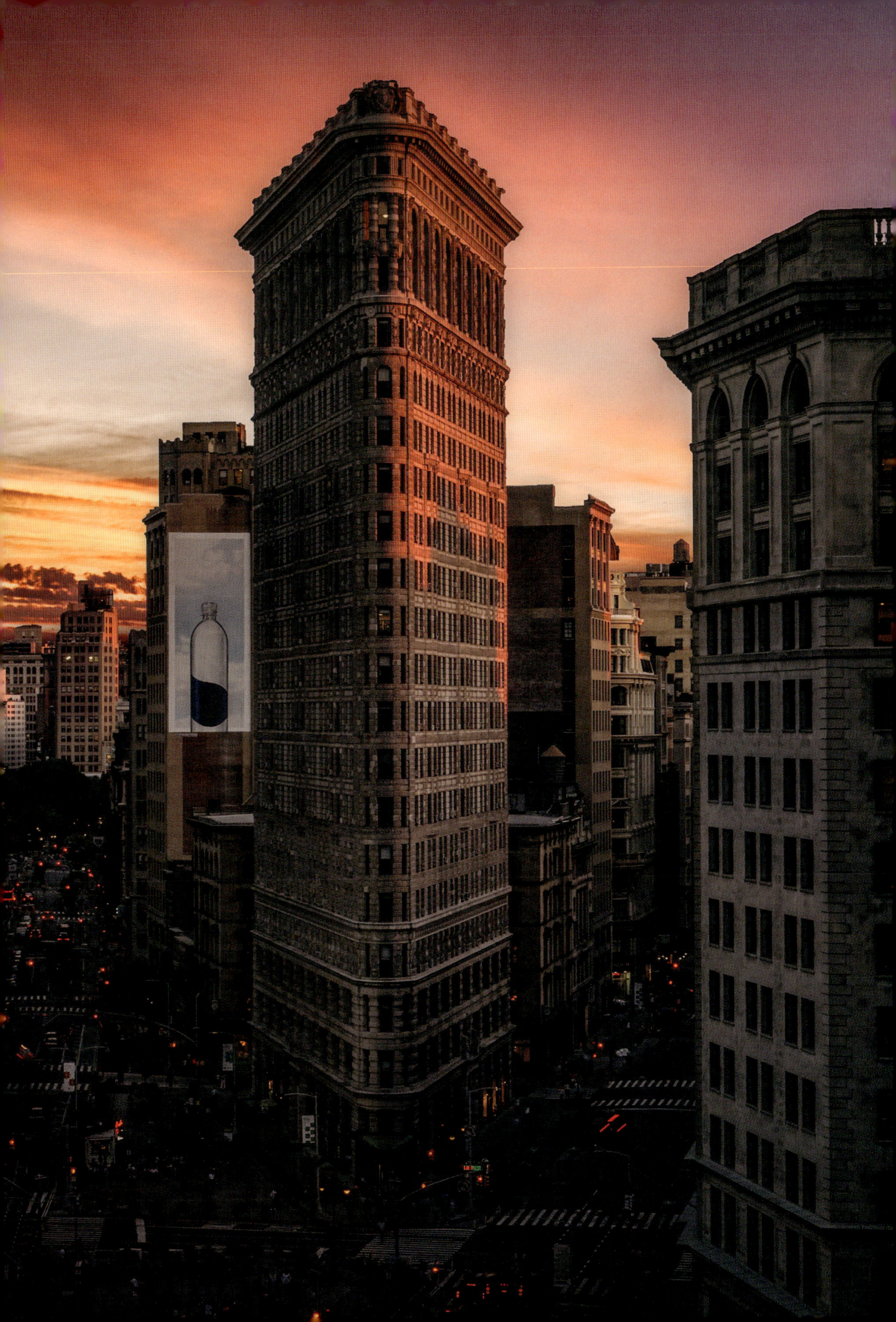

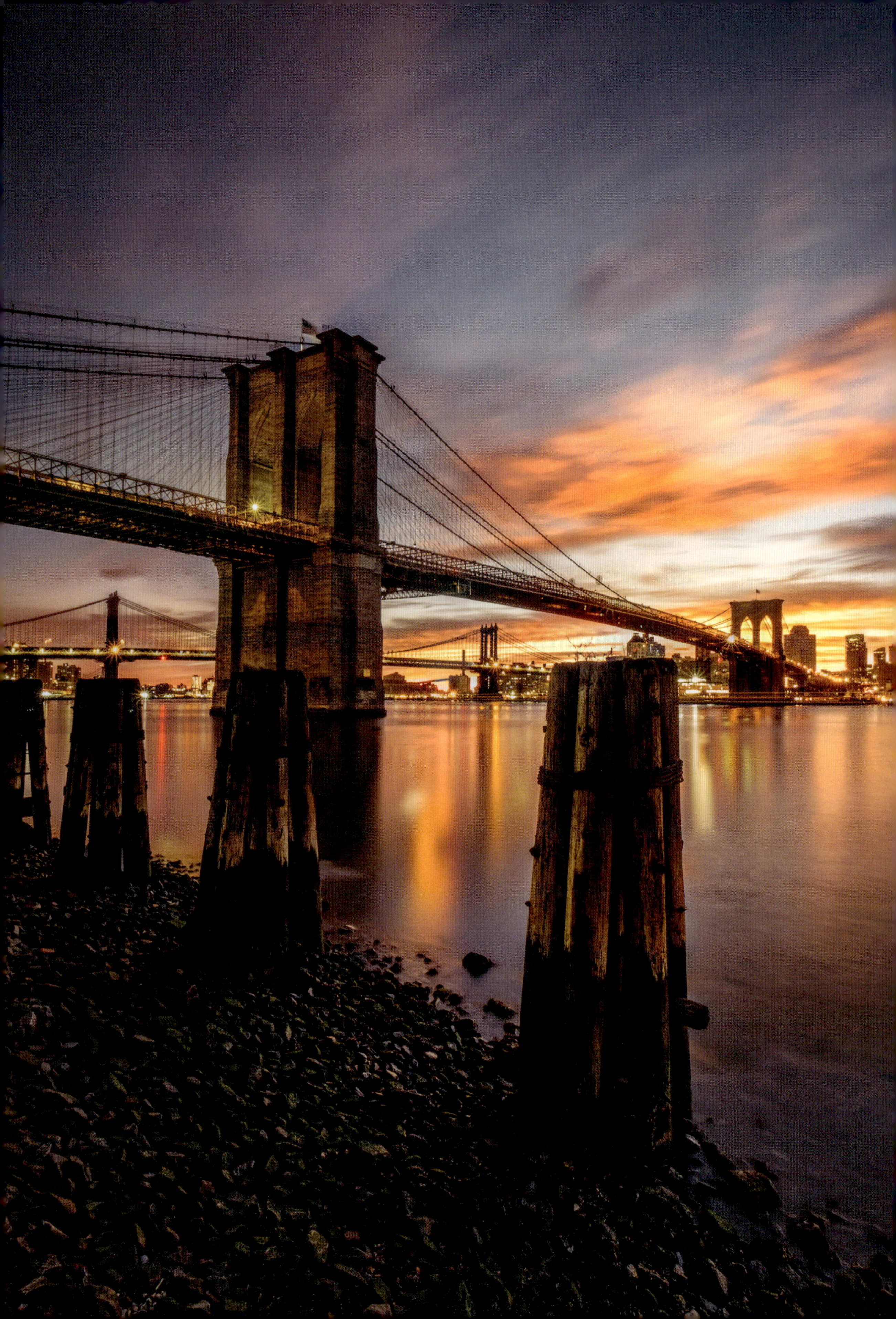

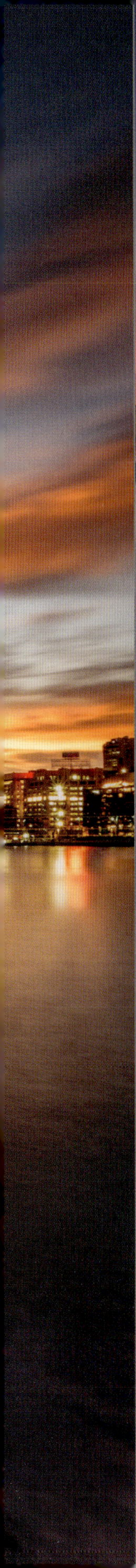

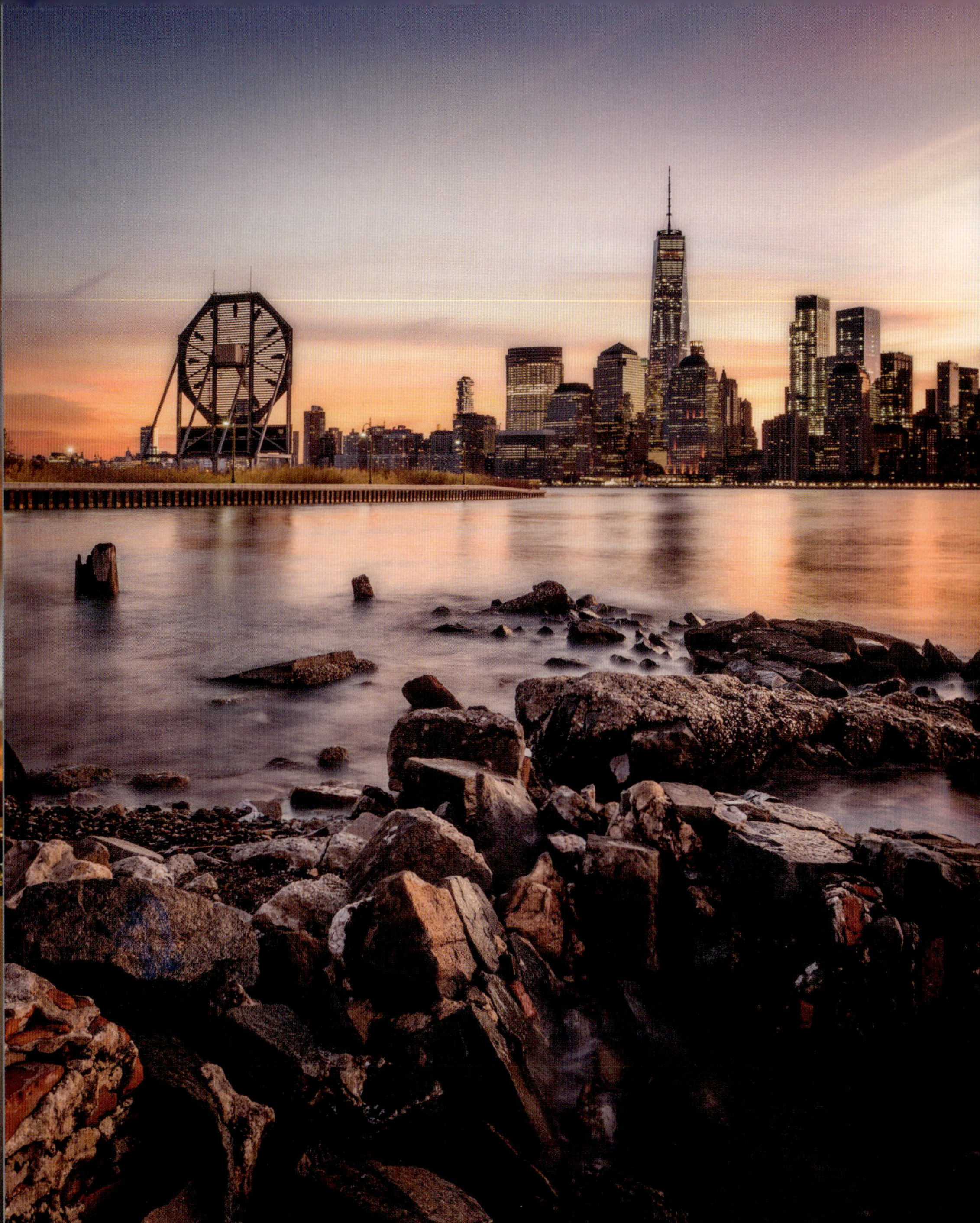

***Morning Light on Brooklyn.*** *(facing page)* Taken on Christmas Eve, the Brooklyn Bridge and Manhattan Bridge stretch across the East River and the morning light illuminates Brooklyn. I met up with some talented photographers this morning and made new friends.

***A Little Extra Effort.*** *(above)* Sometimes, taking a photo requires a little extra effort. To capture this scene, I set my tripod up in the water and had frozen, wet toes. I'm consistently drawn to photographing the rocks along the waterfront and exploring new spots.

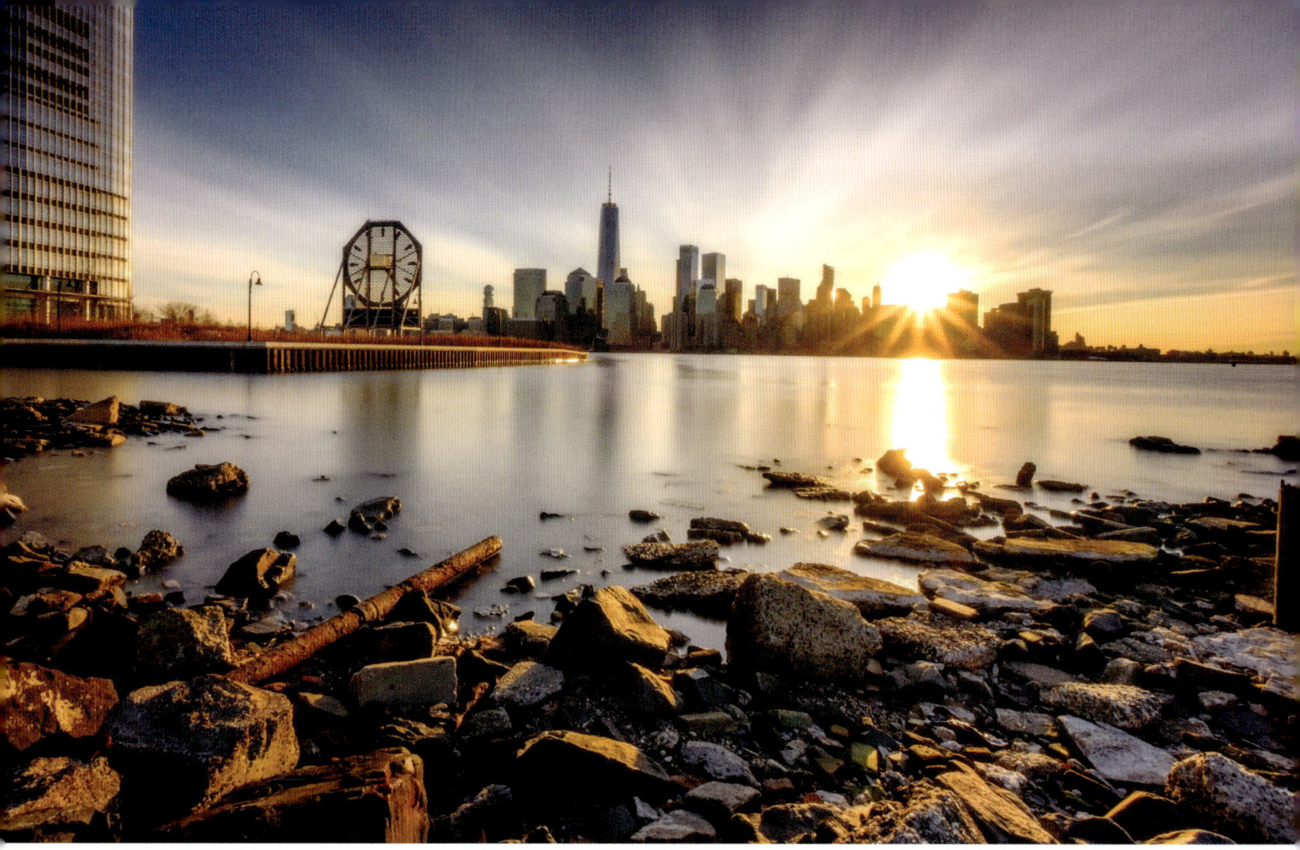

**Dawn Breaks Over Manhattan.** *(above)* The sun makes its first appearance of the day behind Manhattan. The warm morning light glowing along the rocks and the slow crash of the waves are therapeutic to me. Waking up is always difficult—but I never regret it once I'm there.

**A Quiet Morning.** *(bottom left)* I wish that quiet moments like this lasted longer than a few minutes, but that's what makes them special.

**Watching for the Light.** *(bottom right)* One of the main things I focus on in my photos is light. Although I usually prefer colorful clouds, I also enjoy watching the light dance along the skyline in the moments before the sun sets.

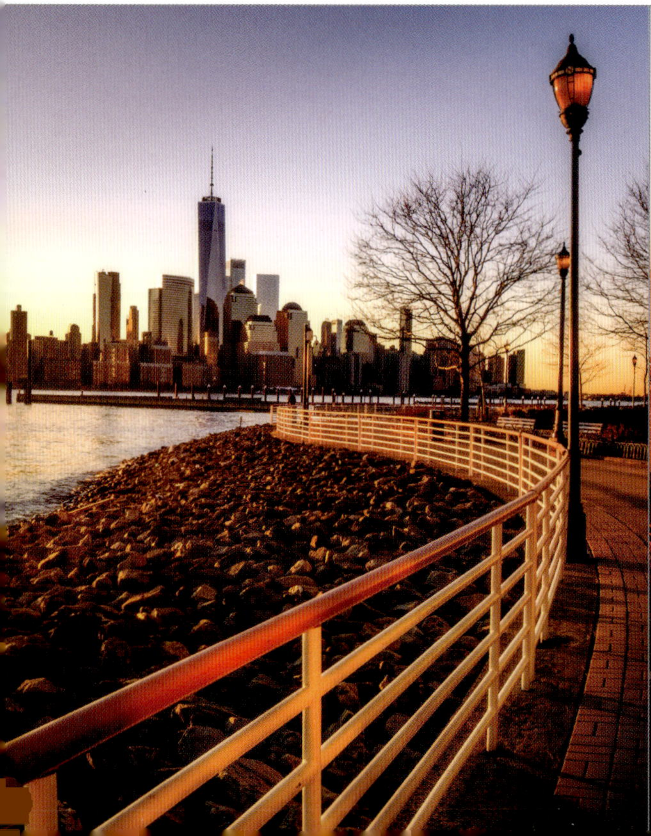

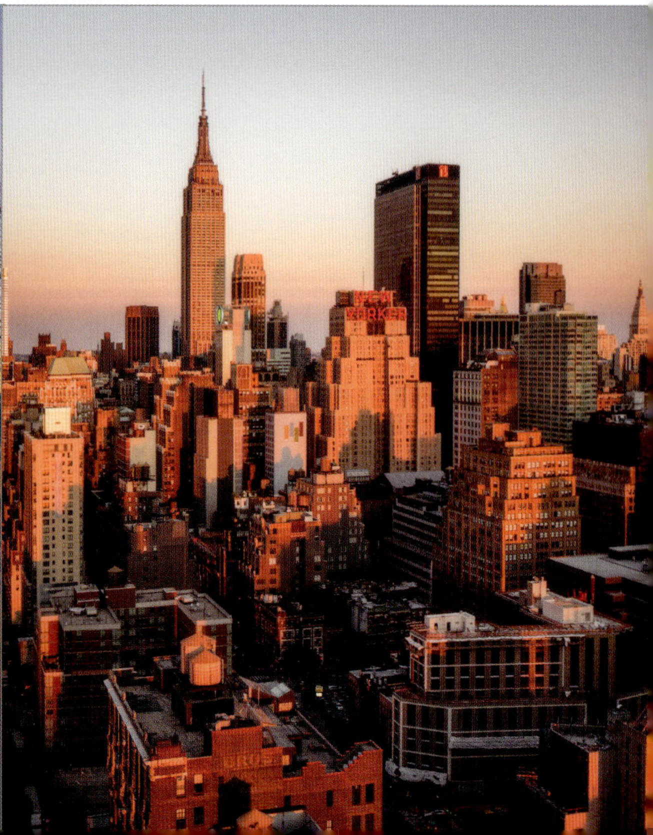

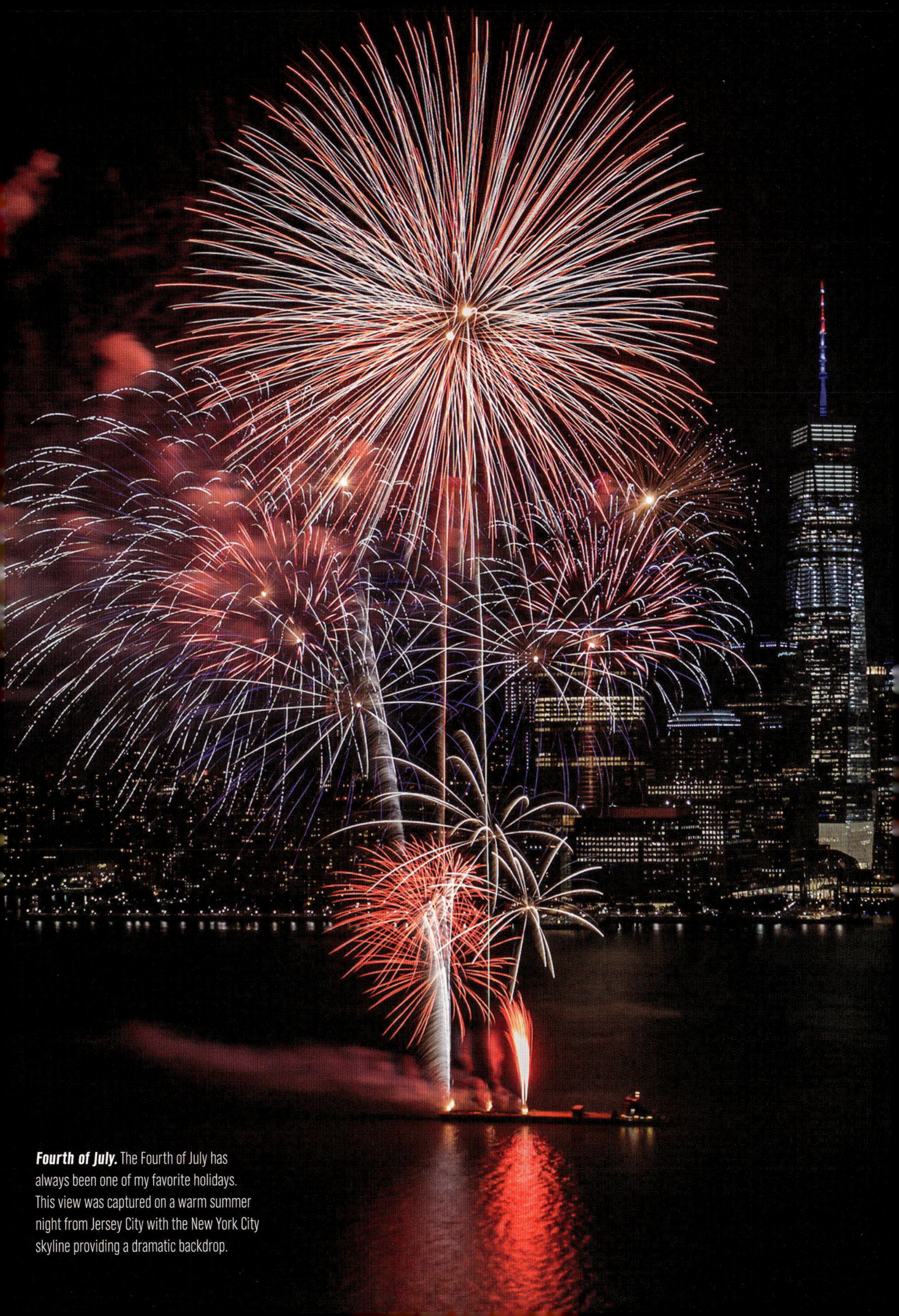

***Fourth of July.*** The Fourth of July has always been one of my favorite holidays. This view was captured on a warm summer night from Jersey City with the New York City skyline providing a dramatic backdrop.

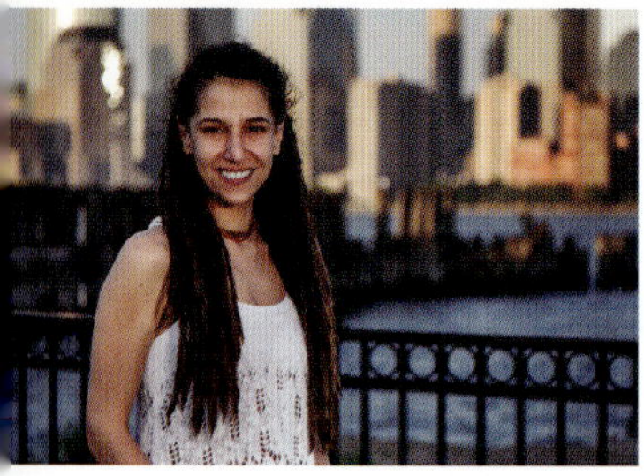

CHAPTER 7

# Karine Sayegh

Instagram: @ksayegh_photography ■ www.facebook.com/ksayeghphotography

I was neither born nor raised in New York City. Rather, I began this marvel called "life" across the Atlantic Ocean along the Mediterranean Sea in a city that was once referred to as the "Paris of the East"—Beirut, Lebanon. The civil war was in full effect at that time and my parents decided that leaving the country was the best bet for stability. Of course, they were right. So, we meandered off to the neighboring country of Syria, where we resided for seven years. Then we came London for a couple of years, Malaysia for a few, and to the Philippines for a solid several more.

It was a remarkable jambalaya of travel, culture, experience, and change, but also a structured one; school, college, work, marriage, kids, etc., were all planned out. So, you can't be surprised when I say that nothing, and I mean *nothing,* compared to the experience of setting foot in New York City.

**The Color of Sunrise.** *(below)* An exquisite winter morning as the sun rises over the Empire State Building, bringing an explosion of miraculous color.

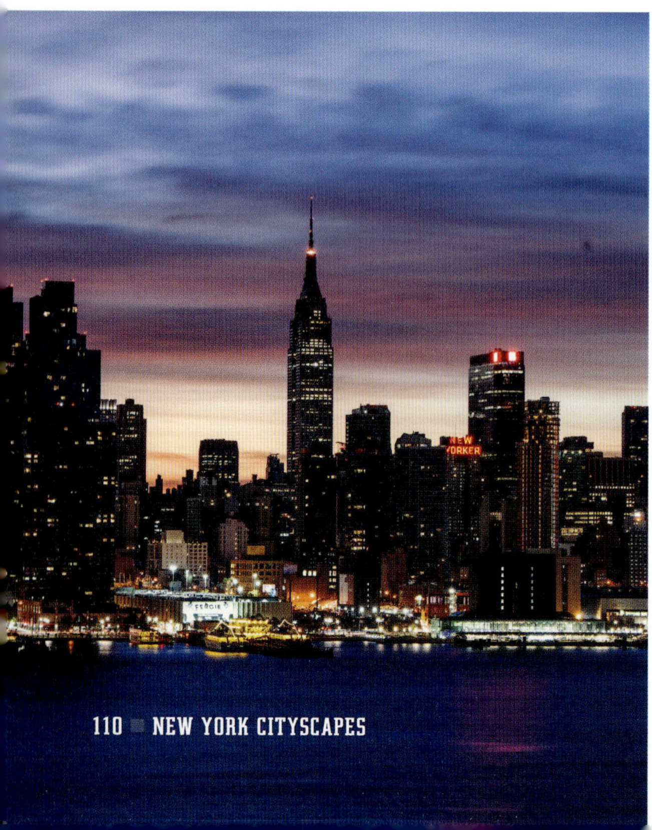

At the age of eighteen, while I was still in Manila, I decided that I wanted to go to New York University (NYU) for my undergraduate degree. Why not, right? It was in New York City, the cultural melting pot of the world, and it was a great liberal arts school with an awesome fine arts program. Harmless, right? Wrong!

From the minute I landed in John F. Kennedy airport, I was petrified! Everything was on overdrive. "Chaos" was the only word I could use to describe it at the time. And, hey, nobody had taught me how to handle *chaos* in my structured plan!

I remember first getting off of the subway stop at West 4th street in the West Village of Manhattan and thinking to myself, "How in the world am I going to make it through the next four years?" The crowds, the density, the sensory overload—I was convinced that New York would engulf me at any minute, then chew me up and spit my bones out like a chicken wing.

Dorm life was another culture shock. It wasn't until I moved off campus, to a quaint Upper East Side neighborhood in Manhattan, that I finally began to find my place in the "world" (the term "world" here equals New York). Ironically, it was New York herself that taught me how to find my place. Our bond grew stronger month after month, year after year. I grew to love her organized chaos, her constant radiating energy—in other words, her *life.* Yes, I refer to New York as a lady, an elegant one, with a mysterious essence in many forms.

Upon graduation, I knew The Big Apple was where I was meant to be—for two main reasons. First, New York City impelled me to pursue my goals without reservation. Second, it afforded me

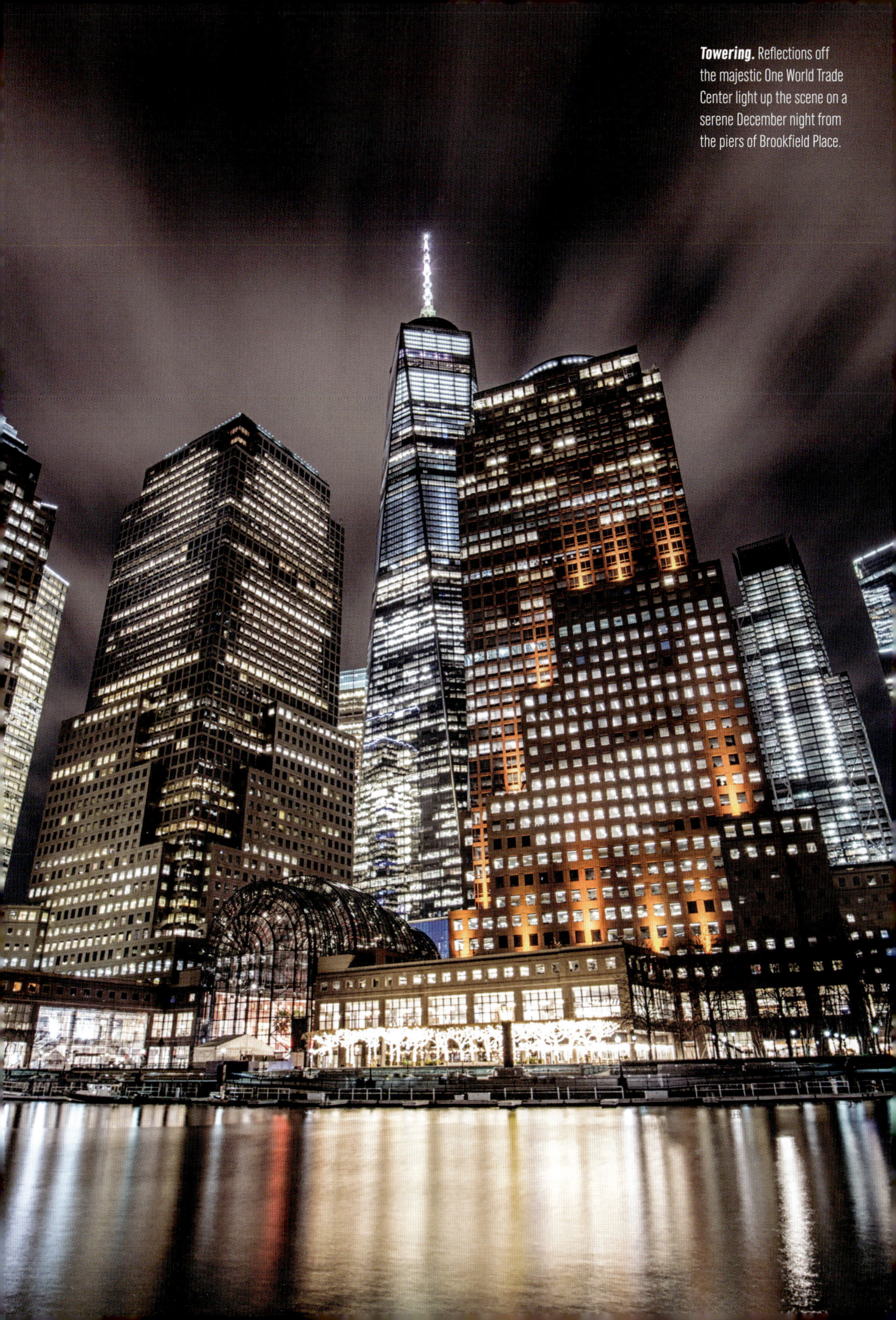

***Towering.*** Reflections off the majestic One World Trade Center light up the scene on a serene December night from the piers of Brookfield Place.

with the outlet to do so creatively. (*Hint:* Photography was a big part of it. I'll get to that in a moment.)

And here I am today. I currently reside across the Hudson River in Jersey City, New Jersey, where I have the valued luxury of experiencing New York City's breathtaking skyline every day; it's one of the reasons I moved from Manhattan. By day, I'm a Human Resource Business Partner at a multi-national professional services firm where my creativity is leveraged through eminence and strategy. By night, on weekends, and anytime in between, I identify as a photographer.

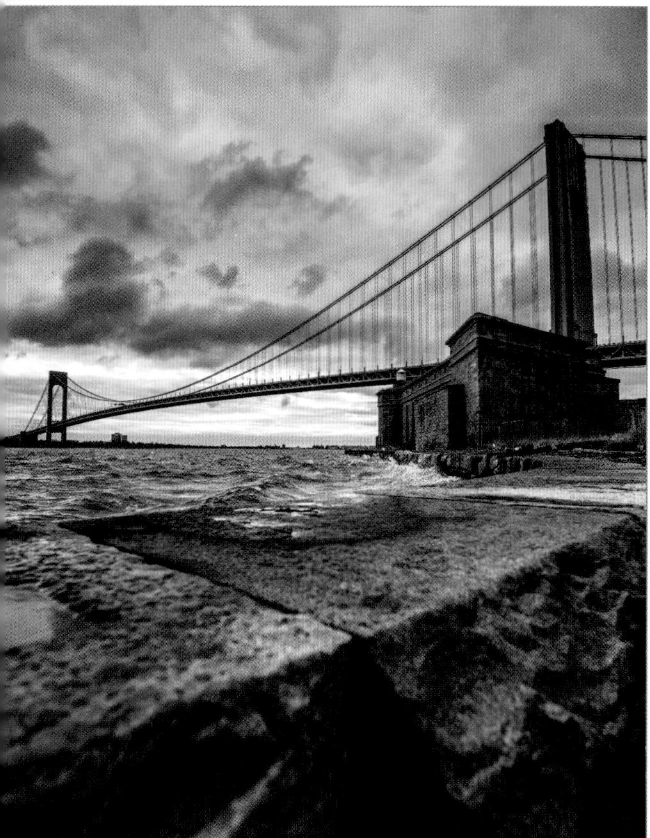

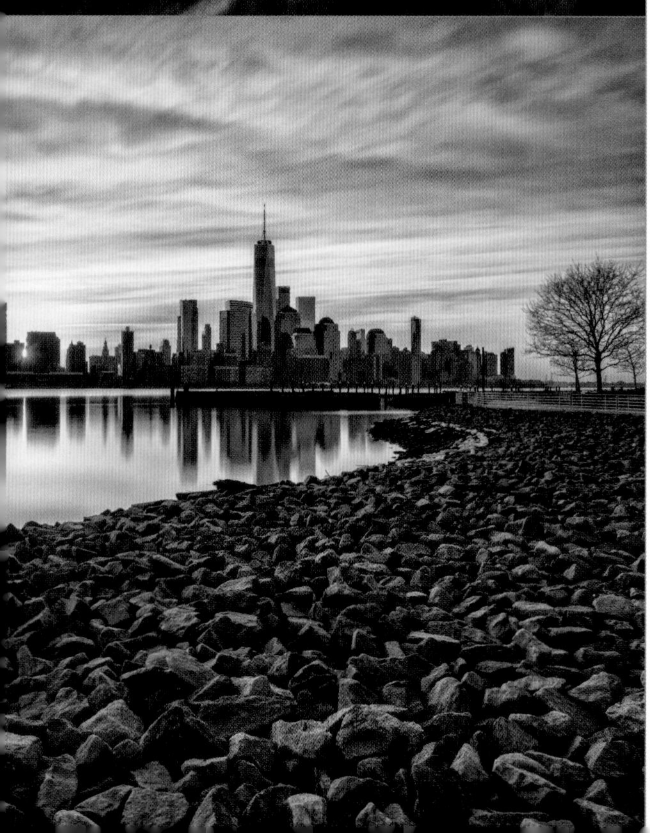

I was first introduced to the wonder of photography during my second year at NYU and immediately fell in love with it. Photography literally transformed the way I experienced my everyday surroundings, allowing me to notice details normally taken for granted: light, shadows, reflections, shapes, colors, angles, and lines—in other words, beauty. It was these details that permitted me to live in the moment, to appreciate the here and now. They showed me that not everything had to be structured and laid out. What once felt ominous about New York City's chaos became—and remains—absolutely glorious.

My photographic inspiration is driven by New York's cityscape—the view of the city. I'm drawn to it because, through all these years, New York proved that she holds no motives or expectations. She seeks nothing and asks for nothing. She's present as-is, through a kind of selflessness and elegance that, to me, defines sheer magnificence and poise. This simple complexity is what I strive to represent through my images.

Going forward, my intention is to continue to hone my eye for a subject and to improve my technical skills with the hope of inspiring and educating others who are passionate about the craft.

Just as important, I'd like to thank my parents and sister for their unconditional support and encouragement through the years, and my fellow photographers for motivating me to try new techniques and explore different locations through their incredible art.

I hope you all like my collection presented here!

**Waves.** *(top left)* New York Harbor's rough waters crash onto Fort Wadsworth, a former military installation located on Staten Island. The Verrazano-Narrows Bridge in the background connects Brooklyn and Staten Island.

**Reflections.** *(bottom left)* One World Trade Center reflects on the Hudson during a peaceful winter morning along the Newport Waterfront.

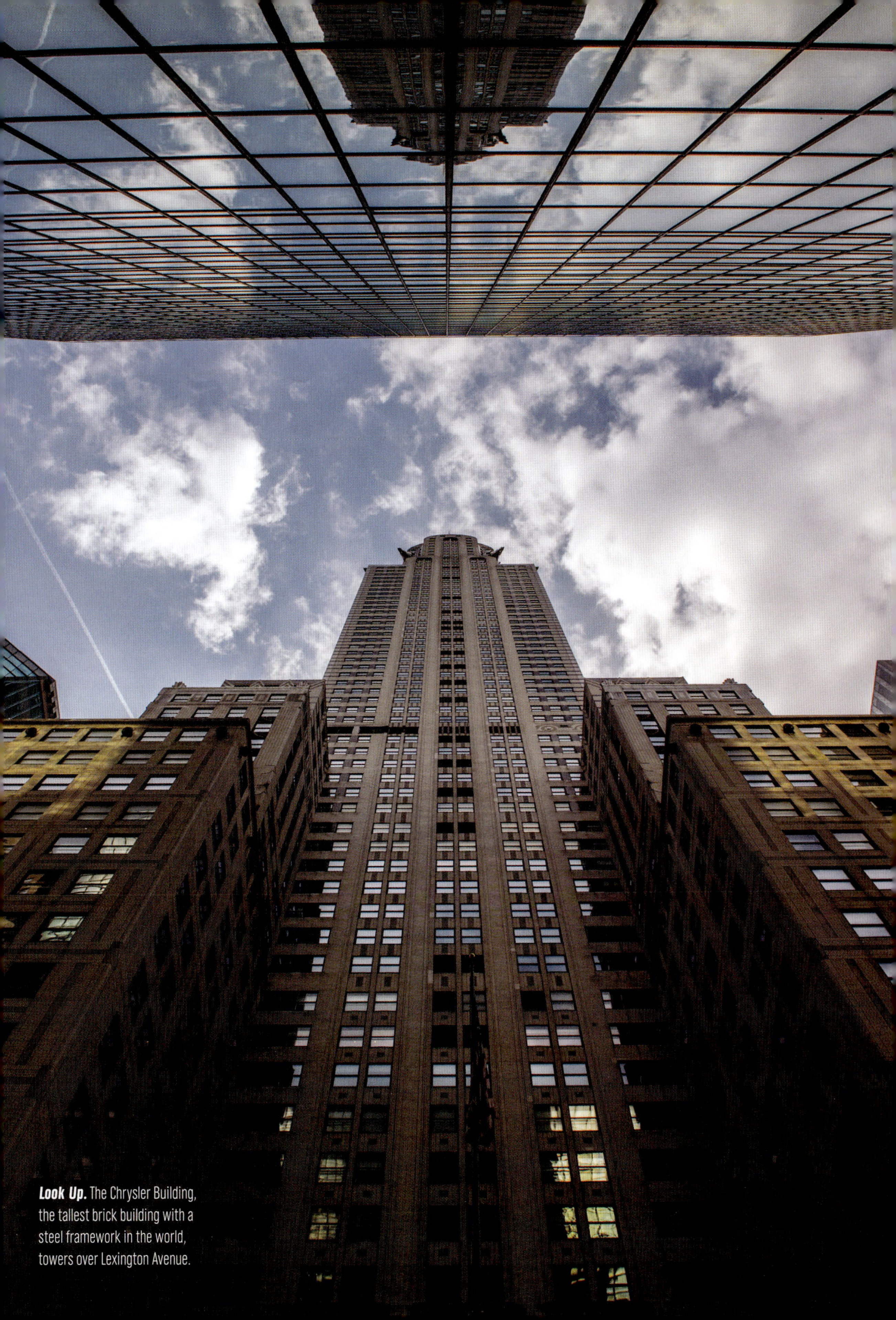

***Look Up.*** The Chrysler Building, the tallest brick building with a steel framework in the world, towers over Lexington Avenue.

**Framed.** *(below)* On a golden Saturday morning, the Freedom Tower (One World Trade Center) was visible from across the Hudson River through a broken pier belonging to the Historic Central Railroad of New Jersey Terminal in Liberty State Park.

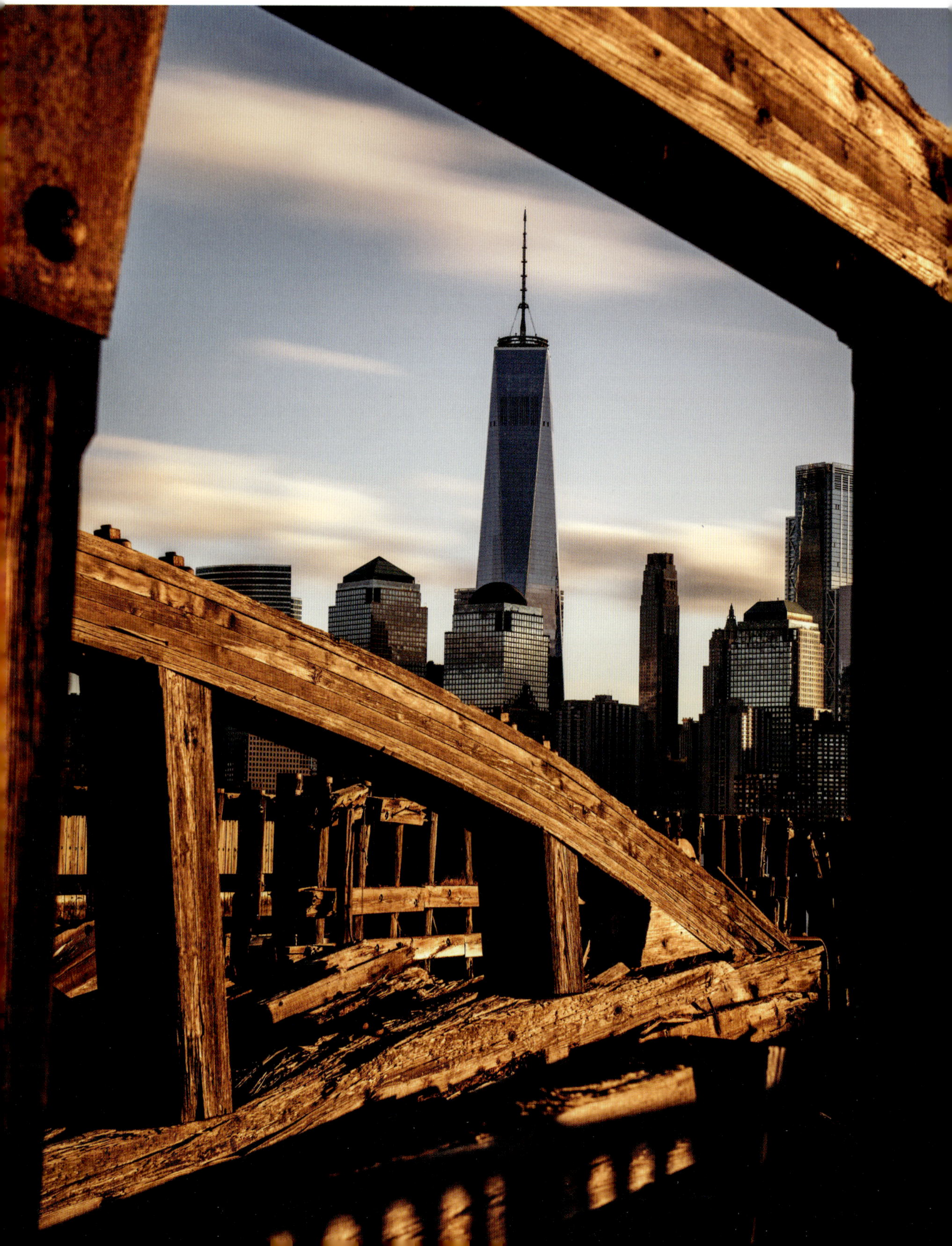

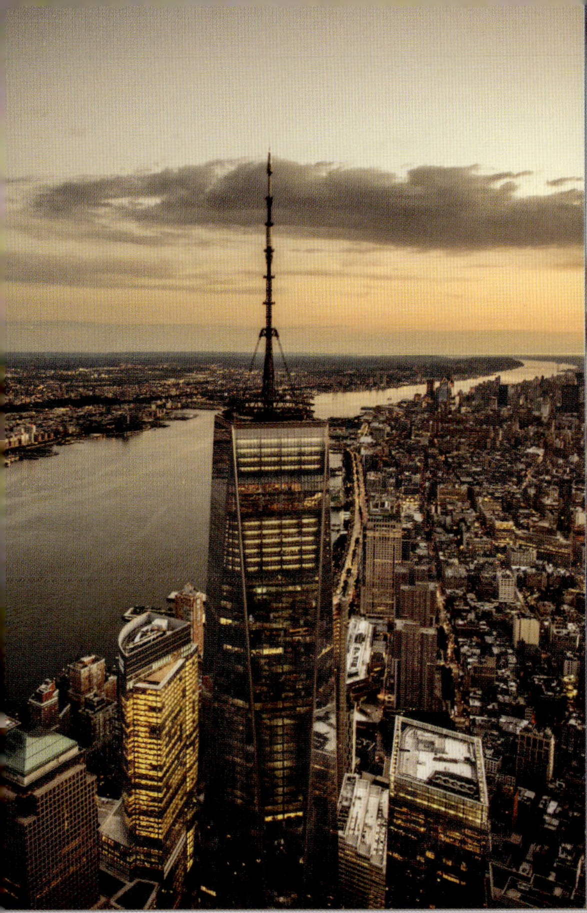

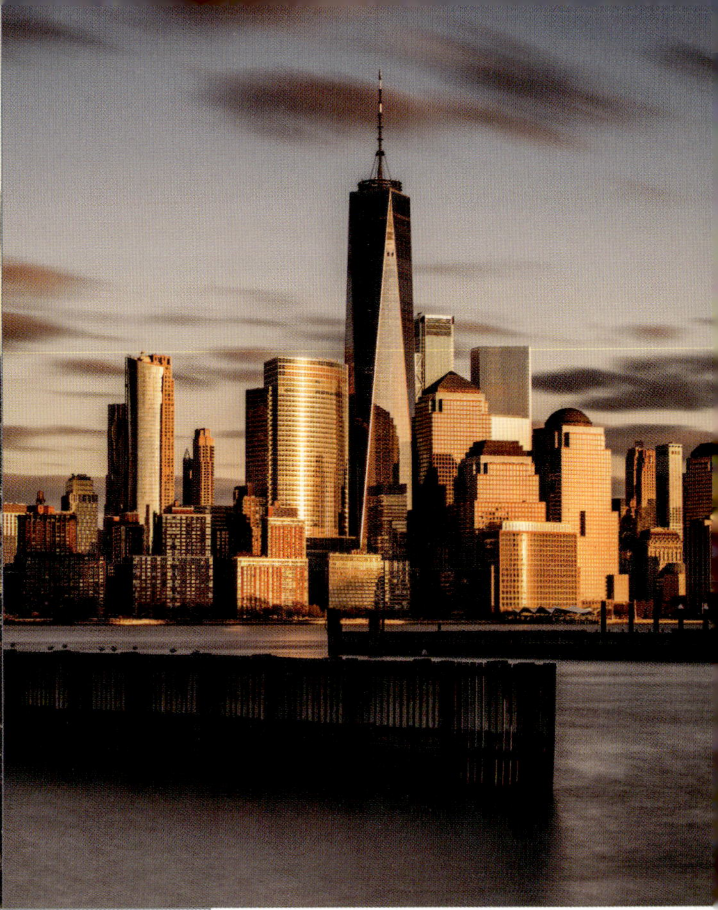

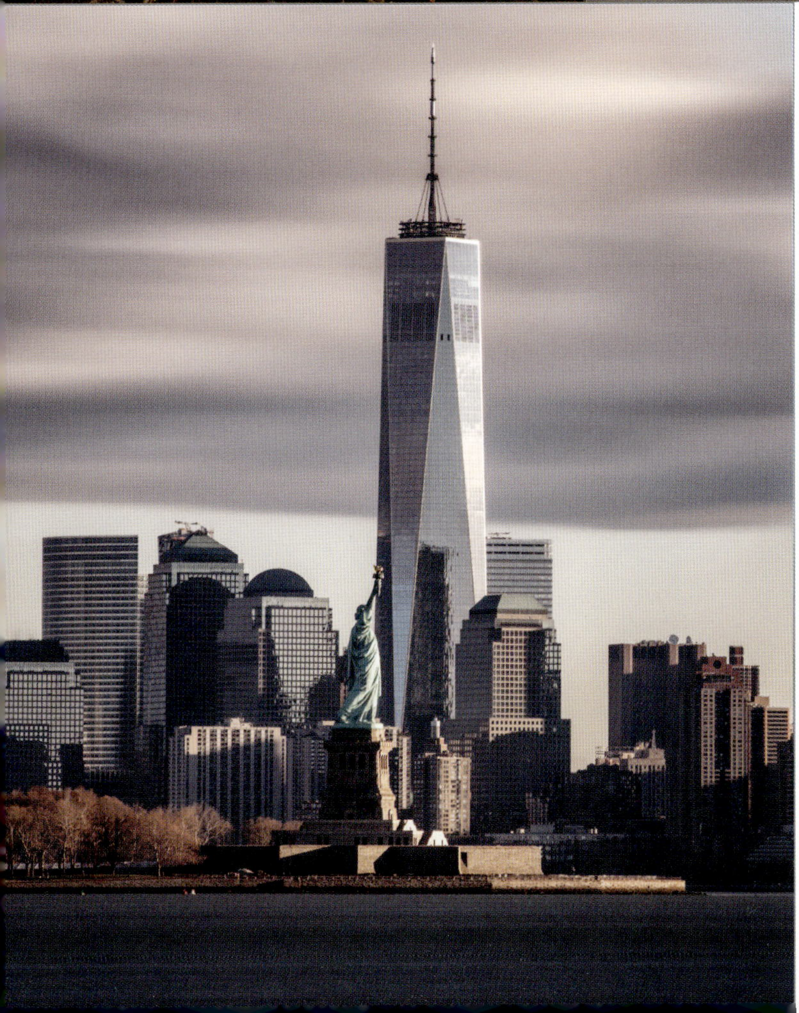

**Golden Hour.** *(top left)* An aerial close-up of the Freedom Tower at dawn as the city begins its day.

**Golden Towers.** *(top right)* The golden glow of the setting sun echoes off of Manhattan's Financial District on a crisp Sunday afternoon.

**Dynamic Duo.** *(left)* This image was taken from a hidden gem of a spot along the coast of Bayonne, New Jersey, where there's a perfectly lined up view of the Freedom Tower and Lady Liberty.

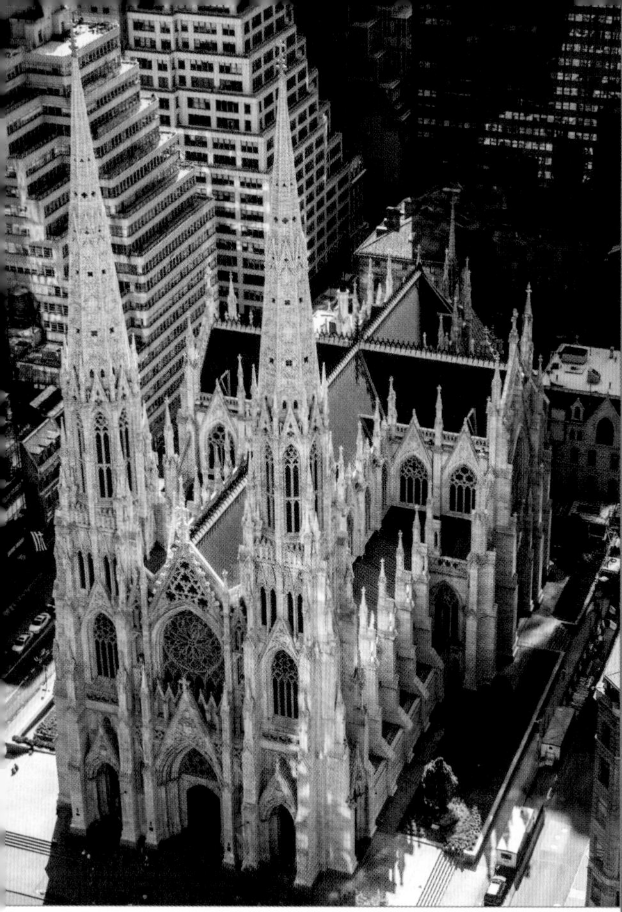

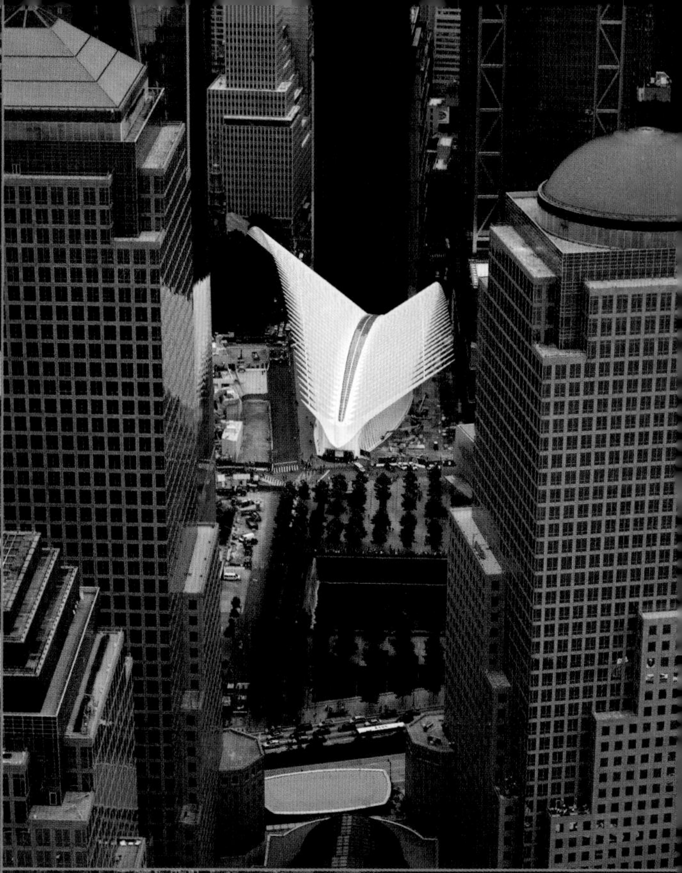

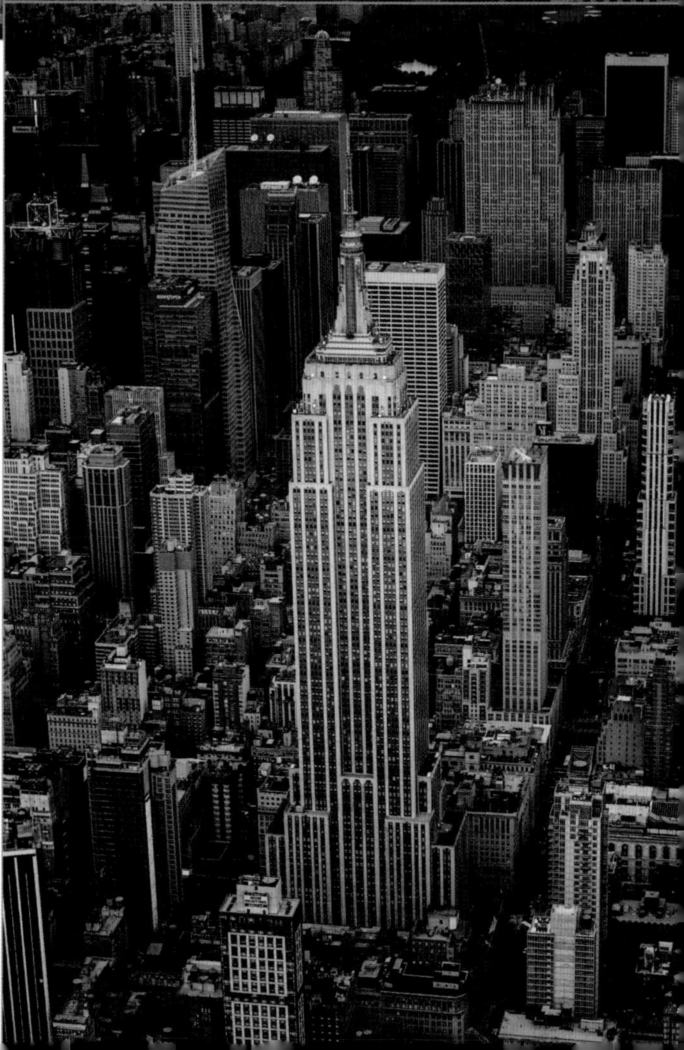

***An Intricate Symbol.*** *(top left)* Viewed from the overlook at Rockefeller Center, this is the iconic Cathedral of St. Patrick (commonly called St. Patrick's Cathedral). Every year, the church is visited by more than five million people of every different nationality and faith.

***Connection.*** *(top right)* This is an aerial view of Oculus, the transportation hub at the rebuilt World Trade Center site.

***The ESB.*** *(bottom right)* In this aerial portrait, the Big Apple's Empire State Building is watching over the city with elegance and finesse.

***The Heart of New York.*** *(facing page)* Flying high over the northern end of Manhattan, I captured this image of Central Park on a glorious summer morning.

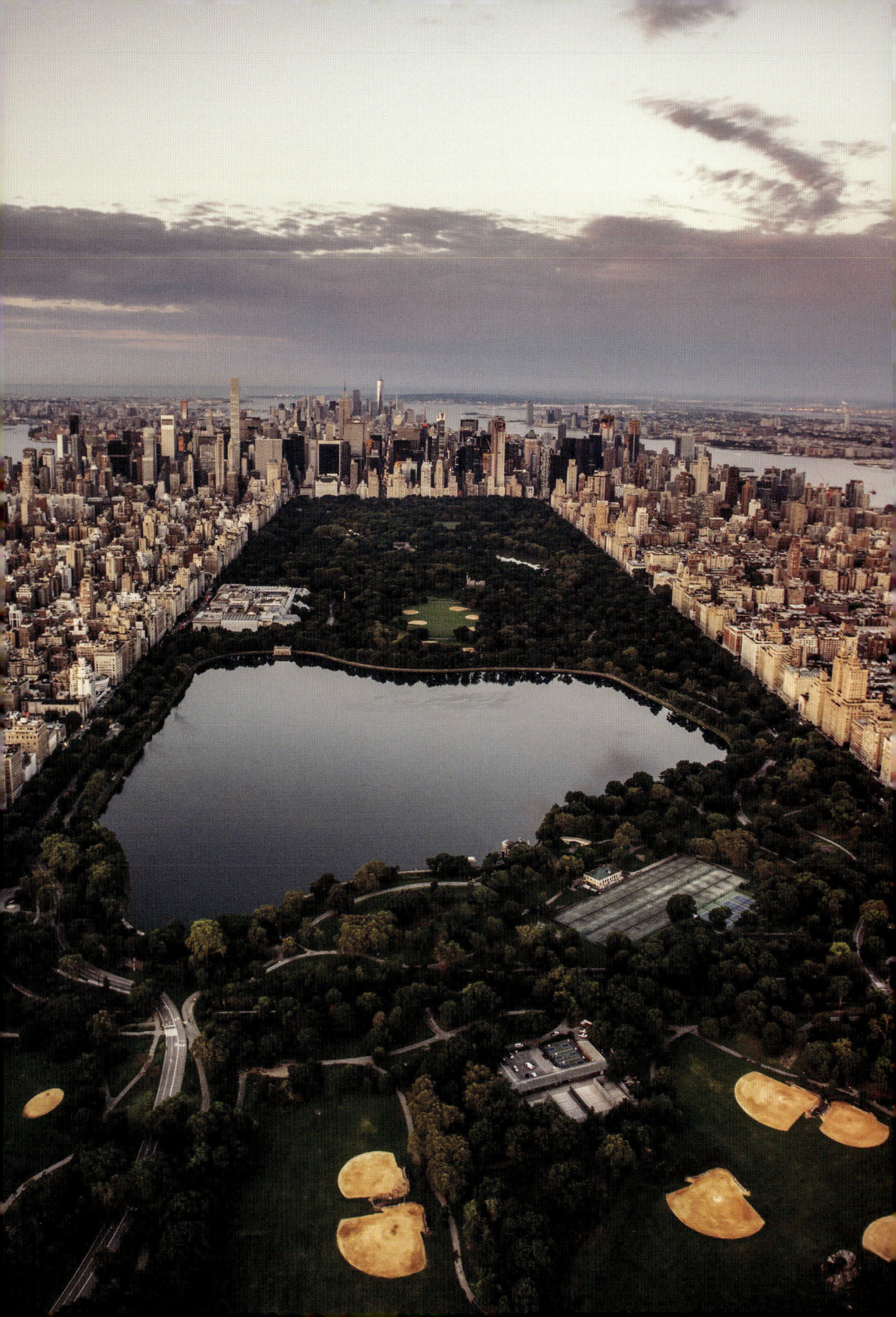

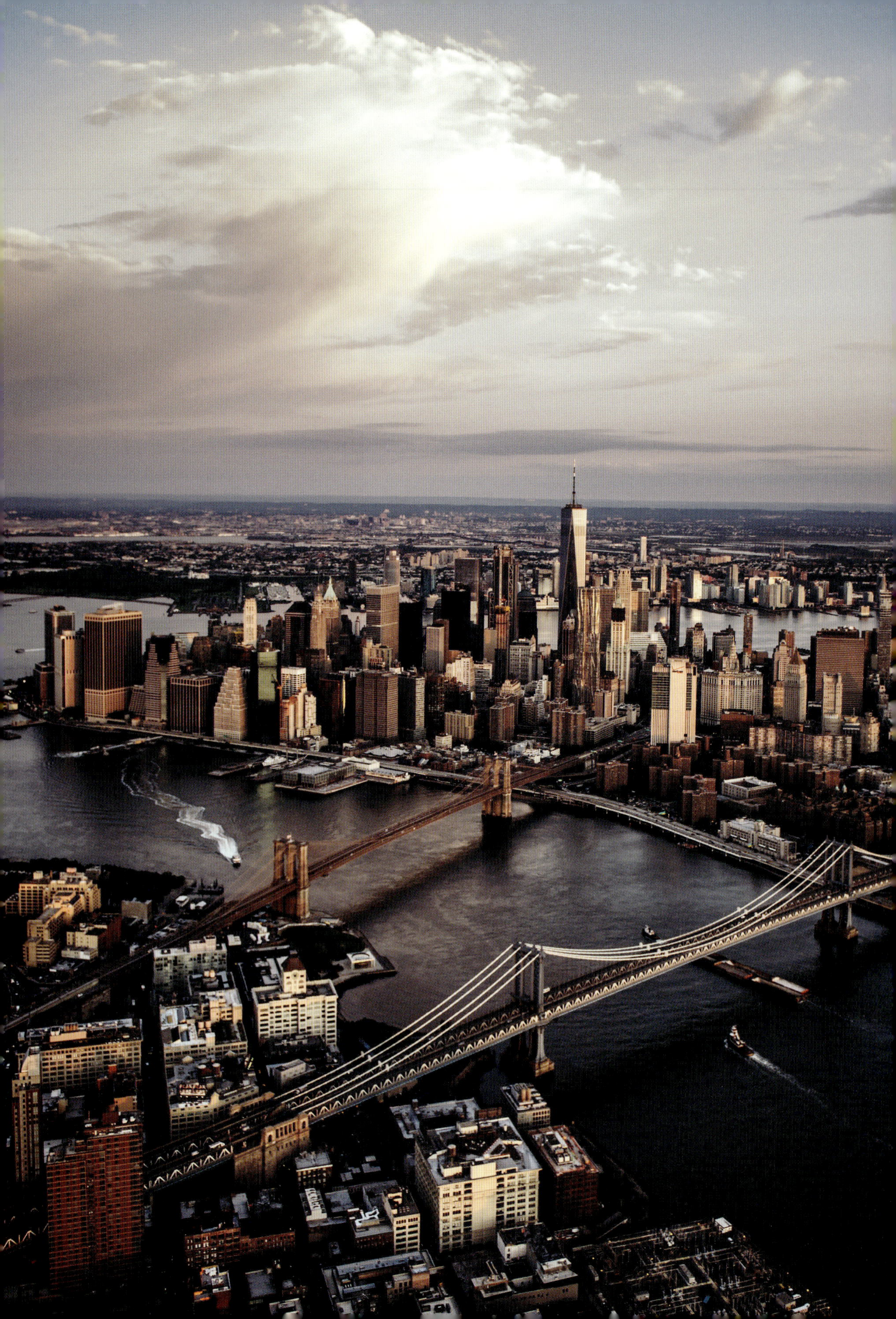

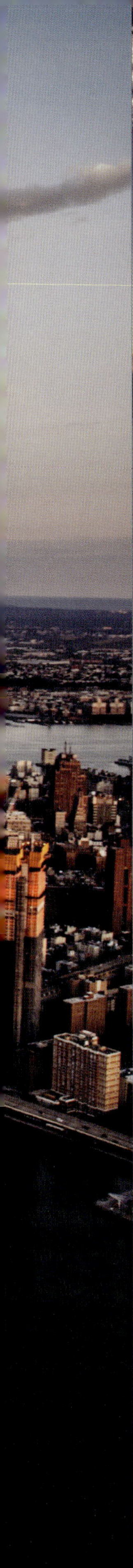

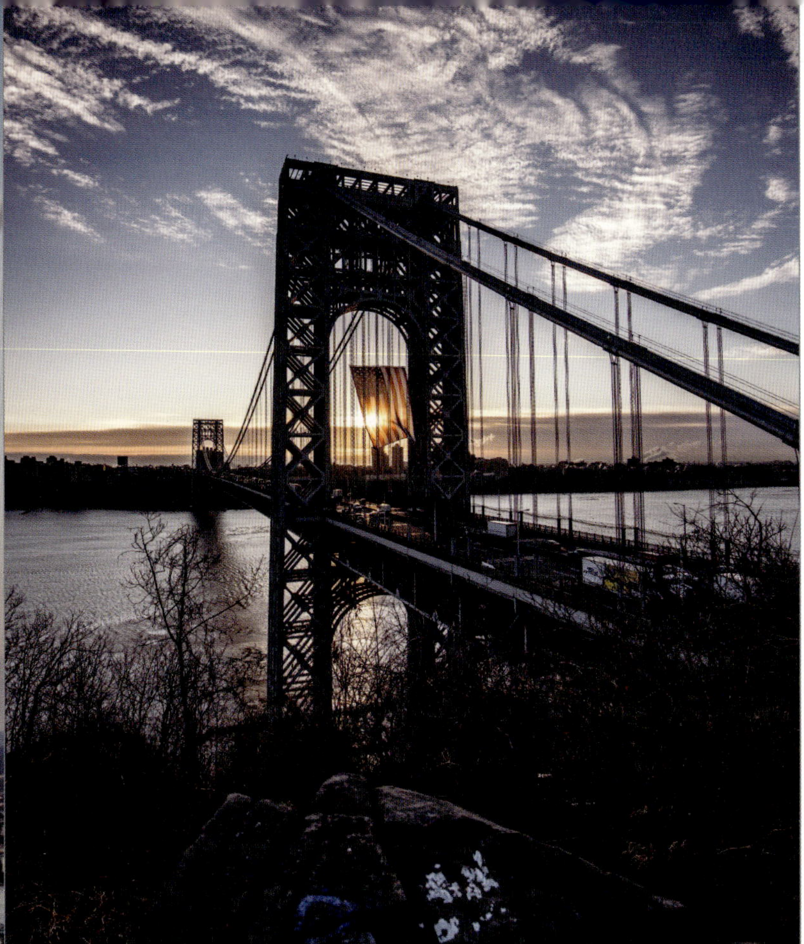

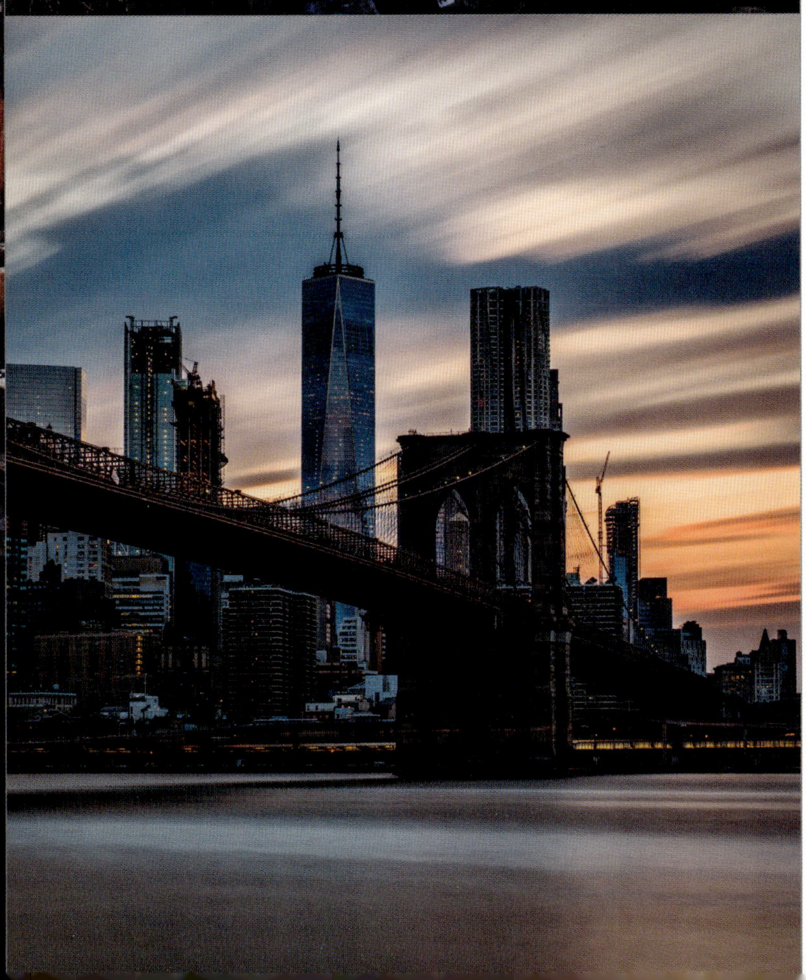

***Bridges.*** *(facing page)* From a sky-high view, we see New York's Brooklyn and Manhattan Bridges connecting lower Manhattan to the borough of Brooklyn.

***POTUS.*** *(top left)* The sun radiates through the world's largest free-hanging American flag, unfurled on the George Washington Bridge in honor of Memorial Day.

***120 Seconds.*** *(bottom left)* The day bids farewell as the sun sets behind Lower Manhattan from Brooklyn Bridge Park.

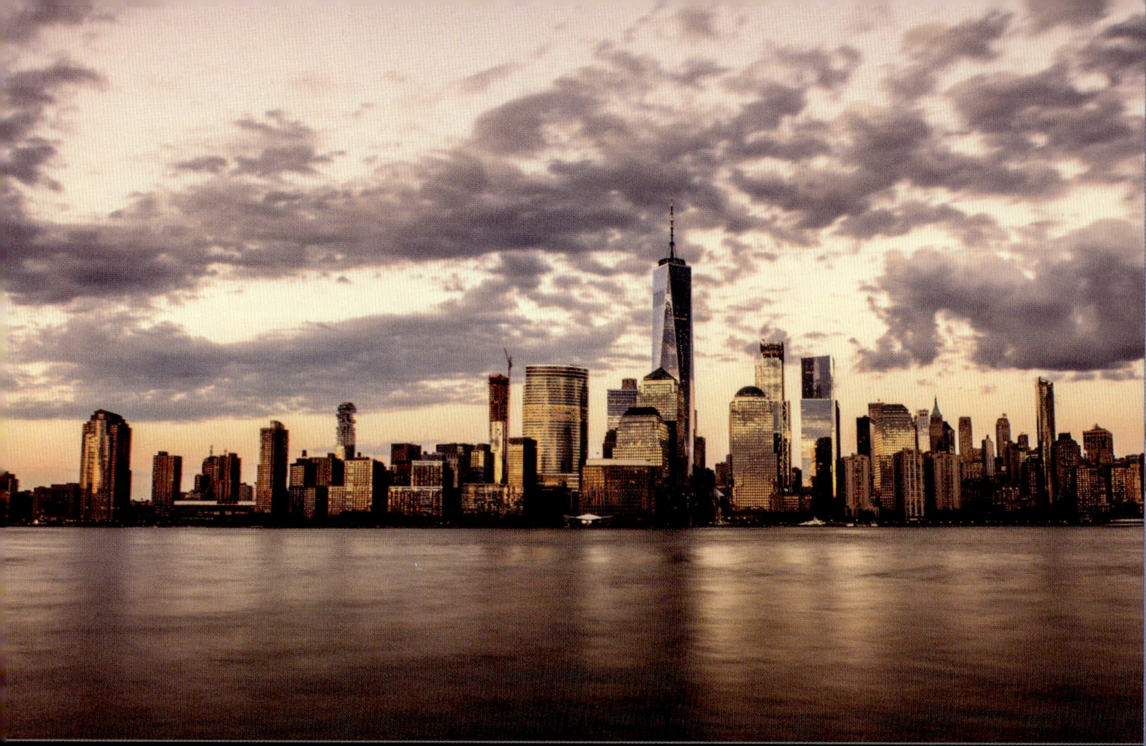

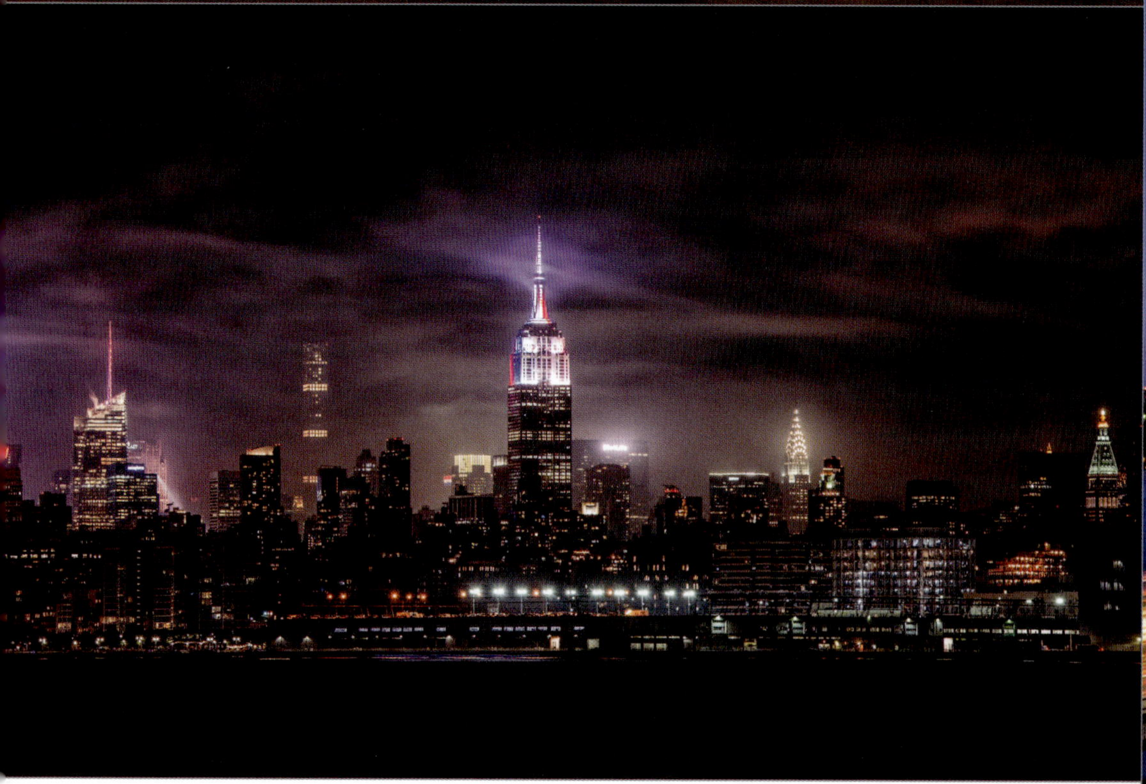

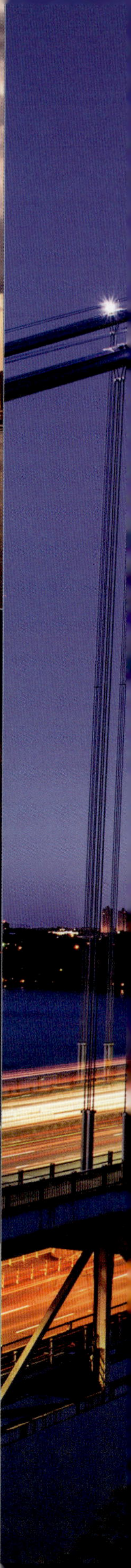

**A Gem.** *(top left)* The majestic skyline of the World Financial District glitters like gold from Exchange Place in Jersey City as the day bids its goodbye.

**Fourth of July.** *(bottom left)* The skyline around the Empire State Building was covered in smoke from the fireworks display.

**Trails.** *(facing page)* Rendered as streaks of light, ongoing traffic speeds along the George Washington Bridge at summer dusk.

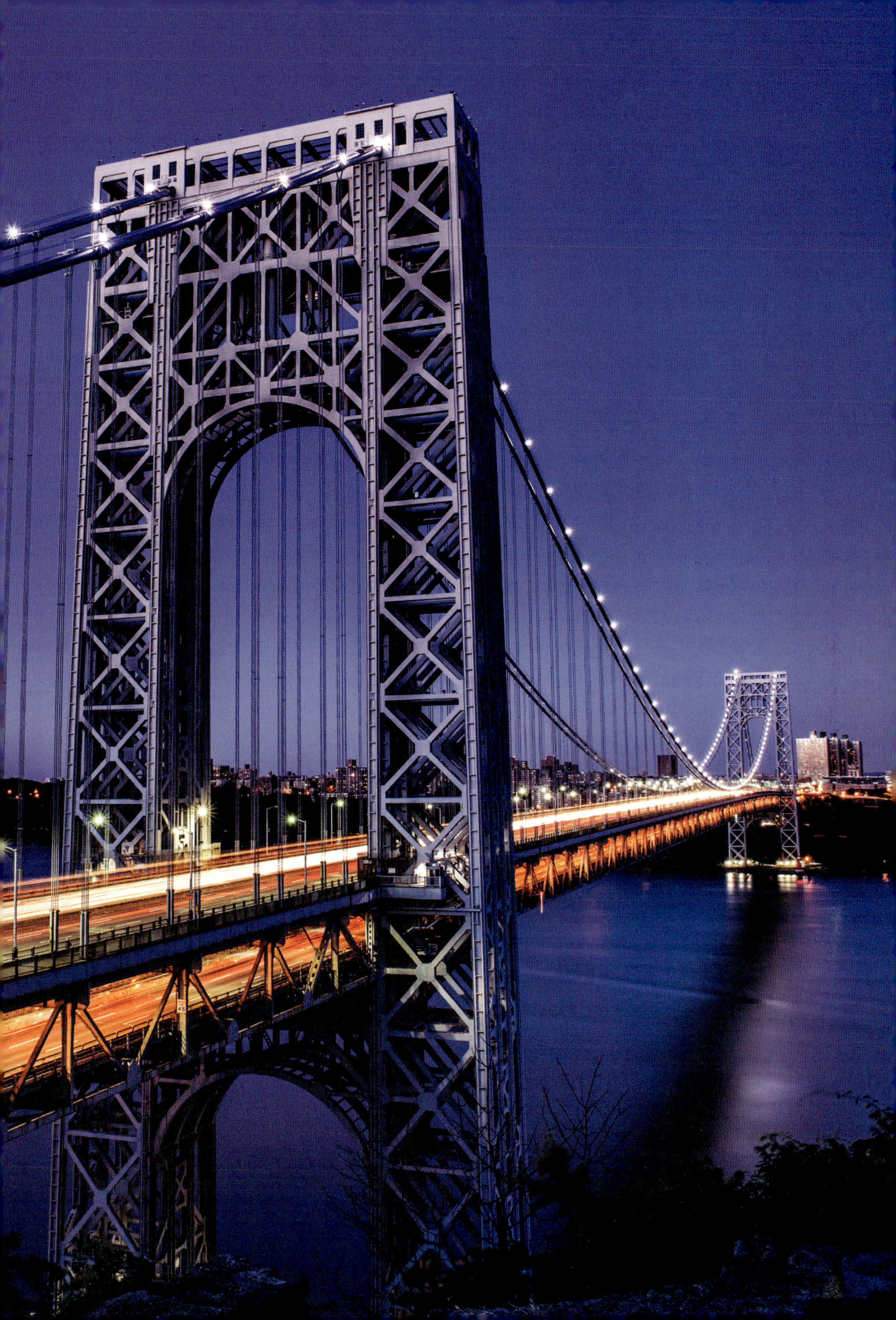

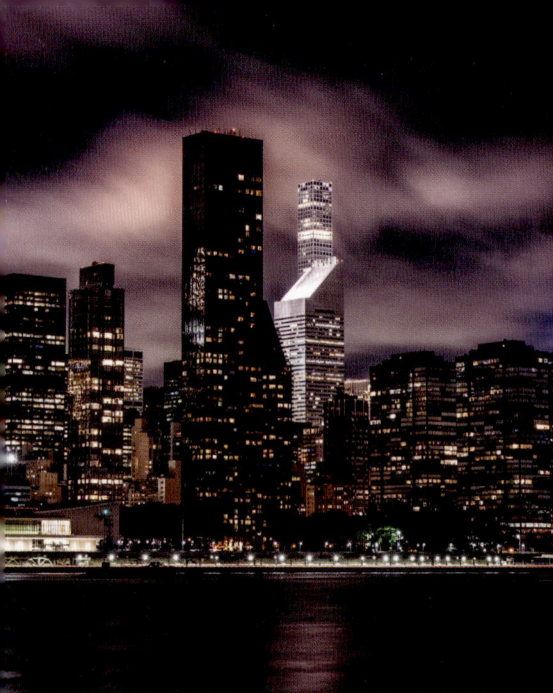

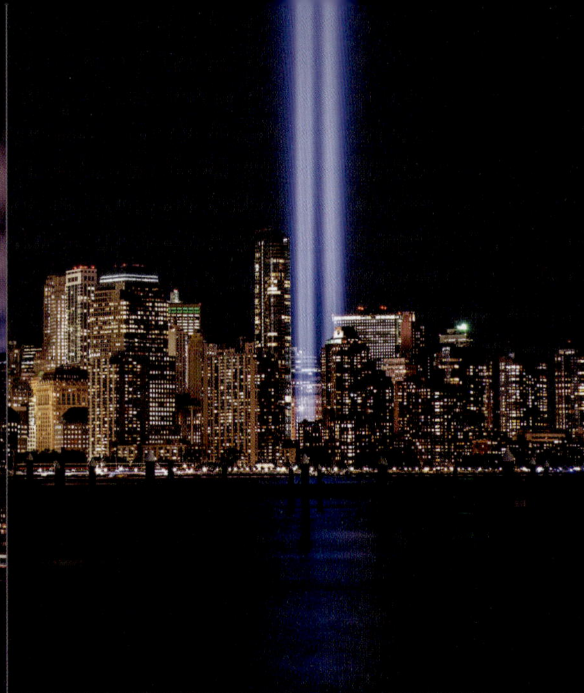

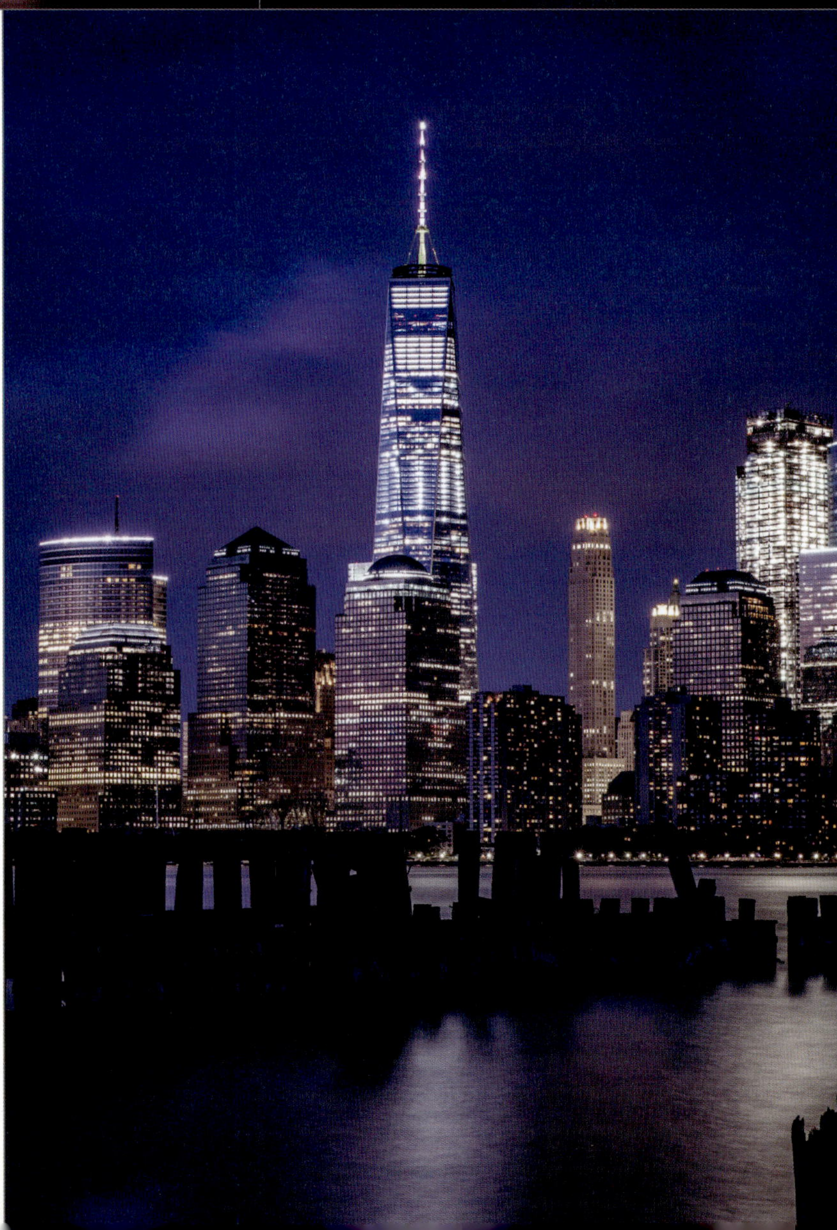

**Nightscape.** *(top left)* Manhattan's 432 Park Avenue viewed from Gantry Plaza State Park in the borough of Queens on a calm summer night.

**Never Forget.** *(top right)* The Tribute in Light, displayed annually on September 11, honors the lives lost and New York City's unbreakable spirit.

**Hues of Blues.** *(right)* Viewed from Jersey City's Liberty State Park, One World Trade Center was shining bright during blue hour.

**Celebration.** *(facing page)* This mesmerizing fireworks display over the Hudson River was in celebration of the 2018 Chinese New Year.

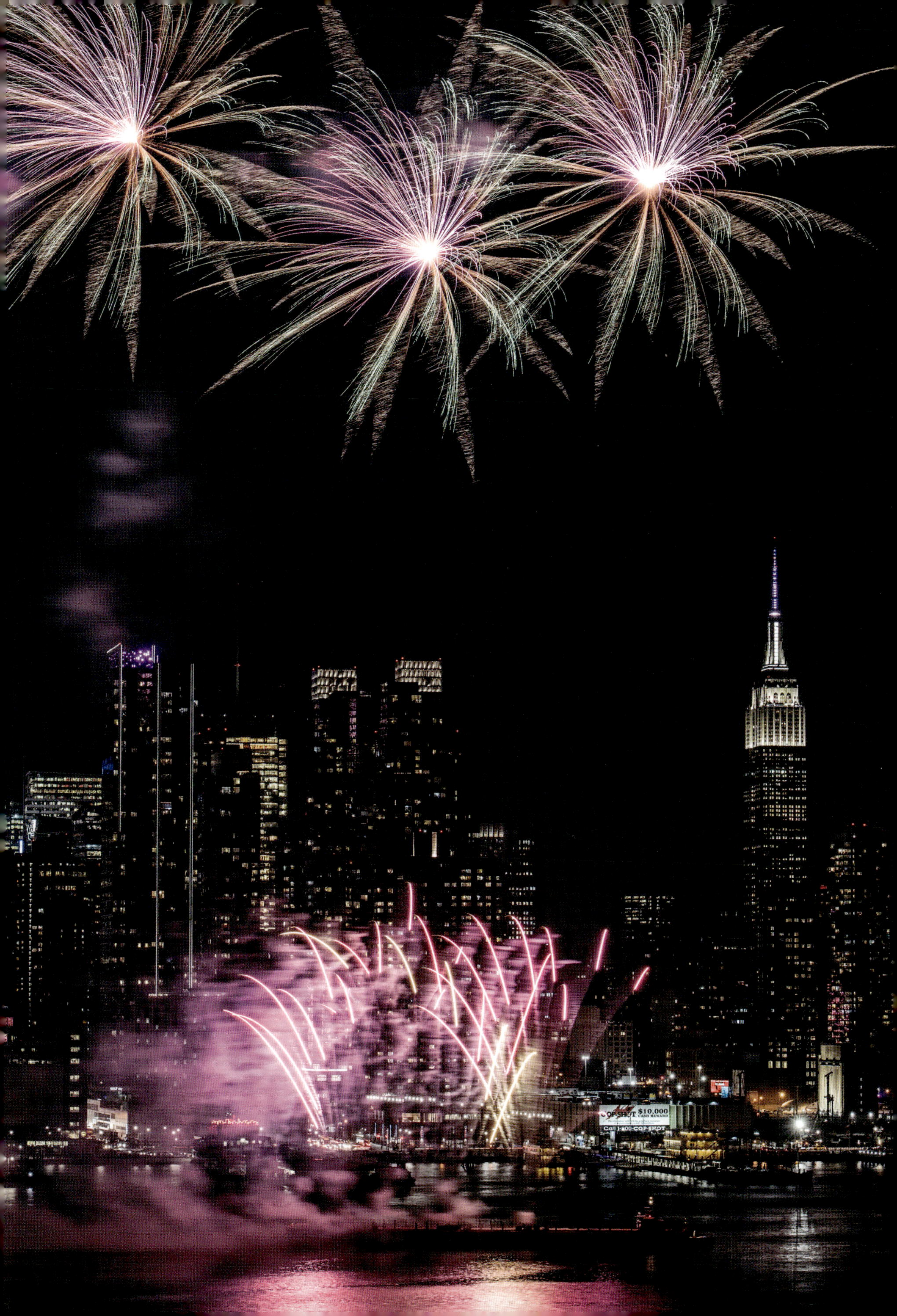
COP-SHOT $10,000
CASH REWARD
Call 1-800-COP-SHOT

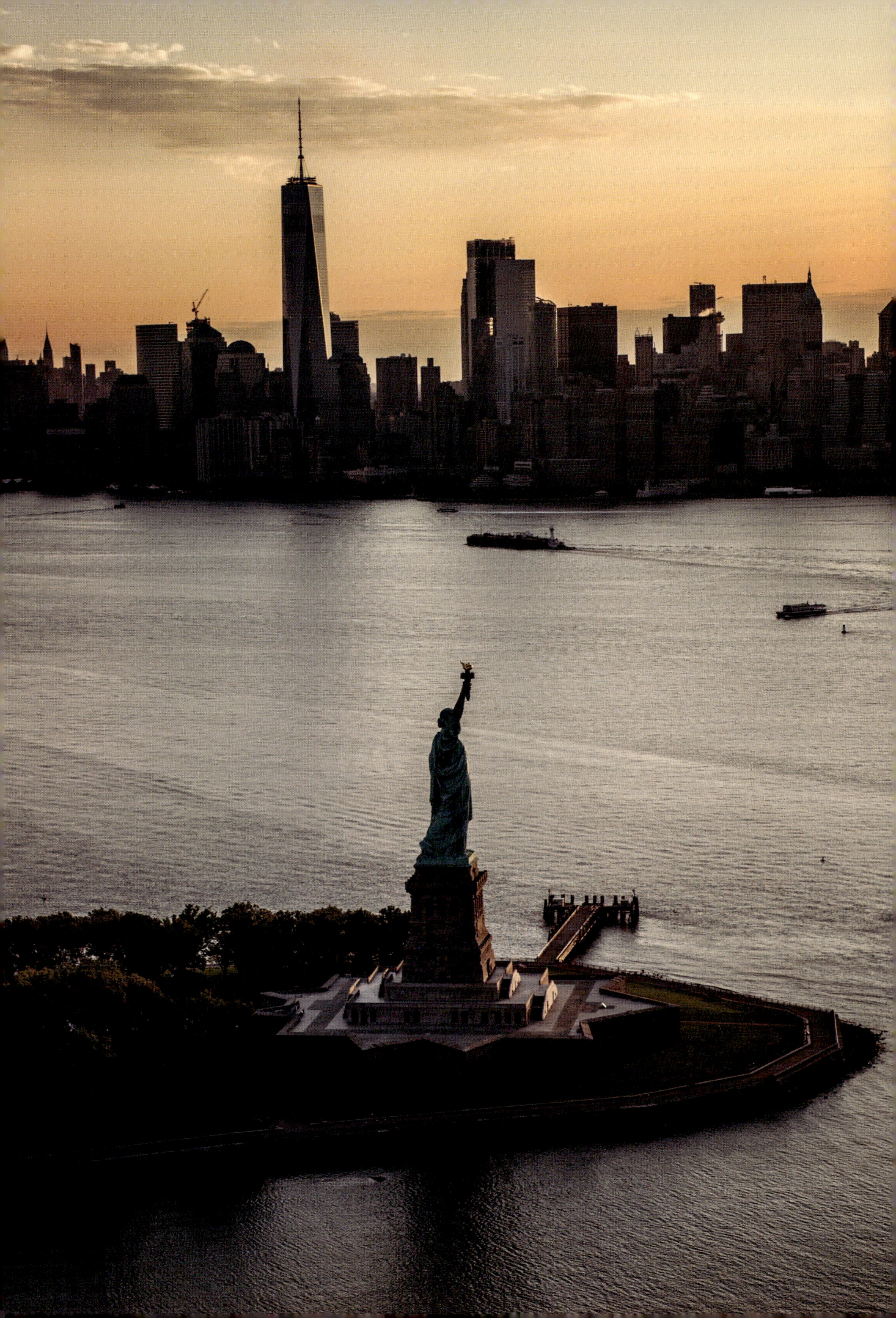

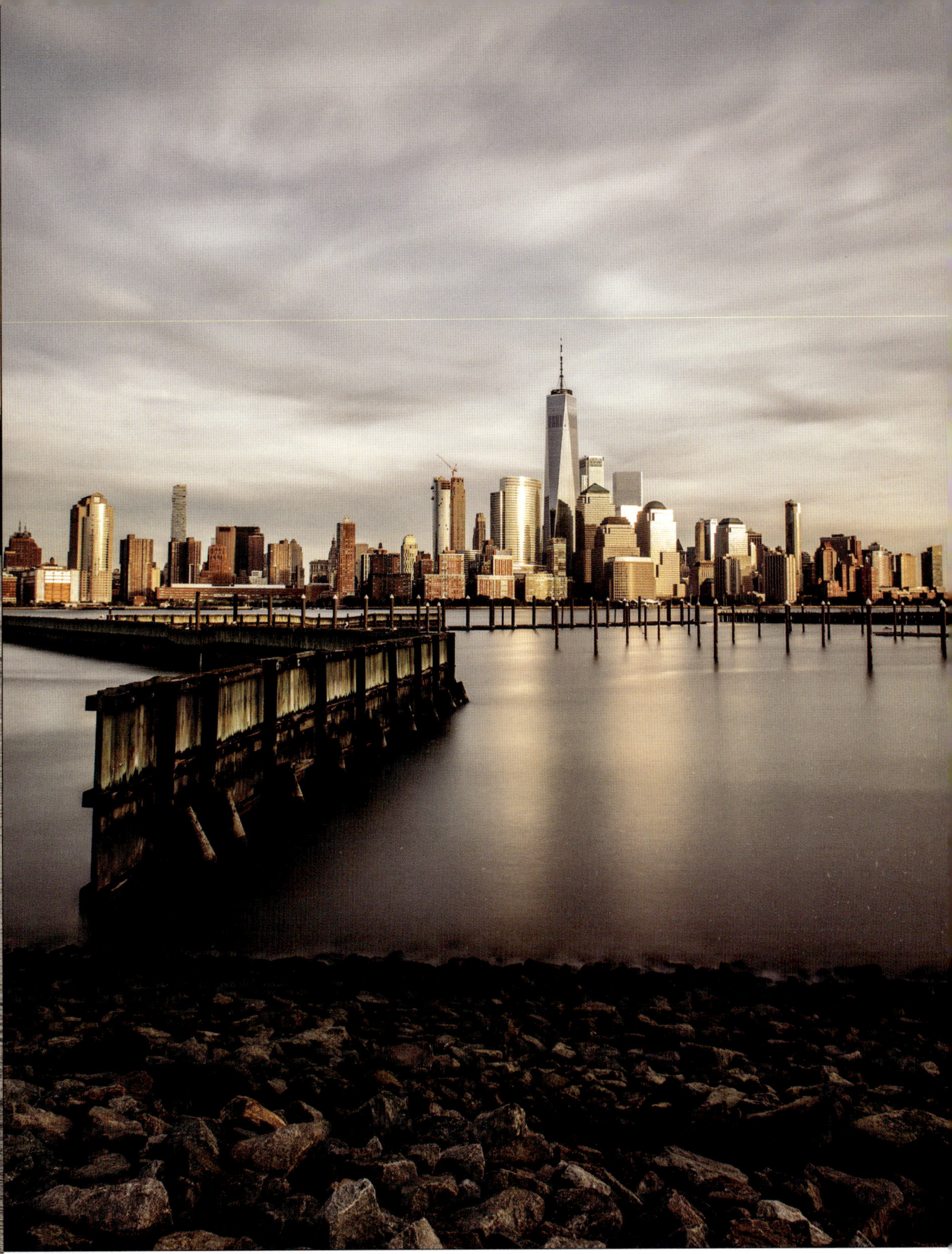

**Zig Zag.** *(above)* With its jagged pier, the Newport Waterfront in Jersey City, New Jersey, is known for its breathtaking view of Manhattan's skyline. Here, the setting sun reflects off the buildings.

**Exemption.** *(facing page)* New York City's two symbols of freedom and liberty are viewed from sky-high at the break of dawn.

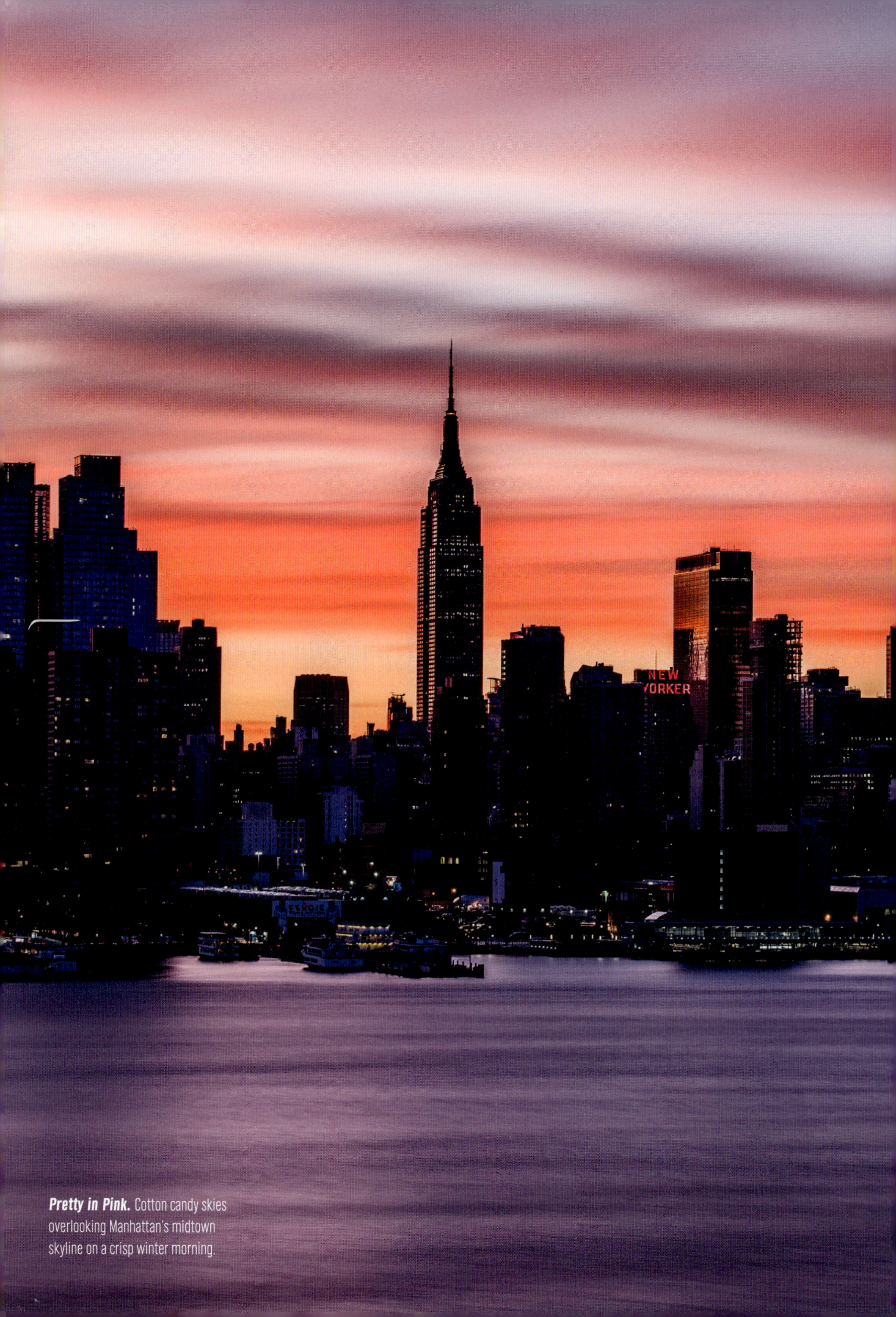


***Pretty in Pink.*** Cotton candy skies overlooking Manhattan's midtown skyline on a crisp winter morning.

# Index